Applying Quality of Life Research

Best Practices

Series editor
Helena Alves, Department of Management and Economics, University of Beira Interior, Covilhã, Portugal

This book series focuses on best practices in specialty areas of Quality of Life research, including among others potentially: community development, quality of work life, marketing, healthcare and public sector management.

In today's world, governments, organizations and individuals alike are paying increasingly more attention to how their activities impact on quality of life at the regional, national and global levels. Whether as a way to tackle global resource shortages, changing environmental circumstances, political conditions, competition, technology or otherwise, the far-reaching impact of decisions made in these and other areas can have a significant impact on populations regardless of their level of development. Many lessons have been learned; yet many are still to be realized. Across a number of volumes on diverse themes, this book series will address key issues that are of significant importance to decision makers and participants across all sectors. The series will be invaluable to anyone with an interest in applying quality of life knowledge in contemporary society.

More information about this series at http://www.springer.com/series/8364

João Leitão • Helena Alves • Norris Krueger
Jacob Park
Editors

Entrepreneurial, Innovative and Sustainable Ecosystems

Best Practices and Implications
for Quality of Life

Springer

Editors
João Leitão
Department of Management and Economics
University of Beira Interior
Covilhã, Portugal

CEG-IST
University of Lisbon
Lisbon, Portugal

Instituto Multidisciplinar de Empresa
Universidad de Salamanca
Salamanca, Spain

Norris Krueger
Center for Global Business Research
University of Phoenix
Phoenix, AZ, USA

Helena Alves
Department of Management and Economics
University of Beira Interior
Covilhã, Portugal

Jacob Park
Green Mountain College
Poultney, VT, USA

ISSN 2213-994X ISSN 2213-9958 (electronic)
Applying Quality of Life Research
ISBN 978-3-319-89029-6 ISBN 978-3-319-71014-3 (eBook)
https://doi.org/10.1007/978-3-319-71014-3

© Springer International Publishing AG 2018
Softcover re-print of the Hardcover 1st edition 2018
This work is subject to copyright. All rights are reserved by the Publisher, whether the whole or part of the material is concerned, specifically the rights of translation, reprinting, reuse of illustrations, recitation, broadcasting, reproduction on microfilms or in any other physical way, and transmission or information storage and retrieval, electronic adaptation, computer software, or by similar or dissimilar methodology now known or hereafter developed.
The use of general descriptive names, registered names, trademarks, service marks, etc. in this publication does not imply, even in the absence of a specific statement, that such names are exempt from the relevant protective laws and regulations and therefore free for general use.
The publisher, the authors and the editors are safe to assume that the advice and information in this book are believed to be true and accurate at the date of publication. Neither the publisher nor the authors or the editors give a warranty, express or implied, with respect to the material contained herein or for any errors or omissions that may have been made. The publisher remains neutral with regard to jurisdictional claims in published maps and institutional affiliations.

Printed on acid-free paper

This Springer imprint is published by Springer Nature
The registered company is Springer International Publishing AG
The registered company address is: Gewerbestrasse 11, 6330 Cham, Switzerland

Preface

The concept of entrepreneurial ecosystems has been attracting considerable attention in the fields of entrepreneurship studies, economic geography and regional studies as well as in policy consulting, seeking to foster firm births as a driver of regional development (Alvedalen and Boschma 2017). However, until now, there has been a lack of knowledge in terms of the best practices and implications for quality of life associated with this type of complex development platform.

Despite its growing relevance for regional policy (Startup Genome 2017; Startup Commons 2017), the concept so far has been applied almost exclusively in (successful) cases, and empirical findings have not been used to advance the ecosystem concept theoretically. Not surprisingly, it has been criticized as being 'underdeveloped' (Stam and Spigel 2016) and 'undertheorized' (Spigel 2017).

The holistic construct of an (E)ntrepreneurial, (I)nnovative and (S)ustainable ecosystem refers to the collective and transversal nature of entrepreneurship, innovation and sustainability. New firms emerge and grow not only because there are entrepreneurs that created and developed them. New ventures emerge also because they are located in an ecosystem made up of private and public stakeholders, which nurture and sustain them, supporting the inventive and innovative action of entrepreneurs.

According to Isenberg (2010), an entrepreneurial ecosystem consists of elements that can be grouped into six domains: (1) a conducive culture (e.g. tolerance of risk and mistakes, positive social status of entrepreneur), (2) facilitating policies and leadership (e.g. regulatory framework incentives, existence of public research institutes), (3) availability of dedicated finance (e.g. business angels, venture capital, microloans, crowdfunding, crowdsourcing, equity funding), (4) relevant human capital (e.g. skilled and unskilled labour, serial entrepreneurs, entrepreneurship training, coaching and mentoring programmes), (5) venture-friendly markets for products (e.g. early adopters for prototypes, reference customers) and (6) a wide set of institutional and infrastructural supports (e.g. legal and accounting advisers, telecommunications and transportation infrastructure, entrepreneurship promoting associations).

Based on this definition, governments can evaluate whether they have an EIS ecosystem and what actions they should take, knowing that each EIS ecosystem is unique and all elements of the ecosystem are interdependent. Successful dynamics often result from the identification of both comparative and competitive advantages founded on natural resources or specific assets, which may be very limited.

Following the previous work by Leitão and Alves (2016), this edited volume aims, firstly, to present a multidimensional approach by providing the state of the art on EIS ecosystems, as well as structural and changing dynamics and their impact on citizens' quality of life. Secondly, it aims to present a set of international benchmarking case studies on good practices and initiatives oriented to the creation and development of EIS ecosystems. Thirdly, it aims to be positioned as a reference guide for scholars, policy makers and practitioners interested in entrepreneurship, public procurement, new public management, innovation and sustainability.

In terms of knowledge transfer, these international benchmarks of EIS ecosystems should be able to be replicated, to foster the creation of entrepreneurial and innovative units and promote sustainable practices, under an open innovation paradigm, which needs to congregate both public and private stakeholders, using co-creation, transparency and participatory practices.

This volume is particularly opportune in that it contributes to the scarce literature on the subject of ecosystems' complexity and their importance in determining the quality of life of different communities and organizations. Nevertheless, it is a first organized attempt which should be continued, as within the complexity characterizing the different phases of an ecosystem's life cycle, namely, creation, development, growth, maturity, decline and regeneration, in pioneering terms, only the entrepreneurial, innovative and sustainable dimensions of ecosystems are portrayed here.

Based on the set of pioneering contributions collected in this volume, an entrepreneurial, innovative and sustainable ecosystem corresponds to what is formed by a natural environment and the communities of entities that inhabit it, interacting with each other and with the environment itself and resulting in a relatively stable system. Consequently, an ecosystem covers the set of communities that form a natural system, including different actors, such as producers, consumers and decomposers, underlining the importance of entrepreneurship, innovation and sustainability as critical anchors of the stages of creation, development and growth of that ecosystem.

Regarding the communities of bodies forming an ecosystem, relations can be established with different characteristics, namely, (1) competitive relationships, which imply a limited resource is disputed by various bodies, and so only the most able survive; (2) predatory relationships, which assume that one body, i.e. a predator, feeds on another, the prey (this type of relationship also allows regulation of the number of species and survival of the fittest, forming a mechanism to self-regulate the ecosystem); (3) parasitical relationships, where one or more smaller bodies, parasites, feed on another larger one, the host, which they live next to; (4) mutual relationships, around which there is a relationship that benefits both associated species; and (5) commensal relationships, where there is a type of relationship where one species is benefited without any detriment to the other.

Preface

However, various open questions deserve additional research efforts and the drawing up of new public policies to contribute in the future to better understanding of the role of ecosystems in determining citizens' quality of life, in different spatial units of analysis (e.g. town, region, country or common economic area) and according to the different phases of the ecosystem's life cycle.

Conceiving, designing and analysing ecosystems, with a view to increasing citizens' quality of life, means deepening knowledge about social network analysis and promoting the eclectic intersection of various branches of knowledge, namely, economics, management, psychology, sociology, mathematics, engineering and information systems, history, anthropology, etc.

Also necessary are metrics associated with key performance indicators (KPIs), which can be used in technological prospection exercises, aiming to improve quality of life, setting out from the different dimensions of ecosystems, in continuous evolution and therefore requiring continuous monitoring and correction.

The volume is formed of two parts. Part I deals with ecosystems' entrepreneurial, innovative and sustainable dimensions (EISE), which served as a basis for the structure of this edited volume. Part II presents a selected set of benchmarking cases originating in India, Mexico, Brazil, Finland, Denmark, Portugal and Italy.

Highlighted in Part I is firstly the work done by Michael Fritsch and Sandra Kublina, who propose four types of regional growth regimes, taking as a reference the type of relationship between new firm creation and the level of economic development. The authors analyse the characteristics of those regimes, aiming to identify the reasons for obtaining different levels of performance regarding growth. They identify typical transitionary tendencies between regimes, clearly suggesting that entrepreneurship is a factor leading to economic development, figuring among the factors that produce long-term effects on economic well-being at the regional level, thereby promoting quality of life.

Secondly, Jamile Rodrigues takes a pioneering look at the subject of local government committed to quality of life in the context of sustainable cities. The emphasis is on the need to create an urban ecosystem that is modelled and modified by people on a daily basis, despite non-sustainable methods being used. Adopting a descriptive and qualitative approach, the author analyses the contribution made by introducing sustainable practices in the city context, concluding that this option promotes not only sustainable local development but also quality of life.

Thirdly, José Luis Vázquez, Ana Lanero, Pablo Gutiérrez and César Sahelices present an innovative view of the contribution of *smart cities* to quality of life, according to citizens' perception. This study analyses the perceptions of a sample of 272 university students in Spain, regarding the local authority's present and ideal level of involvement in six dimensions defining a smart city (smart economy, smart people, smart governance, smart mobility, smart environment and smart living). The results reveal an important gap between real experience in the city and the perceived potential of the dimensions to improve quality of life in the future. The main gaps were detected in the dimensions of smart economy and smart governance.

Fourth, Romano Audhoe, Neil Thompson and Karen Verduijn propose expanding the approach of reference followed in this volume, i.e. integration of the entrepreneurial, innovative and sustainable dimensions, coupling a so far unexplored theoretical perspective of historical-cultural activity. The authors underline the growing importance attributed to entrepreneurial, innovative and sustainable ecosystems, by both political decision-makers and the research community. Connecting to the theoretical approach of new public management, it is recommended that political decision-makers using this type of approach should be more enabled to better understand the links between the stakeholders of EIS ecosystems, which have a determinant role in stimulating the sources leading to local transformation, i.e. entrepreneurship and innovation, towards improving citizens' well-being (i.e. happiness, trust, safety and satisfaction). In this connection, the authors propose and explain a novel framework for analysing and assessing EIS ecosystems, i.e. activity system analysis (ASA), which is a methodological framework, rooted in cultural-historical activity theory (CHAT), assisting researchers by guiding analyses towards specific tensions and contradictions between stakeholders that prevent EIS ecosystems from developing. Additionally, it allows researchers to gain insights into the developmental trajectory of EISE and to understand the learning actions that transform them.

Fifth, Teresa Paiva, Luísa Cagica Carvalho, Cristina Soutinho and Sérgio Leal position product innovation as a mechanism with high value added to promote a region's sustainability, supporting their arguments through exploration of the case study on Douro Skincare. In the context of implementing so-called regional strategies of intelligent specialization (RIS3), the authors present the case of Douro Skincare, a company created by entrepreneurial women and operating in the field of selective biological cosmetics, through the creation, development and production of cosmetic products that use emblematic raw material from the Douro region, one of the oldest wine-producing regions in Europe.

Sixth, Fernando Herrera, Maribel Guerrero and David Urbano describe the determinant role of higher education institutions, as drivers of entrepreneurial and innovative ecosystems. From an evolutionary perspective, the authors position higher education institutions as drivers of entrepreneurial and innovative ecosystems in Mexico. They underline, on one hand, the importance of incentives for the configuration of the triple mission of this type of higher education institution and, on the other, the limited participation and weak involvement of this type of institution in entrepreneurial and innovative activities in the Mexican context.

Seventh, in the business ecosystem context, Zhaojing Huang, Clare Farruk and Yongjiang Shi approach the challenging work of commercialization, which covers the different mechanisms for transferring knowledge and technology, from academia to the market. In an innovative way, the authors approach the subject of commercialization, from the perspectives of scientists whose aim is to develop new products from high-quality research, which can be transferred and valorised. The authors present a theoretical approach, from a business ecosystem perspective, based on a literature review. That theoretical approach is contrasted through the development of a longitudinal case study about the development of a fibre optic sensor analyser with application in the construction industry. As the main results, the authors emphasize, firstly, the need for relationships with partners and other supporting organizations to be established at an earlier stage than is suggested in the literature. Secondly, they highlight the need for scientists to develop a precise understanding of the business ecosystem, to which technology is adjusted, serving as support for the application of instruments of technological and innovative surveillance. Consequently, the anticipated focus on communication and partnerships is pointed out as a critical success factor in commercializing technology.

Part II presents a selected number of benchmarking cases originating in Italy, Mexico, Brazil, Finland, Denmark, Portugal and Italy. In the first case, Ranjini Swamy and Arbind Singh present an interesting support system for the entrepreneurial ecosystem of street sellers, developed by the National Association of Street Vendors of India (NASVI). After the liberalization movement, this system allowed the creation of an entrepreneurial ecosystem based on regulatory procedures defending the interests of street sellers, thereby contributing to improving the quality of life and sustainability of this type of subsistence entrepreneur.

In the second case, Mario Vázquez-Maguirre presents an example of a sustainable ecosystem applied to the situation in Southern Mexico, where the founding element is the community of indigenous social enterprises. The empirical evidence points to this type of company having developed new mechanisms based on their culture and cosmovision, which ultimately generate an ecosystem promoting the community's well-being. Highlighted among the mechanisms are accountability and transparency, legitimacy, equality policies, a participatory organizational structure, social innovation and entrepreneurial orientation. This case also demonstrates unequivocally how an entity's community perspective contributes to improving its employees' and their families' quality of life, making the local economy more dynamic and consolidating an ecosystem that promotes the host community's development. From a public policy perspective, the case also suggests actions that can promote the emergence of new business models to favour the integration of vulnerable communities in the global economy, following an approach of sustainability and collaboration.

In the third case, Ainomaija Haarla, Henri Hakala and Greg O'Shea present an exemplary case of the creation of the *Finnish cellulose entrepreneurial ecosystem*, illustrating the different phases of creating the ecosystem from a community-led initiative which involved three different stages, (1) community of dreams, (2) community of commerce and (3) creation of the ecosystem, which are described in detail in the case, serving as benchmarks for the actors involved. Concerning the main implications, the case reveals unequivocally that entrepreneurial ecosystems can be created and developed following a bottom-up approach, counting with community participation and being led by different types of public funding, as opposed to the more usual top-down approach, representing a better understanding of the associated roles and micro-processes which contributes to better grounding, creation, organization and coordination of the ecosystem's development.

In the fourth case, Simone Sehnem and Hilka Machado analyse the sustainable and social environmental practices of a sample of 50 Brazilian companies located in Santa Catarina. The main results reveal that the majority of environmental practices adopted by the firms studied include the monitoring of risks and opportunities for organizations' activities, due to climatic change. Therefore, the majority separate waste and provide training in health and safety at work. However, they do not incinerate waste, do not use recyclable water and do not take on workers belonging to tribal Indian communities.

In the fifth case, Hugo Pinto and Carla Nogueira develop a pioneering application consisting of mapping an entrepreneurial, innovative and sustainable ecosystem in the Algarve region of Portugal, by resorting to an analysis of social networks focused on innovative projects receiving public funding. Starting from the Algarve case study, the authors use methods of social network structural analysis to map actors and centralities regarding cooperation and innovation in regional development. The mapping of the innovation network in the Algarve is compared to theoretical models of resilient networks with the statistical indicators of hierarchy and homophily. The empirical evidence facilitates the identification of gatekeepers, clusters of activities and constraints and potentialities for enhancement of the regional EIS ecosystem.

In the sixth case, Luís Mendes and Dalila Dias revisit the role of stakeholders in the value creation process, focusing on the sustainable dimension of ecosystems and exploring the relationship between practices of corporate social responsibility (CSR) and total quality management (TQM). Through a literature review, the authors systematize knowledge of how strategies based on CSR and TQM principles may create stakeholders' value and generate sustainable competitive advantages while improving the quality of life. The findings highlight that when thought proactively and strategically, sustainability-based approaches combining CSR and TQM are potential sources for obtaining sustainable competitive advantages and for improving the quality of life of the workforce and citizens in local communities in particular and even of society in general.

In the seventh case, Paula Ungureanu and Diego Maria Macri illustrate how hybrid partnerships help to set up, implement and then innovate business models. The authors exemplify the design of a hybrid partnership for open innovation where six public and private organizations came together with the intention to set up and implement joint innovation projects with a large-scale impact at the regional level. Two business models of hybrid partnerships are discussed in this chapter, the brokering model and the platform model, as well as the mechanisms of transition from the former to the latter. The findings suggest that while the platform model seems more appropriate for complex projects in which a wide number of heterogeneous interests coexist, both models present advantages and disadvantages.

In the eighth case, Alexander Kerl characterizes the development of an innovative ecosystem in an accelerated economic environment, using as the case of reference the Vodafone Open Innovation Program. The author formulates a research question based on an issue frequently faced by multinational companies with an innovative profile, i.e. by what kind of organizational framework are initiatives for multi-cross industry innovation supported, and how can companies utilize this approach to generate new innovation ecosystems? To answer the question, the author describes the organizational model of the Vodafone Open Innovation Program, identifying the structured nature of the programme and the so-called staged intellectual property rights mechanism, as key characteristics potentiating new innovation ecosystems.

Finally, this volume is a step forward in the incomplete and demanding task of building a theoretical body on ecosystems, which requires the future coupling of new dimensions and perspectives of the (formal and informal) structuring and evolution of ecosystems but also the use of qualitative and quantitative methods to measure their evolutionary stage and performance, with a strong motivation to use network approaches in order to improve citizens' and consequently nations' quality of life.

Covilhã, Portugal	João Leitão
Covilhã, Portugal	Helena Alves
Phoenix, AZ, USA	Norris Krueger
Poultney, VT, USA	Jacob Park
August 31, 2017	

References

Alvedalen, J., Boschma, R. (2017). A critical review of entrepreneurial ecosystems research: Towards a future research agenda. *European Planning Studies, 25*(6):887–903.

Isenberg, D. (2010). How to start an entrepreneurial revolution. *Harvard Business Review, 88*(6): 41–50.

Leitão, J., Alves, H. (Eds.) (2016). *Entrepreneurial and innovative practices in public institutions: A quality of life approach.* Applying Quality of Life Research: Best Practices. Springer.

Malecki, E. (2017). *Entrepreneurship, ecosystems, and environments.* Boston: American Association of Geographers Boston.

Spigel, B. (2017). The relational organization of entrepreneurial ecosystems. *Entrepreneurship Theory and Practice, 41*(1):49–72.

Stam, E., Spigel, B. (2016). Entrepreneurial ecosystems. *U.S.E. Discussion Paper Series,* (16–13):1–18.

Start-up Commons. (2017). Start-up ecosystems white paper. http://www.startupcommons.org/. Accessed on 14 Aug 2017.

Contents

Part I Ecosystems' Entrepreneurial, Innovative and Sustainable Dimensions (EISE)

1 Entrepreneurship, Growth, and Regional Growth Regimes 3
Michael Fritsch and Sandra Kublina

2 Local Government Aimed at Quality of Life in Sustainable Cities 35
Jamile Pereira Cunha Rodrigues

3 The Contribution of Smart Cities to Quality of Life from the View of Citizens 55
José Luis Vázquez, Ana Lanero, Pablo Gutiérrez, and César Sahelices

4 Expanding Entrepreneurial, Innovative and Sustainable (EIS) Ecosystems: A Cultural-Historical Activity Theory Perspective 67
Romano Audhoe, Neil Thompson, and Karen Verduijn

5 Product Innovation as Territory Sustainability Added Value: The Case Study of Douro Skincare 91
Teresa Paiva, Luísa Cagica Carvalho, Cristina Soutinho, and Sérgio Leal

6 Entrepreneurship and Innovation Ecosystem's Drivers: The Role of Higher Education Organizations 109
Fernando Herrera, Maribel Guerrero, and David Urbano

7 Commercialisation Journey in Business Ecosystem: From Academy to Market 129
Zhaojing Huang, Clare Farrukh, and Yongjiang Shi

Part II Benchmarking Cases

8 Creating a Supportive Entrepreneurial Ecosystem for Street Vendors: The Case of the National Association of Street Vendors of India (NASVI) 151
Ranjini Swamy and Arbind Singh

9 Sustainable Ecosystems Through Indigenous Social Enterprises 173
Mario Vázquez-Maguirre

10 Re-imagining the Forest: Entrepreneurial Ecosystem Development for Finnish Cellulosic Materials 191
Ainomaija Haarla, Henri Hakala, and Greg O'Shea

11 Sustainable Environmental and Social Practices in Companies in the State of Santa Catarina, Brazil 215
Simone Sehnem and Hilka Pelizza Vier Machado

12 Mapping an Entrepreneurial, Innovative and Sustainable Ecosystem Using Social Network Analysis: An Exploratory Approach of Publicly Funded Innovative Project Data 237
Hugo Pinto and Carla Nogueira

13 Corporate Social Responsibility and Total Quality Management: The Stakeholders' Value Creation Debate Revisited 255
Luís Mendes and Dalila Dias

14 From Broker to Platform Business Models: A Case Study of Best Practices for Business Model Innovation in Hybrid Interorganizational Partnerships 285
Paula Ungureanu and Diego Maria Macri

15 Development of an Innovation Ecosystem in a Fast-Paced Economic Environment: The Case of the Vodafone Open Innovation Program 305
Alexander Kerl

Part I
Ecosystems' Entrepreneurial, Innovative and Sustainable Dimensions (EISE)

Chapter 1
Entrepreneurship, Growth, and Regional Growth Regimes

Michael Fritsch and Sandra Kublina

Abstract We distinguish four types of regional growth regimes based on the relationship between new business formation and economic development. The distinguishing characteristics of these regime types are analyzed in order to identify the reasons for different growth performance. Although growth regimes are highly persistent over time, typical transition patterns between regime types can be identified. We explain these patterns and draw conclusions for policy. The evidence clearly suggests that entrepreneurship is a key driver of economic development and one that has long-run effects on regional economic well-being.

Keywords Entrepreneurship • New business formation • Economic development • Regional growth regimes

JEL Classification L26 • R11 • O11

1.1 Different Patterns of Entrepreneurship, Growth, and Economic Well-Being

The notion of regional growth regimes[1] is based on the idea that the drivers of economic development and well-being may vary considerably across regions. We speak of "growth regimes" in recognition that such differences in economic development may result from a complex interplay of a variety of factors. In investigating the role entrepreneurship plays in growth, we apply a typology based on the of relationship between new business formation and economic development, which was introduced by Audretsch and Fritsch (2002) and further analyzed by Fritsch and Mueller (2006). A particular advantage of our study, compared to previous analyses, is that we have a more comprehensive dataset that covers a considerably longer period of time. We investigate the distinguishing characteristics of the four kinds of growth

---

[1] Audretsch and Fritsch (2002), Fritsch (2004), and Fritsch and Mueller (2006).

M. Fritsch (✉) • S. Kublina
Friedrich Schiller University Jena, Jena, Germany
e-mail: m.fritsch@uni-jena.de; sandra.kublina@gmail.com

© Springer International Publishing AG 2018
J. Leitão et al. (eds.), *Entrepreneurial, Innovative and Sustainable Ecosystems*, Applying Quality of Life Research,
https://doi.org/10.1007/978-3-319-71014-3_1

regime and analyze transitions between these regimes over time. The results help better understand the forces behind different regional growth trajectories and clearly show that the effects of new business formation on regional development can be very long lasting.

The remainder of the paper is organized as follows. First, we introduce the general concept of regional growth regimes and make a distinction between four types of them that is based on the effect of new business formation on regional growth (Sect. 1.2). Section 1.3 elaborates on these four regime types and develops hypotheses about their characteristics. Section 1.4 describes the database and shows the distribution of growth regime types across time and space. We then analyze regime characteristics (Sect. 1.5) and transition patterns between regime types over time (Sect. 1.6). In Sect. 1.7, we provide an interpretation of the development patterns of growth regime types and discuss critical points in the development of the growth regime life cycle. The final section (Sect. 1.8) concludes.

1.2 Regional Growth Regimes

1.2.1 What Is a Regional Growth Regime?

We define a regional growth regime as a set of economic and institutional conditions that influence the level of regional entrepreneurship and growth. Focusing on the effect of new business formation on growth, our typology of regional growth regimes is based on two assumptions for which there is compelling empirical evidence. The first assumption is that the regional context has a significant effect on the level and type of new business formation (for an overview, see Sternberg 2011). The second assumption is that the regional context plays a significant role in the effects that new businesses have on the process of regional development (see Fritsch 2013). Given the role of the economic and institutional context for entrepreneurship, it can be regarded as a "systemic" phenomenon; indeed, one could even speak of a "regional system of entrepreneurship" (Qian et al. 2013) that also constitutes an important part of the regional innovation system (Cooke 2004). The relevant institutional context comprises the formal "rules of the game" (North 1994), such as tax laws and labor legislation, as well as the informal institutions of norms, values, and codes of conduct (Baumol 1990; North 1994), both types of institutes together constituting the regional entrepreneurship "culture."[2] A positive culture of entrepreneurship is marked by a high level of social acceptance and approval of self-employment (Kibler et al. 2014) that result in high levels of new business formation. Recent research indicates that such a culture is also conducive to a positive effect of new

---

[2] An entrepreneurial culture is typically defined as a "positive collective programming of the mind" (Beugelsdijk 2007, 190) or an "aggregate psychological trait" (Freytag and Thurik 2007, 123) of the population oriented toward entrepreneurial values such as individualism, independence, and achievement (e.g., McClelland 1961; Hofstede and McCrae 2004).

business formation on economic development (Glaeser et al. 2015; Fritsch and Wyrwich 2017).

Being part of the regional innovation system, growth regimes are characterized by a certain knowledge stock. Although new firms may generate important knowledge about the (non)viability of business concepts, the focus of growth regimes is on knowledge exploitation via start-ups. Hence, the notion of regional growth regimes applies the "knowledge spillover theory of entrepreneurship" in a regional context (Acs et al. 2013) but also includes those new businesses that are not knowledge-intensive. To the degree new business formation is determined by the regional knowledge stock, the extent and nature of this knowledge, and, particularly, the ability of regional actors to absorb external knowledge and produce new knowledge should determine the number and characteristics of start-ups. There is some overlap between the idea of regional growth regimes and the common concept of technological regimes, which emphasizes the role of certain characteristics of a knowledge base for new business formation (Winter 1984; Audretsch 1995, 47–55; Marsili 2002).

The concept of regional growth regimes suggests that the sources and mechanisms of growth may vary considerably across regions, meaning that regions can be regarded as having different production functions. Accordingly, factors such as new firm formation, large firm presence, innovation, qualification, labor mobility, and the like may not play the same role in all regions. The existence of different growth regimes means that different theories may be required to explain their development and also has important implications for policy aimed at stimulating growth. If the way economic growth occurs differs between regions, then distinct policy strategies may be not only appropriate but necessary for spurring regional development.

1.2.2 Entrepreneurship and Development: Four Types of Regional Growth Regimes

Audretsch and Fritsch (2002) suggest a distinction between four types of regional growth regimes that should account for differences with regard to the role that new firms and entrepreneurship play in development. Analogous to a technological regime, a region's growth regime is called *entrepreneurial* if relatively high growth corresponds with a high level of new firm start-ups and a turbulent enterprise structure. It is assumed that in these regions, growth results from new business formation. In contrast, above-average growth in regions with low start-up rates is probably due to relatively stable, large incumbent enterprises. Audretsch and Fritsch (2002) characterize this combination of new business formation and growth as a *routinized* growth regime (Fig. 1.1). In the routinized regime, new businesses do not play an important role, and their chances for survival and growth are probably much lower than in an entrepreneurial regime.

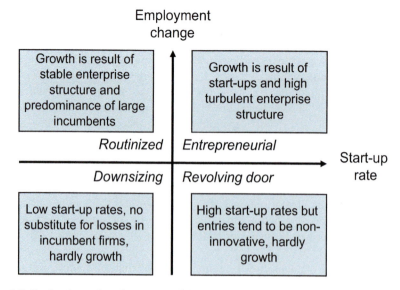

Fig. 1.1 Regional growth regime types and their characteristics (Source: own presentation)

Audretsch and Fritsch (2002) characterize regions with relatively low growth rates but above-average start-up rates as *revolving-door* growth regimes. They conjecture that in such a regime, entries will tend to be non-innovative, supplying basically the same products and using nearly the same technology as the incumbent firms. Finally, relatively low-growth regions characterized by a below-average level of start-up activity are classified as *downsizing* growth regimes. In such regions, the number and quality of start-ups are insufficient to provide enough new jobs or income to compensate for the losses in incumbent firms.[3]

Fritsch and Mueller (2006) analyze transitions between these types of growth regimes and identify patterns that suggest a type of "life cycle" for regional development. These transition patterns are analyzed in detail in Sect. 1.6.

1.3 Characteristics of the Four Growth Regime Types: Hypotheses

There are a number of reasons for expecting that the four growth regimes described above will have distinct characteristics. This section deals with three broad categories of such reasons: the regional knowledge base and the quality of start-ups (Sect.

---

[3] Audretsch et al. (2012) in an analysis of the relationship between regional conditions and the propensity to start a business use the term "entrepreneurial regime" to characterize regions where the members of the labor force have a relatively high propensity for starting an own business. Regions with lower propensities to start a business are characterized as having a "routinized regime."

1.3.1 The Regional Knowledge Base and the Quality of Start-Up

Regional knowledge bases are diverse, comprised, to various degrees, of public and private research and development (R&D), the presence and the activity of higher education institutions, and the qualification of the regional workforce. According to the knowledge spillover theory of entrepreneurship (Acs et al. 2013), the size and quality of the regional knowledge base can have a positive effect on the number of start-ups, particularly on the emergence of those start-ups that exert significant competitive pressure on incumbent firms. Such challenging start-ups can be expected to contribute more to regional growth (Fritsch 2013) than purely imitative new businesses that are never more than marginal, undersized, poor-performance enterprises (also called "Muppets") (Nightingale and Coad 2014). A positive effect of the regional knowledge base, however, is in no way limited to new businesses but can also be a main source of success for incumbent firms. We thus expect to find a larger knowledge base in regions with above-average growth, that is, in those regions classified as being host to either an entrepreneurial or routinized regime as compared to regions with a revolving-door or a downsizing regime.

Although both entrepreneurial and routinized regions may have relatively large knowledge bases, the character of this knowledge can vary according to the technological regime present in them (Winter 1984; Audretsch 1995; Marsili 2002). Hence, in regions with an entrepreneurial growth regime, a high share of the relevant knowledge is expected to be related to an early stage of a product life cycle, whereas in a routinized growth regime, activity and knowledge related to a later stage of the life cycle are expected to prevail. We also expect a high share of knowledge in the later stage of the product life cycle in a downsizing regime. We do not have a clear expectation in this regard for regions with a revolving-door regime. If anything, we may presume that a considerable part of knowledge in these regions is in the entrepreneurial phase of the product life cycle because this would correspond to empirical analyses that show relatively low survival rates of start-ups entering the market at such an early stage (Audretsch 1995).

Using market survival as an indicator for the quality of a start-up, Fritsch and Noseleit (2013a) and Brixy (2014) show that new businesses that manage to survive for a certain period of time have a positive effect on regional development, whereas the effect of start-ups that exit soon after entry is insignificant. We thus expect higher survival rates for newly founded businesses in regions with an entrepreneurial growth regime compared to regions with a revolving-door regime. To the extent that new businesses contribute to employment growth in a routinized regime, we expect higher survival rates in regions with a routinized regime compared to regions with a downsizing regime.

1.3.2 Regional Industry Structure

The industry structure of incumbent firms in a region may be important for a number of reasons. First, it represents a large part of the regional knowledge base that may be exploited by start-ups. Since founders have a strong tendency to set up their venture in an industry in which they have previously worked and have experience with (Fritsch and Falck 2007), the characteristics of the incumbents' knowledge base and the type of technological regime in which these operate will shape the industry structure of future start-ups. Another aspect of the regional industry structure that should have an effect on knowledge exploitation by start-ups is the minimum efficient size of regional industries. Accordingly, regions that have high shares of industries with low minimum efficient size should also experience relatively high levels of new business formation in these industries. Hence, it is expected that these regions will have a high employment share in smaller businesses that act as "seedbeds" for new business formation in the future.[4]

Fritsch and Noseleit (2013b) find that the effect of new business formation on growth is more pronounced in regions with a high share of small business employment. They suspect that this result is due to the fact that young businesses start small and are more likely to compete with other small businesses than with large firms and that this more intense competition between new businesses and incumbents leads to a relatively strong effect on regional growth. We therefore suspect that there will be a higher share of small firm employment in regions with an entrepreneurial regime compared to regions with a revolving-door regime.

Another factor that may have an effect on regional performance is the concentration or variety of the industry structure, although empirical support for this idea is ambiguous (for an overview see Content and Frenken 2016). Frenken et al. (2007) and Boschma and Frenken (2011) argue that it is not industry variety per se, but the related variety of similar or complementary industries, that has positive effects. And, indeed, there is evidence that new business formation can make an important contribution to the emergence of such related variety (Neffke et al. 2011). Noseleit (2013) compares the industry structure of entries with the industry structure of incumbents, as well as with the industry structure of those firms that exit. He finds that dissimilarity of these structures has a pronounced positive effect on regional development in West German regions. Based on these results, we expect that dissimilarity of industry structure between start-ups and exits will be particularly high in regions with an entrepreneurial growth regime and relatively low in regions that are characterized by a revolving-door regime.

The share of regional employees in knowledge-intensive business services (KIBS) may indicate at least two things. First, it can demonstrate a well-developed and relatively rich knowledge base in a region, particularly a high level of labor

---

[4]The relatively high propensity of small-firm employees to start an own firm is well documented by empirical research (Parker 2009; Elfenbein et al. 2010). Another reason small average firm size in a region may lead to a high number of start-ups is that it implies a high density of entrepreneurs who act as role models for potential founders (see Bosma et al. 2012).

division in knowledge-intensive activity. Second, it is an indicator for the availability of knowledge that may be conducive to the competitiveness and development of the local economy. Since local availability of knowledge inputs can be particularly important for the success of start-ups suffering from unbalanced skill sets (Helsley and Strange 2011), we expect a positive relationship between the employment share in KIBS and the success of start-ups. Hence, high shares of KIBS employment should be found particularly in regions with an entrepreneurial growth regime. High shares of KIBS employment may also be found in routinized regimes where large firms have a long-established division of labor with local service suppliers. Specifically, we expect a higher share of KIBS employment in regions with a routinized regime compared with regions characterized by a downsizing regime.[5]

1.3.3 General Regional Entrepreneurial Environment

It is not farfetched to expect that regions with relatively high start-up rates might have favorable conditions for entrepreneurship. These can include easy accessibility of inputs such as labor and finance, as well as a generally held positive attitude toward self-employment (Kibler et al. 2014; Westlund et al. 2014) and a large number of entrepreneurial role models (Bosma et al. 2012). Thus we expect especially high shares of self-employed persons in regions with an entrepreneurial regime and a revolving-door regime as compared to the two other regime types.

Since several empirical studies show that high levels of entrepreneurship tend to be persistent over time (Andersson and Koster 2011; Fotopoulos 2014; Fritsch and Wyrwich 2014), it is expected that most of the transitions between types of growth regime will be between those with a relatively high start-up rate (entrepreneurial, revolving door) and those with a relatively low start-up rate (routinized, downsizing). We thus expect relatively high levels of transition, especially between revolving-door and entrepreneurial regimes as well as between routinized and downsizing regimes.

1.3.4 Summarizing the Hypotheses

Table 1.1 provides a summary of the general characteristics we expect to find in the different types of growth regimes. In Table 1.2, we summarize our expectations regarding the regional characteristics of certain regime types. These expectations are reported in pairwise comparison in line with our empirical approach. With

---

[5] Since KIBS tend to rely heavily on geographic proximity to customers, they tend to be located in larger cities, delivering their services across considerable spatial distance. Hence, the regional share of KIBS employment could be primarily determined by the regional level of urbanization, while their effect may not be limited to the region where they are located. In this case, the effect of the local share of KIBS employment on the success of new businesses in that particular region may be found to be not statistically significant (Keeble and Nachum 2002; Wood 2005).

Table 1.1 Summary of the general regional characteristics

Regional characteristic	Entrepreneurial regime	Revolving-door regime	Routinized regime	Downsizing regime
Regional knowledge base and quality of start-ups	High knowledge intensity and high level of innovation; high share of activity under the conditions of an entrepreneurial technological regime	Low knowledge intensity and low level of innovation; low quality and low survival rates of start-ups	High knowledge intensity and high level of innovative output; high share of activity under the conditions of a routinized technological regime	Low knowledge intensity and low level of innovative output; low survival rates of start-ups; high share of activity under the conditions of a routinized technological regime
Regional industry structure	High share of small firms; high variety of industry structure; high employment share in knowledge-intensive services; entries strongly induce variety of industry structure	Relatively high share of small firms; low level of structural change (industry structure of entries similar to structure of exits); low variety of industry structure	Low share of small firms; low variety of industry structure but high employment share in knowledge-intensive services	High share of large firms; low variety of industry structure; low level of structural change (industry structure of start-ups similar to industry structure of exits)
General regional entrepreneurial environment	Favorable conditions for entrepreneurship, such as high level of peer effects and easy access to supportive infrastructure and other important resources	Low level of supportive infrastructure, but high level of peer effects	Low level of both supportive infrastructure for start-ups and peer effects	Low level of both supportive infrastructure for start-ups and peer effects

regard to the effect of new business formation on regional growth, the most interesting comparisons are between the entrepreneurial and the revolving-door regime as well as between the routinized and the downsizing regime. These are the cases where a relatively high or low level of start-up activity leads to above- or below-average employment growth. Hence, these comparisons should reveal some of the reasons for the opposite development patterns. The most pronounced differences should be found between the two extreme cases with regard to new business formation and growth, i.e., the entrepreneurial regime and the downsizing regime. According to Table 1.2, a relatively small number of differences is to be expected between the revolving-door regime and the downsizing regime.

Table 1.2 Expected differences between growth regime types

Regional characteristics	Indicator	Entrepreneurial vs. revolving door	Entrepreneurial vs. routinized	Entrepreneurial vs. downsizing	Revolving door vs. routinized	Revolving door vs. downsizing	Routinized vs. downsizing
Regional knowledge base and quality of start-ups	Share of highly qualified workforce	+	≈	+	−	≈	+
	Share of private-sector R&D employment	+	≈	+	−	−	+
	Survival rates of new businesses	+	+	+	−	≈	+
Regional industry structure	Employment share of small businesses	+	+	+	+	+	≈
	Similarity of industry structure between entries and exits	−	−	−	≈	≈	≈
	Level of industry diversity	+	+	+	≈	≈	≈
	Share of KIBS employment	+	≈	+	−	≈	+
General entrepreneurial conditions	Self-employment rate	≈	+	+	+	+	≈

"+" denotes "higher" and "−" denotes "lower" values for the first indicated growth regime; "≈" means that we do not expect any significant differences between the two regime types

1.4 Data Issues

1.4.1 Data Sources and Classification into Regime Types

The spatial framework of our analysis is comprised of the 71 planning regions of West Germany,[6] which represent functionally integrated spatial units comparable to labor market areas in the United States. Our data on new business formation are obtained from the German Social Insurance Statistics. This dataset contains every establishment in Germany that employs at least one person obliged to make social insurance contributions (Spengler 2008). The start-up rate is the yearly number of new businesses in the private sector divided by the number of those employed in the private-sector labor force (in 1000s).[7] In contrast to previous studies (Audretsch and Fritsch 2002; Fritsch and Mueller 2006), we exploit a novel and more reliable method of identifying start-ups in the data that is based on workflow analyses (Hethey and Schmieder 2010). Another main advantage of our work over previous studies is our considerably longer time period of more than 30 years, from 1976 to 2011. Data on establishment size distribution, qualification of workforce, R&D employment, and sectoral structure are also obtained from the Social Insurance Statistics; other information is from the Statistical Offices and other sources. All industry-related measures account for changes in the industry classification over time (for details see Eberle et al. 2011).

Classification into the four types of growth regime is based on the average start-up rate for the first 2 years of the respective time period and the percentage of employment change for the whole period. Because the main part of the positive employment effects of new businesses occurs only in the longer run (Fritsch 2013), it is important to relate the indicators for entrepreneurship to growth performance over a sufficiently long period. Fritsch and Mueller (2004) find for West German regions that the strongest positive effect of new business formation on regional employment occurs about 7–8 years after the new entities are set up. To capture such long-term effects, we divide the period of analysis into four relatively long periods of 8 years each: 1976–1984, 1985–1993, 1994–2002, and 2003–2011. Figure 1.2 shows the distribution of regional growth regimes for the period 1994–2002 as an example.

The distinction into the four long-time periods is particularly used for descriptive purposes (see Sect. 1.4.2) and for the empirical analyses of the development of

---

[6] We restrict our analysis to West Germany because many empirical studies indicate that the East German economy in the 1990s was a special case with very specific conditions that cannot be directly compared to those of West Germany (cf. Fritsch 2004). There are actually 74 West German planning regions. For administrative reasons, the cities of Hamburg and Bremen are defined as planning regions even though they are not functional economic units. To avoid distortions, we merged these cities with adjacent planning regions. Hamburg was merged with the region of Schleswig-Holstein South and Hamburg-Umland-South. Bremen was merged with Bremen-Umland. Thus, the number of regions in our sample is 71.

[7] Start-ups in agriculture are not considered in the analysis.

1 Entrepreneurship, Growth, and Regional Growth Regimes

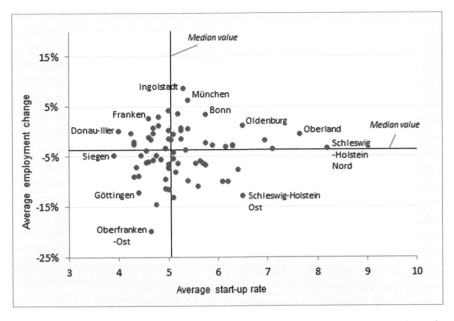

Fig. 1.2 The relationship between new business formation and regional employment change in West German regions, 1994–2002 (Source: own presentation)

growth regime types over time (Sect. 1.6). For the empirical analysis of the distinctive characteristics of the different growth regime types in Sect. 1.5, we define seven partly overlapping time periods (1979–1987, 1983–1991, 1987–1995, 1991–1999, 1995–2003, 1999–2007, 2003–2011) in order to increase the available number of observations. Moreover, this classification does not include the years 1975–1978 for which information about some of the regional characteristics is missing.

1.4.2 The Spatial Distribution of Growth Regime Types

The geographical distribution of the four growth regime types in the two most recent time periods (Fig. 1.3) reveals two remarkable phenomena. First, we find no evidence of an erratic patchwork-like pattern of regional growth regimes, but there are pronounced neighborhood effects in the sense that adjacent regions are frequently assigned to the same type of growth regime. Obviously, the regional context that has an effect on the relationship between entrepreneurial activity and economic development often encompasses more than a single planning region. Second, there is a pronounced tendency of regions to be assigned to the same type of growth regime in subsequent time periods, indicating a certain degree of persistence. As expected, transitions between regime types are mostly between those with relatively high (entrepreneurial and revolving door) and relatively low start-up rates (downsizing

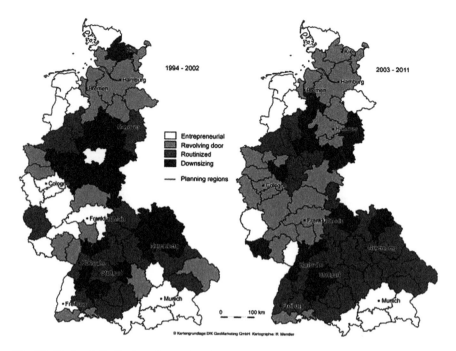

Fig. 1.3 Regional distribution of growth regime types over time (Source: Own presentation)

and routinized), indicating that the regional level of new business formation fluctuates less than regional employment growth.

An example of persistence of regional growth regime type is the southern part of Bavaria, particularly the Munich region and the regions south of it, which are in most or all observation periods classified as entrepreneurial. Also, a number of regions south of Hamburg and south of Frankfurt are always classified as entrepreneurial or revolving door. A downsizing or routinized regime is characteristic of the Ruhr area and of Stuttgart and surrounding regions.

1.5 Empirical Analysis of Regional Growth Regime Characteristics

1.5.1 Variables

Our dependent variable represents the growth regime type as described in Sect. 1.4.1. The following explanatory variables are included in the analysis (see also descriptive statistics in Tables 1.6, 1.7, 1.8, 1.9, 1.10, 1.11 and 1.12 in the Appendix).

- To measure the *regional knowledge base* we employ two variables. First, the *qualification level of the workforce* is captured by the share of private-sector employees with a tertiary degree in total private-sector employment. The second variable is the share of private-sector R&D as measured by the share of R&D employees in private-sector employment.[8]

- Our proxy for *start-up performance and quality of entrants* is captured by start-up survival rates, namely, the share of private-sector start-ups still in existence after 5 years compared to the total number of start-ups in the respective year of foundation.
- *Establishment size* is measured by the share of private-sector employment in establishments with less than 20 employees over total private-sector employment. To reduce the statistical relationship with the start-up indicator—the majority of new businesses start out very small—we exclude the employment in the start-ups that emerged in the respective year.
- We construct several variables to account for *regional industry structure and its development*. The first employs an entropy measure of regional industrial diversity according to Theil (1972) and as used by Fotopoulos (2014). The measure can be constructed in a way that the values vary between 0 and 1, with 0 indicating the presence of only one industry in the region and 1 representing a situation where all industries employ an equal number of employees. The variety measure is based on a distinction of 28 industries.
- We use a measure of the similarity between industry affiliation of start-ups and exits employed by Noseleit (2013). Since the number of employees in start-ups might not be an appropriate indicator of their economic significance, we relate the mere number of start-ups to the number of exits. The similarity measure is calculated as a correlation coefficient between the number of entries and the number of exits in 28 industries (two-digit level). This correlation coefficient can assume values from -1 to $+1$. A high level of correlation indicates a weak influence of entries on changes in the regional sectoral structure.
- The regional *supply of knowledge-intensive services* is measured by the share of employment in KIBS in total private-sector employment.
- As an indicator of the *general entrepreneurial conditions* in a region, we use the self-employment rate, which is calculated as the number of establishments in a region's nonagricultural private-sector industries divided by the regional workforce, thus reflecting the number of entrepreneurial role models in a region.
- In addition to our set of explanatory variables, we also employ a number of *control variables*. Population density is used as a catch-all variable for various regional characteristics (e.g., congestion issues, housing and land prices, infrastructure availability, etc.). To capture effects of different political conditions, we include dummies for the federal state to which a region belongs. Year dummies are included to control for time-specific effects.

---

[8]Another important aspect of the regional knowledge base is the presence and size of higher education institutions such as universities. Unfortunately, detailed information on higher education institutions is not available for the full period of analysis.

Table 1.3 Characteristics of regimes: mean characteristics and t-test of equal means

Indicator	Full sample	Entrepreneurial	Revolving door	Routinized	Down-sizing
Share of highly qualified workforce	0.056	0.054	0.061***	0.053	0.053
Share of private-sector R&D employment	0.024	0.023*	0.026**	0.024	0.025
Survival rates of new businesses	0.573	0.578*	0.552**	0.589	0.571
Employment share of small businesses	0.294	0.323***	0.314***	0.279***	0.264***
Self-employment rate	0.096	0.104***	0.102***	0.093***	0.085***
Similarity of industry structure between entries and exits	0.967	0.964*	0.974***	0.963***	0.967
Level of industry diversity	0.852	0.853	0.844***	0.861***	0.848**
Share of KIBS employment	0.048	0.044	0.061***	0.048	0.039**
Population density (log)	5.405	5.253***	5.572***	5.201***	5.592***
Number of observations	497	108	131	137	121

Asterisks for each regime indicate that the mean of the particular regime is statistically different from the mean of all the rest of the sample, ***statistically significant at the 1% level; **statistically significant at the 5% level; *statistically significant at the 10% level

1.5.2 Characteristics of Regional Growth Regimes: T-tests of Equal Means

In the first step of the statistical analysis, we calculate the mean values for the regional characteristics in the different regime types over the complete observation period and conduct t-tests for significant differences between a particular growth regime type and the rest of the sample (Table 1.3). We find significant differences for all the variables considered.

The results show that regions with an entrepreneurial regime are characterized by a relatively high level of both self-employment and employment in small establishments. They have a relatively high level of industry diversity and relatively low similarity between the industry affiliation of entries and that of exits. Although the share of highly qualified workforce in regions with an entrepreneurial regime is somewhat below average, new businesses in these regions have higher than average survival rates.

Regions with a revolving-door regime have an above-average share of highly qualified workforce, but the survival rates of start-ups are relatively low. As in regions with an entrepreneurial regime, the share of employees in small establishments is relatively high in revolving-door regimes. Regions with a revolving-door regime exhibit the lowest level of industry diversity, while the similarity between the industry structure of exits and entries is the highest. Surprisingly,

1 Entrepreneurship, Growth, and Regional Growth Regimes

regions with a revolving-door regime are characterized by a relatively high share of employment in KIBS.

The characteristics of regions with a routinized regime are rather similar to regions with a downsizing regime. Both types of regions have a below-average share of highly qualified workforce and below-average self-employment rates. The relatively small share of employment in small businesses indicates an on average large establishment size. In regions with a routinized regime type, the similarity between the industry structure of entries and that of exits is relatively low. Below-average similarity of industry structure between entries and exits indicates a relatively high level of structural change in regions with a routinized regime. In regions with a downsizing regime, this type of similarity is about average. Another difference between the two types of regions is that the share of KIBS employment is about average in regions with a routinized regime and significantly below average in regions with a downsizing regime. Furthermore, the population density of downsizing regions is above average, whereas it is below average for regions with a routinized regime. High population density is also a characteristic of regions with a revolving-door regime. In regions with an entrepreneurial regime, population density is significantly below average.

These differences of means tests provide a first impression of the characteristics of regions with different growth regime types, but the impression may be hazy and imprecise for at least two reasons. First, since we always compare the regions of a certain growth regime type with all remaining regions, the sample used for the comparison—all other regions—is not the same across regime types, which makes interpretation difficult. Second, since the variables are related to each other, multivariate analysis should be performed. We thus pairwise compare the characteristics of the different growth regime types by multivariate analyses (for t-tests for equal means of such a pairwise comparison, see Table 1.14 in the Appendix).

1.5.3 Multivariate Analyses of Regime-Type Characteristics

1.5.3.1 Methodology

To test the hypotheses developed in the Sect. 1.3, we use probit regression analysis to estimate the effect of the distinctive set of regional characteristics on the likelihood that the region will belong to the particular regional growth regime. Our dependent variable assumes the value 1 if a region belongs to certain type of growth regime and 0 otherwise. The base model is specified as follows:

$$P\left(Y_{it} = 1 | X_{it}\right) = \beta_0 + \beta_1 HC_{it} + \beta_2 SURV_{it} + \beta_3 RD_{it} + \beta_4 SMALLF_{it} + \beta_5 SIM_{it}$$
$$+ \beta_6 DIV_{it} + \beta_7 KIBS_{it} + \beta_n \chi_{it} + \varepsilon\varepsilon_{it.}$$

with Y_{it} as an indicator for the particular growth regime type of region i in time period t, HC_{it} as the share of employees with a tertiary degree, $SURV_{it}$ as the 5-year

Table 1.4 Distinctive characteristics of regional growth regimes (marginal effects)

Indicator	Entrepreneurial vs. revolving door	Entrepreneurial vs. routinized	Entrepreneurial vs. downsizing	Revolving door vs. routinized	Revolving door vs. downsizing	Routinized vs. downsizing
Share of highly qualified workforce	6.79**	6.25**	0.83	−5.30***	6.67**	15.65***
	(2.79)	(3.17)	(2.35)	(1.99)	(3.39)	(4.51)
Survival rates of new businesses	5.53***	−0.15	2.67***	−1.31	−2.77**	3.24**
	(1.43)	(1.03)	(0.90)	(1.17)	(1.07)	(1.37)
Employment share of small businesses	2.54**	8.05***	8.23***	6.55***	9.54***	3.70*
	(1.17)	(1.07)	(1.06)	(1.00)	(1.89)	(1.92)
Similarity of industry structure between entries and exits	−3.67*	−1.52	0.06	4.19*	0.46	0.52
	(2.09)	(1.33)	(1.19)	(2.23)	(1.39)	(2.00)
Level of industry diversity	3.59*	−1.67	3.53*	−5.39**	0.96	4.10**
	(2.16)	(1.77)	(1.81)	(2.08)	(2.38)	(2.04)
Share of KIBS employment	−1.9	−2.42	−0.16	−0.17	0.7	−9.26**
	(2.48)	(2.93)	(0.66)	(0.60)	(2.37)	(3.77)
Population density (log)	0.06	0.38***	0.16	0.53***	0.31**	−0.31**
	(0.12)	(0.12)	(0.11)	(0.12)	(0.15)	(0.15)
Year dummies	Yes	Yes*	Yes	Yes	Yes*	Yes*
Federal state dummies	Yes	Yes	Yes	Yes	Yes	Yes
Number of observations	239	245	229	268	252	258
Log likelihood	−130.28	−69.93	−72.01	−69.28	−71.54	−124.24
Chi2	41.78	16.28	31.8	24.1	16.54	29.04

Dependent variable: First mentioned regime (= 1) versus second mentioned regime (= 0). Random effects probit regression, standard errors in parentheses. ***statistically significant at the 1% level; **statistically significant at the 5% level; *statistically significant at the 10% level survival rate, RD_{it} as the share of R&D employees in private-sector employment, $SMALLF_{it}$ as the share of employment in establishments with less than 20 employees excluding employment in start-ups of the current year (in alternative specifications, we use the self-employment rate—SER_{it}—instead), SIM_{it} as the level of similarity between the industry structure of the start-ups and that of the exits, DIV_{it} as the regional diversity index, $KIBS_{it}$ as the share of employment in KIBS, χ_{it} as a set of control variables (population density, federal state dummies, year dummies), and ε_{it} as the error term.

We make pairwise comparisons of the growth regime types, resulting in six models. Due to the high correlation between some of the variables of interest, we do not include all these variables in the base model but test the effect of the other variables in separate models. The dependent variable assumes the value 1 for a particular type of growth regime and is 0 for the comparison group. The independent variables relate to the first year of the respective period. We run the regressions with random effects in order to account for time-invariant factors such as affiliation with a certain federal state. This is particularly appropriate because a number of variables show very little change over time so that in a fixed effects setting, their influence would mainly be assigned to the fixed effects.

1.5.3.2 Pairwise Comparison of Characteristics of Regional Growth Regimes

Table 1.4 shows the results of the pairwise comparisons of the different regime types. The results of the analyses support our general hypothesis that the sources and mechanisms driving regional development might vary considerably across types of regional growth regime. We find that regions with an entrepreneurial growth regime have a higher share of highly qualified workforce than regions with a revolving-door and a routinized regime. This finding clearly emphasizes the importance of the regional knowledge base for the number and quality of start-ups. Surprisingly, however, there is no significant difference in this regard between regions with an entrepreneurial regime and a downsizing regime. According to our expectations, regions with either an entrepreneurial or a revolving-door regime have significantly higher shares of small business employment than regions with a routinized or downsizing regime. This higher share of employment in small businesses may be the source of a relatively high number of start-ups, reflecting the relatively high propensity of small firm employees to start an own firm (Parker 2009), as well as a result of high levels of new business formation because most start-ups remain small.

The most interesting pairwise comparisons with regard to employment generation are between high and low start-up regions with above- and below-average employment growth, that is, entrepreneurial versus revolving-door regimes and routinized versus downsizing regimes. In this comparison we find several significant differences. Regions with an entrepreneurial regime have a higher share of qualified workforce and higher rates of new business survival, which probably contribute to a higher share of small business employment. Moreover, regions with an entrepreneurial regime have a lower level of similarity between entries and exits and higher degrees of industry variety.

Comparing the characteristics of a routinized regime with those of a downsizing regime, we find that the former is characterized by a significantly larger share of highly qualified employees, higher rates of new business survival, a higher share of small business employment, and a higher level of industry diversity. Moreover, regions with a routinized regime are characterized by a lower population density as well as by a lower employment share of KIBS. In the comparison of a revolving-door regime to a routinized regime, there is a higher share of highly qualified employees, a larger share of small business employment, a higher degree of similarity between entries and exits, a lower level of industry diversity, and higher population density in regions with a revolving-door regime.

Comparing the two regime types with above-average employment growth—entrepreneurial and routinized—we find a significantly higher share of highly qualified workforce, a higher share of small business employment, and greater population density in regions with an entrepreneurial regime. Similar differences can be found between revolving-door regimes and downsizing regimes. In addition downsizing regions have higher survival rates of new businesses than revolving-door regions.

A number of robustness checks were performed. Due to the high correlation between the share of highly qualified workforce and the share of private-sector R&D employment, we ran the models separately with just one of the two measures. Likewise, different models were run with the small business employment share and the self-employment. Separate models were also run with the measure for overall industry diversity among the regional industries. Since the values of the start-up rate or employment change for some regions are close to the median values, we also ran models where we excluded those regions whose values of the start-up rate and employment change were within a 5% distance on either side of the median values of the respective time period. These robustness checks did not lead to any results significantly different from those obtained from the main model.

As another robustness check, we have defined growth regimes based on sector-adjusted start-up rates that should control for the fact that the composition of industries not only varies across regions but that the relative importance of new and incumbent businesses also varies systematically across industries (for details, see the Appendix of Audretsch and Fritsch 2002). Empirical results do not lead to significant contradictions compared to the base models; however, indicators for industry structure and its change reduced in significance, as was to be expected.

1.6 The Development of Growth Regimes over Time

1.6.1 Transition Probabilities

The spatial distribution of growth regime types in successive time periods (Fig. 1.3) shows, on the one hand, that regions demonstrate a tendency to remain in the same category for subsequent periods. On the other hand, there are quite considerable changes. To analyze these patterns, we first calculate transition probabilities for the different regime types. The results are shown in Fig. 1.4 and in Table 1.13 in the Appendix.

Generally, the probabilities for the transition of regions between different regime types indicate a high level of persistence over time. On average, 42% of the entrepreneurial regions stay entrepreneurial in the following time period. The probability of remaining entrepreneurial is 31% higher than that of switching to revolving door and 2.3 times higher than becoming routinized. Our analysis indicates a low probability for a direct transition from entrepreneurial regime to downsizing regime

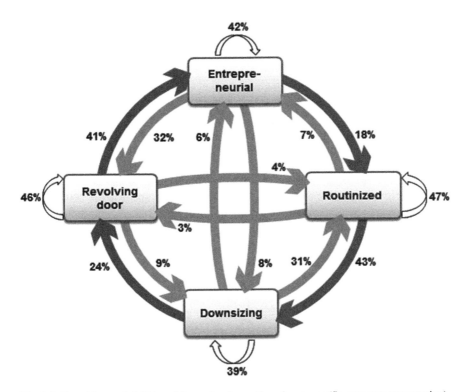

Fig. 1.4 Transition probabilities of the regional growth regime types (Source: own presentation)

(8%). Revolving-door regions have a high probability of either remaining revolving door (46%) or becoming entrepreneurial (41%) in the following time period when compared to the probability of switching to downsizing (9%) or routinized (4%). Routinized regions have a high probability of either remaining routinized (47%) or becoming downsizing (43%). The probability of switching to an entrepreneurial type of regime is relatively low (7%) for these regions. It is remarkable that there is only one instance of a region switching directly from having a routinized regime to having a revolving-door regime in the period of analysis. Once being host to a downsizing regime, a region has the highest probability to remain downsizing (39%) and the lowest probability of experiencing a direct transition to an entrepreneurial regime (6%).

Transition probabilities tend to be higher between the entrepreneurial and the revolving-door types of regime and between routinized and downsizing regimes. Technically speaking, this pattern indicates that changes in the relative level of new business formation tend to be smaller than changes in the relative level of employment growth. Accordingly, the probability of an entrepreneurial regime to become a routinized regime is only 18% as compared to a probability of 32% for an entrepreneurial regime to become a revolving-door type and a probability of 43% for a routinized regime to become downsizing (Fig. 1.4).

Generally, our findings are in line with the analysis of Fritsch and Mueller (2006) and suggest a typical long-term development pattern. Accordingly, if a region with a downsizing regime experiences an increase in new business formation, it will most probably have a revolving-door regime before it eventually attains an entrepreneurial growth regime. Correspondingly, if a region with an entrepreneurial growth regime experiences a decline in the level of new business formation, it will first assume the character of a routinized growth regime before eventually becoming host to a downsizing regime.

These results suggest that at least in some regions, the effect of new business formation on growth occurs with a time lag that is considerably longer than the 10 years suggested by a number of empirical analyses (e.g., Fritsch and Mueller 2004). It may take a long time before the growth effects of an increased level of entrepreneurship become evident, and even if the start-up rate begins to decrease, the growth benefits of higher start-up rates in a region are likely to continue for a number of years.

1.6.2 How Persistent Are Regional Growth Regimes?

Since simple transition probabilities do not account for the panel structure of the data, in a final step, we analyze the statistical significance of the transition probabilities between the different types of growth regimes over time. The simple transition probabilities suggest that the entrepreneurial, as well as the downsizing growth regimes tend to be stable over time, whereas the revolving-door and the routinized

1 Entrepreneurship, Growth, and Regional Growth Regimes

regimes appear to be more temporary in character. Indeed, for the revolving-door and routinized regimes, the probabilities of transitioning to other regime types are nearly the same as the probability of remaining in the same category, whereas for the entrepreneurial and downsizing regimes, the probabilities of remaining in the same category for two subsequent time periods are more pronounced. Moreover, the results suggest a typical development pattern, in which a region with a downsizing regime evolves, via a revolving-door regime, into an entrepreneurial regime that may, in time, transform into a routinized regime with a high probability of becoming a downsizing regime again.

We employ probit analysis to estimate the persistence and transitional nature of the different growth regime types over time. The dependent variable reflects the respective type of growth regime (1 = yes, 0 otherwise), and the independent variables represent the regime type the region belonged to in the previous period. We estimate

$$P(Y_{it} = 1|X_{it}) = \beta_0 + \beta_1 ENTR_{i,t-1} + \beta_2 REVD_{i,t-1} + \beta_3 ROUT_{i,t-1}$$
$$+ \beta_4 DOWN_{i,t-1} + \beta_n X_{it} + \varepsilon_{it}$$

where Y_{it} is an indicator for the growth regime type of a region i in period t; $ENTR_{i,t-1}$, $REVD_{i,t-1}$, $ROUT_{i,t-1}$, and $DOWN_{i,t-1}$ indicate whether the region had an entrepreneurial, revolving-door, routinized, or downsizing growth regime in period t-1 (1 = yes, 0 otherwise); and X_{it} is a set of control variables (federal state dummies, year dummies) with ε_{it} representing the error term.

To avoid overdetermination of the model, we do not include all four variables for the growth regime type in the previous period. Four sequential periods (1976–1984, 1985–1993, 1994–2002, 2003–2011; see Fig. 1.3) are considered, allowing us to observe three transition events for each region. We run the regressions with random effects, thereby controlling for time-invariant factors by including dummies for federal states.

The results of the probit regressions (Table 1.5) indicate that belonging to the entrepreneurial and the downsizing regime type in a certain period significantly increases the probability of belonging to the respective regime type in the following period. No persistence is found for the revolving-door and the routinized regime. Results indicate that being a revolving-door regime significantly decreases the probability of becoming a routinized regime in the next period. Likewise, being an entrepreneurial regime significantly decreases the probability of becoming a routinized regime. The results also show that revolving-door and routinized regimes are especially transitional in nature. Being a region with a revolving-door regime significantly increases the probability of becoming an entrepreneurial regime type in the next period, and regions with a routinized regime have a significant probability of becoming downsizing regimes in the following period.

The multivariate analyses confirm the pattern found for the simple transition probabilities (Sect. 1.6.1) and suggest a certain long-term development pattern for

Table 1.5 Persistence and change of growth regimes over time

Indicator	Entrepreneurial	Revolving door	Routinized	Downsizing
Entrepreneurial (t-1)	1.28***	0.37	−0.71*	0.09
	(0.40)	(0.29)	(0.40)	(0.39)
Revolving door (t-1)	1.53***	0.29	−1.33**	
	(0.42)	(0.40)	(0.52)	
Routinized (t-1)	0.12	−0.65	−0.23	1.27***
	(0.44)	(2.03)	(0.50)	(0.37)
Downsizing (t-1)				0.99***
				(0.34)
Year dummies	Yes*	Yes	Yes	Yes*
Federal state dummies	Yes	Yes	Yes	Yes
Constant	−2.22***	0.27	−0.75	−1.96***
	(0.64)	(0.55)	(0.76)	(0.59)
Number of observations	213	213	213	213
Log likelihood	−87.66	−91.93	−94.56	−97.09
Chi2	34.24	20.67	19.86	34.93

Dependent variable: regime vs. rest of the regimes; random effects probit regression; standard errors in parentheses; ***statistically significant at the 1% level; **statistically significant at the 5% level; *statistically significant at the 10% level

growth regime types. It can be concluded that if a region with low levels of entrepreneurship and low growth (downsizing regime) experiences an increase in new business formation, it will most probably become a revolving-door regime for some time before it eventually becomes an entrepreneurial growth regime, in which new business formation leads to considerable employment growth. Correspondingly, if regions with an entrepreneurial growth regime experience a decline in start-ups, they will first, and for some time, assume the character of a routinized growth regime before they eventually devolve into a downsizing regime.

1.7 Critical Points in the Development of the Growth Regime Life Cycle

The analysis of transitions between different growth regimes suggests that regions are subject to a type of life-cycle development. Taking a situation with no economic activity as a starting point, the emergence of new businesses constitutes first a revolving-door regime, which may, after some time, become an entrepreneurial regime, and then a routinized regime with a certain probability of turning into a downsizing regime. In this life cycle, the entrepreneurial and downsizing regimes tend to be relatively stable, while the revolving-door and routinized regimes are more transitional in character. There are several real-world illustrations of such a life-cycle development. For example, there are regions dominated by a certain industry, such as the automobile industry in Detroit (USA) or the coal and steel industries in the Ruhr area in Germany, that have followed a full life cycle from the emergence of the industry to its decline in a mature stage. However, there are also regions with a more diverse industrial structure that show this type of development.[9]

The life-cycle pattern of development reveals that having an increased level of regional new business formation may not immediately lead to growth but, instead, to a revolving-door regime with a considerable likelihood of becoming an entrepreneurial regime after some time. If regions have succeeded in establishing an entrepreneurial regime, the regime may prove to be stable and persistent. A number of empirical analyses demonstrate that the stability of a region's entrepreneurial orientation may be self-perpetuating and, therefore, persistent over long periods of time (Andersson and Koster 2011; Fritsch and Mueller 2007; Fritsch and Wyrwich 2014). The reasons for this phenomenon are no doubt manifold and as yet only partly understood. Possibly, regions with a relatively high number of start-ups provide many entrepreneurial role models that stimulate further new businesses (Bosma et al. 2012). Moreover, entrepreneurial regions tend to have a high share of employment in small firms, a situation with a great deal of potential for enhanced entrepreneurship. High levels of new business formation, particularly if in new markets, can also generate relatively many entrepreneurial opportunities that induce start-ups. Last, but not least, a regional culture of entrepreneurship may emerge, that is characterized by a high level of social acceptance of self-employment entrepreneurship and a rich supporting infrastructure.

The life-cycle model reveals a danger that regions with an entrepreneurial regime may in the long run become victim of their own success. The constant inflow of new firms with new ideas makes it quite likely that some of these start-ups will grow and become large firms, with the possible consequence that the regional level of entrepreneurship will decrease. For example, the growth of successful firms leads to a decline in the share of small firm employment that constitutes an important seedbed for new businesses. This may reduce the local workforce's propensity to engage in start-ups. Moreover, good availability of well-paid jobs in large firms may make secure dependent employment more preferable to risky self-employment for some would-be entrepreneurs. The region's entrepreneurial spirit may thus wane, resulting in transition to a routinized regime. This is especially likely if the region is dominated by one or a few large firms. Once having reached the stage of a routinized regime, a region loses variety and becomes vulnerable to external shocks. If the innovativeness of the region's established firms declines or market demand falls, the region may become an old industrialized area with low entry rates and below-average employment growth or even decline, that is, it will become host to a downsizing growth regime. Obviously,

---

[9] The development in some regions of Baden-Wuerttemberg (Germany), for example, the region of Stuttgart, may be viewed as an example of such development.

a key task for policy in the life cycle is the establishment and preservation of an entrepreneurial culture that is characterized by high levels of new business formation. The life-cycle model suggests that this is particularly the appropriate strategy for regions with a downsizing regime. This may also be the best way to prevent regions with a routinized regime from becoming downsizing. Empirical evidence suggests that innovation and particularly diversification of the industry structure through entrepreneurial discovery are promising ways by which routinized regions may escape this possible threat (Neffke et al. 2011; Noseleit 2013).

1.8 Implications for Policy and for Further Research

In our analysis we distinguished between four types of regional growth regimes based on the relationship between new business formation and economic development. To identify the reasons for the different growth performance, we analyzed several characteristics to discover if there are distinctive regional aspects that make it more likely a certain region will have a certain type of growth regime. The results show that extent of the regional knowledge base, R&D intensity, the diversity of and entry-induced change in regional industry structure, and a region's general entrepreneurial environment are distinct across different growth regimes. The importance of these factors became particularly clear when comparing regime types that have similar intensity of start-up activity, namely, entrepreneurial and revolving-door regimes and routinized and downsizing regimes.

In investigating the development patterns of the four growth regime types over time, we found that while the downsizing as well as entrepreneurial growth regimes tend to be rather stable over time, the other two types appear to be of a more transitory nature. We identified typical transition patterns between the regime types that indicate relatively long-term positive effects of new business formation on regional development.

All in all, our analysis suggests that entrepreneurship in terms of new business formation is an important resource for initiating and safeguarding well-being under all conditions, that is, for all growth regime types. It may take a great deal of effort to make a region more entrepreneurial, but the reward may be long lasting. Regions home to prospering large firms should try particularly hard to preserve and intensify their entrepreneurial spirit.

Appendix

Table 1.6 Descriptive statistics (all regime types)

Indicator	Number of observations	Mean	Median	Minimum	Maximum	Standard deviation
Share of highly qualified workforce	497	0.056	0.050	0.015	0.185	0.026
Share of private-sector R&D employment	497	0.024	0.022	0.004	0.074	0.013
Survival rates of new businesses	497	0.573	0.570	0.489	0.690	0.036
Employment share of small businesses	497	0.294	0.288	0.191	0.480	0.052
Self-employment rate	497	0.096	0.093	0.059	0.166	0.017
Similarity of industry structure between entries and exits	497	0.967	0.971	0.861	0.993	0.018
Level of industry diversity	497	0.852	0.855	0.781	0.895	0.024
Share of KIBS employment	497	0.048	0.026	0.007	0.314	0.056
Population density (log)	497	5.405	5.263	4.220	7.125	0.667

Table 1.7 Descriptive statistics (entrepreneurial regime)

Indicator	Number of observations	Mean	Median	Minimum	Maximum	Standard deviation
Share of highly qualified workforce	108	0.054	0.043	0.016	0.185	0.031
Share of private-sector R&D employment	108	0.023	0.018	0.004	0.074	0.014
Survival rates of new businesses	108	0.578	0.572	0.503	0.685	0.038
Employment share of small businesses	108	0.323	0.322	0.216	0.480	0.057
Self-employment rate	108	0.104	0.102	0.070	0.159	0.018
Similarity of industry structure between entries and exits	108	0.964	0.970	0.861	0.992	0.021
Level of industry diversity	108	0.853	0.857	0.790	0.890	0.025
Share of KIBS employment	108	0.044	0.025	0.010	0.310	0.050
Population density (log)	108	5.253	5.121	4.220	7.045	0.614

Table 1.8 Descriptive statistics (revolving-door regime)

Indicator	Number of observations	Mean	Median	Minimum	Maximum	Standard deviation
Share of highly qualified workforce	131	0.061	0.057	0.019	0.149	0.027
Share of private-sector R&D employment	131	0.026	0.025	0.007	0.061	0.012
Survival rates of new businesses	131	0.552	0.549	0.489	0.622	0.028
Employment share of small businesses	131	0.314	0.309	0.207	0.469	0.058
Self-employment rate	131	0.102	0.100	0.067	0.166	0.020
Similarity of industry structure between entries and exits	131	0.974	0.976	0.907	0.993	0.015
Level of industry diversity	131	0.844	0.846	0.785	0.895	0.024
Share of KIBS employment	131	0.061	0.032	0.014	0.314	0.070
Population density (log)	131	5.572	5.438	4.234	7.125	0.762

Table 1.9 Descriptive statistics (routinized regime)

Indicator	Number of observations	Mean	Median	Minimum	Maximum	Standard deviation
Share of highly qualified workforce	137	0.053	0.050	0.015	0.130	0.024
Share of private-sector R&D employment	137	0.024	0.020	0.005	0.064	0.013
Survival rates of new businesses	137	0.589	0.589	0.514	0.690	0.036
Employment share of small businesses	137	0.279	0.282	0.191	0.344	0.030
Self-employment rate	137	0.093	0.092	0.064	0.127	0.011
Similarity of industry structure between entries and exits	137	0.963	0.966	0.905	0.989	0.016
Level of industry diversity	137	0.861	0.864	0.800	0.895	0.021
Share of KIBS employment	137	0.048	0.027	0.007	0.207	0.050
Population density (log)	137	5.201	5.130	4.431	6.572	0.474

1 Entrepreneurship, Growth, and Regional Growth Regimes

Table 1.10 Descriptive statistics (downsizing regime)

Indicator	Number of observations	Mean	Median	Minimum	Maximum	Standard deviation
Share of highly qualified workforce	121	0.053	0.048	0.021	0.145	0.022
Share of private-sector R&D employment	121	0.025	0.023	0.009	0.069	0.011
Survival rates of new businesses	121	0.571	0.567	0.500	0.671	0.033
Employment share of small businesses	121	0.264	0.267	0.197	0.368	0.036
Self-employment rate	121	0.085	0.084	0.059	0.128	0.013
Similarity of industry structure between entries and exits	121	0.967	0.971	0.876	0.990	0.019
Level of industry diversity	121	0.848	0.851	0.781	0.892	0.023
Share of KIBS employment	121	0.039	0.023	0.010	0.246	0.049
Population density (log)	121	5.592	5.394	4.564	7.074	0.698

Table 1.11 Correlation matrix

	Indicator	1	2	3	4	5	6	7	8
1	Share of highly qualified workforce	1.0							
2	Share of private-sector R&D employment	0.904*	1.0						
3	Survival rates of new businesses	−0.424*	−0.372*	1.0					
4	Employment share of small businesses	−0.297*	−0.369*	−0.056	1.0				
5	Self-employment rate	−0.091*	−0.192*	−0.054	0.877*	1.0			
6	Similarity of industry structure between entries and exits	0.339*	0.305*	−0.470*	−0.08	−0.082	1.0		
7	Level of industry diversity	−0.277*	−0.175*	0.324*	−0.07	−0.059	−0.155*	1.0	
8	Share of KIBS employment	0.613*	0.469*	−0.284*	−0.002	0.215*	0.220*	−0.327*	1.0
9	Population density (log)	0.561*	0.537*	−0.436*	−0.520*	−0.527*	0.417*	−0.150*	0.206*

*Statistically significant at the 5% level

Table 1.12 Correlation matrix

Indicator (regime type)		1	2	3	4	5	6	7
1	Entrepreneurial	1.0						
2	Revolving door	−0.318*	1.0					
3	Routinized	−0.326*	−0.349*	1.0				
4	Downsizing	−0.318*	−0.339*	−0.349*	1.0			
5	Entrepreneurial (t-1)	0.176*	0.170*	−0.098*	−0.243*	1.0		
6	Revolving door (t-1)	0.301*	0.212*	−0.274*	−0.224*	−0.317*	1.0	
7	Routinized (t-1)	−0.221*	−0.293*	0.370*	0.129	−0.327*	−0.344*	1.0
8	Downsizing (t-1)	−0.242*	−0.087*	0.001	0.322*	−0.323*	−0.339*	−0.349*

*Statistically significant at the 5% level

Table 1.13 Transition probabilities of the regional growth regimes across time periods

	Regime type in 1985–1993, 1994–2002, 2003–2011							
	Entrepreneurial		Revolving door		Routinized		Downsizing	
Regime type in 1976–1984, 1985–1993, 1994–2002	Cases	Share	Cases	Share	Cases	Share	Cases	Share
Entrepreneurial	9	39%	7	30%	5	22%	2	9%
	9	45%	6	30%	3	15%	2	10%
	8	42%	7	37%	3	16%	1	5%
Average transition probability		42%		32%		18%		8%
Revolving door	7	58%	5	42%	0	0%	0	0%
	8	53%	4	27%	0	0%	3	20%
	2	13%	11	69%	2	13%	1	6%
Average transition probability		41%		46%		4%		9%
Routinized	1	8%	1	8%	4	33%	6	50%
	1	7%	0	0%	6	40%	8	53%
	1	6%	0	0%	11	69%	4	25%
Average transition probability		7%		3%		47%		43%
Downsizing	3	13%	3	13%	5	21%	13	54%
	1	5%	6	29%	7	33%	7	33%
	0	0%	6	30%	8	40%	6	30%
Average transition probability		6%		24%		31%		39%

First row, change between 1976–1984 and 1985–1993; second row, change between 1985–1993 and 1994–2002; third row, change between 1994–2002 and 2003–2011; fourth row, average transition probability

Table 1.14 Characteristics of regimes: mean values and t-test of equal means

Indicator	Full sample	Entrepreneurial vs. revolving door	Entrepreneurial vs. routinized	Entrepreneurial vs. downsizing	Revolving door vs. routinized	Revolving door vs. downsizing	Routinized vs. downsizing
Share of highly qualified workforce	0.055	0.054**	1.054	2.054	0.061***	0.061***	0.053
Share of private-sector R&D employment	0.024	0.023**	0.023	0.023*	0.026**	0.026	0.024
Survival rates of new businesses	0.574	0.578**	0.578	0.578*	0.552**	0.552	0.589
Employment share of small businesses	0.295	0.323	0.323***	0.323***	0.314***	0.314***	0.279***
Self-employment rate	0.096	0.104	0.104***	0.104***	0.102***	0.102***	0.093***
Similarity of industry structure between entries and exits	0.967	0.964***	0.964	0.964	0.974***	0.974***	0.963**
Level of industry diversity	0.851	0.853***	1.853***	2.853*	0.844***	0.844	0.861***
Share of KIBS employment	0.049	0.044**	0.044	0.044	0.061**	0.061***	0.048*
Population density (log)	5.406	5.253***	5.253	5.253***	5.572***	5.572	5.201***
Number of observations	497	108	108	108	131	131	137

Asterisks for each regime type indicate that the mean value of the particular regime type is statistically different from the mean value of the other type of regime. ***statistically significant at the 1% level; **statistically significant at the 5% level; *statistically significant at the 10% level

Acknowledgment The research was partially supported by the German Science Foundation (DFG RTG 1411).

References

Acs, Z. J., Audretsch, D. B., & Lehmann, E. E. (2013). The knowledge spillover theory of entrepreneurship. *Small Business Economics, 41*, 757–774. https://doi.org/10.1007/s11187-013-9505-9.

Andersson, M., & Koster, S. (2011). Sources of persistence in regional start-up rates-evidence from Sweden. *Journal of Economic Geography, 11*, 179–201. https://doi.org/10.1093/jeg/lbp069.

Audretsch, D. B. (1995). *Innovation and industry evolution.* Cambridge, MA: MIT Press.

Audretsch, D., & Fritsch, M. (2002). Growth regimes over time and space. *Regional Studies, 36*, 113–124. https://doi.org/10.1080/0034340022012190.

Audretsch, D. B., Falck, O., Feldman, M. P., & Heblich, S. (2012). Local entrepreneurship in context. *Regional Studies, 46*, 379–389. https://doi.org/10.1080/00343404.2010.490209.

Baumol, W. (1990). Entrepreneurship: Productive, Unproductive and Destructive. *Journal of Political Economy, 98*, 893-921.

Beugelsdijk, S. (2007). Entrepreneurial culture, regional innovativeness and economic growth. *Journal of Evolutionary Economics, 17*, 187–210. https://doi.org/10.1007/s00191-006-0048-y.

Boschma, R., & Frenken, K. (2011). The emerging empirics of evolutionary economic geography. *Journal of Economic Geography, 11*, 295–307. https://doi.org/10.1093/jeg/lbq053.

Bosma, N., Hessels, J., Schutjens, V., Praag, M. V., & Verheul, I. (2012). Entrepreneurship and role models. *Journal of Economic Psychology, 33*, 410–424. https://doi.org/10.1016/j.joep.2011.03.004.

Brixy, U. (2014). The significance of entry and exit for regional productivity growth. *Regional Studies, 48*, 1051–1070. https://doi.org/10.1080/00343404.2014.895804.

Content J., & Frenken K (2016) *Indicators and growth effects of related variety at the national and regional level in the EU.* Utrecht University (mimeo).

Cooke, P. (2004). Regional innovation systems: an evolutionary approach. In P. Cooke, M. Heidenreich, & H.-J. Braczyk (Eds.), *Regional innovation systems—The role of governances in a globalized world* (2nd ed.). London: UCL Press.

Eberle, J., Jacobebbinghaus, P., Ludsteck, J., & Witter, J. (2011). *Generation of time consistent industry codes in the face of classification changes. Methodological aspects of labour market data of research data center (FDZ).* Nuremberg: Federal Employment Agency (RDZ Methodenreport 05/2011).

Elfenbein, D. W., Hamilton, B. H., & Zenger, T. R. (2010). The small firm effect and the entrepreneurial spawning of scientists and engineers. *Management Science, 56*, 659–681. https://doi.org/10.1287/mnsc.1090.1130.

Fotopoulos, G. (2014). On the spatial stickiness of UK new firm formation rates. *Journal of Economic Geography, 14*, 651–679. https://doi.org/10.1093/jeg/lbt011.

Frenken, K., Oort, F., & Verburg, T. (2007). Related variety, unrelated variety and regional economic growth. *Regional Studies, 41*, 685–697. https://doi.org/10.1080/00343400601120296.

Freytag, A., & Thurik, R. (2007). Entrepreneurship and its determinants in a cross-country setting. *Journal of Evolutionary Economics, 17*, 117–131. https://doi.org/10.1007/s00191-006-0044-2.

Fritsch, M. (2004). Entrepreneurship, entry and performance of new businesses compared in two growth regimes: East and West Germany. *Journal of Evolutionary Economics, 14*, 525–542. https://doi.org/10.1007/s00191-004-0230-z.

Fritsch, M. (2013). New business formation and regional development: A survey and assessment of the evidence. *Found Trends® Entrepreneurial, 9*, 249–364. https://doi.org/10.1561/0300000043.

Fritsch, M., & Falck, O. (2007). New business formation by industry over space and time: A multidimensional analysis. *Regional Studies, 41*, 157–172. https://doi.org/10.1080/00343400600928301.

Fritsch, M., & Mueller, P. (2004). Effects of new business formation on regional development over time. *Regional Studies, 38*, 961–975. https://doi.org/10.1080/0034340042000280965.

Fritsch, M., & Mueller, P. (2006). The evolution of regional entrepreneurship and growth regimes. In M. Fritsch & J. Schmude (Eds.), *Entrepreneurship in the region* (pp. 225–244). US: Springer.

Fritsch, M., & Mueller, P. (2007). The persistence of regional new business formation-activity over time—assessing the potential of policy promotion programs. *Journal of Evolutionary Economics, 17*, 299–315. https://doi.org/10.1007/s00191-007-0056-6.

Fritsch, M., & Noseleit, F. (2013a). Start-ups, long- and short-term survivors, and their contribution to employment growth. *Journal of Evolutionary Economics, 23*, 719–733. https://doi.org/10.1007/s00191-012-0301-5.

Fritsch, M., & Noseleit, F. (2013b). Indirect employment effects of new business formation across regions: the role of local market conditions. *Papers in Regional Science, 92*, 361–382. https://doi.org/10.1111/j.1435-5957.2012.00475.x.

Fritsch, M., & Wyrwich, M. (2014). The long persistence of regional levels of entrepreneurship: Germany, 1925–2005. *Regional Studies, 48*, 955–973. https://doi.org/10.1080/00343404.2013.816414.

Fritsch, M., & Wyrwich, M. (2017). The effect of entrepreneurship on economic development—An empirical analysis using regional entrepreneurship culture. *Journal of Economic Geography, 17*, 157–189. https://doi.org/10.1093/jeg/lbv049.

Glaeser, E. L., Kerr, S. P., & Kerr, W. R. (2015). Entrepreneurship and urban growth: An empirical assessment with historical mines. *The Review of Economics and Statistics, 97*, 498–520. https://doi.org/10.1162/REST_a_00456.

Helsley, R. W., & Strange, W. C. (2011). Entrepreneurs and cities: Complexity, thickness and balance. *Regional Science and Urban Economics, 41*, 550–559. https://doi.org/10.1016/j.regsciurbeco.2011.04.001.

Hethey, T., & Schmieder, J.F. (2010) *Using worker flows in the analysis of establishment turnover—Evidence from German administrative data.* FDZ Methodenreport 06–2010 EN, Research Data Centre of the Federal Employment Agency (BA) at the Institute for Employment Research (IAB): Nuremberg. https://doi.org/10.3790/schm.133.4.477.

Hofstede, G., & McCrae, R. R. (2004). Personality and culture revisited: Linking traits and dimensions of culture. *Cross-Cultural Research, 38*, 52–88. https://doi.org/10.1177/1069397103259443.

Keeble, D., & Nachum, L. (2002). Why do business service firms cluster? Small consultancies, clustering and decentralization in London and southern England. *Transactions of the Institute of British Geographers, 27*, 67–90. https://doi.org/10.1111/1475-5661.00042.

Kibler, E., Kautonen, T., & Fink, M. (2014). Regional social legitimacy of entrepreneurship: Implications for entrepreneurial intention and start-up behaviour. *Regional Studies, 48*, 995–1015. https://doi.org/10.1080/00343404.2013.851373.

Marsili, O. (2002). Technological regimes and sources of entrepreneurship. *Small Business Economics, 19*, 217–231. https://doi.org/10.1023/A:1019670009693.

McClelland, D. C. (1961). *The achieving society.* Princeton: Van Nostrand Reinhold.

Neffke, F., Henning, M., & Boschma, R. (2011). How do regions diversify over time? Industry relatedness and the development of new growth paths in regions. *Economic Geography, 87*, 237–265. https://doi.org/10.1111/j.1944-8287.2011.01121.x.

Nightingale, P., & Coad, A. (2014). Muppets and gazelles: Political and methodological biases in entrepreneurship research. *Industrial and Corporate Change, 23*, 113–143. https://doi.org/10.1093/icc/dtt057.

North, D. C. (1994). Economic performance through time. *The American Economic Review, 84*, 359–368.

Noseleit, F. (2013). Entrepreneurship, structural change, and economic growth. *Journal of Evolutionary Economics, 23*, 735–766. https://doi.org/10.1007/s00191-012-0291-3.

Parker, S. (2009). Why do small firms produce the entrepreneurs? *Journal Behavioral Experimental Economist Former Journal Sociology-Economist, 38*, 484–494. https://doi.org/10.1016/j.socec.2008.07.013.

Qian, H., Acs, Z., & Stough, R. R. (2013). Regional systems of entrepreneurship: The nexus of human capital, knowledge and new firm formation. *Journal of Economic Geography, 13*, 559–587. https://doi.org/10.1093/jeg/lbs009.

Spengler, A. (2008). The establishment history panel. *Schmollers Jahrbuch, 128*, 501–509. https://doi.org/10.3790/schm.128.3.501.

Sternberg, R. (2011). Regional determinants of entrepreneurial activities—theories and empirical evidence. In M. Fritsch (Ed.), *Handbook of research on entrepreneurship and regional development* (pp. 33–57). Cheltenham: Elgar.

Theil, H. (1972). *Statistical decomposition analysis: With applications in the social and administrative sciences.* Amsterdam: North-Holland Publishing Company.

Westlund, H., Larsson, J. P., & Olsson, A. R. (2014). Start-ups and local entrepreneurial social capital in the Municipalities of Sweden. *Regional Studies, 48*, 974–994. https://doi.org/10.1080/00343404.2013.865836.

Winter, S. G. (1984). Schumpeterian competition in alternative technological regimes. *Journal of Economic Behavior and Organization, 5*, 287–320. https://doi.org/10.1016/0167-2681(84)90004-0.

Wood, P. (2005). A service-informed approach to regional innovation—Or adaptation? *Service Industries Journal, 25*, 429–445. https://doi.org/10.1080/02642060500092063.

Chapter 2
Local Government Aimed at Quality of Life in Sustainable Cities

Jamile Pereira Cunha Rodrigues

Abstract The concept of sustainable development has been more and more adopted by countries around the world. As a strategy of introducing sustainable development within local government, we have seen the advent of sustainable cities that aim their actions at an improvement of the local population's quality of life, together with economic development and environmental preservation. The urban ecosystem is created, modelled and changed by humanity on a daily basis, with humans normally making use of unsustainable methods. For a city to be sustainable, there must be an efficient local government, with the aim of ensuring that the locals have a good quality of life, rather than the mere satisfaction of human needs as defended in Maslow's pyramid. Having needs met is not the same as having good quality of life. For this reason, we can see that the main examples of sustainable cities are all in developed countries, whose cities and towns have already surpassed this threshold, aiming their local government at practices which are really sustainable. Through a descriptive and qualitative method, this paper analyses the contribution of sustainable practices in cities towards improvement in quality of life and comes to the conclusion that the introduction thereof is in line with the promotion of local sustainable development, with improvement to quality of life.

Keywords Sustainable development • Local government • Sustainable cities • Quality of life

2.1 Introduction

The social and environmental issue is firmly at the core of current debates, even though it only appeared at the end of the last century. After many debates, there was the introduction of the need to adopt a sustainable form of development, which upholds social well-being and environmental preservation, without forsaking

---

J.P.C. Rodrigues (✉)
Postgraduate Management School, Federal University of Bahia, Salvador, Brazil
e-mail: jamipcunha@hotmail.com

© Springer International Publishing AG 2018
J. Leitão et al. (eds.), *Entrepreneurial, Innovative and Sustainable Ecosystems*, Applying Quality of Life Research,
https://doi.org/10.1007/978-3-319-71014-3_2

economic development. Some countries have taken on responsibilities with regard to this issue, going as far as taking measures to insert sustainable development in the models of their respective countries. Such actions generate local changes, which can be perceived when we analyse the practices in place in each city.

The cities' need for consumption has been increasing by the day, to meet demand which the cities themselves have created. This has brought pollution, accumulated litter and many other problems which have had a harmful effect on environmental well-being and also on the general well-being of the cities' residents. These social and environmental problems have been made even worse by standards of city planning and also by migration, factors which have also contributed to additional worsening of the quality of life in the cities.

For this reason, in the light of the process of city planning which continues to progress on the planet, researchers, academics, politicians and also the civil society at large now call out for sustainable development combined with economic efficiency, social justice and an environmental balance. It is now possible to find examples of cities which adopt sustainable practices in several different areas, thus taking on their commitment to the issue of sustainable development while they search for a better quality of life.

Sustainable practices taken up by different municipalities help to bring about the concept of sustainable cities, which means those cities that have a standard of development which is sustainable within the economic, social and environmental realms and which seeks to boost quality of life and the environment. Sustainable cities tend to be well planned and well managed and have, as their main management base, the adoption of several different practices in order to remedy the problems that the cities may present. The solution of social and economic problems shall, in the end, have a significant influence on the quality of life as enjoyed by the cities' residents.

The challenge of sustainability of cities consists essentially of making improvements in areas such as housing, urban mobility, security, inclusion, opportunities, governance and also environmental issues: deforestation, insufficient water supply, air and soil pollution, risks of industrial and environmental accidents, poor capacity of disposal of solid waste, lack of green areas, unpaved streets and closeness of sources of environmental hazards.

The purpose of this paper is to present evidence of how sustainable cities take up a style of government that upholds local development in a way that ensures good quality of life for the locals. This issue is both relevant and current, as it encompasses issues regarding sustainable development within the sphere of municipal action, thereby making evident a management model that seeks to improve quality of life in the cities.

The present paper consists of a pure exploratory research study, with the main target of acquisition of knowledge, seeking to update knowledge in areas such as sustainable development and local government. It can be defined as a descriptive and qualitative research study and, as such, is based on induction (Davel 2014). The goal of the paper is to observe, record, analyse and establish correlations between variable facts, thus understanding the relationships that occur in social and political life. The procedures adopted in data collection consist of bibliographic research, focusing mainly on books and scientific articles; study of documents; analysis of secondary data; and due analysis.

2.2 Sustainable Development as a Base

One issue that has been widely discussed nowadays and which is closely related to economic and social issues is that of sustainable development or "development that meets the needs of the present without compromising the ability of future generations to meet their own needs" (World Commission on Environment and Development – WCED 1987). According to WCED (1987), development is defined as being human progress along the social, economic, cultural and political axes, as possible for all countries and at all levels: local, regional and global. The new options for development strive to reduce the impact of society upon the environment.

Bellen (2005) reinforces the definition of sustainable development as arising from a historical process of reappraisal of the relationship that exists between civil society and its natural medium. Sustainable development is a distinct term yet is very close and complementary to that of sustainability, with the former being the means and the latter the end. For the World Summit on Sustainable Development - WSSD (CMDS 2002), this development is constructed upon three main pillars: economic development, social development and environmental protection. The main transversal and critical issues that he has considered are poverty, waste, environmental degradation, net growth of the population, gender equality, prostitution, health, conflict and violence against human rights (Silva and Rauli 2009). These issues are ever present in cities, an important locus for the implementation of sustainable development.

Sachs (1994) addresses this issue using a similar term, that of ecodevelopment. In his discussions on the issue, this author lists five aspects of the feasibility of development: (1) social feasibility, where there is the idea of what a better society actually is, with greater fairness employed in the sharing of goods and income, thereby leading to a shortening of the distance between life levels; (2) economic feasibility, where there is a sharing and better management of public and private funds and measurement of the economic efficiency of macrosocial conditions; (3) ecological feasibility, with reduction of damage caused by exploitation of ecosystems, and also limiting the consumption of fossil fuels, replacing such fuels by abundant renewable resources; also reducing the volume of residue, recycling, limiting the consumption of material goods, and intensifying the search for clean technologies, with the establishment of rules for environmental protection; (4) spatial feasibility, with establishment of a balance between urban and rural areas; and (5) cultural feasibility, research into the roots and translation of the concepts of ecodevelopment for each specific situation, local culture and local ecosystem. It would be convenient if the cities could take these points into account when seeking a more sustainable style of local government; however, it is not common to notice this concern within municipal government.

An interesting aspect of sustainable development is that it needs a balance between the population, the capacity of the environment and productive vitality, through a development philosophy that considers the basic tripod of sustainability: a relationship between economic efficiency with social justice and ecological prudence. According to Jacobi (1999), the dimensions of sustainable development help to interpret the world, making it possible for the prevailing predatory logic to interfere.

For the Centre for Development Alternatives (*Centro de Estudio y Promoción de Asuntos Urbanos* – CEPAUR) (1986), a strategy for sustainable development shall be based on the reorganisation of new local economic orders. According to Sachs (1994), this consists of choosing between different methods of development, considering the environment or not, rather than choosing between development and the environment. This form of development, which takes the environment into account, when taken up as part of city management, helps to make cities more sustainable.

Heuristically, Viola and Leis (1995) group the different versions of sustainable development into three different categories: statist, where environmental quality is a public asset protected by normative and regulatory intervention promoting the state; community, where the base organisations of society have a key role in the adoption of a sustainable society; and market, where it is possible to implement a sustainable society through market logic, defending private appropriation of environmental assets and the protection of the environment by the producers, should the consumers want this. It is mainly through this third category that society has been adopting the basic fundamentals of sustainability. However, the state has come into the act, guiding and standardising actions in working towards a more sustainable form of development, as also the organised civil society. Slowly but surely, it is possible to observe the presence of all three categories, working together towards the implementation of sustainable development.

According to the Brundtland Report, environmental protection is also the responsibility of governments and, as such, government policies are the best tools to achieve this action. The establishment of government policies that uphold sustainable development plays a significant role in implementing the changes required. In the opinion of Ferreira and Ferreira (1995), there is a need to construct development policies which are compatible with new natural and social contracts, which are a base for the construction of a new society. It is also valid to remember that there are some limitations in government policies, with these limitations being generated through poor planning and development, generating operationalisation difficulties. The mere fact that the policy exists does not mean the effectiveness thereof. However, government policies are essential to help towards the preservation of the planet. The government policies for sustainable development are those that incorporate sustainability policies and which seek, through the sensitisation of individual conscience, to bring about the necessary changes to group acts, also being able to preserve the balance in relationships with the environment and also the quality of life of the cities' residents. Considering that the very concept of quality of life is both varied and multidimensional, in this paper, we take up the concept as defined

2 Local Government Aimed at Quality of Life in Sustainable Cities   39

by Minayo et al. (2000), which consider that quality of life contemplates both subjective aspects, such as happiness, personal accomplishment and pleasure, as more objective facets which surpass the satisfaction of basic needs, also including those needs which stem from social and economic development of a certain society.

2.3   The City: An Urban Ecosystem?

Many authors define a city as being an ecosystem, as it transforms energy and matter into products, which are consumed, and subproducts, which is the waste. However, some authors say that a city is not an ecosystem, as in natural systems the waste is recycled, something which does not happen in the urban ecosystem. Thus, the statement that a city would be a kind of urban ecosystem would be incorrect, as self-sufficiency is the main characteristic of an ecosystem.

In contrast, according to Ribeiro (2008), cities are indeed ecosystems created by humankind and which use up the energy generated by the natural ecosystems, according to the city's own interests. This means that a city can be considered as an open ecosystem:

> As a city depends on external energy and matter, it is considered an open ecosystem, where there continues to be interaction between the different natural elements, but at the same time there is a breakage of balance and an acceleration of processes. Apart from the interaction that is evident between natural elements, in cities there is also a strong interconnection of natural, social and constructed components. (Ribeiro 2008, p. 405)

Ecosystems strike a balance between productive, consumer and decomposer organisms, thereby making sure that the substances are recycled. According to Marcondes Helene and Bicudo (1994), cities receive a significant volume of supplies – plants coming from the farms, meat and milk from the livestock, wood from the forest and also many other raw materials – but at the same time do not eliminate all the energy that has accumulated; at the same time, there is no recycling, as these physical, chemical and biological components do not return to nature, from where they came. This cycle is also observed at present because, even though there are cities that do indeed seek this return through recycling, this movement is still not sufficient to deal with the volume of waste that is produced. For this reason, and from the ecological standpoint, most cities are unsustainable, as residues are sent to landfills or are just poured into rivers, as sewage, and in the atmosphere as gas, smoke and dust, thereby giving rise to pollution.

In the opinion of Marcondes Helene and Bicudo (1994), the main factors that distinguish a city from a natural ecosystem are the need for an ever-growing daily consumption of energy obtained from fossil fuels to meet the demand set by transport, industry, houses and services in general; the consumption of materials to an extent greater than what is necessary for the sustenance of life; and increased residue, especially synthetic and toxic chemicals.

If, to be defined as an urban ecosystem, a city needs not only to process and consume the energy produced in natural ecosystems but also to recycle it, by adopting more sustainable practices for the production, consumption and disposal of waste, as well as preservation, one can say that, based on the concept of a sustainable city, a sustainable city is indeed an urban ecosystem, as within the city one can envisage balance and concern with the environment and with the city's residents through sustainable practices that seek to impart a better quality of life, especially through a government style of management in which sustainability comes to the fore.

2.4 Local Government and Sustainability

Disorganised urban growth brings about more and more serious environmental problems, including deforestation, insufficient water supply, air pollution, pollution of the water and the soil, the risk of industrial and environmental accidents, a low capacity for disposal of solid waste, lack of green areas, presence of unpaved streets and closeness of sources of environmental risks. Large cities are ecosystems that have resources that, in many cases, are poorly used. According to Sachs (1994, page 53), "it is only in regions of high population density that the pressure enforced by the environment and the level of available resources are in fact an absolute limit". For this reason, it is so important to address the urban problems that result from this major current unprecedented urban explosion.

Considering the increase in the urban population on a global scale, we can say that this is the century of the urban revolution. Hogan and Carmo (2001) add to this view by saying that the environmental problems are made even worse by the standards of urbanisation and migratory flow, which are now more common in intra- and intercity movements, with a main focus moving towards larger cities, contributing to further worsen the quality of life of the cities' residents. These authors believe that the horizontal growth of cities results in urban spread (horizontal and deconcentrated urban growth which leads to empty spaces in urban locations) or urban agglomeration (a kind of urban cog system which contributes towards the establishment of metropolitan regions). Both of these bring environmental problems in their wake, including the reduction of plant cover, the high costs incurred to provide infrastructure for basic sanitation and increased pollution due to the fact that the cities are near each other.

Both the blending of urban cities, as provided by conurbation, going as far as generating metropolitan areas, as also the horizontal rather than vertical expansion of cities contribute to make the general feel of the environment even worse. Apart from the fact that the spatial development of population in the cities is a problem for sustainability, the industrial concentration in regions of significant economic growth also makes it more difficult to reach the long dreamed-of sustainable development. Currently, there are many cities with areas that are environmentally saturated, without any possibility of providing sustainable existence for their populations and, consequently, of providing good quality of life. In addition, the chaotic urban development in cities results in the degradation of natural resources and also of the landscape, also bringing about congestion, widespread pollution and increased travelling times.

> As they grow in size and in relative importance, cities take on an ever more relevant role in the conformation of the global environment. This growth (...) already takes on the airs of an enormous vicious circle, which increases demand for natural resources and encourages over-exploitation, and this, in turn, generates degradation of the environment and increased poverty, thereby activating migration for major centres... If we wish to enjoy a better world, it is essential that we acknowledge and accept the global nature of urban problems, and also do everything we can to make cities more humane places to live in – and more benign from the environmental standpoint. (Marcondes Helene and Bicudo 1994, page 23)

According to Sachs (1994), the quest for active and innovative strategies for sustainable urban development shall include elements such as a management model; cooperation between civil society, government and companies; replacement of the assistential policy by a policy which provides a stimulus for local populations; saving of resources and reduction of waste; and research of new technological solutions and improvement of the environment and of the general social conditions of the cities' residents through urban rehabilitation. This would be a government model that would be efficient for sustainable development.

The current government administration has to deal with a range of conflicts between environmental preservation, economic and population growth and social equality, with the cities having the task of striking a balance between these challenges. In this way, each municipality shall be responsible for structuring its local administration with a view to sustainable development. According to Silva and Rauli (2009, page 94), "sustainability is not given by any formula, which means that its reach is by no means limited to only one subject, but rather to the whole set of efforts, derived from public and private articulation, on both a local and a global scale".

According to Lefebvre (1979), the city is a reflection of the humanised landscape, where natural space is turned into a product of the social. The production of space has the state as the leading player. Carlos (2007) shows that the city is really revealed through its usage and also through social and spatial praxis, giving a meaning to life. In his opinion, urban space is a usage value in which life is transformed through a transformation of the location, as regulated by the laws of the state.

Considering the growing environmental concerns, it is essential to come up with ways of inserting this theme in the universe of local administration. In the opinion of Jacobi (1999), the practices which are currently being adopted by the municipal government in this regard show that it is very important that there is the political will to implement actions guided by the principles of sustainability. Thus, the municipality allows the "intersectorial political articulation for social development, which expands the field of analysis and performance, including concepts such as quality of life, exercising rights, and expansion of competences (Jacobi 1999, page 31)".

At present, there are several countries facing the challenge of striking a balance, within their local administration, between the dynamics of the economy, on the one hand, with social balance and environmental sustainability. The spread of the concepts of sustainable development means that every day, there are more cases of adoption of alternative management practices, to make cities sustainable. This is the case of Brazil, a country which, even though it does not cater to all basic needs of all its residents, does show some efforts in local administration in some cities, seeking to make them sustainable, as is the case of Curitiba. This happens because of the structuring of its policies with independence and focus on the municipalities, which therefore have to deal with economic, social and environmental issues alone. This decentralisation has made a positive contribution towards the implementation of sustainable practices in the municipalities.

However, this is the exception rather than the rule. Brazilian cities have grown in disorderly fashion and now, already at an unsustainable level, they need attention aimed at an urban policy which carries out the social role of cities, through a more conscientious style of management. According to Schenini and Nascimento (2002, page 7), "in sustainable Government administration, the participants, be they leaders, managers or employees, tackle the management problem of finding and installing appropriate technologies, for their different needs".

Partnerships with civil society in the search for quick actions of government management, for solving problems such as focus on consumption, rapid process of urban development and increased demand for basic services (Cidades Sustentáveis 2015) have helped Brazil to advance at a sluggish pace, with regard to this issue. This was how the model known as sustainable government management (GPS) came about, with the proposal of promoting synergy of flow, including the institutional, social and cultural, scientific and technological sectors, starting with local governments. In this way, they try to harmonise the processes and also the impact of local development, making it more sustainable and participative and with better quality of life.

For Schenini and Nascimento (2002), specific actions and sustainable procedures should be incorporated into a variety of activities in the Brazilian public organisations to provide them with the features of sustainable public organisations, as shown in Table 2.1. They are:

Besides the actions cited in Table 2.1, is necessary to emphasise the adoption of the Environmental Agenda of Public Administration. For each action, many other procedures can be listed. So, the researchers concluded that the public administration should consider the global changes in the actions of improvement on municipalities.

According to Schenini and Nascimento (2002), there are specific sustainable actions and procedures to be included in the different activities carried out by Brazilian government organisations that amount to sustainable government management policy. These are:

Compliance with legislation and environmental standards
Use of clean management technologies, such as AS 8000, geospatial information systems (GISs), government accounting and environmental finance and sustainable purchases and tenders

2 Local Government Aimed at Quality of Life in Sustainable Cities

Table 2.1 Actions and sustainable procedures for public organisations in Brazil

Sustainable actions	Types of procedures
Compliance with environmental legislation and standards	Follow laws and decrees
Adoption of agenda 21	Adopt a sustainable strategic planning
Use of clean management technologies	AS 8000
	Geospatial information systems-GIS
	Accounting and public environmental finance
	Environmental communications
	ISO 14,000 (environmental management system)
	Taxation as restrictive action against pollution
	Environmental audit
	Environmental improvement and recovery projects
	Environmental protection plan to the flora, fauna and natural resources
	"Brown Agenda" (sanitary, health and environmental quality)
	Supplies of not environmentally degrading raw materials and inputs
	Strategic partnerships and alliances for viability of ecological projects
	Urban land planning (environmental master plan)
	Environmental zoning of the city
Use of clean operating technologies	Basic infrastructure and energy balances
	Prevention systems (environmental accidents, fires, floods and windstorms)
	Monitoring systems (water, air, noise, soil, vegetation, physical, chemical and biological accidents, emergency dikes, dams, nature reserves and risk municipality of impact)
	Urban solid waste management
	Water and sewage treatment
	Watershed management
	Landscaping and ecological urbanism
	Waste from rural areas
Promotion of environmental recovery	Use of renewable natural resources
	Creating generators of clean technologies
	Development of physical and biological recovery projects to degraded areas
Management and supervision	Health surveillance
	EIS (environment impact studies) and EIR (environment impact report)
	Administrative sanctions

Source: Self-prepared

Ecological communications

ISO 14000 (environmental management system – EMS)

Taxation as a way to limit pollution

Environmental audits

Ecological projects for environmental recovery and improvement

A plan for the environmental protection of plant life, animal life and natural resources

The Brown agenda – sanitary and environmental quality and supply of raw materials and other supplies that do not degrade the environment

Partnerships and strategic alliances to make ecological projects feasible

Urban territory plan – ecological city plan and ecological zoning of the municipality

Use of clean operational technologies, such as basic infrastructure and energy balances, prevention systems (to prevent against ecological accidents, fire, floods and wind), monitoring systems (for water, air, noise, soil, vegetation, physical risk, chemical and biological accidents, emergency dykes, dams, natural reserves and risk of impact on the city), management of urban solid waste, water treatment and sewerage, management of hydrographic basins, landscaping and ecological city planning and rural waste

Actions for nurturing and recovery of the environment

Actions for control and inspection

Adoption of the Environmental Government Administration Agenda (A3P)

In this way, the global changes shall be considered by local government administration, within the actions for the enhancement of the local administration of the municipalities. Analysing the guidelines of Agenda 21 (1992), we see that the government institutions are also responsible for the sustainable management of the environment. For Abreu and Silva (2010, page 5), government administration shall also allow "economic citizenship in the institutions". This requires involvement of the workforce, changes in management and adoption of ethics within government administration.

It is not just the social and environmental aspects that need to be considered. A system of public management that can make a city sustainable needs to be clean, transparent and free from disrespect and corruption in the treatment of its citizens and, most importantly, must have guaranteed at least the two levels of basic needs defined in Maslow's pyramid shown in Fig. 2.1.

As shown in Fig. 2.1, Abraham Maslow brings a list of values that represent human needs, divided into basic needs (physiological needs and security), psychological needs (esteem, love and relationships) and self-accomplishment needs (personal fulfilment). However, one cannot speak of well-being and quality of life in places where people do not even have access to basics such as food, clean water, sanitation, housing and security. However, certain sustainable practices, such as sanitary and environment education, selective refuse collection and reduction of pollution, help to meet the basic needs of human beings, also nurturing sustainable management.

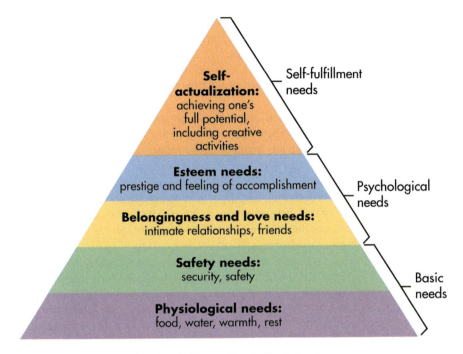

Fig. 2.1 Maslow's hierarchy of needs (Source: Simply Psychology)

Government administration also needs to include sustainable practices within the environmental, social, territorial, political, health and cultural spheres, also as a way of being an example of what is required from other institutions and sectors within society. In the quest to construct a form of social organisation which is ecologically fair and materially feasible, tools must be used to rally round and train government agents, diagnose human impact, promote justice and social control and uphold common good for everyone (Abreu and Silva 2010). This means that sustainable government administration is an important aspect to be incorporated into government organisations by the administrators who intend to make their cities more sustainable.

2.5 Sustainable Cities and Quality of Life

Sustainable cities are those which are well planned and managed based on the adoption of several practices which intend to solve social and environmental problems, leading to an improvement in the quality of life enjoyed by the cities' residents. Authors defend that there is no ready model for a sustainable city; however, there are guidelines to be followed that link the cities to a form of planning that is socially and environmentally fair.

Sustainable cities adopt best practices aimed at the general well-being of the population, governance, common natural assets, consumption and responsible production, among others (Ahmed and Coutinho 2009). The issue of sustainability in cities must include environmental issues; social issues, such as housing, urban mobility, inclusion and security; and government administration and governance (Souza and Awad 2012).

For Marcondes Helene and Bicudo (1994), an ideal sustainable city should include proposals for greater urban sustainability, with the city containing housing close to places of work in the city centre, thereby reducing the need for travel and making the city more centralised, and preference given to pedestrians, bicycles and public transport on the streets, thereby saving energy and reducing the emission of polluting gases and thus becoming less dependent on cars, in addition to the use of renewable sources of energy, selective refuse collection and plant cultivation on the roof. These actions favour the environment and also make an inevitable contribution towards improvement of environmental quality and quality of life in the cities. In addition, there is a need for maintenance of ecological processes and diversity of the biological and physical medium, through careful handling of natural resources.

One must not forget that quality of life depends on more than just having basic needs met. For a city to become sustainable to the point that it offers quality of life to its residents, the city must already have met at least its basic needs, expanding its attention to other aspects. This is why the greatest examples of sustainable cities come from developed countries, where there is a more structured local administration which has overcome the stage of meeting basic needs for survival of the human being, as defended in Maslow's pyramid. Figure 2.2 shows the stages for the local administrations to implement sustainable cities.

Figure 2.2 presents a summary of this article. It shows the city as an urban ecosystem with unsustainable processes, managed by local government with the main aim of meeting the basic needs of the city's residents. This first stage of the scheme is known as Stage A. Many cities have stagnated at Stage A, struggling to manage to meet these basic needs, and with the possibility of suffering interference from actions of corruption, siphoning off of funds and others. To implement the concept of sustainable cities, it is necessary to move on to stage B, modelling local management based on sustainable practices seeking to obtain better quality of life in cities.

Sustainable cities consist of only one action aimed at the practice of local government management for sustainable development, and for this reason, its implementation should be expanded to as many cities of the country as possible. However, Marcondes Helene and Bicudo (1994, page 40) say that each city is a specific case, and each one should consider the local culture, traditions and environmental characteristics, to discover their own sustainability. Thus, "there is no simple description of a sustainable city, as there is no single description of a sustainable society".

Other actions which also seek to achieve environmental preservation and increased quality of life for the cities' residents are expansion of green areas and nature reserves, reduction of illegal deforestation in the municipality, environmental restructuring based on environmental policies, implementation of certification of

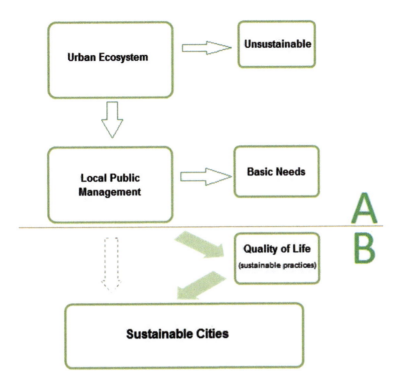

Fig. 2.2 Stages of local government administration seeking to implement sustainable cities (Source: self-prepared)

environmental sustainability, construction of appropriate pavements, availability of basic public services close to where the people live, depollution of rivers, reduction of the pollution of the air, reduction of unemployment, provision of worthy housing and, more importantly, the adoption of environmental education as a base of projects for change and for the ecological awareness of the population.

The implementation of sustainable cities should be like basing them on the principles of traditional communities, in which the people were guardians of natural habitats, with the preservation of the environment, without polluting in any way, and by taking up a form of subsistence economy without any excess production, and with social equality and social justice. It is quite evident that the sustainable cities of today do not, and will not ever, come close to this standard of preservation and sustainability. However, they should base themselves on this standard, as "traditional cultures make changes to the environment, but do not degrade it (Marcondes Helene and Bicudo 1994, page 35)". Also according to these authors, truly sustainable societies are those that exercise social control over the environment, knowing it well, and blending it in to the local culture, acting below the full capacity that ecosystems can support.

> Considering the definition of sustainability and the conduct of traditional communities, we define sustainable societies as being those that, in some way, recognise that they depend on exchange relationships that they maintain with nature in order to survive and, acting in a way to make common well-being permanent, respect the integrity of their own culture, their historical development, and the natural environment. (Marcondes Helene and Bicudo 1994, page 38)

If we consider strictly what these authors address, we cannot affirm that there are sustainable cities. However, we are going in the right direction. The proposals and sustainable practices of the cities are implemented in isolated areas, but it is expected that they slowly integrate local culture, expanding them to as many municipal areas as possible.

It is possible to say that a sustainable city is the one which establishes an alliance between their policies for preservation of the environment with quality of life for citizens, as the former contributes to the latter. Government policies establish conditions for the advent of sustainable cities, to the extent that such policies introduce laws by which local administration has to adopt practices that are socially and environmentally responsible, such as those policies that deal with solid residue, water resources, urban mobility, organic and sustainable production, the environment and environmental education.

According to Roseland (1992), there are several cases of cities which adopt practices within their quest to become sustainable, starting with isolated attempts made by groups and communities of sectors from cities, at the end of the last century: Minneapolis, in the United States, adopted a measure for restriction of packaging of foodstuffs and beverages in 1989, making it mandatory to reduce and recycle waste; Portland, also in the United States, adopted measures for the selective collection of 150,000 tonnes of organic waste per year, with the same objective; and Niagara Falls, in Canada, has adopted measures to implement offloading in toilets and household showers with low flow of water, for new construction projects as from 1990, seeking the preservation of water resources. Such practices make a direct contribution towards the improvement of quality of life and environmental quality in these cities, bringing reduction of waste and saving of water as important consequences.

Current examples of cities that have become more sustainable include Seoul, in South Korea, where there is one of the best systems of sustainable public transport; London, in the United Kingdom, where the River Thames has been depolluted; Évora, in Portugal, where there is a zero carbon plan; Copenhagen, in Denmark, which is considered as the Green Capital of Europe (Programa Cidades Sustentáveis 2015).

In Brazil, the issue of sustainable cities arose with the proposal for construction of the Brazilian Agenda 21 (Porto 2008), which gives, in Chapter 28, greater attention to cities, as many of the problems and solutions as present comes from local activities. According to the Brazilian Ministry for the Environment (MMA 2015a), Agenda 21 is a reference for the development and implementation of sustainable government policies, thereby promoting sustainable development and acting as a tool of democratic administration for cities and also validating the proposals of the city statute and their city plans.

Currently, in Brazil, there is a Sustainable Cities Programme. With the proposal of promoting synergy between several different sectors, in order to harmonise processes and impact of development at a local level, seeking to make them more sustainable, sustainable cities arise as a model of sustainable government administration (Programa Cidades Sustentáveis 2015). The existence of the Sustainable Cities Programme is based on the organisation of civil society in order to contribute towards the sustainability of Brazilian cities, being carried out together with the Ethos Institute, the Brazilian Social Network for Fair and Sustainable Cities and the Our São Paulo Network.

Even though this is not an initiative taken by local government, but rather by organised civil society, the programme acts in partnership with local government, thereby contributing towards the adoption of sustainable government policies to benefit the environment and improvements to the citizens' quality of life. This is the case of the National Policy for Solid Waste (*Política Nacional de Resíduos Sólidos*), which has made little progress over the last few years, mainly with regard to selective refuse collection and also the treatment of waste. Reverse logistics, for example, has also been a problem for the development of this policy. Unfortunately, we see the lack of applicability of many Brazilian policies, especially those with social and environmental purposes, and for this reason, the programme has become so important for the implementation of sustainable cities in Brazil.

According to MMA (2015a), the Brazilian Agenda 21 clearly shows the importance of inserting the environmental dimension in sectorial urban policies, such as sanitation, housing, water supply and planning of urban space, considering criteria and indicators which suggest improvements to the quality of life.

Marcondes Helene and Bicudo (1994) show that, in Brazil, the city of Curitiba, in the state of Paraná, started its urban actions towards sustainability in the middle of the 1960s, by taking up the following measures: for public transport, the creation of express bus lanes, seeking to save energy and making Curitiba's public transport the quickest and the cheapest in the country; to meet the needs of pedestrians and cyclists, the city has installed a lengthy cycle path, also implementing priority for pedestrians in the city centre, revitalising squares in an additional move towards sustainability; with the same ultimate goal, some roads were completely close to cars, reducing traffic; for policies regarding the use of the soil, a densification programme was adopted, recovering urban spaces; for integration of policies for transport and soil use, they encouraged the presence of a mix of housing, jobs and services in the different neighbourhoods.

In fact, this city is an international model for sustainability and for energy preservation. The local practices have led to improved mobility, reduction of pollution, improvement of public spaces, increase of green areas, reduction of time and cost involved in travel, directly contributing to boost quality of life and general environmental quality in the city.

In Brazil, there are other examples of cities that are taking up sustainable practices in several different areas, thereby taking up a commitment to the issue of sustainable development, seeking to improve the quality of life of the local population and also the people's well-being. The municipality of Bonito, in the Brazilian State of Mato Grosso do Sul, has the Sustainable Tourism Programme which reduces impact on nature; Rio Branco, a municipality in the Brazilian state of Acre, has a unit for treatment of solid waste, which is a reference for local management; João Pessoa, in Paraíba, is a reference in the management of protected areas; Extrema, in the state of Minas Gerais, in 2007 implemented the Water Producer Project, through recovery and preservation of protected areas; Curitiba, in the state of Paraná, has the Green Exchange Programme since 1991, being considered the most sustainable city in Brazil (Programa Cidades Sustentáveis 2015).

There are additional examples, both national and international, of cities that already have the sustainable city seal. With these actions at municipal level, we can slowly change the country and move it towards a really sustainable style of development, with the main gain being better quality of life and better environmental quality in the cities.

To replicate examples of sustainable cities, there is a need to enhance and expand this initiative. There are several terms concerning cities where sustainable practices could be inserted. Normally, actions are taken up gradually by the administrators. Marcondes Helene and Bicudo (1994) show that the transition to make society more sustainable requires the inclusion of tangible aspects related to urban environmental issues (quality of the air, transport, use of the soil and preservation of energy) and also intangible aspects (security, public health, gender equality, environmental education and global environmental responsibility). For this reason, it is important to strengthen the local levels for decision-making, thus becoming more skilled in the process of distinction, establishing priorities and appropriate solutions.

The implementation of sustainable development on a local, national, or global scale requires analysis, adaptation and planning, actions that shall bring more effective results for the improvement of the quality of life and environmental quality, for the cities' residents.

2.6 Conclusion

Sustainable development is an extremely relevant issue these days and is already well ingrained in debates and actions taken by public and private organisations and in society as a whole, bringing in its concept a range of theoretical contributions. The perception of environmental degradation, pollution, diseases and social injustice is making the population aware of this issue. The current scenario is one of unsustainability of contemporary society, which has come about due to factors such as concentration of the population in a limited space, very rapid population growth, degradation of natural resources, productive systems that cause pollution and an unlimited expansion of material consumption. Some nations are now engaged in this new perspective of development which has been causing changes to their styles of administration, at local and global levels.

It was in this context that sustainable cities appeared as the result of actions of local government management for sustainable development. Sustainable cities are a model for the implementation of sustainable development at municipal level, and whenever possible, this model is expanded to global level, with the consideration of natural, cultural, social and political factors for each location as part of the transition.

It is also worth remembering that the tackling of environmental and social issues also requires political willpower. It is possible to confirm that, even though there are many cases of sustainable cities that were started by isolated attempts by groups, communities or sectors within the cities themselves, the perpetuation thereof requires more than an own intention. For this reason, to disseminate this model of sustainable government management, it is necessary for government policies to intervene. In Brazil, the social, environmental and development policies are mandatorily contributing so that the cities may become sustainable. However, their effectiveness is still timid, as shown by the issue of the solid waste policy as presented in this article.

We can also see, however, that the actions and policies currently taken up in the quest for sustainable cities in Brazil are still very few, when compared with sustainable cities elsewhere in the world. This is perfectly understandable, when we remember that Brazil is a developing country that is still struggling to meet the basic needs of citizens of several cities. For this reason, the state needs to present clearer courses of action to tackle the serious social and environmental problems. There are many actions working towards an increase in the environment and in society, to be adopted, and also, as the problem has already got under way, it is time to improve these actions and make them more sophisticated, by adopting the following: renewable energy, depollution of rivers and sea, environmental education at schools, effectiveness in compliance with the terms of legislation in force, a minimum green area set for each district, excellence in provision of health services, cultural activities and leisure for the population, worthy housing and the eradication of hunger and extreme poverty, among others.

> It is quite evident that in Brazil there is a significant difference between rhetoric and reality: environmental legislation accompanies the international experience and has new instruments of great sophistication in place; however, the real conditions for the application thereof are extremely restrictive (…) At the same time, the environmental, populational, scientific and technology policies, as well as the social policies aimed at quality of life, are totally disconnected and detached from the Government strategies for development. (Ferreira and Ferreira 1995, page 31)

The social side of sustainable development should be intensely worked on, as there are still serious shortcomings in social equality. Once again, it is the responsibility of government policies to serve this demand.

Considering the fact that we are dealing with a local government administration that can make a city sustainable to the point that actions are focused on provision of quality of life to the city's residents, we are now talking about cities that have a satisfactory level of human development and which have already surpassed the guarantee of at least the two levels of basic needs as defined in Maslow's pyramid, including aspects of social and environmental responsibility. It is quite clear that actions like those taken up by Brazil, as shown as examples, are quite valid, as they shall contribute towards progress with sustainability; however, it is very difficult to qualify a city as being sustainable, due to one-off actions, when in the next district there are people who are still living under highly precarious conditions.

In the light of the points here raised, we conclude that sustainable practices in cities do indeed contribute for an improvement in the quality of life of those people residing in the cities and to implement sustainable development at local level.

Regarding their practical implications, this work addresses the importance of establishment of public-private partnerships for the implementation of sustainability in the cities and also shows the important dimensions of insertion in local government administration that seeks to establish a sustainable city. The examples here shown present the positive results that have been obtained within this initiative.

It is hoped that this document may promote sustainable models for local public administration focused on the quality of life of the cities' residents. As a suggestion and also as guidance for future work, we suggest the establishment of a schedule with generic steps and the actions to be taken so that the city may become a sustainable city, together with guidance about how to study and reflect about, the characteristics that are intrinsic to each city. In addition, the creation of indicators that show the level of sustainability of a given city is also suggested.

References

Abreu, D.Q., & Silva J.J.M.C. (2010). *A gestão pública sustentável do ambiente e a perícia ambiental* [Environmental public management and environmental assessment]. GesPublicaGov. http://www.gespublica.gov.br/biblioteca/pasta.2010-12-08.2954571235/GESTaO%20 PUBLICA %20SUSTENTAVEL.pdf. Acessed 23 Mar 2015.

Agenda 21. (1992). *Conferência das Nações Unidas sobre Meio Ambiente e Desenvolvimento 1992* [United Nations Conference on Environment and Development in 1992]. Rio de Janeiro-Brasil: Ed. do Ministério do Meio Ambiente.

Ahmed, F., & Coutinho, R. (2009). *Cidades Sustentáveis no Brasil e sua tutela jurídica* [Sustainable Cities in Brazil and its legal protection] (178 p). Rio de Janeiro: Lumen Juris.

Bellen, H. M. V. (2005). *Indicadores de sustentabilidade: Uma análise comparativa* [Sustainability indicators: a comparative analysis]. Rio de Janeiro: FGV.

Carlos, A. F. A. (2007). *O Espaço Urbano: Novos Escritos sobre a Cidade* [Urban space: New writings about the city] (123 p). São Paulo: FFLCH – USP.

CEPAUR. (1986). *Desarrollo a escala humana: una opción para el futuro* [Development on a human scale: An option for the future]. Santiago: CEPAUR.

Cidades Sustentávies (2015). Gestão Pública Sustentável (Sustainable public management). CidadesSustentáveis. http://www.cidadessustentaveis.org.br/gps. Accessed 22 July 2015.

Comissão Mundial sobre Meio Ambiente e Desenvolvimento – CMMAD. (1991). *Nosso futuro comum* [Our commun future]. Rio de Janeiro: Fundação Getúlio Vargas.

Cúpula Mundial sobre o Desenvolvimento Sustentável – CMDS (2002). RIO +10 (World Summit on Sustainable Development – WSSD RIO +10). Johannesburgo, África do Sul.

Davel, E. (2014). *Pesquisa Qualitativa* [Qualitative research]. Salvador: Imagem. 55 slides, color.

Ferreira, L.C., & Ferreira, L.C. (1995). Limites Ecossistêmicos: novos dilemas e desafios para o Estado e para a sociedade (Ecosystem boundaries: new dilemmas and challenges for the State and for society). In: *Dilemas socioambientais e desenvolvimento sustentável*, Daniel Joseph Hogan e Paulo Freire Vieira (orgs.), Editora Campinas, 2. ed. Campinas.

2 Local Government Aimed at Quality of Life in Sustainable Cities

Hogan, D.J., & Carmo, L.R. (2001). Distribuição espacial da população e sustentabilidade: alternativas de urbanização no estado de São Paulo, Brasil (Spatial distribution of the population and sustainability: urbanization alternatives in São Paulo, Brazil). *Ideias: A questão ambiental e as ciências sociais*, Campinas, v. 2, n. 8, Semestral, pp. 152–190.

Jacobi, P. (1999). Meio Ambiente e Sustentabilidade (Environment and sustainability). In: CEPAM (Org.). O município no século XXI: cenários e perspectivas. Ed. especial. São Paulo, pp. 175–184.

Lefebvre, H. (1979). Space: Social product and use value. In J. Freiberg (Ed.), *Critical sociology: European perspective*. New York: Irvington Publishers.

Marcondes Helene, M. E., & Bicudo, M. B. (1994). *Cenário Mundial: sociedades sustentáveis* [World Scenario: sustainable societies]. São Paulo: Scipione.

Ministério do Meio Ambiente – MMA (2015a). *Caderno de Debate Agenda 21 e Sustentabilidade: Agenda 21 e a sustentabilidade das cidades* (Discussion Paper Agenda 21 and sustainability: Agenda 21 and sustainability in the cities). MMA. http://www.mma.gov.br/estruturas/agenda21/_arquivos/caderno_verde.pdf. Acessed 13 Oct 2015.

Ministério do Meio Ambiente – MMA (2015b). *Cidades sustentáveis* (Sustainable cities). MMA. http://www.mma.gov.br/cidades-sustentaveis/aguas-urbanas. Acessed 13 abr 2015.

Minayo, M.C.S., Hartz, Z.M.A., & Buss, P.M. (2000). Qualidade de vida e saúde: um debate necessário (Quality of life and health: a necessary debate). *Ciência & Saúde Coletiva*, Rio de Janeiro, v. 5, n. 1, pp. 7–18.

Porto, R.G. (2008). *Estudo de impacto ambiental versus estudo de impacto de vizinhança: análise comparativa à luz da legislação pátria na perspectiva de cidades sustentáveis'* (Environmental impact study versus neighbourhood impact study: comparative analysis in the light of country legislation in the perspective of sustainable cities). Dissertação, Pontifícia Universidade Católica de São Paulo.

Programa Cidades Sustentáveis, Sustainable Cities Programa (2015). *Gestão Pública Sustentável* (Sustainable public management). *Cidades Sustentáveis*. http://www.cidadessustentaveis.org.br/gps. Acessed 28 Mar 2015.

Ribeiro, H. (2008). Poluição Urbana (Urban pollution), In: ISA. Almanaque Brasil Socioambiental (pp. 405–408). São Paulo: Instituto Socioambiental.

Roseland, M. (1992). *Toward sustainable communities: a resource book for municipal and local governments*. Ottawa: Natural Round Table on the Environment and the Economy.

Sachs, I. (1994). *Estratégias de transição para o século XXI* [Transition strategies for the 21st century]. Cadernos de Desenvolvimento e Meio Ambiente, no 2 (pp. 47–62). Curitiba: UFPR, .

Schenini, P.C., & Nascimento, D.T. (2002). *Gestão Pública Sustentável* (Sustainable public management). In: *Revista de Ciências da Administração*, v.4, n. 08, jul/dez. 2002.

Silva, C.L., & Rauli, F.C. (2009). Avaliação de políticas públicas para o desenvolvimento sustentável: um estudo de caso dos programas de educação de Curitiba de 1998 a 2005 (Evaluation of public policies for sustainable development: a case study of education programs of Curitiba to 1998 to 2005). *Semestre Económico*, v. 12, n° 23, Enero – Junio de, pp. 77–96.

Simply Psychology. (2017). Maslow's Hierarchy of Needs. https://www.simplypsychology.org/maslow.html. Accessed 7 Jan 2017.

Souza, C. L., & Awad, J. C. M. (2012). *Cidades Sustentáveis, Cidades Inteligentes* [Sustainable cities, smart cities] (278 p). São Paulo: Bookman.

Viola, E.J., & Leis, H.R. (1995). Evolução das políticas ambientais no brasil, 1971–1991: do bissetorialismo preservacionista para o multissetorialismo orientado para o desenvolvimento sustentável (Evolution of environmental policies in Brazil, 1971–1991: from preservationist bisectorialism to multisectorialism oriented towards sustainable development). In: J. Hogan & P. F. Vieira (orgs.) *Dilemas socioambientais e desenvolvimento sustentável* (pp. 73–102). Campinas: Ed. Unicamp.

WCED. (1987). *Our common future*. Oxford: Oxford University Press.

Chapter 3
The Contribution of Smart Cities to Quality of Life from the View of Citizens

José Luis Vázquez, Ana Lanero, Pablo Gutiérrez, and César Sahelices

Abstract This study analyses the perceptions of a sample of 272 university students in Spain regarding current and ideal involvement of the municipality in six dimensions defining a smart city (smart economy, smart people, smart governance, smart mobility, smart environment and smart living). Data was collected through a questionnaire and analysed with descriptive statistical analysis and Student t-tests. Results point to an important gap between students' real experience in the city and the perceived potential of the analysed dimensions to improve future quality of live. Main gaps were found in the dimensions of smart economy and smart governance.

Keywords Smart cities • Quality of life • Sustainability • Citizens • University students • Spain

3.1 Introduction

In recent years, the concept of smart city has gained increasing attention in governance and urban planning (Caragliu et al. 2011; Mosannenzadeh and Vettorato 2014; Washburn et al. 2010). Although there is not an agreed definition, most authors mention the application of information and communication technologies (ICT) as basic foundation and transversal facilitator of public services, sustainability and efficiency (Neirotti et al. 2014). Accordingly, the European Union (EU) is devoting constant efforts to devising a strategy for achieving urban growth in a smart way for its metropolitan areas (Caragliu et al. 2011), by investing in ICT research and innovation and developing policies to improve the quality of life of citizens and make cities more sustainable in view of Europe's targets for 2020. Particularly, the Digital Agenda for Europe (European Commission 2015) is an

J.L. Vázquez • A. Lanero (✉) • P. Gutiérrez • C. Sahelices
Faculty of Economics and Business Sciences, University of León, León, Spain
e-mail: jose-luis.vaquez@unileon.es; ana.lanero@unileon.es; pablo.gutierrez@unileon.es; cesar.sahelices@unileon.es

© Springer International Publishing AG 2018
J. Leitão et al. (eds.), *Entrepreneurial, Innovative and Sustainable Ecosystems*, Applying Quality of Life Research,
https://doi.org/10.1007/978-3-319-71014-3_3

initiative set out to define the key enabling role that the use of ICT will have to play in the new European scene. It aims to maximize the social and economic potential of ICT, most notably the Internet, to foster innovation, economic growth and improvements in daily life for both citizen and businesses.

Consequently, it is expected that wider development and more effective use of digital technologies will provide citizens with a better quality of life, through better health care, safer and more efficient transport solutions, cleaner environment, new media opportunities and easier access to public services and cultural content (European Commission 2015). From this conceptualization of smart cities and their impact on citizen welfare, it is understood that services provided by either local administrations or public-private consortia should be repackaged in a collaborative, sustainable and creative way, thus making the most of any opportunity and potential for socioeconomic development and quality of life improvement.

Likewise, citizens are fundamental actors in the smart growth of cities, given their role as main users and requestors of urban services and their increasing participation in the management of the city. However, citizens do not seem to play a really relevant role in smart cities design, which remains in the hands of politicians, municipal technicians and managers of urban services firms (Centre of Innovation of the Public Service and IE Business School 2015). Related to the previous, citizens might not have a proper knowledge and understanding of smart cities-related concepts and variables and their consequences in daily and future living.

This paper uses the defining dimensions of smart cites identified in the previous literature (Giffinger et al. 2007) to analyse the assessment that a sample of Spanish university students made of the city they live in. Young citizens are chosen for the study because they are common ICT users and, therefore, have the ability to assess their presence in the city. In addition, university students' opinion regarding the potential of smart cities dimensions to improve their quality of life is analysed, according to the existing gap between their current and ideal perceptions. Next sections review the previous literature on the dimensions of the concept of smart city and stress their relationship with quality of life and the fundamental role that citizens should play as main actors of urban spaces. From this theoretical framework, the main results of the empirical study carried out are presented, and its main conclusions are discussed.

3.2 Literature Review

3.2.1 Smart Cities Dimensions

The concept of smart city is wide, giving rise to definitions of different reach, from the most restrictive to the most extensive. In general, it is assumed that smart cities involve the extensive and intensive application of ICT to several spheres of functioning in a city, including public services, water supply and consumption management, improvement of transport and mobility, citizen security and civil protection, creation of favourable environment for business and economic activity and transparency and citizen participation (AMETIC 2012).

From this general framework, Giffinger et al. (2007) proposed a *Ranking of European Medium-Sized Cities* aimed at identifying strengths and weaknesses of urban spaces in a comparative way, based on a combination of local circumstances and activities carried out by politics, business and the inhabitants. According to the fields of activity defined in the previous literature, the authors identify six characteristics to describe a smart city: smart economy, smart people, smart governance, smart mobility, smart environment and smart living.

Smart economy includes factors all around economic competitiveness and innovation, entrepreneurship, trademarks, productivity and flexibility of the labour market as well as the integration in the national and international markets (Giffinger et al. 2007). From this view, it is crucial for a smart city to create a beneficial environment to get economic outcomes as business and job creation, workforce development and productive improvement (Kogan and Lee 2014). Related to this, several authors stress the importance of fostering entrepreneurial initiatives, innovative spirit and competitiveness as essential values for productivity improvement and economic growth (Caragliu et al. 2009; Neirotti et al. 2014; Topetta 2010). Similarly, this dimension relates to investment in ICT services to develop new products and the integration of international markets (Neirotti et al. 2014).

Smart people are described by the level of qualification and education of the citizens, the quality of social interactions regarding integration and public life and the openness towards the outer world (Giffinger et al. 2007). According to Kogan and Lee (2014), smart cities initiatives allow members of the city to participate in the governance and management of the city and become active users. From this view, citizens can collaborate with the city in several aspects, as providers of quality social interactions, providers/consumers of information and data and generators of ideas and initiatives. Therefore, civic engagement and active participation represent key sources of city development. Related to this idea, smart cities aim to foster more informed, educated and participatory citizens by using ICT applications and services (Kogan and Lee 2014). In this regard, development of citizens' e-skills and promotion of digital education to create more opportunities for students and teachers are considered key factors within this dimension (Dirks et al. 2009; Neirotti et al. 2014; Washburn et al. 2010). Additionally, several authors stress the idea of enhancing citizens' affinity to lifelong learning and fostering social and ethnic plurality (Directorate-General for Internal Policies 2014).

Smart governance comprises aspects of political participation, services for citizens and the functioning of the administration (Giffinger et al. 2007). On one hand, smart governance refers to good management with open data, transparency and participatory decision-making democracy supported by ICT (Kogan and Lee 2014; Neirotti et al. 2014). It is defined as an administration, which integrates information, communication and operational technologies; optimizes planning, management and operations across multiple domains, process areas and jurisdictions; and generates sustainable public value. On the other hand, some other factors related to the dimension of smart governance refer to effective public services for citizens, business and institutions and integration of public, private, civil and European organizations (Directorate-General for Internal Policies 2014).

Smart mobility refers to aspects of local and international accessibility and to the availability of ICT and modern and sustainable transport systems (Giffinger et al. 2007). Particularly, the previous literature on smart cities recalls the relevance of local and international accessibility and put the emphasis on improving logistics flows by effectively integrating business needs with traffic conditions and geographical and environmental issues (Caragliu et al. 2009; Neirotti et al. 2014; Toppeta 2010). In this regard, Neirotti et al. (2014) identify several innovative ways to provide the transport of people in cities, such as vehicles based on environment-friendly fuels and propulsion systems, and emphasis on walking and cycling. In addition, ICT infrastructures for traffic monitoring and control can be used to save time, energy consumption and costs and to optimize logistics (Neirotti et al. 2014).

Smart environment is described by attractive natural conditions (climate, green space, etc.), pollution, resource management and environmental protection (Giffinger et al. 2007). According to Kogan and Lee (2014), smart environment is based on green technologies and doing-more-with-less principle. Core to the concept of a smart city is the use of technology to protect the environment and better manage natural resources (pollution control, green renewable energies, etc.), with the ultimate goal of increasing sustainability (Caragliu et al. 2009; Neirotti et al. 2014). Of a particular interest is the protection of natural resources and the related infrastructure, such as waterways and sewers and green spaces such as parks (Kogan and Lee 2014). Similarly, some authors stress the usage of ICT to enable measurement and information exchange about energy consumption and incentives to increase resources reuse and recycling (Caragliu et al. 2009; Giffinger et al. 2007; Toppeta 2010).

Finally, smart living comprises various aspects of quality of life as culture, health, safety, housing, tourism, etc. (Giffinger et al. 2007). In the area of culture, the literature insists on facilitating the diffusion of information related to cultural activities and motivating people to be involved in them. Examples of initiatives are: cultural facilities, applications that provide insight into the waiting time to access a particular monument, city and museums guides available for smartphones, etc. (Neirotti et al. 2014). ICT can also be used to support disease prevention, diagnosis and treatment, assuring all citizens efficient facilities and services in the health-care system. Telemonitoring and telecare are examples of this kind of initiatives (Dirks et al. 2009; Neirotti et al. 2014). Another important aspect within this dimension is the protection of citizens' integrity and their goods, as well as optimization of emergency services based on big data collection through technology applications (Dirks et al. 2009; Neirotti et al. 2014). Related to the previous, improvement of technology accessibility and adaptation of sustainable building technologies to gain energy efficiency, security, accessibility and usability are core elements of smart living (Directorate-General for Internal Policies 2014).

3.2.2 *Quality of Life in Smart Cities*

From the previous description of the main dimensions of smart cities, it follows that quality of life must be the main goal of urban planning. In this respect, Marsa-Maestre et al. (2008) use the adjective *smart* to characterize an environment that is able to acquire and apply knowledge about its inhabitants and their surroundings to meet comfort and efficiency goals. In similar terms, Neirotti et al. (2014) state that the number of smart initiatives launched by a municipality reflects the efforts made to improve the quality of life of the citizens.

Within the same framework, Kogan and Lee (2014) state that a smart city remains a city which uses ICT to go beyond economic targets, to deliver sustainable, quality of life improvements for its citizens, its industry and the local environment. Likewise, Komninos et al. (2011) connect smart cities to notions of global competitiveness, sustainability, empowerment and quality of life.

In more specific terms, Mosannenzadeh and Vettorato (2014) note that, although a common definition is not yet established, experts agree that smart cities are urban areas that aim to help human beings overcome their problems. Particularly, these authors consider smart cities as sustainable and efficient urban areas with "high quality of life that aims to address urban challenges (improve mobility, optimize use of resources, improve health and safety, improve social development, support economic growth and participatory governance) by application of ICT in its infrastructure and services, collaboration between its key stakeholders (citizens, universities, government, industry), integration of its main domains (environment, mobility, governance, community, industry, and services), and investment in social capital" (pp. 691–692).

Based on this reasoning, an empirical analysis by Caragliu et al. (2011) found that the quality of the urban environment, the level of education and the accessibility to ICT for public administration – as dimensions of their definition of smart cities – were positively correlated with urban wealth. Similarly, a study carried out in Spain found that citizens consider quality of life improvement and public services quality as the main utilities of smart cities, followed by mentions to environmental sustainability and transparency in public management (Centre of Innovation of the Public Service and IE Business School 2015).

In short, smart cities' infrastructures are equipped with advanced technological solutions to facilitate citizens' interactions with urban elements, making their lives easier. In this context, citizens are not only engaged and informed in the relationship between their activities, their neighbourhoods and the wider urban ecosystems, but are actively encouraged to see the city itself as something they can collectively tune, such that it is efficient, interactive, engaging, adaptive and flexible (ARUP 2011). At the same time, ICT give city governments a way of involving citizens more directly in the direction and operation of their city and, by doing so, create a platform through which the city can learn from their actions.

3.2.3 Citizens as Key Actors on Smart Cities

Because quality of life is unavoidably linked to the concept of smart city, citizens' experiences are of crucial importance in the process of urban planning. Accordingly, the literature suggests people as one main group of stakeholders involved in creation of smart cities (Cosgrave et al. 2013; Lombardi et al. 2012; Yovanof and Hazapis 2009). For instance, Giffinger et al. (2007) define a smart city as a well-performing city built on the *smart* combination of endowments and activities of self-decisive, independent and aware citizens.

Similarly, although the application of ICT to several citizen spheres is a common element to most definitions of smart cities, some experts point that technological solutions can be considered as just one of the various approaches to urban planning and living that have the aim of improving the social, environmental and economic sustainability of a city (Neirotti et al. 2014). Moreover, Caragliu et al. (2011) state that smart cities depend not only on the endowment of hard infrastructure (physical capital) but also on the availability and quality of knowledge communication (intellectual capital) and social infrastructure (social capital). Similarly, Kogan and Lee (2014) affirm that ICT is not a sufficient condition for a city to become smart and that citizen engagement and governance represent two key success factors along with other enablers.

Beyond such a consideration, as pointed by Neirotti et al. (2014), the various positions agree on the fact that a smart city should be able to optimize the use and exploitation of both tangible (e.g. transport infrastructures, energy distribution networks, natural resources) and intangible assets (e.g. human capital, intellectual capital of companies and organizational capital in public administration bodies). Thus, smart urban spaces are considered as a meeting place where the public sector, private interest and citizens can come together to generate new value, collaborate and innovate (Leydesdorff and Deakin 2011; Yawson 2009; Walravens 2015). From this view, smart cities can only be successful if they act as local innovation platforms that bring together all involved stakeholders (Shepard and Simeti 2013).

Therefore, the goal of the application of ICT to urban planning and quality of life improvement in cities should not be only that citizens get informed and more involved in their neighbourhoods and other urban ecosystems, but that they feel active agents in their cities and see them as spaces that can be altered in an efficient, interactive, adaptive and flexible way (ARUP 2011). However, some evidence points that citizens might not have a proper knowledge and understanding of smart cities-related concepts and variables and their consequences in daily and future living. For instance, a recent study carried out in Spain concludes that only one half of citizens affirm that they know and understand what a smart city is. In addition, most of them link the concept to technology, environmental sustainability and efficiency in urban services management. In this context, Spanish citizens also consider that the cities they live in are poorly smart (Centre of Innovation of the Public Service and IE Business School 2015).

In order to go deeper into these findings, next sections describe the methodology and results of a previous study carried out in a Spanish city to analyse the opinion of a sample of young citizens regarding the smart practices adopted according to the six dimensions identified previously, as well as their ideal vision of these dimensions to improve their perceived quality of life.

3.3 Methodology

3.3.1 Sample

A self-report study was carried out with a sample of 272 university students at the Faculty of Economic and Business Sciences of the University of León. This city is situated in the Northwest of Spain, within the autonomous community of Castilla y León. At the moment of the survey, the city of León had a total population of 127,817 inhabitants (National Institute of Statistics 2016), spread out in an area of 39.03 Km². Nowadays, the city council is working in the project *León XXI-21*, aimed to design smart urban spaces similar to other Spanish cities. However, up to now, the city has not been analysed by any national or international ranking. Thus, this study seeks to know the citizen perception regarding the dimensions of smart cities described previously, as well as their potential contribution to quality of life improvement.

The study relied in a sample of young university students, because of their greater closeness to ICT applications in comparison to other collectives of the general population. From the total of respondents, 208 (76.47%) were habitual citizens, whereas the remaining 62 respondents (23.53%) were living temporally in the city. Regarding the sociodemographic characteristics of respondents, 100 were males (36.8%) and 172 females (63.2%), aged 18–26 years ($M = 20.05$; $DT = 1.65$).

3.3.2 Procedure

A questionnaire was developed for data collection. To ensure content validity of the scales, a deductive approach was followed that was based on a thorough review of the specialized literature and other similar instruments (Hinkin 1995). In addition, the selection of the indicators was based on three experts' judgement and the results of a pretest conducted with a small group of undergraduate students who were consulted about the difficulty and their understanding of the content. To minimize social desirability and acquiescence biases, respondents were requested to respond to the survey anonymously and as honestly as possible (Podsakoff et al. 2003).

In particular, respondents were presented a list of 25 indicators defining several practices of smart cities, around the six dimensions of smart economy, smart people, smart governance, smart mobility, smart environment and smart living.

The smart economy dimension was defined by six indicators related to the application of ICT to the economic growth and competitiveness of the city (e.g. support for entrepreneurship and business start-up through intelligent incubators).

The smart people dimension was composed of five items concerning the development of digital skills to improve participation and efficient use of urban services (e.g. development of citizens' e-skills to use the ICT applications and services of the city).

The smart governance dimension was measured with three items on citizen participation and efficient public management (e.g. creation of a society based on open data, transparency and a participatory decision-making democracy supported by ICT – e-governance, e-democracy, etc.).

The smart mobility dimension was defined by three indicators of local and international accessibility supported by ICT (e.g. development and emphasis on logistics flows and modern, sustainable and safe public means of transport).

The smart environment dimension was composed of three items related to the application of technological advances to environmental protection and responsible consumption (e.g. usage of ICT to enable measurement and information exchange about energy consumption in real time between providers and users).

Finally, the smart living dimension was assessed through five indicators of citizen life (e.g. usage of ICT for the diffusion of information and citizen involvement in cultural activities and tourism).

For each item, respondents were requested to indicate firstly their perceptions of current involvement of the city. Next, they had to assess the importance that each practice should have to improve citizen experience and quality of life. In both cases, responses were ranged in a five-point Likert-type scale from 1 (*no current/ideal involvement*) to 5 (*maximum current/ideal involvement*).

Two indexes of current and ideal involvement were calculated for the six dimensions, according to the mean obtained for the total sample in the indicators assigned to each scale. Then, six *Student t-tests* for related samples were carried out to analyse the existence of statistically significant differences between the punctuations of current and ideal involvement obtained for each dimension.

3.4 Results

Figure 3.1 displays the mean scores obtained by the total sample in the six dimensions of perceived current involvement in smart urban practices. In general, it is appreciated a poor assessment in the six factors analysed, with mean scores under the intermediate value of 3 in the five-point Likert scale. In particular, respondents seemed to share a negative perception of the city in issues related to transparent and

3 The Contribution of Smart Cities to Quality of Life from the View of Citizens

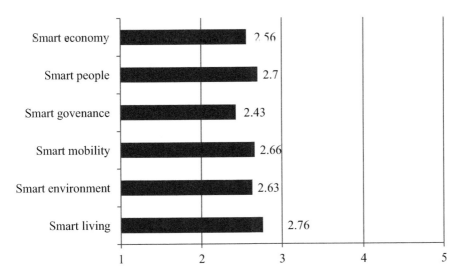

Fig. 3.1 Current involvement in smart urban practices (mean scores)

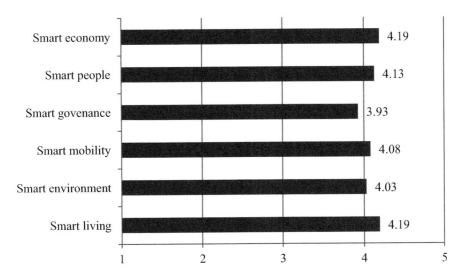

Fig. 3.2 Ideal involvement in smart urban practices (mean scores)

democratic governance ($M = 2.43$), as well as to ICT application to economic performance and local competitiveness improvement ($M = 2.56$). Although global mean scores were also considerably low, a better assessment was observed in the scales of smart living ($M = 2.76$) and smart people ($M = 2.70$).

On the other side, Fig. 3.2 shows the mean scores in the six dimensions studied when respondents were asked on the ideal involvement of the city in smart urban practices to improve their experiences as citizens and perceived quality of life. In

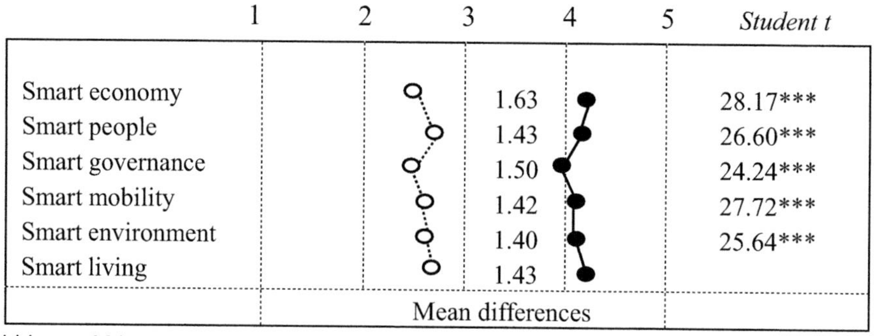

	1	2	3	4	5	*Student t*
Smart economy			1.63			28.17***
Smart people			1.43			26.60***
Smart governance			1.50			24.24***
Smart mobility			1.42			27.72***
Smart environment			1.40			25.64***
Smart living			1.43			
		Mean differences				

*** p < .001.

Fig. 3.3 Differences between current and ideal involvement in smart urban practices

general terms, considerably greater punctuations were obtained, most of them above 4 in the five-point Likert scale. Specifically, the factors in which a greater involvement is demanded corresponded to the dimensions of smart economy and smart living ($M = 4.19$ in both cases), followed by smart people ($M = 4.13$), smart mobility ($M = 4.08$) and smart environment ($M = 4.03$). The lowest mean score corresponded this time to smart governance ($M = 3.93$).

To test statistically the existing differences between perceptions of current and ideal urban involvement in smart practices, six *Student t-tests* were performed (Fig. 3.3). For all the dimensions analysed, differences were statistically significant. The most important gaps corresponded to smart economy ($t = 28.17$, $p < 0.001$, $dif = 1.63$) and smart governance ($t = 24.24$, $p < 0.001$, $dif = 1.50$). The lowest discrepancies corresponded to the dimensions of smart environment ($t = 25.64$, $p < 0.001$, $dif = 1.40$) and smart mobility ($t = 27.72$, $p < 0.001$, $dif = 1.42$).

3.5 Conclusions

The concept of smart city is strongly linked to urban planning's commitment to quality of life, what gives citizens a leading role as main requestors of public services and fundamental actors of citizen participation. Nevertheless, the smart design of most cities usually remains in the hands of public or private agents with a scarce consideration of citizens' opinions regarding the convenience and usefulness of the implemented improvements and their impact on quality of life. Related to this, the knowledge that citizens have on the concept of smart cities and their dimensions can be seriously questioned (Centre of Innovation of the Public Service and IE Business School 2015).

In this context, the study presented in this chapter was aimed to analyse the assessment that a sample of young university students made of the city they lived in, as well as their opinion regarding the contribution of smart urban planning to their

3 The Contribution of Smart Cities to Quality of Life from the View of Citizens

quality of life. For doing that, the existing gaps between current and ideal perceptions of six dimensions defining a smart city (Giffinger et al. 2007) were analysed: smart economy, smart people, smart governance, smart mobility, smart environment and smart living.

In general terms, the results of the study point to the conclusion that university students perceive a poor involvement of the municipality in practices of smart economy and governance. In fact, the main gaps between current and ideal perceived involvement appear linked to these two dimensions. Thus, our findings suggest the convenience of reinforcing the involvement of the city in practices related to the application of ICT to the improvement of economic growth and local competitiveness, as well as the transparent functioning of public administration and citizen participation.

Paradoxically, smart governance was the factor less associated to quality of life from the point of view of respondents. On the other side, the most valued dimensions were smart economy, smart living and smart people. Thus, application of ICT to aspects related to daily life in the city – cultural issues, health services, security, etc. – seems to be the key to improve citizen's positive experiences and quality of life. Similar conclusions can be said regarding the improvement of citizen digital skills to reinforce their social interactions and participation in public spaces.

Finally, the dimensions of smart mobility and smart environment were associated to intermediate assessments in the study, both in terms of current perceived involvement and ideal perceived involvement. In sum, it can be concluded that those aspects related to improvements in local and international mobility, as well as to efficient resources management, are considered important but of less priority when assessing the potential of ICT to improve students' quality of life.

As final clarification, it is worth pointing that the conclusions of this study need to be interpreted in the context of some methodological limitations that should be addressed in future research. Basically, while analysing the opinion of university students is a valuable starting point in the research on citizen perception regarding basic concepts of smart urban planning, future studies should consider more heterogeneous profiles that are more representative of the general population. Those approaches would allow identifying segments of citizens with different needs and experiences in the city, giving rise to adapted practices of urban planning to improve citizen quality of life.

References

AMETIC. (2012). *Smart cities*. Madrid: Foro TIC para la Sostenibilidad.
ARUP. (2011). *The smart solution for cities*. ARUP.
Caragliu, A., Del Bo, C., & Nijkamp, P. (2011). Smart cities in Europe. *Journal of Urban Technology, 18*, 65–82.
Centre of Innovation of the Public Service and IE Business School. (2015). *Smart cities. La transformación de las ciudades*. Madrid: Centre of Innovation of the Public Service and IE Business School.

Cosgrave, E., Arbuthnot, K., & Tryfonas, T. (2013). Living labs, innovation districts and information marketplaces: A systems approach for smart cities. *Procedia Computer Science, 16*, 668–677.

Directorate-General for Internal Policies. (2014). *Mapping smart cities in the EU*. European Parliament.

Dirks, S., Keeling, M., & Dencik, J. (2009). *How smart is your city*. IBM Institute for Business Value.

European Commission. (2015). *Digital agenda for Europe. A Europe 2020 initiative*. Brussels: European Commission.

Giffinger, R., et al. (2007). *Smart cities: Ranking of European medium-sized cities*. Vienna: Centre of Regional Science (SRF), Vienna University of Technology.

Hinkin, T. R. (1995). A review of scale development practices in the study of organizations. *Journal of Management, 21*, 967–988.

Kogan, N., & Lee, K. L. (2014). Exploratory research on the success and challenges of smart city projects. *Asia Pacific Journal of Information Systems, 24*, 141–188.

Komninos, N., Schaffers, H., & Pallot, M. (2011). Developing a policy road map for smart cities and the future Internet. In *eChallenges e-2011 Conference Proceedings*. P & M Cunningham.

Leydesdorff, L., & Deakin, M. (2011). The triple-helix model of smart cities: A neo-evolutionary perspective. *Journal of Urban Technology, 18*, 53–63.

Lombardi, P., Giordano, S., Farouh, H., & Yousef, W. (2012). Modelling the smart city performance. *Innovation: The European Journal of Social Science Research, 25*(2), 137–149.

Marsa-Maestre, I., López-Carmona, M. A., Velasco, J. R., & Navarro, A. (2008). Mobile agents for service personalization in smart environments. *Journal of Networks, 3*(5), 30–41.

Mosannenzadeh, F., & Vettorato, D. (2014). Defining smart city. A conceptual framework based on keyword analysis. *Journal of Land Use, Mobility and Environment*, (Special Issue):683–694.

National Institute of Statistics. (2016). *Cifras oficiales de población*. http://www.ine.es

Neirotti, P., De Marco, A., Cagliano, A. C., Mangano, G., & Scorrano, F. (2014). Current trends in smart city initiatives: Some stylised facts. *Cities, 38*, 25–36.

Podsakoff, P. M., MacKenzie, S. B., Lee, J.-Y., & Podsakoff, N. P. (2003). Common method biases in behavioural research: A critical review of the literature and recommended remedies. *Journal of Applied Psychology, 88*(5), 879–902.

Shepard, M., & Simeti, A. (2013). What's so smart about the smart citizen? In D. Hemment & A. Townsend (Eds.), *Smart Citizens* (Vol. 4). Manchester: Future Everything Publications.

Toppeta, D. (2010). *The smart city vision: How innovation and ICT can build smart, "livable", sustainable cities*. The Innovation Knowledge Foundation.

Walravens, N. (2015). Mobile city applications for Brussels citizens: Smart city trends, challenges and a reality check. *Telematics and Informatics, 32*, 282–299.

Washburn, D., et al. (2010). *Helping CIOs understand "smart city" initiatives: Defining the smart city, its drivers, and the role of the CIO*. Cambridge, MA: Forrester Research.

Yawson, R. M. (2009). The ecological system of innovation: A new architectural framework for a functional evidence-based platform for science and innovation policy. In *The Future of Innovation Proceedings of the XXIV ISPIM 2009 Conference*. Vienna.

Yovanof, G. S., & Hazapis, G. N. (2009). An architectural framework and enabling wireless technologies for digital cities & intelligent urban environments. *Wireless Personal Communications, 49*, 445–463.

Chapter 4
Expanding Entrepreneurial, Innovative and Sustainable (EIS) Ecosystems: A Cultural-Historical Activity Theory Perspective

Romano Audhoe, Neil Thompson, and Karen Verduijn

Abstract The value of Entrepreneurial, Innovative and Sustainable (EIS) ecosystems has seen increasing recognition from policymakers and researchers alike. Policymakers employing New Public Management (NPM) have come to understand that the intricate links between diverse EIS stakeholders play a vital role in advancing sources of local transformation – entrepreneurship and innovation – to enhance citizen wellbeing (e.g. happiness, trust, safety and satisfaction). A persistent challenge to both academic and policy research, however, is uncovering how and why EIS ecosystem stakeholders do or do not interact to produce positive outcomes. In this chapter, we propose and explain a novel framework for analysing and assessing EIS ecosystems: activity system analysis (ASA). This methodological framework, rooted in cultural-historical activity theory (CHAT), assists researchers by guiding analyses towards specific tensions and contradictions between stakeholders that prevent EIS ecosystems from developing. ASA does this by moving the analysis from ambiguous framework and systemic conditions (e.g. cultural, social and material attributes) towards the activities and objectives by stakeholders in specific locales. Additionally, it allows researchers to gain insights in the developmental trajectory of EIS ecosystems and to understand the learning actions that transform them. Ultimately, this chapter provides guidelines for performing activity-oriented research on EIS ecosystems so as to uncover the intricacies of an EIS ecosystem's functioning. Adopting the ASA approach will enable policymakers to better understand how to improve EIS ecosystems and the quality of life for their citizens.

Keywords Activity systems • EIS ecosystems • Entrepreneurship • Community • Expansive learning cycle

---

R. Audhoe (✉) • N. Thompson • K. Verduijn
School of Economics and Business, VU University Amsterdam, Amsterdam, The Netherlands
e-mail: romano.audhoe@outlook.com; n.a.thompson@vu.nl; karen.verduijn@vu.nl

© Springer International Publishing AG 2018
J. Leitão et al. (eds.), *Entrepreneurial, Innovative and Sustainable Ecosystems*, Applying Quality of Life Research,
https://doi.org/10.1007/978-3-319-71014-3_4

4.1 Introduction

The bureaucratic processes that were once firmly rooted in governmental practice have transitioned to a new management philosophy called New Public Management (Hood 1995). Under this philosophy, policymakers aim to embrace sustainable and inclusive businesses to improve the quality of life for citizens (Osborne 2010; Thomas 2013). It is no surprise then that entrepreneurship, known for its vital role in urban renewal, job creation and innovation (Decker et al. 2014; Stam 2014), has been a central focus of NPM. Entrepreneurs working with a sustainable orientation are actively modifying markets and institutions towards a more pro-environmental and social condition, thus introducing and diffusing new sustainable products and services (Thompson et al. 2011, 2015). It is widely accepted that entrepreneurship does not happen in a vacuum, but rather as the result of coordinated actions among many stakeholders (Mason and Brown 2013; Stam and Spigel 2016). Such notions have dovetailed into a keen interest in the development and successes of Entrepreneurial, Innovative and Sustainable (EIS) ecosystems consisting of private and public stakeholders that support sustainable and innovative action of entrepreneurs (Feld 2012; Suresh and Ramraj 2012). Recent research in this area has succeeded in identifying the different components or elements that are manifest in successful cases of entrepreneurial ecosystems (Isenberg 2010; Spigel 2015). For instance, Spigel (2015) details the material attributes (policies, universities, infrastructure, open markets, supportive systems), social attributes (networks, worker talent, investment capital, mentors and role models) and cultural attributes (supportive and history of entrepreneurship) needed for productive entrepreneurship. In alignment with the goals of NPM, the notion of EIS ecosystems informs potential policy actions that will encourage a flourishing environment for innovative and sustainable entrepreneurship.

However, there remains two major opportunities to further our understanding of EIS ecosystems that will enhance quality of life for citizens. First, existing research has systematically overlooked the existence and importance of the diversity of entrepreneurship communities within them. Entrepreneurship communities are groups of individuals and organizations, such as nascent and serial entrepreneurs interacting (physically, digitally or in markets) who interact based on a common interest in a particular domain (Cohen 2006). Examples of entrepreneurship communities are information technology (software/Internet), biotech, cleantech, natural foods, Lifestyles of Health and Sustainability (LOHAS) and so on. Studies by Horst (2008) and Horwitch and Mulloth (2010) among others have shown that it is through the grassroots process of sharing information and experiences with the community that entrepreneurs learn from each other, have an opportunity to develop personally and professionally (Wenger 1999) and expand opportunities for participation (Feld 2012) which influences entrepreneurial emergence and success (Popoviciu and Popoviciu 2011). Meanwhile, researchers, policymakers and practitioners acknowledge that actors and factors of the ecosystem are interdependent (Stam and Spigel 2016) and that successful outcomes often result from the identification of both comparative and competitive advantages (Mason and Brown 2013). But to date, the fact that EIS ecosystems consist of several entrepreneurship communities, each having a different repertoire of actions, styles, artefacts, concepts, discourses and histories, remains under-acknowledged. The result is that policymakers develop plans and policies to promote and increase sustainable and innovative entrepreneurship in general, without acknowledging that each entrepreneurship community has different needs or systemic constraints.

Second, there is still a lack of understanding of how and why (ongoing) interactions between different parties within EIS ecosystems take place, how these interactions develop over time, and why they may prevent EIS ecosystems from developing (Mack and Mayer 2016). The dynamics of EIS ecosystems are important because they reveal how historical ties between companies, people and entrepreneurial communities have developed (Zahra and Nambisan 2012), which lead to transformation in EIS ecosystems. For instance, entrepreneurial activity in Finland once centred solely around Nokia, yet nowadays it revolves around a vibrant start-up community (Mason and Brown 2013). Following Feld (2012), we recognize in this chapter that EIS ecosystems not only include multiple entrepreneurship communities, but that their dynamic development is linked to their interaction and systemic conflicts with investment, government, research and education communities. In order for policymakers to improve the quality of life for their citizens, a deep understanding of entrepreneurship communities and their interactions with other communities involved in EIS ecosystems is indispensable.

Considering these two oversights, the purpose of this chapter is twofold. First, we aim to develop a new conceptual framework of EIS ecosystems that explains the dynamics and interactions within entrepreneurship communities as well as between investment, government, research, education and other communities. Second, we develop and discuss methods for understanding, developing and intervening in EIS ecosystems for policymakers and researchers. To achieve these objectives, we employ the framework of activity systems from cultural-historical activity theory (CHAT). Originally developed by Vygotsky (1978) and Leont'ev (1978, 1981) and later extended by Engeström (1993, 1987, 2001), CHAT provides a framework for conceptualizing and studying EIS ecosystems as multiple interactive activity systems (Kuutti 1996). Next, we explain the contradictions within and between activity systems that explain the development and expansion of an EIS ecosystem through collective learning. Finally, we discuss activity system analysis (ASA) as a way for policymakers and researchers to understand, develop, resolve contradictions and support the dynamic activities of EIS ecosystems. In particular, we outline how the ASA method can help investigators make sense of complex real-world data sets in a manageable and meaningful manner. It provides a valid framework to use as a guide while building reliable interpretations of data about EIS ecosystems. Thus, ASA provides opportunities for investigators to (a) work with a manageable unit of analysis, (b) find systemic implications, (c) understand systemic contradictions and tensions, (d) communicate findings from the analyses and (e) implement informed actions to support EIS ecosystems (Yamagata-Lynch 2010). Accordingly, this chapter serves as a guide for policymakers, scholars, practitioners or other investigators to assist in better visualizing EIS ecosystems, thus enabling them to make better informed choices in deciding on how to improve the quality of lives for citizens.

4.2 Literature Review and Motivation

This section briefly reviews the existing literature on Entrepreneurial, Innovative and Sustainable (EIS) ecosystems with reference to the improved quality of life that EIS ecosystems bring about from the perspective of New Public Management (NPM). Following this review, we discuss two opportunities for conceptual development that motivates this chapter.

4.2.1 Entrepreneurial, Innovative and Sustainable Ecosystems

The mission of NPM is to not only effectuate renewal and growth to cities but also to enhance the quality of life for its citizens (Osborne 2010; Thomas 2013). A key mechanism for achieving this mission is the support of innovative and sustainable entrepreneurship (Stam 2014). Research on sustainable entrepreneurship suggests that it can be an 'innovative, market-oriented and personality driven form of creating economic and societal value by means of break-through environmentally or socially beneficial market or institutional innovations' (Schaltegger and Wagner 2011, p. 226). Dean and McMullen (2007) and Cohen and Winn (2007) argue that various market failures represent opportunities for sustainable entrepreneurs to reduce socially and environmentally degrading economic behaviours. Since sustainable entrepreneurs find bottom-up solutions to these problems, they help redirect the path of socio-economic development towards sustainable development (see Hekkert and Negro 2009).

The limited but growing literature on entrepreneurial ecosystems begins with the observation that entrepreneurs do not perform activities in a social vacuum (Drakopoulou Dodd and Anderson 2007; Steyaert and Katz 2004; Suresh and Ramraj 2012). Rather a growing body of evidence suggests that external support is essential to increasing the number of and survival rates of entrepreneurs in a particular region or city (Mason and Brown 2013; Yasuyuki and Watkins 2014). In fact, the coordinated action among a variety of stakeholders is necessary in order to pave the way for (aspiring) entrepreneurs to set up and grow their own businesses. Stam and Spigel (2016) define an entrepreneurial ecosystem as a set of interdependent actors and factors coordinated in such a way that they enable productive entrepreneurship within a particular territory. The academic study of entrepreneurial ecosystems examines how ecosystems can be arranged to generate competitive advantages for cities, regions and nation-states (Boyd Cohen 2006; Feld 2012; Pitelis 2012; Suresh and Ramraj 2012). The value of an EIS ecosystems construct is evident not only as a means to help stable economies grow but also as an approach to realize cocreated value that has implications for quality of life of its citizens and declining economies (Suresh and Ramraj 2012). As such, EIS ecosystems serve the needs of New Public Management (NPM) in its goal of moving public policy away from bureaucratic administration and towards creating sustainable, flourishing communities through renewal, entrepreneurship and growth (Osborne 2010).

The research on entrepreneurial ecosystems connects with ongoing theoretical discussions regarding the role of context in entrepreneurship (Welter 2011) as well as recognizing entrepreneurship as an inherently socially embedded process (Steyaert and Katz 2004). The entrepreneurial ecosystem concept is important in this literature as it recognizes the complexity and diversity of interactions between components such that outcomes of one organizational process may be used as raw material in another process. Among the components being discussed, Isenberg (2010) suggests entrepreneurial ecosystems consist of elements that can be grouped into six domains: (1) a conducive culture (e.g. tolerance of risk and mistakes, positive social status of entrepreneur), (2) facilitating policies and leadership (e.g. regulatory framework incentives, existence of public research institutes), (3) availability of dedicated finance (e.g. business angels, venture capital, microloans, crowdfunding, crowdsourcing, equity funding), (4) relevant human capital (e.g. skilled and unskilled labour, serial entrepreneurs, entrepreneurship training, coaching and mentoring programmes), (5) venture-friendly markets for products (e.g. early adopters for prototypes, reference customers) and (6) a wide set of institutional and infrastructural supports (e.g. legal and accounting advisers, telecommunications and transportation infrastructure, entrepreneurship promoting associations). Recently, Stam and Spigel (2016) build from these ideas to create a conceptual framework based on framework conditions (formal institutions, culture, physical infrastructure, demand) and systemic conditions ('a broad, deep talent pool', financial capital, leadership, 'mentors and advisors giving back across all stages', supportive large established organizations and supportive policies). In their conceptual model, systemic and framework conditions of entrepreneurial ecosystems encourage entrepreneurial activity that results in aggregate value creation for a particular region or city.

4.2.2 Limitations of Current Models

We argue that there remain two opportunities to greatly increase our understanding of EIS ecosystems. The first is the empirical acknowledgement that EIS ecosystems are very often made up of multiple communities (Wenger 1999), each with their own shared repertoire of actions, styles, artefacts, concepts, discourses and histories. The notion of community suggests that entrepreneurship includes an element of situated learning (Pitelis 2012) – the handed-down ways of doing and being that persist through time. For example, successful and impactful start-ups in cleantech require the acquisition of human, social, technological and financial capital through engagement with individuals and organizations within a community who are themselves knowledgeable about cleantech. Thus, the structural and changing dynamics of these communities have differential but measurable impacts on entrepreneurial emergence and success (Horwitch and Mulloth 2010). As Feld (2012) notes, the thriving entrepreneurial ecosystem in Boulder, Colorado, includes multiple communities related to information technology (software/Internet), biotech, cleantech, natural foods and Lifestyles of Health and Sustainability (LOHAS). Knowing how to succeed in these communities is a matter of displaying the socially defined competence sustained by the community (Haugh 2007); thus the knowledge and competence necessary for successful entrepreneurship in one community are historically and socially defined (Wenger 1999). Despite its intuitive appeal, existing conceptual models, such as those previously reviewed, emphasize acquiring or supporting the necessary components for a flourishing EIS ecosystem (resources, policies, etc.) without recognizing the crucial role of communities.

Second, the conceptual frameworks that focus on listing the distinct elements or components are certainly valuable, yet they tend to overlook the inherently dynamic and developmental nature of EIS ecosystems (Mack and Mayer 2016). This is problematic since EIS ecosystems are born and grown out of ongoing processes that serve the needs of both public and private stakeholders (Spigel 2016). Therefore, it is essential for policymakers, entrepreneurs and governments to understand how EIS ecosystems evolve and develop over time in order to design interventions or promotional policies to encourage them. Understanding what propels the formation and expansion of EIS ecosystems thus enables one to engage more deeply in the ongoing activities within these ecosystems and to adjust actions and policies accordingly, to benefit the entrepreneurs within these communities. This can only be achieved by taking note of the history and context that help shape the EIS ecosystems (Zahra and Nambisan 2012). To illustrate this point, we can turn to the entrepreneurial ecosystem of Switzerland, whose medical technology community emerged as a result of growth and development in engineering advancements within the Swiss watch industry (Vogel 2013). Accordingly, what is needed is a framework that enables policymakers, academics and practitioners to identify and analyse those important activities over time, while also accounting for the cultural and historical background of communities which have shaped these activities.

Finally, existing conceptual frameworks lack connection to a specific methodological procedure to understand and support EIS ecosystems. The main challenges to proponents of EIS ecosystems are not only conceptualizing real-world EIS ecosystems but also extracting meaningful information from massive and complex data. Conceptual frameworks that list elements or factors that are necessary for flourishing EIS ecosystems downplay the systemic relations between different communities that comprise them. In particular, it is hard to visualize systemic contradictions and tensions that influence a series of related activities, as well as how communities modify and create new activities while adapting to environments. Systemic contradictions do not happen accidentally or arbitrarily but reflect the incompatible incentives or interests between communities. Understanding real-world ecosystems involves complicated data collection, analysis and presentation that make communicating findings with others difficult. It can also be challenging for investigators to coordinate at multiple levels to arrive a meaningful conclusion about the development or barriers to EIS ecosystems. Finally, these challenges ultimately mean it remains difficult to stimulate EIS ecosystems to enhance citizen wellbeing (e.g. happiness, trust, safety and satisfaction). In the next section, we develop a new conceptual model of EIS ecosystems that seeks to solve these issues.

4.3 EIS Ecosystems as Multi-interactive Activity Systems: A New Conceptual Framework

In response to the critiques above, we draw on cultural-historical activity theory (CHAT), to develop a new conceptual model of EIS ecosystems that acknowledges evolving, interacting communities. In particular, we employ CHAT's notion of an activity system to conceptualize a community. After explaining the elements of an activity system and the outcomes of interacting activity systems, we move on to describe the formation and expansion of EIS ecosystems. In doing so, we employ a model of expansive and collective learning developed by CHAT scholar Engeström (1987, 1990, 1999, 2001). Throughout this section, we draw on empirical research to provide examples of our conceptual model as well as indicate spillover benefits for citizen wellbeing.

4.3.1 Activity Systems

Rooted in a tradition of adopting practice-based theory in the social sciences (Foot and Fi 2001; Nicolini 2012; Roth 2007; Yamagata-Lynch 2007), CHAT is a cross-disciplinary theoretical framework that argues researchers, policymakers and practitioners should seek to understand and analyse object-oriented activity in order to study how humans intentionally and unintentionally transform natural and social reality. At the centre of CHAT is the notion that an activity is not something a person or organization does, but is a collective effort of communities. Thus activities are not viewed as units of discrete individual behaviour. Consequently, activity systems are conceptualized as an indivisible, molar unit of analysis, that cannot be disaggregated into its substantive parts (Leont'ev 1978), as shown in Fig. 4.1. Importantly, activities are longer-term formations – their objects are transformed into outcomes not at once but through an iterative process that typically consists of several steps or phases. Actions are shorter-term processes that are conscious, goal-oriented and facilitated by tools. Therefore, activities consist of actions or chains of actions that are subject to concrete conditions (Kuutti 1996). In the following section, we describe and give empirical examples of each element of an activity system, before moving on to discuss its implications for the formation and expansion of EIS ecosystems.

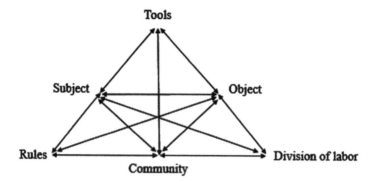

Fig. 4.1 An activity system (Engeström 1987, p. 78)

4.3.2 Object of the Activity System

The object element distinguishes one activity system from another (Leont'ev 1978), which means understanding an activity system requires understanding its object. For example, the shared object of a community of entrepreneurs might be to improve environmental conditions and citizen wellbeing by establishing cleantech ventures (e.g. wind, solar, bio, etc.). Objects can be thought of as consisting of three dimensions – a thing to be acted upon, an objectified motive and a desired outcome. In CHAT, each object has all three of these facets, and any of these facets may be constructed or perceived differently by various members of the community. For example, entrepreneurs may interpret cleantech (thing to be acted upon), business models (motive) and flourishing ventures (desired outcome) differently than other entrepreneurs in the community. The process of shared object formation within an activity system arises from a state of need on the part of one or more actors, such as the need for an alternative to fossil fuels, cleaner air in cities or more equitable supply chains. Accordingly, it is the shared object that gives an activity system a determined direction, a horizon towards which it orients – but just as a horizon is never reached, an object is never fully accomplished (Engeström and Miettinen 1999). In other words, the object of flourishing cleantech ventures is necessarily open to further expansion and redefinition as conditions change.

4.3.3 Subject of the Activity System

The subject(s) (or actors) of an activity system are individuals and organizations taking part in actions towards some object. Going back to our example, entrepreneurs and their immediate colleagues are the subjects that take action towards the shared object of flourishing cleantech ventures. The actions of subjects towards any object involve interaction between aspects of the subjects' personal experience, his or her relationship to the community of significant others with whom the object is pursued and cultural-historical properties of the object. As such, an individual subject (or even a collective subject) cannot arbitrarily define or construct the object of an activity. Rather, a subject's perception of an object is both facilitated and constrained by historically accumulated constructions of the object (Foot 2002), as well as by the community of significant others oriented towards the same object. For example, the various ways that generations of people involved in energy and cleantech – whether as providers or receivers – construct what cleantech is (and is not), which influences how individual entrepreneurs (subject) at a particular point in time constructs the object of flourishing cleantech ventures. Accordingly, the historical layers of object constructions both enable and constrain the entrepreneurs' perception of and engagement with the object, in both ideational and material ways (Engeström 1990). At any point in time, participants in an activity may be at different stages in the reciprocal processes of need and object formation, thus differing in their abilities to perceive and articulate the object of the activity in which they are engaged. In other words, an entrepreneur's past professional experience, position in the power structure, role within the team and idiosyncratic characteristics of each particular case influence each entrepreneur's construction of the object of the activity.

4.3.4 Tools of the Activity System

CHAT scholars argue that a subject's actions towards an object in activity systems are never 'direct', but always mediated by means of the use of tools and signs, sometimes called 'mediational means' (Wertsch 1994). Tools can be either material or conceptual, e.g. physical technologies or mental/textual plans or schemas. For example, cleantech entrepreneurship involves multiple types of environmental technologies (e.g. solar panels, bioenergy, wind turbines, etc.). In every activity system, participants draw upon pre-existing tools as well as use cultural-historical resources to create new tools with which to engage, enact and pursue the object of their activity. Tools are important because they provide a historical record of the relationship between subjects and the object of their activity. That is, each tool employed in an activity system reveals something about the relationship between actors and their object concept at the point in time in which the tool was appropriated or created. For example, modern solar panels for creation of clean energy are situated in ongoing discussions of climate change, which were neither occurring nor available by tools earlier in human history.

It is important to point out that tools can simultaneously enable certain forms of action and constrain others. For example, cleantech involves multiple types of environmental technologies (e.g. solar panels, bioenergy, wind turbines, etc.) that provide an entrepreneur (the subject) with a particular way of formulating and testing business models (the object). Each technology consists of properties that both enable and constrain the uses to which it can be put. On the other hand, any single environmental technology orients problems and solutions in one way – rendering other potential technologies less important or even invisible. For instance, consider a cleantech entrepreneur (subject) that develops and sells solar-powered products to achieve an objective of viable business and promote a greener world. While this entrepreneur is bound by the limits of current solar technology (tool), it also allows him to utilize solar panels in working towards the objective. As such, many kinds of tools are employed in a complex activity system. However, since tools are subject to innovation, their purpose may change over time. For instance, the way in which people use computers (tool) has changed enormously over the past few decades – and may continue to do so in the future. The point is that there is no inherent characteristic of any tool (i.e. a human-constructed instrument, in either material or conceptual form) that will permanently determine its role and function in an activity system.

4.3.5 Community, Rules and Division of Labour of the Activity System

In addition to tools, core to the undertaking of activities are communities, rules and division of labour. The community within an activity system consists of the individuals and organizations who share with the subject an interest in and involvement with the same object. The interactions between the subject and the community that engages a shared object can be thought of as the 'communicative relations' of the activity (Engeström 1999, p. 32). As explained previously, communities are implicated in the process of making and interpreting meaning – and thus fundamental to all forms of learning, communicating and acting. Keeping with our illustration, cleantech ventures' ability to meet their objectives depends on its members knowing how to successfully implement and commercialize their technology. Because achieving this objective requires the acquisition of human, social, technological and financial capital through engagement with individuals and organizations who are themselves knowledgeable about cleantech, knowledge is not bound to the individual members or to an organization but a matter of displaying the socially defined competence sustained by the community (Haugh 2007). Within the cleantech community of Boston, for example, serial entrepreneurs play a key role in the knowledge creation and facilitation, as they develop and identify talent, invest in educating prospective entrepreneurs, start incubators and host start-up competitions (Van Stijn and Van Rijnsoever 2014).

Relations between the subject and the community are mediated by the last two components: (1) the rules that regulate the subject's actions towards an object and relations with other participants in the activity and (2) the division of labour, understood as what is being done by whom towards the object, including both the relatively horizontal division of tasks and the vertical division of power, positions, access to resources and rewards (Engeström 1987). First, rules in an activity system primarily mediate what the subject does vis-à-vis the object of the activity (i.e. how the subject acts in relation to the object, including the tools employed and the ways they are used). For instance, cleantech ventures' selling of a sustainable product is subject to many formal laws (e.g. business tax, labour, product safety, intellectual property, nondisclosure, etc.) as well as norms in the community about behaving entrepreneurially and the importance of sustainable development. Second, activities are constrained and enabled by rules that govern relations between subjects and the community. Such rules and norms stem not only from the community of this particular activity but also from the broader cultural, economic and political context. In the case of cleantech entrepreneurship community, rules and norms may dictate that subjects profess pro-environmental and pro-entrepreneurial values.

Finally, the division of labour refers to how the tasks are shared among the community. For example, cleantech entrepreneurs' actions towards an object are both supported and constrained by the corresponding actions of supportive staff (e.g. those who manage working capital, apply for property rights, assist in hiring, etc.) as well as outside the subject's organization (e.g. other entrepreneurs who develop and identify talent, invest in educating prospective entrepreneurs, start incubators and host start-up competitions). For example, many cleantech entrepreneurs divide their tasks and projects with co-founders or employees in order to achieve efficiency and overcome knowledge constraints. Furthermore, members of the entrepreneurship community that have an interest in cleantech play different roles, such as building relations with local governments, hosting developmental workshops or encouraging the next generation of entrepreneurs. Historical explanation of who does what in relation to the object (i.e. which members of the community engage with subjects) is typically mediated by sociohistorical power structures and patterns of relations both within the community and between a community and the larger culture/society of which it is part. For instance, serial entrepreneurs tend to come into contact with local governments when considering how to develop EIS ecosystems.

4.3.6 EIS Ecosystems as Multi-interactive Activity Systems

In this section, we develop a novel view of EIS ecosystems as multi-interactive activity systems that provide unparalleled citizen wellbeing. To do so, we review two ways in which activity systems interact – shared objects and supportive activities – and discuss their relevance for flourishing EIS ecosystems. Since the interactions between multiple activity systems in EIS ecosystems are complex, we will delve more into their tensions and contradictions in Sect. 3.7.

First, when two activity systems interact, it is possible that their objects obtain collective meanings, which may lead to a third object – a collective object for both activity systems, as seen in Fig. 4.2. For example, an activity system that revolves around the object of increasing sustainable entrepreneurship may require that its government (subject) takes certain actions. Now suppose that another activity system aims to develop sustainable business models (object) for that particular region. In this second activity system, entrepreneurs (subject) may seek to utilize the

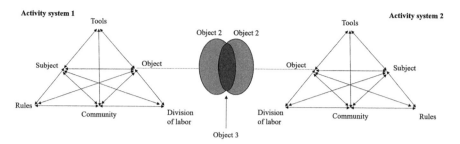

Fig. 4.2 Two interacting activity systems with shared object (Engeström 2001)

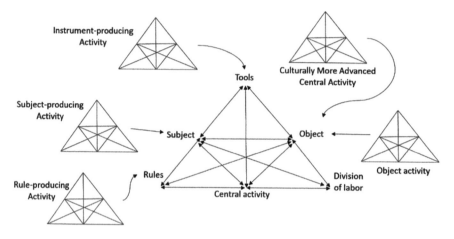

Fig. 4.3 EIS ecosystems as multiple, interconnected activity systems (Based on Engeström 2001)

resources in the community. Together, the government and the entrepreneurs may form a third shared object of developing greater access to resources that promote entrepreneurship within the city (object 3). Yet, while the government and the entrepreneurs in this case have formed a common goal, they may draw on different tools to pursue them. For instance, the government may set up a programme to support entrepreneurial activity (e.g. the StartupAmsterdam initiative explained by the Amsterdam government (StartupAmsterdam 2015) and the StartupDelta project (2015)), while the entrepreneurs may decide to organize some entrepreneurial events to attract more human capital, entrepreneurs and investors to the city. Our overall premise is that all of the different communities involved in any functioning EIS ecosystem have both individual and collective objects. As we will discuss later, developing an EIS ecosystem therefore requires the effort and commitment to forge shared objects that benefit all parties involved.

The second way in which EIS ecosystems are constituted by multi-interactive activity systems is acknowledging the interrelation of activities that influence each other's systems (Engeström 2001; Foot 2001). Figure 4.3 reveals the complexity and multivoicedness of EIS ecosystems as being composed of interdependent activity systems. In this model, a central activity system may be influenced by other instrument-, subject-, rule- and object-producing activity systems. For example, the activities of the community of science and engineering institutions (instrument-producing activity system) may influence the capabilities of environmental technologies that entrepreneurs active in the cleantech community (central activity system) use to achieve their objective of developing sustainable business models. Similarly, subject-producing activity systems (such as education communities) may influence the personal and professional development of future entrepreneurs. On the other hand, rule-producing activity systems (such as local, provincial and national governments) may produce formal and informal rules and norms that enable or constrain cleantech entrepreneurs who are active in the central activity system. In the region of Öresund, for example, the objectives of cleantech entrepreneurs (central activity system) were enabled by the rules of the government (rule-producing activity system) to achieve their 'low-carbon goals' (Kiryushin et al. 2013). Lastly, other communities, such as NGOs, researchers, writers and public intellectuals, may influence the ongoing development of the object of a central activity system (object activity systems). For example, the scientific realization and public discussions that fossil fuels have a negative influence on the global climate spurred the notion of sustainable development that continues to influence the objectives of entrepreneurs in the cleantech community (central activity system). In the next section, we will delve more into the different layers that comprise tensions and contradictions in the next section.

4.3.7 Contradictions, Learning and Expansion of EIS Ecosystems

We argued above that EIS ecosystems consist of multiple, interacting activity systems. In this section, we propose that the contradictions inherent in and between activity systems that make up an EIS ecosystem are complex in nature. We build from Engeström's (2001) four layers of contradictions – primary, secondary, tertiary and quaternary – to explain common contradictions among and between activity systems that hinder the development of EIS ecosystems, as shown in Fig. 4.4. However, rather than be seen as a negative development, contradictions reveal opportunities for creative innovations, for new ways of structuring and enacting activities and EIS ecosystems. Therefore, contradictions should be seen as the 'places' from which innovations in EIS ecosystems emerge (Foot 2014). Foot and Groleau (2011) elaborated the ways in which contradictions provoke collective epistemic actions, which lead to the ascent from abstract ideas to concrete knowledge, as shown in Table 4.1.

Primary contradictions (numbered 1 in Fig. 4.4) challenge the most fundamental aspects of the elements of an activity system (i.e. object, subject, tools, rules,

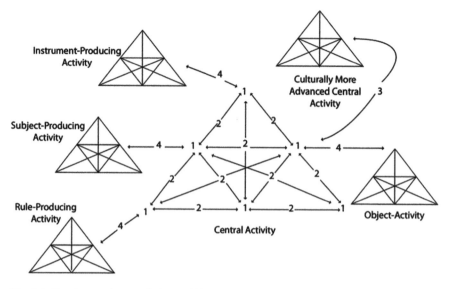

Fig. 4.4 Four layers of contradictions within and between activity systems (Engeström 2001)

Table 4.1 Four layers of contradictions and corresponding learning actions (Foot and Groleau 2011)

Levels of contradictions and corresponding learning actions		
Levels of contradiction	Characteristics of contradiction levels	Corresponding learning actions
Primary	Occurs between the use value and exchange value of any corner of an activity system	Questioning
Secondary	Develops between two corners of an activity system	Analysing
		Modelling
Tertiary	Arises when the object of a more developed activity is introduced in the central activity system	Examining model
		Implementing model
		Evaluating progress
Quaternary	Occurs between central activity and neighbouring activities triggered by tertiary contradictions	Consolidating new practice
		Questioning

community, division of labour). A primary contradiction is due to the dual construction of everything and everyone as both having inherent use value and being an exchangeable commodity within market-based socio-economic relations (Foot and Groleau 2011). In this sense, they lead people, entrepreneurs and organizations to question, critique and even reject some aspects of an accepted practice or existing wisdom. Keeping with our example, cleantech entrepreneurs (subjects) facing tensions in its object caused by the duality of both wanting to reduce environmental degradation (use value) and wanting to generate a profit (exchange value) lead these entrepreneurs to question their own practice or business model and even reject those typically accepted in their industry. Subjects try to overcome primary contradictions when they surface by vocalizing or questioning the legitimacy of some element of the activity system. For example, some entrepreneurs may question the motives of others for prioritizing a certain environmental technology over another, even questioning the efficacy of the technology and/or the profit motivation. The object of a typical sustainable entrepreneur in an EIS ecosystem is inextricably dual – in this case, fostering sustainable development and increasing private revenue (see Haigh and Hoffman 2012, 2014; Schaltegger and Wagner 2011).

Secondary contradictions (numbered 2 in Fig. 4.4) occur between different nodes of an activity system and provoke analysing and modelling actions among participants (e.g. tools and rules, community and subject or object and division of labour). For example, a secondary contradiction can be seen between the nondisclosure laws (i.e. rules) signed upon demands by investors that constrain a cleantech entrepreneur from sharing details of a new solar panel technology and the scientific advancement of solar panel technology (i.e. a tool) that requires openly sharing information about the details of that technology. To resolve this secondary contradiction, cleantech entrepreneurs may engage in analyses to find out why nondisclosure causes a conflict for scientific development. Upon analysis, cleantech entrepreneurs may move on by modelling the newly found explanatory relationship in some publicly observable and transmittable medium.

Tertiary contradictions (numbered 3 in Fig. 4.4) emerge with the implementation of a new model in the central activity system, which spurs actions to analyse the sources of these contradictions. The motive for introducing a new object to an activity system is typically to find relief from one or more secondary contradictions and the tensions stemming from them. As an example of a tertiary-level contradiction, imagine that academic scientists believe that the sharing of information freely with international colleagues advances the purposes of sustainable development. If these scientists talked positively about freely accessible information for the benefit of technological development to the cleantech entrepreneurs (subjects), the possibility of open knowledge transfer as an alternative to the current object of a profitable business model supported by secrecy could precipitate a tertiary contradiction between the existing object (flourishing cleantech ventures) and the new one (open innovation), resulting in rifts among entrepreneurs who wanted to retain the status quo and those interested in open innovation.

Finally, quaternary contradictions (numbered 4 in Fig. 4.4) occur between activity systems and result in the process of consolidating a new practice aimed at solving a tertiary contradiction (Foot and Groleau 2011). Consolidating a new practice or model, in our example, translates into setting up processes and procedures for cleantech entrepreneurs to implement and support the movement from prioritizing profitability to prioritizing equitable access to information. This transformation of the activity systems, nevertheless, leads to substantive changes in the venture's relations with the venture capitalists. In the instance of resource acquisition contradiction, cleantech entrepreneurs may seek to acquire financial resources by implementing a new model but inadvertently cause disturbances with their relations to the rule-producing activity system of the government. In this case, cleantech entrepreneurs take action to realign their activities with neighbouring activity systems, holding meetings and negotiations about the role of private and public value in their community. These discussions may precipitate a new round of questioning actions with and between activity systems, restarting the expansive cycle.

The four layers of contradictions capture the idea of an expanding cycle of development of EIS ecosystems. The evolution and expansion of an EIS ecosystem are thus a collective learning process that necessarily includes contradictions within and between activity systems. In other words, we explain the evolution and expansion of EIS ecosystems as the result of actions aimed at resolving the four layers of contradictions within and between activity systems. New participants are stimulated to enter the EIS ecosystem when they perceive solutions to problems within or between activity systems and believe that their proposed solutions will result in sustainable and independent sources of financial and other resources. This notion attends to the multivoicedness related to the plurality of and in an EIS ecosystem, acknowledging that within each activity system, there are multiple points of view, traditions and interests, each with their own (diverse) histories and contradictions. In the next section, we explain activity system analysis as a method for analysing contradictions, innovation and expansion of EIS ecosystems. This method helps to gain a better understanding of its developmental path (Foot 2014) enabling policymakers to intervene and take action to support EIS ecosystems, thus improving citizen quality of life.

4.4 Activity System Analysis for Analysing and Supporting EIS Ecosystems

In this section, we discuss activity system analysis as a method to understand, analyse, intervene and support EIS ecosystems. We provide a roadmap for ASA applied to the context of EIS ecosystems, thus serving as a guide for investigators to assist in better visualizing and supporting EIS ecosystems. Flourishing EIS ecosystems improve the quality of life of its citizens by providing better access to health, education and natural environment opportunities. While activity system analysis (ASA) is new to the EIS ecosystem literature, scholars in a variety of fields are already applying this method in analysing (professional) activities (Foot 2014; Foot and Fi 2001; Yamagata-Lynch 2010). For instance, it has been used to capture the processes involved in organizational change (Barab et al. 2004; Yamagata-Lynch and Smaldino 2007), identify guidelines for designing constructivist learning environments (Jonassen 1999; Jonassen and Rohrer-Murphy 1999), identify systemic contradictions and tensions that shape developments in educational settings (Barab et al. 2002; Roth and Tobin 2002), and demonstrate historical developments in organizational learning (Yamagata-Lynch 2003).

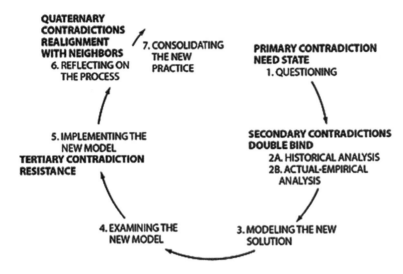

Fig. 4.5 Sequence of epistemic actions in an expansive learning cycle (Engeström 1999)

4.4.1 Analysing and Supporting EIS Ecosystems Through the Learning Cycle

ASA starts with identifying and mapping existing activity systems in a particular spatial area and questioning the absence of desired entrepreneurship communities in an EIS ecosystem (shown in Fig. 4.5). The identification of desired communities requires researchers and policymakers to consider the distinct object of the central activity system. Having identified activity systems, investigators should spend time understanding the elements of each activity system, mapping the people involved as subjects and community, the rules and division of labour that govern their interactions and the tools subjects use to accomplish their objectives. The empirical methods for accomplishing this are interviews and ethnographic work. Having the voices of all relevant communities represented is important, since it allows investigators to understand the multiple interrelated perspectives and distinguish between the different needs and wants of the activity systems within the EIS ecosystem. Next, researchers and policymakers need to identify the secondary contradictions within a particular activity system. This can be achieved by performing a historical and empirical analysis in which they examine the contradictions between the different components of a particular central activity system. One approach to finding secondary contradictions is to look for ongoing conflicts in between the nodes of a central activity system using interviews with subjects and members of the community.

The third step in the learning process occurs when investigators take an active role in (a) cocreating new joint objects between different activity systems and (b) co-developing new models in a collaborative effort to resolve secondary contradictions of a particular activity system. Here, it is important to outline the shared objects that emerge when policymakers' activity system meets a central activity system. Once again, this requires close collaboration with relevant stakeholders in the target activity system to ensure that all viewpoints are accounted for. The new model should serve as a plan of action, outlining the future developmental trajectory of the activity system. Step four of the process entails implementing and examining the new model (i.e. looking for tensions/contradictions that could emerge). Not surprisingly, implementing the model requires the participation of the members of the activity system. Policymakers should bear in mind that change – in any form – is usually met with some resistance. Therefore, it is helpful for researchers and policymakers to investigate the sources and possible solutions to the resistance of the new model for the central activity system.

Once the model has been implemented, policymakers should reflect on the process and seek to identify quaternary contradictions. Identifying these contradictions is a matter of recognizing disturbances that previous interventions and support policies have had in the network of relations between a central activity system and its neighbours. This includes investigating the influences of other activity systems on the central activity system, as well as the disturbances that the central activity system may create for relations with other activity systems (i.e. that receive the output of the central activity system or are otherwise affected by its outcomes). For instance, in Denmark a collective effort of national ministries and regional communities helped to support its cleantech industry. However, one decision to withdraw the subsidy on the wind turbine industry backfired, as it almost put an end to the industry itself. Fortunately, the industry was able to survive by entering new export markets (Potter et al. 2012).

4.5 Discussion

Under the philosophy of New Public Management, policymakers no longer seek to pursue economic growth alone, but aim to enhance the quality of life for citizens as well (Thomas 2013). The recognition that entrepreneurship plays a vital role in innovativeness, economic growth and attracting international talent has captured the attention of policymakers, researchers and practitioners (Decker et al. 2014; Wennekers and Thurik 1999). Interest in the role, and functioning of EIS ecosystems, has consequently grown substantially (Mack and Mayer 2016; Mason and Brown 2013; Motoyama et al. 2014). In this chapter, we have briefly discussed the current state of the literature of EIS ecosystems. We have argued that while the present literature has greatly enhanced our understanding of EIS ecosystems and its distinct elements, it also has clear shortcomings. Our first argument is that the current literature has overlooked the notion that EIS ecosystems are comprised of multiple communities (cf. cleantech, LOHAS, biotech, ICT, etc.). This is problematic, since policies designed to promote entrepreneurship tend to neglect the specific needs of different communities within EIS ecosystems. Our second argument is that the literature falls short of capturing the dynamics that transform EIS ecosystems over time. We have emphasized that building EIS ecosystems requires more than just its distinct elements (e.g.). This understanding has led us to ask the question of how to deal with its dynamic and systemic nature.

In this chapter, we have drawn on CHAT to propose and explain ASA as a novel framework to analysing EIS ecosystems. We have argued that ASA will help academics and NPM-minded policymakers to better conceptualize, understand, analyse, intervene and support EIS ecosystems in their development. Ultimately, ASA will help them improve the quality of life for citizens. Our argument is twofold. First of all, we contend that existing measures to the development of EIS ecosystems generalize across communities without recognizing that different communities within EIS ecosystems (e.g. cleantech, LOHAS) exist and therefore have different needs. The current emphasis in the literature on the distinct elements of EIS ecosystems is limited in that these conceptual models do not capture the role that contradictions and tensions within and between communities have for the development of EIS ecosystems. Secondly, we have reasoned that existing conceptual frameworks that list elements or factors downplay the systemic relations between different communities that comprise it. As a result, it is hard to visualize how systemic contradictions and tensions influence a series of related activities and how communities modify and create new activities while adapting to their environment.

Understanding EIS ecosystems can be a challenging endeavour, since it requires the collection and analysis of large and complicated data sets. The difficulty of figuring out how to present the findings to others in an insightful manner adds to the complexity. Additionally, it can also be demanding for investigators to coordinate at multiple levels to arrive at meaningful conclusions about the development or barriers to EIS ecosystems. Faced with these challenges, our new conceptual framework contributes to NPM by conceptualizing EIS ecosystems as multi-interactive activity systems. While our framework represents a leap forward in furthering our understanding of EIS ecosystems, it also reveals the complexity and interrelatedness of activities. Through ASA, researchers and policymakers can come to understand the systemic contradictions and the resulting learning actions that transform and develop EIS ecosystems. ASA enables researchers and policymakers to coordinate action for collective learning by relying on its detailed methodology. Using ASA may seem daunting at first due to the web of multiple interrelated activities and layers of contradictions. Once the different levels of contradiction have been identified, however, researchers and policymakers can draw on Engeström's expansive learning cycle to track development and/or take intervening action in EIS ecosystems. There is a growing recognition that ASA can help researchers and policymakers to understand complex human activities in an insightful and understandable manner (Yamagata-Lynch 2007). In particular, it can help them to understand how, when and why people interact and take certain actions based on the cultural and historical trajectories of activities. This enables researchers and policymakers to understand how current activities have been influenced, transformed and developed over time. Following the developmental trajectory of EIS ecosystems helps researchers and policymakers to both understand why changes in activity systems occur and when to take intervening action to relieve some of the contradictions. This allows them to implement policies that can help to improve the quality of life of citizens within the EIS ecosystems.

References

Barab, S. A., Barnett, M., Yamagata-Lynch, L., Squire, K., & Keating, T. (2002). Using activity theory to understand the systemic tensions characterizing a technology-rich introductory astronomy course. *Mind, Culture, and Activity, 9*(2), 76–107. https://doi.org/10.1207/S15327884MCA0902_02.

Barab, S., Schatz, S., & Scheckler, R. (2004). Using activity theory to conceptualize online community and using online community to conceptualize activity theory. *Mind, Culture, and Activity, 11*(1), 25–47. https://doi.org/10.1207/s15327884mca1101.

Cohen, B. (2006). Sustainable valley entrepreneurial ecosystems. *Business Strategy and the Environment, 15*(1), 1–14. https://doi.org/10.1002/bse.428.

Cohen, B., & Winn, M. I. (2007). Market imperfections, opportunity and sustainable entrepreneurship. *Journal of Business Venturing, 22*(1), 29–49.

Cole, M., & Engeström, Y. (1993). A cultural-historical approach to distributed cognition. In G. Salomon (Ed.), *Distributed cognitions* (pp. 1–46). New York: Cambridge University Press.

Dean, T. J., & McMullen, J. S. (2007). Toward a theory of sustainable entrepreneurship: Reducing environmental degradation through entrepreneurial action. *Journal of Business Venturing, 22*(1), 50–76. http://doi.org/DOI. https://doi.org/10.1016/j.jbusvent.2005.09.003.

Decker, R., Haltiwanger, J., Jarmin, R., & Miranda, J. (2014). The role of entrepreneurship in US job creation and economic dynamism. *Journal of Economic Perspectives, 28*(3), 3–24. https://doi.org/10.1257/jep.28.3.3.

Drakopoulou Dodd, S., & Anderson, A. R. (2007). Mumpsimus and the Mything of the individualistic entrepreneur. *International Small Business Journal, 25*(4), 341–360. https://doi.org/10.1177/0266242607078561.

Engeström, Y. (1987). *Learning by expanding: An activity theoretical approach to developmental research.* Helsinki: Orienta-Konsultit Oy. https://doi.org/10.1016/j.intcom.2007.07.003.

Engeström, Y. (1990). *Learning, working and imagining: Twelve studies in activity theory.* Helsinki: Orienta-Konsultit.

Engeström, Y. (1999). Innovative learning in work teams: Analyzing cycles of knowledge creation in practice. In Y. Engeström, R. Miettinen, & R. L. Punamäki (Eds.), *Perspectives on activity theory* (pp. 377–404). New York: Cambridge University Press.

Engeström, Y. (2001). Expansive learning at work: Toward an activity theoretical reconceptualization. *Journal of Education and Work, 14*(1), 133–156. https://doi.org/10.1080/13639080020028747.

Engeström, Y., & Miettinen, R. (1999). Introduction. In Y. Engeström, R. Miettinen, & R. L. Punamäki (Eds.), *Perspectives on activity theory* (pp. 1–18). New York: Cambridge University Press.

Feld, B. (2012). *Startup communities: Building an entrepreneurial ecosystem in your City.* Hoboken: Wiley.

Foot, K. A. (2001). Cultural-historical activity theory as practice theory: Illuminating the development of conflict-monitoring network. *Communication Theory, 11*(1995), 56–83. https://doi.org/10.1111/j.1468-2885.2001.tb00233.x.

4 Expanding Entrepreneurial, Innovative and Sustainable (EIS) Ecosystems... 87

Foot, K. A. (2002). Pursuing an evolving object: A case study in object formation and identification. *Mind, Culture, and Activity, 9*(2), 132–149. https://doi.org/10.1207/S15327884MCA0902.

Foot, K. A. (2014). Cultural-historical activity theory: Exploring a theory to inform practice and research. *Journal of Human Behavior in the Social Environment, 24*(3), 329–347. https://doi.org/10.1080/10911359.2013.831011.

Foot, K. A., & Fi, K. F. (2001). Cultural-historical activity theory as practical theory: Illuminating the development of a conflict monitoring network. *Published in Communication Theory, 11*(1), 56–83.

Foot, K. A., & Groleau, C. (2011). Contradictions, transitions, and materiality in organizing processes: An activity theory perspective. *First Monday, 16*(6), 1–18.

Haigh, N., & Hoffman, A. J. (2012). Hybrid organizations. The next chapter of sustainable business. *Organizational Dynamics, 41*(2), 126–134. https://doi.org/10.1016/j.orgdyn.2012.01.006.

Haigh, N., & Hoffman, A. (2014). The new heretics: Hybrid organizations and the challenges they present to corporate sustainability. *Organization & Environment, 27*(3), 223–241. https://doi.org/10.1177/1086026614545345.

Haugh, H. (2007). Community-led social venture creation. *Entrepreneurship Theory and Practice*, 161–182.

Hekkert, M. P., & Negro, S. O. (2009). Functions of innovation systems as a framework to understand sustainable technological change: Empirical evidence for earlier claims. *Technological Forecasting and Social Change, 76*(4), 584–594.

Hood, C. (1995). The "new public management" in the 1980s: Variations on a theme. *Accounting, Organizations and Society, 20*(2–3), 93–109. https://doi.org/10.1016/0361-3682(93)E0001-W.

Horwitch, M., & Mulloth, B. (2010). The interlinking of entrepreneurs, grassroots movements, public policy and hubs of innovation: The rise of Cleantech in new York City. *Journal of High Technology Management Research, 21*(1), 23–30. https://doi.org/10.1016/j.hitech.2010.02.004.

Isenberg, D. J. (2010). The big idea: How to start an entrepreneurial revolution. *Harvard Business Review, 88*(6). https://doi.org/10.1353/abr.2012.0147.

Jonassen, D. H. (1999). Designing constructivist learning environments. *Instructional Design Theories and Models: A New Paradigm of Instructional Theory, 2*, 215–239.

Jonassen, D. H., & Rohrer-Murphy, L. (1999). Activity theory as a framework for designing constructivist learning environments. *Educational Technology Research and Development, 47*(I), 61–79. https://doi.org/10.1007/BF02299477.

Kiryushin, P., Mulloth, B., & Iakovleva, T. (2013). Developing cross – border regional innovation systems with clean technology entrepreneurship: The case of Øresund. *Internation Journal of Innovation and Regional Development Journal Innovation and Regional Development, 5*(2), 179–195. https://doi.org/10.1504/IJIRD.2013.055237.

Kuutti, K. (1996). Activity theory as a potential framework for human-computer interaction research. In B. A. Nardi (Ed.), *Context and consciousness* (pp. 17–44). Cambridge, MA: MIT press.

Leont'ev, A. N. (1978). *Activity, consciousness, and personality*. Englewood Cliffs: Prentice-Hall.

Leont'ev, A. N. (1981). *Problems of the development of the mind*. Moscow: Progress.

Mack, E., & Mayer, H. (2016). The evolutionary dynamics of entrepreneurial ecosystems. *Article Urban Studies Urban Studies Journal Limited, 53*(10), 2118–2133. https://doi.org/10.1177/0042098015586547.

Mason, C., & Brown, R. (2013). *Entrepreneurial ecosystems and growth oriented entrepreneurship.* OECD LEED Programme & Dutch Ministry of Economic Affairs.

Motoyama, Y., Konczal, J., Bell-masterson, J., & Morelix, A. (2014). *Think locally, act locally: Building a robust entrepreneurial ecosystem. Kauffman Foundation Reports.* https://doi.org/10.1016/j.jcin.2013.04.001.

Nicolini, D. (2012). *Practice theory, work, and organization: An introduction* (Vol. 3). Oxford: Oxford University Press.

Osborne, S. P. (Ed.). (2010). *The new public governance? Emerging perspectives on the theory and practice of public governance.* New York: Routledge.

Pitelis, C. (2012). Clusters, entrepreneurial ecosystem co-creation, and appropriability: A conceptual framework. *Industrial and Corporate Change, 21*(6), 1359–1388. https://doi.org/10.1093/icc/dts008.

Popoviciu, I., & Popoviciu, S. A. (2011). Social entrepreneurship, social enterprise and the principles of a community of practice. *Revista de Cercetare Si Interventie Sociala, 33*(1), 44–55.

Potter, J., Miranda, G., Cooke, P., Chapple, K., Rehfeld, D., Theyel, G., & Rosenboim, M. (2012). *Clean-tech clustering as an engine for local development: The Negev Region, Israel* (OECD Local Economic and Employment Working Papers). https://doi.org/10.1787/5k98p4wm6kmv-en. OECD.

Roth, W. M. (2007). Emotion at work: A contribution to third-generation cultural-historical activity theory. *Mind, Culture, and Activity, 14*(1–2), 40–63. https://doi.org/10.1080/10749030701307705.

Roth, W. M., & Tobin, K. (2002). Redesigning an "urban" teacher education program: An activity theory perspective. *Mind, Culture, and Activity, 9*(2), 108–131.

Schaltegger, S., & Wagner, M. (2011). Sustainable entrepreneurship and sustainability innovation: Categories and interactions. *Business Strategy and the Environment, 20*(4), 222–237. https://doi.org/10.1002/bse.682.

Spigel, B. (2015). The relational organization of entrepreneurial ecosystems. *Entrepreneurship Theory and Practice, 44*(0), n/a–n/a. https://doi.org/10.1111/etap.12167.

Spigel, B. (2016). Developing and governing entrepreneurial ecosystems: The structure of entrepreneurial support programs in Edinburgh, Scotland. *International Journal of Innovation and Regional, 7*(2), 17–19.

Stam, E. (2014). *The Dutch entrepreneurial ecosystem*. Utrecht: Birch Research Llp.

Stam, E., & Spigel, B. (2016). Entrepreneurial Ecosystems. In R. Blackburn, D. De Clercq, J. Heinonen, & Z. Wang (Eds.), *Handbook for entrepreneurship and small business*. London: Sage.

Startup Delta. (2015). *Startup delta report.* Amsterdam. https://wtce.nl/wp-content/uploads/160630-Results-StartupDelta-V5.pdf. Accessed 30 Oct 2016.

StartupAmsterdam. (2015). *Visie en actieprogramma StartupAmsterdam.* Amsterdam. https://tweakimg.net/files/upload/StartupAmsterdam%20plan%20PDF%20Totaal%20070115.pdf. Accessed 30 Oct 2016.

Steyaert, C., & Katz, J. (2004). Reclaiming the space of entrepreneurship in society: Geographical, discursive and social dimensions. *Entrepreneurship & Regional Development, 16*(3), 179–196. https://doi.org/10.1080/0898562042000197135.

Suresh, J., & Ramraj, R. (2012). Entrepreneurial ecosystem: Case study on the influence of environmental factors on entrepreneurial success. *European Journal of Business and Management, 4*(16), 95–102.

Thomas, J. C. (2013). Citizen, customer, partner: Rethinking the place of the public in public management. *Public Administration Review, 73*(6), 786–796. https://doi.org/10.1111/puar.12109.

Thompson, N. A., Kiefer, K., & York, J. G. (2011). Distinctions not dichotomies: Exploring social, sustainable, and environmental entrepreneurship. In: *Social and sustainable entrepreneurship* (Advances in entrepreneurship, firm emergence and growth) (pp. 201–229) (Vol. 13). Bingley: Emerald Books.

Thompson, N. A., Herrmann, A. M., & Hekkert, M. P. (2015). How sustainable entrepreneurs engage in institutional change: Insights from biomass torrefaction in the Netherlands. *Journal of Cleaner Production, 106*, 608–618. https://doi.org/10.1016/j.jclepro.2014.08.011.

Van der Horst, D. (2008). Social enterprise and renewable energy: Emerging initiatives and communities of practice. *Social Enterprise Journal, 4*(3), 171–185. https://doi.org/10.1108/17508610810922686.

Van Stijn, N., & Van Rijnsoever, F. (2014). *Climate-KIC scout report -the Boston start-up ecosystem supporting entrepreneurship in a highly academic environment.* Utrecht. http://www.startupinsights.org/wp-content/uploads/2014/09/Climate-KIC-Scout-Report-Boston.pdf. Accessed 30 Oct 2016.

Vogel, P. (2013). *Building and assessing entrepreneurial ecosystems*. The Hague: OECD LEED Programme.

Vygotsky, L. S. (1978). *Mind in society: The development of higher psychological processes*. Cambridge: Harvard University Press.

Welter, F. (2011). Contextualizing entrepreneurship – conceptual challenges and ways forward. *Entrepreneurship Theory and Practice, 35*(1), 165–184. https://doi.org/10.1111/j.1540-6520.2010.00427.x.

Wenger, E. (1999). *Communities of practice: Learning, meaning, and identity*. Cambridge: Cambridge University Press.

Wennekers, S., & Thurik, R. (1999). Linking entrepreneurship and economic growth. *Small Business Economics, 13*(1), 27–55.

Wertsch, J. V. (1994). The primacy of mediated action in sociocultural studies. *Mind, Culture, and Activity, 1*(4), 202–208.

Yamagata-Lynch, L. C. (2003). Using activity theory as an analytic lens for examining technology professional development in schools. *Mind, Culture, and Activity, 10*(2), 100–119.

Yamagata-Lynch, L. C. (2007). Confronting analytical dilemmas for understanding complex human interactions in design-based research from a cultural – Historical activity theory (CHAT) framework. *Journal of the Learning Sciences, 16*(4), 451–484.

Yamagata-Lynch, L. C. (2010). *Activity systems analysis methods. Springer*. London: Springer.

Yamagata-Lynch, L. C., & Smaldino, S. (2007). Using activity theory to evaluate and improve K-12 school and university partnerships. *Evaluation and Program Planning, 30*(4), 364–380.

Yasuyuki, & Watkins, K. M. M. (2014). *Examining the connections within the startup ecosystem: A case study of St. Louis*, (September), 1–32.

Zahra, S. A., & Nambisan, S. (2012). Entrepreneurship and strategic thinking in business ecosystems. *Business Horizons, 55*(3), 219–229.

Chapter 5
Product Innovation as Territory Sustainability Added Value: The Case Study of Douro Skincare

Teresa Paiva, Luísa Cagica Carvalho, Cristina Soutinho, and Sérgio Leal

Abstract Within a smart specialization context, regions and businesses have to develop their innovation and product delivery with added value to supply market needs in a different perspective. As the territory sustainability within the Portuguese smart specialization strategy (RIS3) is defined, we propose to exemplify through a case study a good practice in answering these new challenges. The case study explores the growth and regional involvement of Douro Skincare, a company created by women that operates in the field of selective biological cosmetics through the creation, development, and production of cosmetic lines that are based on emblematic raw materials of the Douro region, one of the oldest wine-growing areas, located in the north of our country, Portugal. It uses Douro grapes and PORT WINE DNA ™ (Douro Nuclear Aroma), created from the first Port wine from entirely organic production, to develop cosmetic lines produced with endogenous products. These types of territorial intensive products (TIPs) are associated directly with the region and are intensively endogenous, an answer to the challenges created within RIS3.

Keywords Territory sustainability • Smart specialization • Product innovation • Regional brands and marketing • TIPs

---

T. Paiva (✉)
Unidade de Investigação de Desenvolvimento do Interior, Instituto Politécnico da Guarda, Guarda, Portugal
e-mail: tpaiva@ipg.pt

L.C. Carvalho
Universidade Aberta & CEFAGE, Universidade de Évora, Évora, Portugal

C. Soutinho
PEEP – Educar para Empreender, Porto, Portugal

S. Leal
PEEP – Educar para Empreender, Porto, Portugal

Departamento de Química e Bioquímica, FCUL, Lisbon, Portugal

© Springer International Publishing AG 2018
J. Leitão et al. (eds.), *Entrepreneurial, Innovative and Sustainable Ecosystems*, Applying Quality of Life Research,
https://doi.org/10.1007/978-3-319-71014-3_5

5.1 Introduction

The national development strategies, promoted by the European Union policy for economic growth and development, are currently defining the actions of the different Portuguese stakeholders. One of the main objectives of this policy is to guide the activity with economic and social impact, namely, business activity. With this in mind, it's very interesting to analyze how a Portuguese business company may impact its activity, prosecuting innovation and other actual and important goals as tourism and sustainability, through territorial intensive products. These objectives are in line with the mainstream concerns of economic development and growth as well as of a modern sustainable business model.

In our article, we will address these questions by giving a short but pertinent literature review on the main scientific subjects we have to reach to fully answer the questions we developed to make our research. We will follow the case study methodology that permits us a complete insight of the business activity as it allows us to not only collect the data but also to understand why the events occurred as they did. So, our article will present one part of the literature review and another part for the methodology description followed by the case study portrayal, ending with the main discussions of the results of the research.

5.2 Literature Review

5.2.1 Smart Specialization Strategy

As stated by Foray et al. (2009), the different assets and features of each region have to be aligned so the innovation policies have visible impacts on competitiveness, economic growth, and employment. This is what they called the smart specialization paradigm.

The contextual character of innovation requires that innovation policies are formatted in such a way as to maximize the external interactions and to facilitate the flow of knowledge but in line with the specifics of the patterns of regional innovation (McCann and Ortega-Argilés 2011; Camagni and Capello 2012). So, the smart specialization principle is based on the belief that innovation strategy and region competitiveness are due to the characteristics and assets within the territory.

This specialization and its concentration of resources aim to increase underlying economies of scale but carry risks of lock-in (conditions the economic structure ability of the region to change its technological trajectory in face of an external demand shock). To overcome these risks, the concept of smart specialization evolved in the direction of "specialized diversification" (McCann and Ortega-Argilés 2011; CEC 2010), promoting I&D strategies and innovation leading to an upgrade and diversification of the productive structure around technology and market relatedness (ESPON 2012).

Therefore, smart specialization involves the matching of knowledge and human capital accumulated with regions' economic structure (Capello 2013) and an analysis of the potential competitive advantages definition that is able to respond to the international evolution demand.

The main distinction between smart specialization and traditional industrial and innovation policies is the process defined as "entrepreneurial discovery" which is the interactive process in which market forces and the private sector are discovering and producing information about new activities and the government assesses the outcomes and empowers those actors that are most capable of realizing the potential (Foray 2012; Hausmann and Rodrik 2003). This entrepreneurial process empowers entrepreneurs to combine the necessary knowledge about science, technology, and engineering with knowledge of market growth and potential in order to identify the most promising activities. In this learning process, entrepreneurial actors have to play the leading role as they pinpoint the needed adaptations to local skills, materials, environmental conditions, and market access conditions and will entail gathering localized information and the formation of social capital assets (OECD 2013). In this context, entrepreneurial actors are not only the people creating new companies but also innovators in established companies, in academia, or in the public sector.

Smart specialization in RIS3 context consists of a strategic approach to economic development mainly focused on research and innovation. This concept is based on the principle that the concentration of knowledge resources and their connection to a limited number of priority economic activities will enable the countries and regions to be, and remain to be, competitive in the global economy. The smart specialization approach suggests regions, especially those regions which are not leaders in any of the major science and technology domains, to invest in R&D and innovation on few key priorities (OECD 2013).

In Portugal, the smart specialization strategy was thought at a national level and in a regional context. Each region of the country, accordingly with the national and regional government existing (North, Centre; Lisbon and Tagus Valley; Alentejo, Algarve, Azores, and Madeira), had to think and define its own RIS3. The implementation of the intelligent specialization regional strategy was founded on distinctive characteristics and the existing potential and affirming competitive international emerging, so it is essential to assess the regional scientific critical mass, business base and the existence and potential of articulation with power users. In the Northern region, this evaluation has identified eight priority areas (Life Sciences and Health; Resources of the Sea and Economy; Human Capital and Specialized Services; Culture, Creation and Fashion; Industries of Mobility and Advanced Production Systems Environment; Symbolic Capital Technologies; Tourism Services; and Agro-environment and Food Systems) (CCDRN 2014). It is in these last two domains that the products of our case study may be integrated since not only they seem to fit in the appreciation of cultural resources and territory, taking advantage of intensive scientific and technological capacities, in particular in the fields of tourism and marketing, as defined for the symbolic capital technologies and tourism services domain, but also they fit in the agro-environment and food systems since they articulate the agriculture potential of the region with an added value product with scientific and technological skills and enterprise with a related product development, even if this product is not food.

5.2.2 Product Innovation, Sustainability, and Added Value

Innovation, as defined in the *Oslo Manual* of the OECD (1997), distinguishes mainly between process, product, and organizational innovation:

- Process innovations occur when a given amount of output (goods, services) can be produced with less input.
- Product innovations require improvements to existing goods (or services) or the development of new goods. Product innovations in machinery in one firm are often process innovations in another firm.
- Organizational innovations include new forms of management, e.g., total quality management.

The general definition of innovation is neutral concerning the content of change and open in all directions. In contrast, putting emphasis on innovation toward sustainable development is motivated by concern about direction and content of progress (Rennings 2000). Thus, the additional attribute of innovations toward sustainability is that they reduce environmental burdens at least in one item and, thus, contribute to the improvement of the situation (Fig. 5.1).

Progress is often still understood simply as innovation in firms, with a strong focus on technological progress. Since many problems of sustainable use of nature and land are not primarily technological questions, this may lead to a "technology bias." Natural resources can often be characterized as open access regimes, and unsustainable use stems from inappropriate institutional arrangements (Rennings 2000).

The increasing awareness of the environmental theme by consumers had consequences in the corporate world, which began by considering the development of new products more in line with the environmental concerns of the markets (Paiva and Proença 2011). This consumer recognition of its ecological responsibility has become a concern in protecting and preserving the environment in an increasingly important aspect of the lives of consumers and their buying decisions (Paiva and Proença 2011). In this sense, the additional value that can be provided by products to meet these concerns differentiates them and adds value to the product in terms of the benefit it provides to the market.

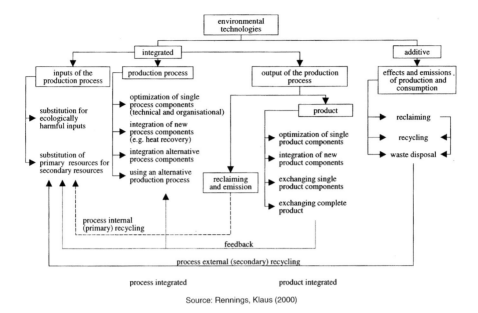

Fig. 5.1 Preventive environmental technologies (Source: Rennings 2000)

5.2.3 Tourism and TIPs

Today TIPs are part of the heritage in a territory and could provide a special cultural tourism experience. In the last few years, the Council of Europe for Cultural Routes has encouraged the creation and exploitation of some itineraries, as cultural routes, such as "The Routes of the Olive Tree" or the "Iter Vitis – Wine Routes in European countries." These thematic routes promote thematic tourism and the protection of cultural heritage through the utilization of typical products (Asero and Patti 2009). The touristic potential of these typical products is higher when they are identified with quality labels and brands that protect their identity and are associated with the endogenous features from the territory where they are produced.

In the case of the wine tourism it's possible to identify different stages associated with wine production, since the grape plantations and their landscape (for instance in the case of Portugal, Douro is a United Nations Educational, Scientific and Cultural Organization (UNESCO) World Heritage)were the first wine Demarcated Region in the world and several tourists come just to see this particular landscape); to production in the wineries, taste and gastronomy; contact with the farms where the wine is produced and all the environment and experiences provided within rural tourism (Carvalho 2014).

Ohe and Kurihara (2013) suggest that local food production and rural tourism are joint products, and wine is a predominant TIP associated with rural tourism in numerous researches. Table 5.1 presents a state of the art of TIPs and tourism.

Table 5.1 State of the art: TIPs and tourism

Topic	Subtopic	Publication
Local food and tourism	Rural development/rural tourism	Renko et al. (2010), Sims (2009, 2010), and Vaz et al. (2009)
	Authenticity	Sims (2009)
	Rural cultural heritage	Szlanyinka (2009) and Ohe and Ciani (2011)
	Food tourism	Hall et al. (2003)
	Wine tourism	Hall et al. (2000) and Kim et al. (2009)
	Social effects	Everett and Aitchison (2008) and Brandth and Haugen (2011)
	Rural development/rural tourism	Renko et al. (2010), Sims (2009, 2010), and Vaz et al. (2009)
	Culinary tourism	Montanari and Staniscia (2009), and Horng and Tsai (2010)
	Organic agriculture and agro-ecotourism	Kuo et al. (2006)
Rural tourism		Bélisle (1983), Ohe (2008), and Telfer and Wall (1996)
Economic effects of local food and tourism	Differentiation of tourism destinations	Haven-Tang and Jones (2006)
	Food consumption by tourists	Kim et al. (2009) and Skuras et al. (2006)
	Backward economic linkage	Telfer and Wall (2000)
	Hedonic pricing approach	Ohe and Ciani (2011)
Economies of scope	Agricultural and rural field	Azzam (1998), Chavas (2008), Chavas et al. (2010), Fernandez-Cornejo et al. (1992), Hartarska et al. (2011), and Melhim and Shumway (2011)
	Agricultural cooperatives	Kondo (1997) and Schroeder (1992)
	Nonagricultural field	Chavas et al. (2012) and Proir (1996)
	Theoretical development	Baumol et al. (1988), Chavas and Kim (2007), and Panzar and Willig (1981)

Source: Ohe and Kurihara (2013)

5.2.4 Brand and Marketing Linked with Regional Products

Brand as defined by Kotler et al. (1994) is a name or image to establish a product position as the property of a specific brand owner that gives them value. It serves also to differentiate a product which benefits consumers in a way that is more than its functional characteristics (de Chernatony and Macdonald 2003). There are diverse types of brands that do not easily equate with the classic notion of a brand owned and operated by a single enterprise (Charters et al. 2011). That is the case of the corporate umbrella, leader brands, and the place-related brands (country, regional, and destination brands).

These territorial brands are not created through consumer orientation but are rather a result-oriented production, as core characteristics of the product depend on the environment (Charters and Spielmann 2014). Regional or local brands are based in one area and have the advantage of association with a region of origin, especially when the region of origin is particularly important as a cue for high added-value products (Van Ittersum et al. 2003).

These types of brands may include products which trade off a region or place as well as products which are situated in a single region (Van Ittersum et al. 2003), like "Douro region." However, the products are not defined by the collective memberships of the regional brand, nor they have to be produced in the region with an indissoluble environmental relationship to it (Charters et al. 2011).

As observed by Perrouty et al. (2006), the region of origin may serve as a cue to link product benefits with a region, and in some situations consumers may prefer to buy those products. This factor is especially true for more highly involved consumers.

The theoretical and empirical literature on consumer-perceived brand benefits suggests classifying the benefits according to different dimensions: functional benefit (Sheth et al. 1991; de Chernatony 1993), price benefit (Zeithaml 1988; Dodds et al. 1991), social benefit (Sheth et al. 1991; Ambler 1997; Bhat and Reddy 1998; Long and Schiffman 2000), and emotional benefit (Sheth et al. 1991; de Chernatony 1993; Ambler 1997; Bhat and Reddy 1998; Long and Schiffman 2000). So, the importance of that countries, regions, places, and other geographical entities, that behave like brands, are gaining acceptance and value for regional branding (Papadopoulos and Heslop 2002). There are studies that confirmed that national and other places are powerful stereotypes that influence behavior in all types of target markets.

5.3 Methodology

This is a descriptive study where we have used interviews to design a case study. This case study uses a qualitative methodology, based on Yin (2004), to select and analyze information collected by the interviewers and other secondary information sources. According to Yin (2004), case study research enables to investigate important topics not easily covered by other methods. Conversely, other methods cover many topics better than a case study does. Firstly, the case study method is pertinent when the research addresses either a descriptive question (what happened?) or an explanatory question (how or why did something happen?). Secondly, it is useful when we want to illuminate a particular situation, to get a close (i.e., in-depth and first-hand) understanding of it.

According to Eisenhardt (1989), building theory from case study research implies following certain steps. Table 5.2 presents the methodological guide for this research based on guidelines provided by Eisenhardt (1989).

Table 5.2 The process of building theory from case study

Step	Activity	Reason
Getting started	Definition of research question:	Focuses efforts:
	How territorial intensive products promote regional tourism?	TIPs and tourism, female entrepreneurship, female entrepreneurial profile, regional development
Selecting case	Specific population:	Local firm that uses local products to produce innovative products (managed by women)
	Douro Skincare	
Entering the field	Flexible and opportunistic data collection	Allows investigators to take advantage of methods and unique case features
Analyzing data	Within-case analysis	Gains familiarity with data and preliminary theory generation
		Cross-case pattern search using divergent techniques
Shaping hypotheses	Iterative tabulation of evidence for each sharpens construct definition, construct validity, and construct measurability replication, not sampling, logic across	Confirms, extends, and sharpens theory cases
		Search evidence for "why" behind builds internal validity relationships
Enfolding literature	Comparison with conflicting literature Comparison with similar literature	Builds internal validity, raises theoretical level, sharpens generalizability, improves construct definition, and raises theoretical level construct definitions
Reaching closure	Theoretical saturation when possible	Ends process when marginal improvement becomes small

Source: Eisenhardt (1989) adapted

We will use qualitative evaluation methods during the development of the research process.

Interviews are particularly useful for getting the story behind a participant's experiences. The interviewer can pursue in-depth information around the topic (McNamara 1999).

There are several types of interviews, namely: informal, conversational interview; general interview guide approach; standardized, open-ended interview; and closed, fixed-response interview.[1] The type of interview that we used was the general

---

[1] https://en.wikipedia.org/wiki/Interview_(research), retrieved on July 29, 2016

Informal, conversational interview – no predetermined questions are asked, in order to remain as open and adaptable as possible to the interviewee's nature and priorities; during the interview the interviewer "goes with the flow."

General interview guide approach – the guide approach is intended to ensure that the same general areas of information are collected from each interviewee; this provides more focus than the conversational approach but still allows a degree of freedom and adaptability in getting the information from the interviewee.

Standardized, open-ended interview – the same open-ended questions are asked to all interviewees; this approach facilitates faster interviews that can be more easily analyzed and compared.

5 Product Innovation as Territory Sustainability Added Value: The Case Study...

Table 5.3 Interviewees

Interviewee	Function	Type of interview	Interview date	Place
Mariana Andrade	Director/founder	Face to face	2016.07.05	Matosinhos
Marta Enes	Brand manager	Face to face	2016.07.05	UPTEC – Porto
Susana Cruz	Regulatory affairs	Skype	2016.07.12	DGESTE – Porto/London

interview guide approach. In annex 1 it is possible to find the guide used in the interviews, and Table 5.3 identifies the interviewees.

All interviews were audio recorded and useful for the analysis, and we have used semi-structured interviews that contain components of structured and unstructured interviews. We prepared a set of the same questions to be answered by all interviewees; however, additional questions were asked during interviews to clarify and/or further expand certain issues.

Among the main advantages of semi-structured interviews, we can include the following: (1) the possibility of access to richer information (contextualized through the words of the interviewees and their perspectives), (2) the possibility of the researcher to clarify some aspects following the interview that structured interview or questionnaire does not allow, and (3) the possibility of collecting many important data that can generate quantitative and qualitative information.

The literature review allows proposing the following hypotheses:

H1: Product innovation allocating regional resources, within a smart specialization strategy, contributes for territory added value through entrepreneurial process.
H2: The entrepreneurial project using TIPs influences positively regional tourism.
H3: The use of TIPs influences positively marketing brand.

Table 5.4 presents general and specific objectives and hypotheses tested in this case study.

5.4 Case Study

This section presents the case study selected "Douro Skincare."

Closed, fixed-response interview – where all interviewees are asked the same questions and asked to choose answers from among the same set of alternatives. This format is useful for those not practiced in interviewing.

Table 5.4 Objectives and hypotheses

General objective	Specific objectives	Hypotheses
Understand how product innovation contributes to the territory sustainability added value	Understand the entrepreneurial process related to product innovation and added value	*H1: Product innovation allocating regional resources, within a smart specialization strategy, contributes for territory added value through entrepreneurial process*
	Understand how the product innovation is linked to territory sustainability and added value	
	Realize the relation between TIPs and tourism	*H2: The entrepreneurial project using TIPs influences positively regional tourism*
	Understand how they develop the brand and their relation with region	*H3: The use of TIPs influences positively marketing brand*

5.4.1 Brief Description of Douro Skincare

Douro Skincare company is intended to act in the area of selective cosmetics, through the creation, development, and production of lines of products and brands which have high-quality standards and meet the required European regulations and market demand.

Through a business-to-business (B2B) model, it focuses on innovation and technology, enhancing the parallel strand of biological products and raw materials, environmental sustainability, and social responsibility. Increasing the promotion of the products and concepts, it became a "line of fusion cosmetics" as a result, by valuing the Northern country emblematic raw materials from the Douro region, especially those that give rise to Port wine.

5.4.2 Process of Business and Product Creation and RIS3

The idea came up when the founder was in front of river Douro in Oporto and noticed that all the cosmetics that were being used belonged to a foreign brand. That was when she first identified a business opportunity. The founding partner already knew some lesser known brands that sold well online and that resulted from raw materials from certain regions, that is, having a value attached, and it attracted the buyers' attention. She was not feeling motivated at work at the time due to a company merger, and that was when she felt the need to change and create a new product, and thus a new professional activity came to reality.

As she liked the Douro region a lot, she thought that a range of cosmetic products could be developed from raw materials of this iconic territory of northern Portugal.

Given the characteristics of the region and its products, mainly Port Wine, she came up with the idea of using vinotherapy but innovating the concept.

Regarding the technical part of the idea, the first step was to contact the manufacturers to see what were the raw materials that they would have an interest in using, which resulted in Port wine, including the seeds of grapes.

The allocation of human resources came primarily because they all knew each other and had similar ideas besides the same academic background and pharmaceutical studies, being the gender just a coincidence and not an option. One of the members is currently working on the technical/operational part of the business, whereas another works on the regulatory part, and the founding partner manages the business and idealizes the cosmetic lines and product development. They pointed out that part of the investigation was the result of a partnership with the University of Porto through its Faculty of Engineering. A team of professors had investigated the process of extracting alcohol from beer keeping the aromas, a process that was then applied in the beer industry. And that was when they thought about applying a similar process to Port wine, extracting its aroma.

Since that moment, they have come across various barriers along their path. The first one was financial as usual. The fact of having to arrange to finance, was very challenging, but they managed to overcome this phase after having applied to the National Strategic Reference Framework, QREN (Quadro de Referência Estratégica Nacional) funds, and to a microcredit (which helped in the production part because they could not get the product done on time and didn't have inventory nor samples) and an SME investment.

Since in Portugal the technology involved in cosmetics production was not very advanced yet, it was difficult to find the appropriate partners to produce the chemical formulas Douro Skincare had created. It was only at the third attempt and after an international experience in the UK that they managed to find a producer in Portugal, and it was then possible to stabilize the partner. Another obstacle that arose from the company's sustainable packaging requirements was the need to buy bottles with specific characteristics, airless glass bottles; therefore, to buy only 500 bottles would be very expensive, and they needed to overcome this and they did. After the first failed experiment that resulted from their own experience, because they analyzed not only the budget they had but ultimately the quality of the final product, they requested samples in order to decide whether it was really what they wanted for the products.

In short, the main obstacles are those that arise out of the business plan that is made in advance. They suffered a setback when they hired a carrier that didn't assure that the glass packaging was properly packaged and transported; that was when almost half of the glass bottles that arrived were broken. Thus, they had to balance the investment and find the money to cope with the waiting period required for the production of new glass bottles, through the development of secondary products for other companies.

It was this business decision that allowed them to cope with the current expenses, but it was also what made the company deviate a little from the concept of D'Vine, to which they managed to return to within a year.

So, instead of producing the ten products that they had developed formulas for, paid for, and made the development tests, they started with four products, only to work as sampling, and then, when they contracted with the first distributor, with whom they combined special conditions, he financed the production of four more products, and they were left with a line of eight products.

5.4.3 Relation Between Product Innovation and Territory Sustainability and Added Value

Even though their products aren't exclusively organic or bio, the product correlation with the environment is very important for the brand concept and consequently a concern in acting accordingly to the natural environment preservation are followed, balanced with a profitable perspective of business management. Therefore, some solutions were found, from the wine production and fragrance used to the packaging characteristics. But the environmental sustainable allegation doesn't have, yet, a strong response from the market, which makes these options more difficult to follow. In spite of that reality, the company uses grapes from organic production and organic wine although not exclusive for their production. They use organic grapeseed oil extract that is made in an industry that manufactures ingredients for cosmetics. Although there is always waste, the grapes are also used in wine production.

As there are no cosmetic factories in the Douro region, they face another challenge as there are some aspects of sustainability that make the product more expensive, for example, the fact that the fragrance of Port wine is certified by Ecocert. The Ecocert Group is a leader in the control and certification of organic production worldwide, which, in addition to its capacity and know-how, makes use of its logo, additional guarantee of the quality of the service provided and value added for the recognition, in trust, of the products of its operators by many millions of consumers. But this process of certification it is much more expensive, reflecting its costs in the final price of the products.

As far as the packing is concerned, the bottles are made of glass, airless, and opaque, thus reducing the number of preservatives to be added, and if it is sheltered from the air and light, the packaging itself contributes to the stability of the product throughout the shelf life.

The bottles also have an Ecocert certificate, and the glass and plastic used are 100% recyclable. They also allow using 95% of the amount of product inside because the bottle has a plunger and airless pump, which is not aerosol, that makes the product go up making utilization rate practically total.

D'Vine's carton has the FSC (Forest Stewardship Council) symbol that certifies it comes from sustainable forests, and their serigraphy is not made hot, which would be polluting, but rather it is a cold carton stamping, and there is only one printer in Portugal that has a cold stamping machine, which immediately increases the price

5 Product Innovation as Territory Sustainability Added Value: The Case Study... 103

of the packaging. There is no extra printing regarding the manufacturer's instructions for use, which are printed on the inside of the carton package.

There is a real concern with sustainability in the production of the cosmetics as well. As for the formulation of the product itself, they tried to avoid petroleum products although petrochemicals are widely used in cosmetics, such as paraffin, petrolatum, and silicone because they are cheap and completely inept.

If a company replaces petrochemicals with more active ingredients or vegetable extracts, the product increases in price.

Take an exfoliant, for example; there is a current controversy because the exfoliating balls are responsible for its abrasive effect and many of them are plastic polymers that can be bought, of any type and diameter depending on the level of abrasion that is intended. But this is changing; the UK was the first country to abolish these spheres, so our entrepreneurs tried to make an exfoliant without these spheres replacing them by a powdered walnut shell or powdered grape seed and put a film to mitigate the abrasion, getting a more enzymatic rather than mechanical exfoliator. This process also makes prices higher.

5.4.4 Realize the Relation Between TIPs and Tourism

This product is manufactured with local raw materials, such as biological Port wine, bottled, certified, and sealed, thus making the Douro brand completely associated with the Douro Skincare brand. The name of its main line of products D'Vine derives from Douro (D) and its vine.

One of the entrepreneurs said "we use local raw materials, to establish a direct relation with the Douro region. And if we used local products in the SPAS, we would establish a stronger relation with the region besides the landscape."

However, another entrepreneur revealed her reluctance in limiting the product to the region, when she said, "we selected Ana Moura (Portuguese well-known Fado singer) as the brand ambassador. She refers that they wouldn't want that DVine became just a line of regional products. They intended to promote a sophisticated and modern line of fusion cosmetics using Douro's references as an image capable of influencing behavior in a certain type of target market, women with buying power that relates to the uniqueness of the product and the region it portraits.

The product is intended to be much more than a cosmetic that uses an extract from a pipe of an autochthonous grape of the Douro."

They use Port wine and grape extracts due to the fact that these two components are certified products subjected to a rigorous quality control; they are not handmade products. The products are developed through an R&D process that verifies in all phases of their development and production the quality of the product and of the raw materials with suppliers.

Concerning the impact of Douro Skincare in local economy, they do not have enough data to register the impact of the firm on local economy yet; however they reveal some perceptions due to their participation in international fairs and events that took place in several countries (France, Brazil, Japan, etc.) where people were curious about the cosmetics made with grapes and Port wine, and they wanted to know where the Douro region was and how they could visit it. This way, they were also promoting the Douro region through their products when referring to the raw materials' origin and the beauty of the territory.

Having the Douro as a brand could create more synergies; however, the market approach of the firm is broader. They have already established partnerships with hotels, and they have already sent samples to an international hotel chain that owns hotels in the region, to provide amenities from their lines. Sometimes local hotels and pharmacies also request products that are more directed to the tourist market, such as soaps or candles, which the company is considering to produce in a next phase, but for the moment, the company promotes a structured line of cosmetic products.

Nonetheless, the association with the Douro region as a brand also creates some barriers. They had some problems in using the brand Port wine. Initially, they wanted to use the label PORT WINE DNA, Douro Nuclear Aroma, playing with the acronym for human DNA, but they were just allowed to use Douro Nuclear Aroma, and they couldn't register the brand due to the barriers associated with "protected denomination of the region" that limited the disclosure.

In what sales are concerned, so far and since the beginning of September of 2015, they sold 100,000 Euros. The figures of 2016 were not closed by the time of the interviews yet, but they expect to have tripled that value till the end of the year.

5.4.5 Understand How They Develop the Brand and Their Relation with the Region

The marketing strategy of Douro Skincare is based on the definition of the brand concept. It's a B2B2C business in which the privileged relation and contact are with distributors and intermediaries, and the brand has little connection with the final consumer, in spite of the business responsibility in the product image and positioning definition. The uniqueness and product differentiation are essential for a clear positioning and directed to a chic and demanding woman that is not subdued to normal elements.

The products also have in its brand the association with the Douro region and its wine for the obvious relationship between the natural beauty of the region and the attractiveness that the products intend to offer along with the uniqueness of Port wine aromas and colors added to the products and their packaging. Even the lines of the fusion cosmetics follow a specific glossary related to wine using words such as harvest to identify the lines and the age target of the creams, for example. They had to find an advantage because they already knew that people associated grape polyphenols as anti-aging substances and that resveratrol is regenerative so they wanted to make a line that added something else since they thought that vinotherapy no longer brought innovation.

These grapes and this wine come from the Douro, a harsh environment, from a soil that is not favorable to the development of plants; otherwise, men would not have to build terraces to control the thermal amplitudes and the incidence of light; it is an unfavorable soil and therefore only fortified plants could grow there. These characteristics of the soil add character and distinction to the raw materials they use in the cosmetic lines and therefore to their products as well.

The completion of the differentiation of Douro Skincare is not made through price since they are not capable of mass production and consequently they try to link their products as selective cosmetics and not to derma cosmetics despite using pharmacies as retailers. The difference between the two is that the latest is linked to a medicinal perspective, thought to be prepared to protect several skin types.

The selective cosmetics intend to offer beauty, in a healthy way, in this case mainly through natural and sustainable arguments, adding performance ingredients to biological raw materials, but they are not mass market products.

Sometimes their products are mistaken by biological cosmetics because of the Douro, the vine, the wine, and the use of grapes, but they are not. Some lines even have gold in the composition, although they have the preponderance of plant extracts; they also have performance ingredients such as Enzyme Q10 and hyaluronic acid that are cosmetic top sellers, more associated with cosmetics rather than perfumery, which have a performance on the skin.

5.4.6 Future and Challenges

Douro Skincare has two major goals for the future which are the sales increase in Portugal and the internationalization of the company and its brand.

They intend to upgrade the national market by having visibility and a strong distribution, consolidating the business value chain.

To export is a very important and determinant feature for the growth of the company, but they are aware of the differentiation between the regulations of the countries that they have to adapt to and the cultural issues they have to incorporate into the products in order to be accepted. These concerns are due to the goal to export to the Middle East countries, but also Japan, Brazil, or the USA.

For example, during their visit at a fair in Dubai, although people appreciated the presence of gold in the formulas and the wine aromas, the Muslim religion does not allow wine consumption, and their products claim the aromatic profile of the wine, Port wine. In this context, they are considering having a line that explored the Douro's almond and not the wine to cover these markets.

Not only market diversification is essential but also product variety. They are already testing some new products to complement the actual offer with the constant concern of listening to the market desires and needs. The company is only 3 years and it is still consolidating its market position.

5.5 Discussion of Results and Concluding Remarks

In terms of the research work and comprehension of the innovation factor of the company and its products within the smart specialization strategy, it is clear that there is strong investment in an innovation process based on a technological process that gives origin to a product innovation in the sense of a new form of producing cosmetics with a green market positioning in spite of their nonconsumer recognition as an environmentally friendly product. Maybe Douro Skincare hasn't felt this consumer recognition, mainly in their product sales or business income; nevertheless, the product in itself has a green positioning as it uses some organic resources and mostly because it has a very strong link to natural resources of a region.

The innovation process described not only has a technological improvement in the process of production definition due to a new application of a known technology but also seeks to reach the diverse dimensions of the innovation process, as described in the literature review. As the discussion provided by the case study concludes that Douro Skincare is directly related to Douro trademark, however, it follows a global approach that dispels the association with regional tourism.

As announced on the company's website, the regions of mountain viticulture are those that present greater scale, greater historical significance, greater continuity, and a greater biological variety of the grape varieties perfected here. Alto Douro is thus a striking example of landscape illustrating different stages of human history. In order to cultivate the vineyard on the slopes of the Douro and its tributaries, men had to produce soil and build terraces, traditionally supported by shale walls and, more recently, by vineyard leveling and "up" forms, susceptible to mechanization. The landscape of the Douro vineyard is today a complex and dynamic architecture, witnessing the continuous work of transforming the mountains into "hanging gardens," according to the expression of Jaime Cortesão (Portuguese writer).

Literature review underlines a positive relation between TIPs and tourism (Ohe and Kurihara 2013; see Table 5.1); however, Douro Skincare doesn't have a direct relation with tourism and regional development due to their market target. This firm aims to achieve global markets with a product with high-quality standards and developed with the rigorous process and intensive R&D. Nevertheless, the association with the Douro could influence indirectly the promotion of the tourism in this region.

Yet, it is possible to find a relationship between Douro region as a brand and the consumers mainly in the sustainable perspective, but the mental connection to the region is already evident. As argued by several authors (e.g., Van Ittersum et al. 2003; Charters and Spielmann 2014), we may observe a direct connection with Douro region and its two most important assets: beauty and nature. In this sense, we may call the business and its products clearly trying to take advantage of a well-known region, linked to the main raw material used and a strong mental and emotional connection with the splendor and natural environment of the region. There is a stronger relationship to develop between these allegations and the consumers,

5 Product Innovation as Territory Sustainability Added Value: The Case Study...

Table 5.5 Validation of hypotheses

Hypotheses	Validation	References
H1: Product innovation allocating regional resources, within a smart specialization strategy, contributes for territory added value through entrepreneurial process	Valid	CCDRN (2014), Rennings (2000), and Paiva and Proença (2011)
H2: The entrepreneurial project using TIPs influences positively regional tourism	Reject	Ohe and Kurihara (2013)
H3: The use of TIPs influences positively marketing brand	Valid	Van Ittersum et al. (2003)
		Charters and Spielmann (2014)

mainly in the sustainable perspective, but the mental connection to the region is already evident.

With all this in mind, we also may add that smart specialization strategy of the region is also addressed here since there is a clear impact of the business activity with the region and its growth and development concerns and the RIS3 for the North Region of Portugal. This company and its products are in tune with the strategic policies defined for this region in terms of agro-environment. We believe that the smart specialization axes of the North Region of Health and Advanced Production Systems Environment are also addressed here, but the connection is not so strong and evident.

So, we may conclude that two of the three research questions were positively answered by the business activity, strategy, and positioning of Douro Skincare (see Table 5.5). Further research aims to develop a broader study considering other topics such as internationalization that, also, could provide more insights in order to validate the full impact of the business activity.

References

Ambler, T. (1997). How much of brand equity is explained by trust? *Management Decision, 35*(4), 283–292.

Asero, V., & Patti, S. (2009). Developing the tourist market through the exploitation of the typical products. *The Annals of Dunarea de Jos*, University of Galati, Fascicle I/2009, Year XV, 5–14.

Bhat, S., & Reddy, S. K. (1998). Symbolic and functional positioning of brands. *Journal of Consumer Marketing, 15*(1), 32–43.

Camagni, R., & Capello, R. (2012). *Regional innovation patterns and the EU regional policy reform: Towards smart innovation policies*. Proceedings of the 52nd ERSA Conference in Bratislava.

Capello, R. (2013). Knowledge, innovation, and regional performance: Toward smart innovation policies. *Introductory Remarks to the Special Issue, Growth, and Change, 44*(2), 185–194.

Carvalho, L. (2014). *From winery to rural tourism experience: A perfect married couple*. IX Congresso Internacional Sobre Turismo Rural e Desenvolvimento Sustentável (CITURDES), 9–10 setembro, São Paulo, Brasil.

CCDRN. (2014). *Estratégia Regional de Especialização Inteligente – Norte2020*. Comissão de Coordenação da Região Norte.

CEC – Commission of the European Communities. (2010). *Europe 2020. A strategy for smart, suitable and inclusive growth*. Communication from the Commission, COM (2010) 2020.

Charters, S., & Spielmann, N. (2014). Characteristics of strong territorial brands: The case of champagne. *Journal of Business Research, 67*(2014), 1461–1467.

Charters, S., Mitchell, R., Menival, D. (2011). *The territorial brand in wine*. 6th AWBR International Conference, 9–10 June, Bordeaux Management School, France.

de Chernatony, L. (1993). Categorizing brands: Evolutionary processes underpinned by two key dimensions. *Journal of Marketing Management, 9*(2), 173–188.

de Chernatony, L., & Macdonald, M. (2003). *Creating powerful brands*. Oxford: Butterworth-Heinemann.

Dodds, W. B., Monroe, K. B., & Grewal, D. (1991). Effects of price, brand, and store information on buyers' product evaluations. *Journal of Marketing Research, 28*(August), 307–319.

Eisenhardt, K. (1989). Building theories from case study research. *The Academy of Management Review, 14*(4), 532–550.

ESPON. (2012). *Knowledge, innovation, territory (KIT)*. Final Report available online http://www.espon.eu/main/Menu_Projects/Menu_AppliedResearch/kit.html. Accessed 26 Dec 2016.

Foray, D. (2012). Economic fundamentals of smart specialisation. *Ekonomiaz*, special issue.

Foray, D., David, P.A., Hall, B. (2009). *Smart specialisation – The concept*. http://ec.europa.eu/invest-inresearch/pdf/download_en/kfg_policy_brief_no9.pdf?11111. Accessed 26 Dec 2016.

Hausmann, R., & Rodrik, D. (2003). Economic development as a self-discovery. *Journal of Development Economics, 72*, 2.

Kotler, P., Chandler, P. C., et al. (1994). *Marketing*. Sydney: Prentice Hall.

Long, M. M., & Schiffman, L. G. (2000). Consumption values and relationships: Segmenting the market for frequency programs. *Journal of Consumer Marketing, 17*(3), 214–232.

McCann, P., & Ortega-Argilés, R. (2011). *Smart specialisation, regional growth and applications to EU cohesion policy* (Work document of IEB 2011/14). Institut d'Economia de Barcelona, Barcelona.

McNamara, C. (1999). *General guidelines for conducting interviews*. Minnesota.

OECD. (1997). *OECD proposed guidelines for collecting and interpreting technological innovation data – Oslo-manual*. Eurostat: OECD.

OECD. (2013). *Innovation-driven growth in regions: The role of smart specialisation*. Paris: OECD Publications.

Ohe, Y., & Kurihara, S. (2013). Evaluating the complementary relationship between local brand farm products and rural tourism: Evidence from Japan. *Tourism Management, 35*, 278–283.

Paiva, T., & Proença, R. (2011). *Marketing Verde*. Edited by Atual, Portugal.

Papadopoulos, N., & Heslop, L. (2002). Country equity and country branding: Problems and prospects. *Journal of Product & Brand Management, 9*(4–5), 294–314.

Perrouty, J. P., d'Hauteville, F., et al. (2006). The influence of wine attributes on the region of origin equity: An analysis of the moderating effect of consumer's perceived expertise. *Agribusiness, 22*(3), 323–341.

Rennings, K. (2000). Redefining innovation – eco-innovation research and the contribution from ecological economics. *Ecological Economics, 32*(2000), 319–332.

Sheth, J. N., Newman, B. I., & Gross, B. L. (1991). Why we buy what we buy: A theory of consumption values. *Journal of Business Research, 22*, 159–175.

Van Ittersum, K., Candel, M. J., et al. (2003). The influence of the image of a product's region of origin on product evaluation. *Journal of Business Research, 56*, 215–226.

Yin, R. (2004). *Case study methods*. COSMOS Corporation. Revised draft, January 20, 2004. http://www.cosmoscorp.com/docs/aeradraft.pdf. Accessed 26 Dec 2016.

Zeithaml, V. A. (1988). Consumer perceptions of price, quality and value: Means-end model and synthesis of evidence. *Journal of Marketing, 52*(July), 2–22.

Chapter 6
Entrepreneurship and Innovation Ecosystem's Drivers: The Role of Higher Education Organizations

Fernando Herrera, Maribel Guerrero, and David Urbano

Abstract Extant empirical entrepreneurship studies recognize that the main challenge of emerging economies is transforming into entrepreneurial societies. Following this perspective, the involvement of several actors (government, universities, entrepreneurs, investors, etc.) is required in this evolutionary process. In this regard, emerging economies' governments promote the configuration of entrepreneurial ecosystems to achieve this transformation. Even in previous insights, the role of each actor is an interesting attention for academics and policy makers. In this sense, this chapter tries to provide a better understanding about the role of higher education organizations as driver of entrepreneurship and innovation ecosystems in Mexico. Our analysis provides evidence about the relevance of incentives in configuration of triple mission of Mexican higher education organizations as well as their lower participation in the involvement of innovation and entrepreneurial activities.

Keywords Entrepreneurship • Innovation • Higher education organizations • Mexico

---

F. Herrera
Engineering and Science Department, Tecnologico de Monterrey, León, Mexico

M. Guerrero (✉)
Newcastle Business School, Northumbria University, Newcastle upon Tyne, UK
e-mail: maribel.guerrero@northumbria.ac.uk

D. Urbano
Department of Business, Universitat Autónoma de Barcelona, Barcelona, Spain

© Springer International Publishing AG 2018
J. Leitão et al. (eds.), *Entrepreneurial, Innovative and Sustainable Ecosystems*, Applying Quality of Life Research,
https://doi.org/10.1007/978-3-319-71014-3_6

6.1 Introduction

During the past few decades, the configurations of new knowledge-intensive environments have required fertile settings for innovative and entrepreneurial activities. Both types of activities play a crucial role in the economy, and many studies have examined the factors that influence these activities (Autio et al. 2014). Despite innovation and entrepreneurship being multidimensional processes, empirical studies continue to employ models that presume that these phenomena occur at a single point in time (McMullen and Dimov 2013). Those facts explain why the triple- or quadruple-helix concepts have been operationalized in different ways (e.g., with/without government intervention, closed/opened, administrated/entrepreneurially, etc.), in different spaces (e.g., global, national, regional, local), and in different contexts (e.g., organizational, technological, social, etc.).

Because of this diversity, there has been growing interest in the study of how organizations transform their roles and practices in the development and strengthening of national innovation and entrepreneurial ecosystems (Etzkowitz and Leydesdorff 2000). According to Autio et al. (2014), in both temporal and spatial contexts, entrepreneurial innovation is the result of a variety of elements that compare the attributes of national innovation systems, entrepreneurship, contextual influences, and the main benefits for the actors involved in this process. Applying this perspective, how different agents operate, collaborate, make decisions, identify benefits, or transform their roles is still an interesting research area (Cunningham and Link 2015), particularly in emerging or transitional economies (Wright et al. 2005). For instance, these types of economies comprise countries[1] that face a rapid pace of development and government policies that favor economic liberalization and the transition from centrally planned economies (Wright et al. 2005).

In general, emerging economies invest in more productive capacity and adopt a free market or mixed economy to move toward an innovative economy (Meyer et al. 2009). In these scenarios, governments create subsidies to promote entrepreneurship innovation through compulsory university partnerships as a strategy to stimulate regional economic development (Cohen et al. 2002; Thompson 1999). Therefore, questions about how institutions influence organizational/individual entrepreneurial and innovative decisions have been relatively unexplored (Hoskisson et al. 2000; Meyer et al. 2009), particularly in emerging economies, where there is significant organizational heterogeneity represented by incumbent enterprises (primarily busi-

---

[1] According to Hoskisson et al. (2000), some countries identified as emerging or transitional economies are (in alphabetical order) Albania, Argentina, Armenia, Azerbaijan, Bangladesh, Belarus, Bosnia and Herzegovina, Botswana, Brazil, Bulgaria, Chile, China, Colombia, Cote d'Ivoire, Croatia, Czech Republic, Ecuador, Egypt, Estonia, Georgia, Ghana, Greece, Hungary, India, Indonesia, Israel, Jamaica, Jordan, Kazakhstan, Kenya, Korea, Kyrgyzstan, Latvia, Lithuania, Macedonia, Malaysia, Mauritius, Mexico, Moldova, Morocco, Nigeria, Pakistan, Peru, the Philippines, Poland, Portugal, Romania, Russia, Saudi Arabia, Slovakia, Slovenia, South Africa, Sri Lanka, Taiwan, Tajikistan, Thailand, Trinidad and Tobago, Tunisia, Turkey, Turkmenistan, Ukraine, Uzbekistan, Venezuela, and Zimbabwe.

ness groups, state-owned enterprises, and privatized firms), entrepreneurial start-ups, and foreign entrants. Based on those arguments, the purpose of this research is to provide a better understanding about the micro-foundations of entrepreneurial and innovation ecosystems explained through their main actors, particularly, exploring the role of higher education organizations. To achieve this objective, adopting institutional economic theory and case study approach, we analyzed the case of the drivers of the Mexican innovation and entrepreneurship ecosystems.

This chapter is organized as follows. Section 6.2 presents the link between entrepreneurship and innovation. Section 6.3 integrates the methodological design. Section 6.4 describes the main agents that allow for the understanding of the entrepreneurship and innovation ecosystem of an emerging economy (Mexico), as well as of the role of higher education organizations such as drivers of innovation and entrepreneurship ecosystems in the light of previous studies. Finally, Sect. 6.5 summarizes the concluding remarks.

6.2 Theoretical Framework

Entrepreneurship and innovation have always been strongly related. According to Schumpeter (1934), creative destruction is present when entrepreneurs introduce radically new products, services, and processes to the marketplace. Baumol (2002) also argues that entrepreneurship and innovation were the true source of national competitive advantage because new ventures broke the established development paths and undermined established competencies. In this regard, associating entrepreneurship with innovation, many nations, regions, and states have adopted policies to stimulate innovation by entrepreneurial firms with the aim to facilitate economic growth (Autio et al. 2014). For instance, several policies include local, regional, and national initiatives to promote technology-based entrepreneurship (Mustar and Wright 2010; Grimaldi et al. 2011).

Based on this perspective, we assume that institutions, defined as the rules of the game in the society, not only encourage the formal and informal factors (policies, culture, etc.) but also are linked to the drivers of each socioeconomic transformation process in the society (North 1990). In this regard, Zahra and Wright (2011) argue that the innovation literature, and especially the National System Innovation (NSI) literature, was mostly about structure and organizations, while the entrepreneurship literature has been mostly about the individual or the firm. For one side, NSI focused on the complex relationships of cooperation, communication, and feedback among organizations in both the process of innovation and the innovative performance across countries (Carlsson et al. 2002). This orientation has been criticized because the existing literature provides only limited insights into the drivers and mechanisms that can explain their evolution and growth over time (Castellacci and Natera 2013). For the other side, the entrepreneurship literature traditionally focused on independent ventures as well as on the organizational mode within which entrepreneurial initiatives took place intrapreneurship (Parker 2011). Based on this theoretical gap, Autio et al. (2014) propose that the concept of entrepreneurial innovation ecosystems distinguishes between the different types of contexts that influence it such as industrial, organizational, and social contexts—overlain by temporal and spatial contexts.

An entrepreneurial and innovation ecosystem could be understood as a set of interconnected actors (potential and existing), entrepreneurial organizations (e.g., firms, venture capitalists, business angels, banks, public sector agencies), innovative organizations (e.g., universities, research centers), and entrepreneurial and innovative processes (e.g. business birth, high growth firms, serial entrepreneurs, degree of entrepreneurial and innovative mentality within firms, and levels of ambition) that formally and informally coalesce to connect, mediated by government initiatives oriented to the performance of the local entrepreneurial environment (Mason and Brown 2014, p. 5). Generally, an entrepreneurial and innovation ecosystem emerges in locations that have place-specific assets/attributes. It represents a shift from traditional economic thinking on firms/markets (management societies) to new economic thinking involving different agents in the society, market, and organizations (entrepreneurial societies) (Audretsch and Thurik 2004). Typically, successful ecosystems have emerged under a unique set of pre-existing circumstances as well as with subsequently created conditions. For instance, Isenberg (2010) identified certain pillars that comprise a successful entrepreneurial innovation ecosystem, including accessible markets (both domestic and foreign), talented human capital and a qualified workforce, access to private/public sources of funding, an adequate support system and regulatory frameworks, and cultural support, among others. Nevertheless, these optimal conditions or pillars are not presented in all types of economies.

Within an emerging economy, policy makers usually try to translate successful formulas applied by developed economies, such as fostering ecosystems to promote innovation and entrepreneurship as the best transitional instrument (Wright et al. 2005). Traditionally, in a scenario characterized by several constraints, governments have eschewed a linear model encouraging universities and government laboratories to embrace the cause of innovation and technology commercialization (Cohen et al. 2002). In other words, in response to the widespread view that public research is too distant from industry in most sectors (with notable exceptions), they have called on universities and government R&D labs to implement their science and engineering strategies (Cohen et al. 2002, p. 2). In many developed countries, collaborative research is subsidized by public policy programs that provide resources for projects involving universities and enterprises (Caloghirou et al. 2001; Almus and Czarnitzki 2003; Grimaldi et al. 2011). Astrom et al. (2008) have defended the important role of public subsidies in supporting all types of collaboration, but in emerging economies, where the compulsory character of university-enterprise partnerships for access to subsidies allows for an effective exchange of knowledge, this type of collaboration is the most widespread (Boschma 2005). In addition, there is evidence to support the existence of long-standing partnerships between universities and enterprises and the fact that universities continue to aggressively seek industrial sponsorship. These partnerships persist despite the fact that government subsidies and grants create strong administrative burdens for companies, as government support is considered to be highly inflexible since it does not allow for the change of partners and the programs cannot end before a given date (Van de Vrande et al. 2009; Urbano and Guerrero 2013).

As a result, the university's significance increases in terms of its impact on the economy (Audretsch 2014). As universities are located in the intersection of the education, research, and transference processes, they are considered a key access agent in any entrepreneurship and innovation ecosystem. Traditionally, universities tend to be large organizations that by nature are not very entrepreneurial in their focus; however, the incorporation of an entrepreneurial orientation into a university's missions could change this convention (Hannan and Freeman 1984; Kirby et al. 2011). The core activities of universities have been universally recognized as teaching and research, but currently universities have undergone internal transformations in order to adapt to external conditions and to legitimize their role in the economy, giving place to a new kind of university: the entrepreneurial university (Guerrero and Urbano 2012, 2014; Guerrero et al. 2015).

6.3 Methodology

6.3.1 Case Study Approach

This analysis uses a qualitative perspective to investigate the complex phenomenon of the entrepreneurship innovation ecosystems, where the interaction between the phenomenon and the context is unclear (Yin 1984). In particular, we take a single case study approach (Yin 1984; Eisenhardt 1989, 2007) with the purpose of understanding the knowledge concerning the role of higher education organizations as drivers of entrepreneurship and innovation ecosystems. As a result, case study research involves the examination of a contemporary phenomenon in its natural setting (Yin 1984), and it is especially appropriate for research for providing the analysis of a phenomenon in a specific setting. Adopting the theoretical criteria to identify emerging economies (Hoskisson et al. 2000; Wright et al. 2005), the case of the Mexican entrepreneurial and innovation ecosystems was selected to analyze this contemporary phenomenon in-depth within its real-life context, especially when the boundaries between this phenomenon and the university role are not clearly evident (Eisenhardt 1989, 2007; Yin 1984).

Mexico is an interesting example of an emerging economy, as classified by the International Monetary Fund (2015).[2] Since the first editions of the Global Competitiveness Index, Mexico is classified as an efficiency-driven country (Porter and Schwab 2008, p. 9). This means that the country's main advantage comes from producing more advanced products and services highly efficiently.

---

[2] For further details, [http://www.imf.org/external/pubs/ft/weo/2008/01/weodata/groups.htm#oem].

Heavy investment in efficient infrastructure, business-friendly government administration, strong investment incentives, improving skills, and better access to investment capital allow for major improvements in productivity. The trade of products and services and human capital movements between countries has enormous effects on an economy's productivity and efficiency, especially for efficiency-driven countries such as Mexico. However, the challenge is to reinforce the ability to produce innovative products and services at the global technology frontier using the most advanced methods to become the dominant source of competitive advantage (Solleiro and Castañón 2005), in other words, a transformation of an *efficiency-driven economy* to an *innovation-driven economy*. In this context, Mexican higher education organizations are characterized by law, rules, and conditions that are introduced within a legal, economic, cultural, and social context of each country; and these are influenced by the level of development achieved (factor-efficiency-innovation driven). Mexicans face a big challenge for higher education organizations because many problems and gaps must be solved beforehand. In the past three decades, governmental agencies have been introducing supporting programs to promote collaboration between enterprises and knowledge creation agents in order to improve innovation and knowledge transfer and to achieve a higher development state. Therefore, it is important to analyze that Mexico needs to improve the drivers to economic development, especially human capital (Solow 1956), knowledge capital (Romer 1990), and entrepreneurship capital (Audretsch 2014).

Data were gathered by different methods and tools applying the concept of triangulation proposed by Yin (1984). In particular, we collected data using secondary sources such as the International Monetary Fund, World Bank, Mexican government (National Development Plans, from 1983 to 2018, *Diario Oficial*, Presidency, Chamber of Deputies), National Council for Science and Technology (CONACYT), Ministry of Economy, INADEM, Fondo PYME, Ministry of Education (SEP), National Association of Universities and Higher Education Organizations (ANUIES), Global Entrepreneurship Monitor (GEM), World Economic Forum (WEF), National Institute of Statistics and Geography (INEGI), World Intellectual Property Organization (WIPO), Organisation for Economic Co-operation and Development (OECD), Times Higher Education, and the El Financiero. The data collection was conducted over a 6-month period (September 2015 to March 2016). Regarding data analysis, procedures suggested by Yin (1984) and Eisenhardt (1989, 2007) were adopted. In particular, we used a general analytic approach that prioritizes information through the development of categories of data and the examination of similarities.

6.3.2 Understanding the Mexican Entrepreneurship and Innovation Strategies

During the past 32 years, Mexico has experienced a deep process of transformation. After the 1982 financial crisis created very critical conditions for the Mexican economy, it was necessary to introduce structural changes to design and apply economic policies in order to drive stability and development for Mexico and Mexicans. According to the World Bank Indicators, Mexico's economy, politics, and society have rapidly transformed from an efficiency-driven economy to an innovation-driven economy. The Mexican government has implemented certain strategies to stimulate regional economic development and the transition from an efficiency economy to an innovation economy. Figure 6.1 shows the government's economic development objectives during the past three decades.

The first initiative was the National Development Plan applied during the Miguel de la Madrid Hurtado administration (1983–1988). The main challenge during this period was maintaining and reinforcing the independence of the nation (Gobierno de la República 2015b). Its focus was to build a society under the principles of the state's rights and to guarantee individual and collective freedom in an integral democratic system with social justice conditions (pp. 3–4). Based on these challenges, the economic and social development strategy was oriented to an economic restructuring and a structural change.

The second initiative was the modernization plan implemented during the Carlos Salinas de Gortari administration (1989–1994). In this period, the main focuses were the defense of sovereignty, the expansion of democratic scenarios, the recovery of the economy, and the improvement of productivity (Gobierno de la República 2015c). However, after a 5-year period of stability and national recovery, another crisis occurred during the last year of this administration. As a consequence, during the Ernesto Zedillo Ponce de Leon administration (1995–2000), the main challenge was

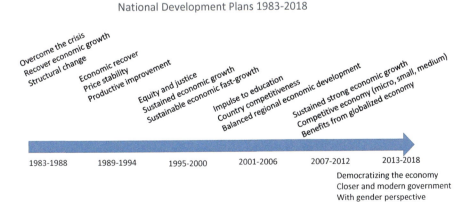

Fig. 6.1 Evolution of national development plans

to face the most severe crisis in Mexico. In this scenario, strategies were devised to reinforce national sovereignty, to consolidate a social harmony, to build a complete democratic development system, to improve socioeconomic development, and to promote a sustained/sustainable economic fast growth (Gobierno de la República 2015d).

Mexico started a new political era with the Vicente Fox Quesada administration (2001–2006). Its main strategy was to launch Mexico toward an accelerated growth through collaborative public relationships including education, social cohesion, human development, economic course, competitiveness, and public security, among others (Gobierno de la República 2015e). The following Felipe Calderón Hinojosa administration (2007–2012) focused on sustainable human development based on five axes: law enforcement and security, competitive job creation and equal opportunities, environmental sustainability, effective democracy, and responsible foreign policy (Gobierno de la República 2015f). December 2012 saw the start of the Enrique Peña Nieto administration, with its general objective to lead Mexico to its full potential and achieve the central idea that Mexico is a place where each person is able to write his/her own successful story and be happy (Gobierno de la República 2015a). Peña Nieto's planning was based on inclusion, peace, prosperity, qualified education, and worldwide responsibility, with productivity, modernization, and gender perspectives as transversal strategies.

Based on our review of those National Development Plans, we confirm that Mexico is trying to implement strategies to move from a factor-driven economy to an efficiency-driven economy and is now oriented to introduce an innovation economy to achieve the status of an innovation-driven economy (Global Entrepreneurship Monitor 2015). Today, economic development is characterized by a deeply competitive international environment and a knowledge-based economy. Mexico is classified by the World Economic Forum (2014) as an efficient-based economy. According to the National Development Plan 2013–2018 (Gobierno de la República 2015a), Mexico is searching for a strategy and processes to enhance this level and achieve a new development level based on innovation and knowledge. Therefore, this evolutionary perspective helps us to understand the configuration of the Mexican entrepreneurship and innovation ecosystems that will be explained in the next section.

6.4 Results and Discussions

6.4.1 Mexican Innovation Ecosystem

Supported by the Innovation Law (Diario Oficial 2014), the Mexican Science, Technology and Innovation System is integrated by (i) the National Council for Science and Technology (CONACYT), (ii) the Mexican government, (iii) the Mexican industry, and (iv) higher education systems. Figure 6.2 shows the main agents involved in the Mexican Science, Technology and Innovation System (Diario Oficial 2014).

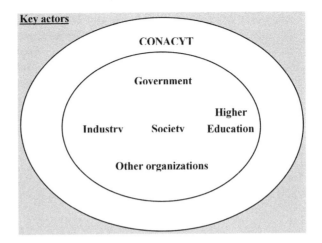

Fig. 6.2 Mexican Science, Technology and Innovation System (Diario Oficial 2014)

6.4.1.1 National Council for Science and Technology

The first agent is the National Council for Science and Technology (CONACYT), which is a decentralized public organization responsible for the design, development, and implementation of the main scientific and technological policies. Since its foundation in 1970, based on the national priorities and in collaboration with all the other agents, CONACYT promotes the reinforcement of human capital (scholarships and evaluation of national researchers), the development of scientific/technological activities (research funding, supporting innovative enterprises, etc.) in strategic areas (e.g., communication, biotechnology, advanced materials, manufacture design, socioeconomic development, social innovations), and the implementation of each administration (CONACYT 2015a).

CONACYT was involved with the development and implementation of the Scientific and Technological Research Law in 1999 and the Science and Technology Law in 2002 (Pérez-Hernández and Calderón-Martínez 2014). During the Calderón administration (2007–2012),[3] the Mexican Science, Technology and Innovation System faced a decentralization strategy across the 31 states that integrate Mexico. According to the INEGI (2016), the exercised budget by CONACYT was 202 million pesos in 1990 and 18,421 million pesos in 2013. As a result, during the past decade, Mexican knowledge production—measured by the number of patents of Mexican residents, trademarks, and industrial designs—has increased from 1% in 2000 to 3% in 2014 (WIPO 2016). The distribution of those patents has been primarily in pharmaceutical, engineering, and medical areas, and the 2014 top higher education applicants were the UNAM and the ITESM.

In this regard, CONACYT has implemented several initiatives to foster innovation throughout the collaboration among different agents (enterprises, research centers, higher education organizations). Some examples include innovation incentives

---

[3] For further details, review Gobierno de los Estados Unidos Mexicanos (2007).

such as the Programa de Estimulos a la Innovación (PEI), with three modalities (Innovapyme, Finnova, and Innovatec) and an investment of more than 7447 million pesos since 2009 and programs such as the Mixed Founding (FOMIX), the Technological Modernization Program (PMT), the Technological Consultant Register (RCCT), and the Innovation and Technology International Fund (FONCICYT), among others. It is important to note that the results obtained during the past decade from those supporting programs were lower than expected because they have also been influenced by factors such as the lack of collaboration from enterprises, the lack of human capital, the lack of trained employees, and higher cost in production factors. Simultaneously, CONACYT has implemented incentives for the development of human capital, including Sistema Nacional de Investigadores (SNI) and Sabatic stancies in foreing institucions (CONACYT 2015b).

6.4.1.2 Government

The second agent is represented by the Mexican government, which has implemented programs to facilitate the development of basic/applied research, technology, and innovation. According to the *Diario Oficial* (2014) and OECD (2010, 2012), during the Calderón administration, Mexico spent 378,021 million pesos to develop scientific activities and technology that represented around 37% of the gross domestic product (GDP). In general terms, federal government expenses in science and technology increased from 2035 million pesos (28% of GDP) in 1990 to 68,317 million pesos (42%) in 2013 (INEGI 2016). Typically, the distribution of expenditures for national science and technology has been 56.5% toward research and development of experimental activities, 23.9% toward education and training for scientists and technicians, and 19.5% toward the services of science and technology. The main funders have been the government (49.3%), private sector (44.5%), and universities (6.2%).

6.4.1.3 Industry

The third agent is represented by more than three million economic units. In general, small and medium enterprises (SMEs) represent more than 99% of all Mexican firms. They have accounted for more than 70% of all employment since 1993, and they generate more than 50% of the GDP (Hausmann et al. 2009). Mexico is also characterized as one of the world's most entrepreneurial countries in terms of the percentage of its population who has started or is in the process of starting a new venture (Flores et al. 2013). Yet there is evidence that Mexico is not friendly to entrepreneurs. It is estimated that between 60% and 90% of new ventures are started in the informal sector. While job growth expectations and realizations arguably constitute the most visible medium-term impact of entrepreneurship, innovative orientation impacts structural renewal in the long-term. Mexico has made room for entrepreneurship, but it does not seem to foster the kind of entrepreneurship required for economic growth. In terms of innovation, only one-third of new entrepreneurs identified in the total entrepreneurial activity develop new products or services for their customers, when in innovation-driven economies it is almost one-half of new entrepreneurs (Flores et al. 2013).

6.4.1.4 Higher Education Organizations

The last agent is represented by higher education systems, comprising technological institutes, technological universities, intercultural universities, polytechnic universities, federal public universities, regional public universities, higher teacher education universities, private universities, and public research (SEP 2012). Therefore, Mexican higher education systems are characterized by diversity and heterogeneity as well the normative of the Mexican Ministry of Education (SEP 2015a, b). The laws and regulations associated with Mexican higher education systems are Article 3 of the Constitution, Article 38 of the Organic Law of Federal Public Administration, the General Law of Education, the Science and Technology Law (SEP 2015a), the local laws from each state of the country, and specific organic laws and regulations of each local organization. There are also some associations such as the ANUIES (National Association of Universities and Higher Education Organizations) that include 179 members (ANUIES 2015). Interestingly, the origin of higher education resources is from private organizations (31.7%), from autonomous organizations (31.2%), and from public funding distributed by the federation (13.4%) and the states (17.8%) (SEP 2012). In addition, according to Silas Casilla (2005), the Mexican private education system has shown three tendencies since 2000: (i) diversification and growth; (ii) differences in contributions, impact, and quality with respect to public organizations; and (iii) the focus to attend to the demands of poor people who have not got any place in a public university. In terms of quality, according to the Times Higher Education, World University Ranking 2014–2015, Mexican universities are not found in the first 400 positions (The Times Higher Education, 2015). However, in the classification presented by the Shanghai Ranking in the Academic Ranking of World Universities (Top 500), the National Autonomous University of Mexico (UNAM) is found only in the 201–300 range and within the best 400 worldwide only in 2014 (Ranking Shanghai 2015).

6.4.2 Mexican Entrepreneurship Ecosystem

In Mexico, an entrepreneurial ecosystem is a system integrated by a set of economic agents linked and working to create, develop, and consolidate conditions to promote entrepreneurial activity and micro, small, and medium enterprise (MiPyME) development (INADEM 2015). According to the INADEM (2015), the Mexican entrepreneurial ecosystem is integrated by (i) private and public sources of funds, such as venture capitalists, banks, subsidies, and so on; (ii) chambers of commerce; (iii) higher education organizations and research centers; (iv) public and private incubators and accelerators; and (v) other public/private organizations (Fig. 6.3). Similar

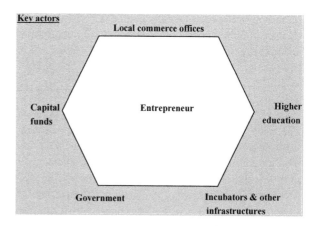

Fig. 6.3 Mexican entrepreneurial ecosystem (INADEM 2015)

to an innovation ecosystem, the entrepreneurial ecosystem works across the 31 states and with the support of universities.

6.4.2.1 Chambers of Commerce

These organizations and entrepreneur associations play a relevant role in any entrepreneurial ecosystem because they know the main needs and have strong channels of communication among the agents. In other words, these organizations are the main translators between the enterprises and local agents such as the government, universities, and employee associations.

6.4.2.2 Capital Funds

Funding tends to be the main element associated with the creation and growth of new/established ventures. For this reason, venture capitalist, business angels, crowdfunding, and banks are some of the most common sources of funding. Any entrepreneurial ecosystem requires strong financial mechanisms that allow entrepreneurs access not only to start-up capital but also capital for growth. Some examples include the creation of investors' clubs or networks, the establishment of loan programs to support entrepreneurial activity (e.g., programs developed by Santander Bank, BBVA Bancomer, Nacional Financiera, Banamex, Banregio, and Banorte), the development of co-inversion modalities (public-private), and the creation of crowdfunding platforms.

6.4.2.3 Higher Education Organizations

Many higher education organizations contribute to entrepreneurial ecosystems by providing talent, resources, and capabilities through their activities as well as supporting infrastructures (technology transfer offices, incubators, and accelerators). In this regard, Pérez-Hernández and Calderón-Martínez (2014) have shown that the support of higher education organizations contributes to the development of innovation as well as knowledge transfer and commercialization, where the efficiency of technology transfer offices (OTT) has been fundamental. For instance, many entrepreneurship educational programs and infrastructures developed by higher education organizations are classified/registered/certified by the INADEM according to the level of impact produced (e.g., university incubators and accelerators).

6.4.2.4 Incubators and Accelerators

With its integration of a national network of incubators and accelerators, INADEM tries to ensure solid entrepreneurial support, in particular for the different stages of the entrepreneurial process. For instance, INADEM's records show 196 basic incubators registered, including 24 high-impact incubators and 24 accelerators (INADEM 2014). The creation and operation of incubators across the country are an important factor in obtaining successful start-up rates. INADEM classifies these infrastructures into high-impact of basic-impact categories. In general, two models proposed by the Instituto Politécnico Nacional and the Tecnológico de Monterrey are examples of that.

6.4.2.5 Government

Over the past three decades, the Ministry of Economy has been responsible for the strategies associated with the creation and development of ventures. In the current Peña Nieto administration (2013–2018),[4] the main focus has been to foster economic development via innovation and new/established enterprises, with strategies in place to reinforce several elements of the Mexican entrepreneurial ecosystem, such as governmental supports, financing, entrepreneurial capabilities and culture, and technology. With this aim, this administration has created the National Institute of the Entrepreneur (INADEM), which is linked to the Ministry of Economy, as well as modifying existing legislation (e.g., education, foreign investment, telecommunications, tax system, and labor) to develop the entrepreneurial ecosystem.

During the Fox and Calderón administrations, the main program in support of entrepreneurship was the Small and Medium Enterprise Fund (Fondo PYME), an important advancement to improve entrepreneurial capabilities in Mexico managed by the Ministry of Economy between 2004 and 2012. During this time, many higher

---

[4] For further details, review Gobierno de los Estados Unidos Mexicanos (2013).

education organizations were important actors offering support via knowledge, experience, and networking. In the current Peña Nieto administration (2013–2018), two programs have been designed as the platform to encourage entrepreneurship: the Entrepreneurial Development Program (Programa de Desarrollo Empresarial) and the Entrepreneur and Financing Program (Programa de Emprendedores y Financiamiento). These mechanisms were introduced to improve entrepreneurial activity and increase the value of Mexican products and services (Secretaría de Economía 2016a, b, c). As a result, between 2004 and 2012, a total of 76,087 enterprises were created, with an employment generation of 395,674 and with the support of more than 32,015 million pesos (Fondo PyME 2016). Between 2014 and 2016, INADEM has invested more than 26,968 million pesos (El Financiero 2016).

6.4.3 The Role of Higher Education Organizations as Drivers of Entrepreneurship and Innovation Activities in Mexico

In the majority of socioeconomic scenarios, universities play a relevant role in entrepreneurial innovation processes, not only by reinforcing a governmental strategy to stimulate economic development (Hoskisson et al. 2000; Guerrero et al. 2015) but also by providing adequate environments in which the university community can develop innovative and entrepreneurial initiatives (Audretsch 2014; Guerrero et al. 2015). In this regard, several authors such as Guerrero and Urbano (2012), Urbano and Guerrero (2013), and Audretsch (2014) have shown the current higher education organizations' missions: education and training to community members, knowledge generation and transference, and fostering entrepreneurship and innovation.

In this regard, our previous section provides some insights into the relevant role and alignment of universities in the evolution of Mexican innovation and entrepreneurship ecosystems. Some of those insights have also been shown in previous studies about the interaction channels between universities and industry in Mexico (De Fuentes and Dutrénit 2012). However, in-depth analysis is still required of the efficiency/productivity relationships among the agents involved in both innovation and entrepreneurial ecosystems, particularly, how Mexican universities are facing their roles/strategies to drive entrepreneurial innovations. Nevertheless, we also need to take into account that in emerging economies, the participation of universities as the promoter of entrepreneurial innovations has been limited and it is not homogenous.

In the Mexican case, higher education organizations have a relevant presence in both innovation and entrepreneurship processes. According to INEGI (2015), there are 5739 higher education organizations, 443 research centers, and 21,259 business units in Mexico that provide other linked services, such as professional, scientific, and technical services. Unfortunately, not all those higher education organizations are working simultaneously toward the three missions (teaching, research, transference, and commercialization) or their transformation process. Only 10% of higher educa-

Pillar	US-Bay Area	US-Others Cities	United States	United Kingdom	Switzer-land	Ireland	Spain	Singapore	Pakistan	India	Australia	Mexico
Accessible Markets	92%	83%	86%	82%	89%	79%	67%	70%	78%	72%	71%	52%
Human Capital Workforce	93%	87%	90%	79%	67%	74%	90%	50%	92%	72%	79%	65%
Funding and Finance	91%	76%	82%	68%	61%	53%	43%	65%	22%	44%	67%	52%
Mentors/Advisers/Support Systems	91%	72%	79%	68%	56%	53%	29%	40%	58%	28%	54%	48%
Regulatory Framework/Infrastructure	67%	57%	61%	57%	61%	63%	48%	80%	31%	28%	54%	52%
Education and Training	80%	62%	70%	61%	61%	37%	62%	40%	39%	22%	33%	30%
Major Universities as Catalysts	88%	67%	75%	68%	67%	37%	38%	65%	22%	11%	38%	35%
Cultural Support	90%	64%	75%	50%	39%	42%	24%	40%	25%	17%	29%	22%
Average Score	86%	71%	77%	67%	63%	55%	50%	56%	46%	37%	53%	45%
Heat Map Key	Highest % of Respondents											
	Approximately Half % of Respondents											
	Lowest % of Respondents											

Fig. 6.4 Entrepreneurial ecosystem heat map by country. Pillars most important (World Economic Forum 2013, p. 13)

tion organizations and 17% of research centers are registered in the National Register for Scientific and Technological Organizations and Enterprises (CONACYT 2015c).

Applying the World Economic Forum benchmarking approach,[5] in comparison with other ecosystems from more advanced economies, Fig. 6.4 shows that the Mexican entrepreneurial ecosystem suffers from several deficits in the majority of the pillars, particularly, in cultural support, education/training, and universities such as catalysts of entrepreneurship (World Economic Forum 2013). Therefore, in order to develop human capital, generate knowledge, and foster innovative/entrepreneurial initiatives (Guerrero et al. 2015), Mexican higher education organizations need to introduce diversified support mechanisms (Bramwell and Wolfe 2008); to act proactively in the entrepreneurship innovation, enhancing links with all the agents involved in those ecosystems (Mian 1997; Etzkowitz 2003; Mueller 2007; Perkemann and Walsh 2007); and to generate more competitive collaborations for value creation (Chesbrough et al. 2006). Definitely, higher education organizations could bring competitive advantages (resources and capabilities) to drive entrepreneurship innovation activity in Mexico. Those competitive advantages could be encouraged by talent, human capital, incubators, accelerators, open innovation collaborations, generation and transference of knowledge, as well as value creation for socioeconomic development.

6.5 Conclusion

The analysis of the involvement of Mexican higher education organizations in innovation and entrepreneurship ecosystems reflects the existence of incentives to accomplish their triple mission but also a poor participation in the involvement of

---

[5] The World Economic Forum (2013) recognizes the importance to create and operate an entrepreneurial ecosystem as well as proposes some pillars to the growth/success of ventures such as accessible markets, human capital, funding, support systems, regulatory framework, education/training, and cultural support.

innovation and entrepreneurial activities. A plausible explanation is that the Mexican higher education system context is complex, diverse, and contrasting. In addition, the majority of Mexican higher education organizations are only attending to teaching, and only some of them are also focused on research. As a result, only a few universities are using their resources/capabilities to transform themselves into competitive organizations that contribute to the generation of talent and qualified people, higher-quality research, strong knowledge transfer and commercialization, and value creation (Amit and Schoemaker 1993; Barney 1991; Boyd 1991; Grant 1991; Wernerfelt 1984). Successful examples include the CINVESTAV, the IPN, the Tecnológico de Monterrey, and the UNAM.

Based on this evidence, the main implication of this chapter is oriented toward policy makers. Of course, the efforts made by CONACYT and the Ministry of Economy in the configuration of the Mexican innovation and entrepreneurship ecosystems are recognized. However, the obtained results are not sufficient due to the lack of participation among enterprises, higher education organizations, and research centers. It is necessary that each participant works together systematically and systemically, using an open innovation approach, to capitalize in a complementary way on each other's resources and capabilities to generate entrepreneurial innovation activity. Both the Ministries of Education and Economy must recognize the relevant role of universities and encourage, motivate, and involve universities in the development and implementation of innovation and entrepreneurship strategies.

This work only explores the role of higher education organizations in innovation and entrepreneurship activities. Therefore, this work also illuminates a good research opportunity to continue the exploration of this phenomenon using different theoretical/methodological approaches, particularly, to understand why Mexican higher education organizations are only attending to teaching and training activities; to identify which factors influence the main outcomes of innovation and entrepreneurship supporting programs; to recognize which are the best practices of most representative Mexican entrepreneurial universities to understand the reasons and factors that drive their success; and finally to determine which types of collaboration among production agents and knowledge agents are more adequate to stimulate economic development by government agencies.

Acknowledgments The authors acknowledge the support received by the Mexican National Institute of Statistics and Geography (INEGI), National Science and Technology Council (CONACYT), and Ministry of Education (SEP) to access the databases. Fernando Herrera acknowledges the PhD scholarship and support from the Tecnológico de Monterrey (ITESM). Maribel Guerrero acknowledges the financial support from Santander Universidades (Iberoamerica Scholarship for Young Researchers). David Urbano acknowledges the financial support from projects ECO2013-44027-P (Spanish Ministry of Economy and Competitiveness) and 2014-SGR-1626 (Economy and Knowledge Department—Catalan government).

References

Almus, M., & Czarnitzki, D. (2003). The effects of public R&D subsidies on firms' innovation activities: The case of eastern Germany. *Journal of Business and Economic Statistics, 2*(2), 226–236.

Amit, R., & Schoemaker, P. J. H. (1993). Strategic assets and organizational rent. *Strategic Management Journal, 14*(1), 33–46.

ANUIES. (2015). *Higher Education Institutions*. México: Asociación Nacional de Universidades e Instituciones de Educación Superior. http://www.anuies.mx/anuies/instituciones-de-educacion-superior/. Accessed 4 Sept 2015.

Astrom, T., Eriksson, M. L., Niklasson, L., & Arnold, E. (2008). *International comparison of five institute systems*. Copenhagen: Forsknings-og Innovationsstyrelsen, Copenhagen.

Audretsch, D. (2014). From the entrepreneurial university to the university for the entrepreneurial society. *The Journal of Technology Transfer, 39*, 313–321.

Audretsch, D., & Thurik, R. (2004). A model of the entrepreneurial economy. *International Journal of Entrepreneurship Education, 2*(2), 143–166.

Autio, E., Kenney, M., Mustar, P., Siegel, D., & Wright, M. (2014). Entrepreneurial innovation: The importance of context. *Research Policy, 43*(7), 1097–1108.

Barney, J. B. (1991). Firm resources and sustained competitive advantage. *Journal of Management, 17*, 99–120.

Baumol, W. J. (2002). *The free-market innovation machine: Analyzing the growth miracle of capitalism*. Princeton: Princeton University Press.

Boschma, R. (2005). Proximity and innovation: A critical assessment. *Regional Studies, 39*(1), 61–74.

Boyd, B. K. (1991). Strategic planning and financial performance: A meta-analytic review. *Journal of Management Studies, 28*(4), 353–374.

Bramwell, A., & Wolfe, D. (2008). Universities and regional economic development: The entrepreneurial University of Waterloo. *Research Policy, 37*, 1175–1187.

Caloghirou, Y., Tsakanikas, A., & Vonortas, N. S. (2001). University-industry cooperation in the context of the European framework programmes. *Journal of Technology Transfer, 26*(1–2), 153–161.

Carlsson, B., Jacobsson, S., Holmén, M., & Rickne, A. (2002). Innovation systems: Analytical and methodological issues. *Research Policy, 31*(2), 233–245.

Castellacci, F., & Natera, J. M. (2013). The dynamics of national innovation systems: A panel cointegration analysis of the coevolution between innovative capability and absorptive capacity. *Research Policy, 42*(3), 579–594.

Chesbrough, H., Vanhaverbeke, W., & West, J. (2006). Open innovation: A new paradigm for understanding industrial innovation. In *Open innovation: Researching a new paradigm* (pp. 1–27). New York: Oxford University Press.

Cohen, W. M., Nelson, R. R., & Walsh, J. P. (2002). Links and impacts: The influence of public research on industrial R&D. *Management Science, 48*(1), 1–23.

CONACYT. (2015a). *Antecedents of the National Council of Science and Technology*. México: CONACYT. http://www.conacyt.gob.mx/index.php/el-conacyt. Accessed 14 Apr 2015.

CONACYT. (2015b). *Innovation Incentives Programmes*. México: CONACYT. http://www.conacyt.gob.mx/index.php/fondos-y-apoyos/programade-estimulos-a-la-innovacion. Accessed 9 Sep 2015.

CONACYT. (2015c). *National Registry of Scientific and Technological Institutions and Companies-(RENIECYT)*. Mexico: CONACYT. http://www.conacyt.mx/index.php/el-conacyt/registro-nacional-de-instituciones-y-empresas-cientificas-ytecnologicas-reniecyt. Accessed 14 Apr 2015.

Cunningham, J. A., & Link, A. N. (2015). Fostering university-industry R&D collaborations in European Union countries. *International Entrepreneurship and Management Journal, 11*(4), 849–860.

De Fuentes, C., & Dutrénit, G. (2012). Best channels of academia–industry interaction for long-term benefit. *Research Policy, 41*, 1666–1682.

Diario Oficial. (2014). *National National Council for Science and Technology*. México: Presidencia de la República. http://www.fiderh.org.mx/21_ciencia_y_tecnologia.pdf. Accessed 14 Oct 2015.

Education Times Higher. (2015). *Times higher education*. World university ranking. https://www.timeshighereducation.co.uk/world-university-rankings/2015/world-university-rankings#/sort/0/direction/asc. Accessed 9 Sep 2015.

Eisenhardt, K. (1989). Building theories from case study research. *Academy of Management Review, 14*(4), 532–550.

Eisenhardt, K. (2007). Theory building from cases: Opportunities and challenges. *Academy of Management Journal, 50*(1), 25–32.

El Financiero. (2016). *Enterprises and Pyme funds*. http://www.elfinanciero.com.mx/empresas/quitan-mil-mdp-a-fondo-emprendedor.html. Accessed 10 Jan 2016.

Etzkowitz, H. (2003). Research groups as 'quasi-firms': The invention of the entrepreneurial university. *Research Policy, 32*, 109–121.

Etzkowitz, H., & Leydesdorff, L. (2000). The dynamics of innovation: From national systems and "Mode 2" to a triple helix of university–industry–government relations. *Research Policy, 29*(2), 109–123.

Flores, M., Campos, M., Naranjo, E., Lucatero, I., & Lopez, N. (2013). *GEM Mexico 2013 report*. México: GEM México.

Fondo PYME. (2016). *Annual report*. México: Secretaría de Economía. http://www.fondopyme.gob.mx/kardex/2012/reportes/historico_consulta_publica.asp. Accessed 10 Jan 2016.

Global Entrepreneurship Monitor. (2015). *Country profiles*. http//:www.gemconsortium.org/conuntry-profile/87. Accessed 29 Oct 2015.

Gobierno de la República. (2015a). *National Development Plan 2013–2018*. México: Presidencia de la República. http://pnd.gob.mx/. Accessed 4 Dec 2015.

Gobierno de la República. (2015b). *Official Journal*. Second Section. México: Presidencia de la República. www.dof.gob.mx/nota_detalle.php? codigo=4805999&fecha=31/05/1983. Accessed 7 Dec 2015.

Gobierno de la República. (2015c). *Salinas' Administration*. México: Presidencia de la República. http://ordenjuridico.gob.mx/Publicaciones/CDs2011/CDPaneacionD/pdf/PND%201989-1994.pdf. Accessed 7 Dec 2015.

Gobierno de la República. (2015d). *Zedillo's Administration*. México: Presidencia de la República. http://zedillo.presidencia.gob.mx/pages/pnd.pdf. Accessed 7 Dec 2015.

Gobierno de la República. (2015e). *Fox's Administration*. México: Presidencia de la República. http://www.diputados.gob.mx/LeyesBiblio/compila/pnd.htm. Accessed 7 Dec 2015.

Gobierno de la República. (2015f). *Calderon's Administration*. México: Presidencia de la República. http://pnd.calderon.presidencia.gob.mx/. Accessed 8 Dec 2015.

Gobierno de los Estados Unidos Mexicanos. (2007). *Plan Nacional de Desarrollo 2007–2012*. México: Presidencia de la República [http://pnd.calderon.presidencia.gob.mx/pdf/PND_2007-2012.pdf], last access October 2015.

Gobierno de los Estados Unidos Mexicanos. (2013). *Plan Nacional de Desarrollo 2013–2018*. México: Presidencia de la República. [http://pnd.gob.mx/wp-content/uploads/2013/05/PND.pdf], last access October 2015.

Grant, R. B. (1991). A resource-based theory of competitive advantage: Implications for strategy formulation. *California Management Review, 33*, 114–135.

Grimaldi, R., Kenney, M., Siegel, D., & Wright, M. (2011). 30 years after Bayh–Dole: Reassessing academic entrepreneurship. *Research Policy, 40*(8), 1045–1057.

Guerrero, M., & Urbano, D. (2012). The development of an entrepreneurial university. *Journal of Technology Transfer, 37*(1), 43–74.

Guerrero, M., & Urbano, D. (2014). Academics' start-up intentions and knowledge filters: An individual perspective of the knowledge spillover theory of entrepreneurship. *Small Business Economics, 43*(1), 57–74.

Guerrero, M., Cunningham, J. A., & Urbano, D. (2015). Economic impact of entrepreneurial universities' activities: An exploratory study of the United Kingdom. *Research Policy, 44*(3), 748–764.

Hannan, M. T., & Freeman, J. (1984). Structural inertia and organizational change. *American Sociological Review, 29*, 149–164.

Hausmann, R., Lozoya, E., & Mia, I. (2009). *The Mexico competitiveness report 2009*. Geneva: World Economic Forum.

Hoskisson, R. E., Eden, L., Lau, C. M., & Wright, M. (2000). Strategy in emerging economies. *Academy of Management Journal, 43*(3), 249–267.

INADEM. (2014). *Incubators*. México. http://www.redincubadoras.inadem.gob.mx/. Accessed 15 Nov 2014.

INADEM. (2015). *Programmes for entrepreneurial development*. México. https://www.inadem.gob.mx/templates/protostar/direccion_general_de_programas_de_desarrollo_empresarial.php. Accessed 4 Sep 2015.

INEGI. (2015). *National Statistical Directory of Economic Units*. México: INEGI. http://www3.inegi.org.mx/sistemas/mapa/denue/default.aspx. Accessed 9 Dec 2015.

INEGI. (2016). *Science and Technology Statistics*. México: INEGI. http://www3.inegi.org.mx/sistemas/temas/default.aspx?s=est&c=19007. Accessed 10 Jan 2016.

International Monetary Fund. (2015). *Data and statistics. World economic and financial surveys. World economic outlook. Country composition of WEO groups*. http://www.imf.org/external/pubs/ft/weo/2008/01/weodata/groups.htm#oem. Accessed 20 Oct 2015.

Isenberg, D. J. (2010). How to start an entrepreneurial revolution. *Harvard Business Review, 88*(6), 40–50.

Kirby, D., Guerrero, M., & Urbano, D. (2011). Making universities more entrepreneurial: Developing a model. *Canadian Journal of Administrative Sciences, 28*, 302–316.

Mason, C., & Brown, R. (2014). *Entrepreneurial ecosystems and growth oriented entrepreneurship*. Paper prepared for a workshop of the OECD LEED Programme and the Dutch Ministry of Economic Affairs. The Hague, Netherlands, 7 Nov 2013.

McMullen, J. S., & Dimov, D. (2013). Time and the entrepreneurial journey: The problems and promise of studying entrepreneurship as a process. *Journal of Management Studies, 50*(8), 1481–1512.

Meyer, K. E., Estrin, S., Bhaumik, S., & Peng, M. W. (2009). Institutions, resources, and entry strategies in emerging economies. *Strategic Management Journal, 30*(1), 61–80.

Mian, S. A. (1997). Assessing and managing the university technology business incubator: An integrative framework. *Journal of Business Venturing, 12*, 251–285.

Mueller, P. (2007). Exploiting entrepreneurial opportunities: The impact of entrepreneurship on growth. *Small Business Economics, 28*, 355–362.

Mustar, P., & Wright, M. (2010). Convergence or path dependency in policies to foster the creation of university spin-off firms? A comparison of France and the United Kingdom. *Journal of Technology Transfer, 35*(1), 42–65.

North, D. (1990). *Institutions, institutional change and economic performance*. Cambridge: Cambridge University Press.

OECD. (2010). *High-growth enterprises: What governments can do to make a difference. OECD studies on SMEs and entrepreneurship*. Paris: OECD Publishing. https://doi.org/10.1787/9789264048782-en.

OECD. (2012). *Science, technology and industry outlook 2012*. Paris: OECD.

Parker, S. C. (2011). Intrapreneurship or entrepreneurship? *Journal of Business Venturing, 26*(1), 19–34.

Pérez-Hernández, P., & Calderón-Martínez, G. (2014). Analysis of the technology commercialization process in two Mexican higher education institutions. *Journal of Technology Management & Innovation, 9*(3), 196–209.

Perkmann, M., & Walsh, K. (2007). University-industry relationship and open innovation: Towards a research agenda. *International Journal of Management Reviews, 9*(4), 259–280.

Porter, M., & Schwab, K. (2008). *Global competitiveness report 2008–2009*. Cologny: World Economic Forum.

Ranking Shanghai. (2015). *Academic ranking of world universities (top 500)*. Shanghai: Universidad Jiao Tong. http://www.shanghairanking.com/es/ARWU2015.html. Accessed 9 Sep 2015.

Romer, P. (1990). Endogenous technological change. *The Journal of Political Economy, 98*(5), S71–S102.

Schumpeter, J. A. (1934). *The theory of economic development: An inquiry into profits, capital, credit, interest and the business cycle* (trans: Redvers Opie). Cambridge: Harvard University Press

Secretaría de Economía. (2016a). *Antecedents*. México: Fondo PYME. www.fondopyme.gob.mx/docs/Antecedentes_Fondo_Pyme.ppt. Accessed 10 Jan 2016.

Secretaría de Economía. (2016b). *PYME Funds 2006–2012*. México: Secretaría de Economía. http://www.2006-2012.economia.gob.mx/mexicoemprende/fondo-pyme-int. Accessed 10 Jan 2016.

Secretaría de Economía. (2016c). *INADEM*. México: Secretaría de Economía. https://www.inadem.gob.mx/index.php/conoce-inadem. Accessed 10 Jan 2016.

SEP. (2012). *Mexican educational system, 2011–2012 indicators*. México: Secretaría de Educación Pública.

SEP. (2015a). *Normativity*. México: Secretaría de Educación. http://www.ses.sep.gob.mx/acerca-de-la-ses/normatividad. Accessed 9 Sep 2015.

SEP. (2015b). *Higher Education Institutions*. Mexico: Secretaría de Educación. http://www.ses.sep.gob.mx/instituciones-de-educacion-superior. Accessed 4 Sep 2015.

Silas Casilla, J. C. (2005). Realidades y tendencias en la educación superior privada mexicana. *Perfiles Educativos, 27*(109–110), 7–37.

Solleiro, J. L., & Castañón, R. (2005). Competitiveness and innovation systems: The challenges for Mexico's insertion in the global context. *Technovation, 25*(9), 1059–1070.

Solow, R. (1956). A contribution to the theory of economic growth. *The Quarterly Journal of Economics, 70*(1), 65–94.

Thompson, J. L. (1999). A strategic perspective of entrepreneurship. *International Journal of Entrepreneurial Behavior & Research, 5*(6), 279–296.

The Times Higher Education. (2015). *World university ranking*. London. https://www.timeshighereducation.co.uk/world-universityrankings/2015/world-university-rankings#/sort/0/direction/asc. Accessed 9 Sep 2015.

Urbano, D., & Guerrero, M. (2013). Entrepreneurial universities socioeconomic impacts of academic entrepreneurship in a European region. *Economic Development Quarterly, 27*(1), 40–55.

Van de Vrande, V., De Jong, J. P., Vanhaverbeke, W., & De Rochemont, M. (2009). Open innovation in SMEs: Trends, motives and management challenges. *Technovation, 29*(6), 423–437.

Wernerfelt, B. (1984). A resource-based view of the firm. *Strategic Management Journal, 5*(2), 171–180.

World Economic Forum. (2013). *Entrepreneurial ecosystems around the globe and company growth dynamics. Report summary for the annual meeting of the new champions 2013*. http://www3.weforum.org/docs/WEF_EntrepreneurialEcosystems_Report_2013.pdf. Accessed 10 Jan 2016.

World Economic Forum. (2014). *Global competitiveness report 2012–2013*. Schwab, K.- Full data edition. http://www3.weforum.org/docs/WEF_GlobalCompetitivenessReport_2012-13.pdf. Accessed 20 Jan 2016.

World Inetellectual Property Organization (WIPO). (2016). *Statistics*. http://www.wipo.int/ipstats/en/statistics/country_profile/profile.jsp?code=MX. Accessed 10 Jan 2016.

Wright, M., Filatotchev, I., Hoskisson, R. E., & Peng, M. W. (2005). Strategy research in emerging economies: Challenging the conventional wisdom. *Journal of Management Studies, 42*(1), 1–33.

Yin, R. (1984). *Case study research design and methods*. Thousand Oaks: Sage.

Zahra, S., & Wright, M. (2011). Entrepreneurship's next act. *Academy of Management Perspectives, 25*, 67–83.

Chapter 7
Commercialisation Journey in Business Ecosystem: From Academy to Market

Zhaojing Huang, Clare Farrukh, and Yongjiang Shi

Abstract Scientists are becoming more entrepreneurial in trying to commercialise their findings as new technologies and products. However, academic research focuses very little on the commercialisation process and the management tools needed by entrepreneurial scientists. This paper looks at commercialisation from scientists' viewpoint seeking to develop new products from successful research. It takes a business ecosystem perspective and presents a theoretical framework developed by mapping diverse literature. This framework is then compared to data collected during a longitudinal case study on the development of a fibre optic sensor analyser with application in the construction industry. A key finding is that relationships with partners and other supporting organisations need to be formed earlier than the literature currently suggests and that an awareness of the business ecosystem within which the technology fits is as important to scientists as knowledge of available innovation and technology management tools. Hence an early focus on communication and partnership is highlighted as an important factor for commercialisation success.

Keywords Commercialisation process • Business ecosystems • Innovation and entrepreneur

7.1 Introduction

In an attempt to speed the uptake of research to give benefit to society, as well as potentially reap rewards to feed back into ongoing research, research institutes are assuming a much more important role in bringing new technology to the market. Increasingly researchers and scientists are becoming new entrepreneurs, trying to commercialise their scientific findings as new technologies or products. Although

---

Z. Huang (✉) • C. Farrukh (✉) • Y. Shi
Institute for Manufacturing, University of Cambridge, Cambridge, UK
e-mail: huangzj@cantab.net; cjp2@eng.cam.ac.uk; ys@eng.cam.ac.uk

© Springer International Publishing AG 2018
J. Leitão et al. (eds.), *Entrepreneurial, Innovative and Sustainable Ecosystems*, Applying Quality of Life Research,
https://doi.org/10.1007/978-3-319-71014-3_7

different parts of the process are supported by innovation and technology management techniques, academic research focuses very little on the whole commercialisation process. There is also a lack of approaches documented in the literature to provide guidance for scientists in their commercialisation journey. Therefore, this work (Huang 2015) aims to investigate the question 'How can a group of scientists commercialise a new product from a successful piece of research?' To do this a wide-ranging literature review has been carried out to piece together the commercialisation process within a business ecosystem view, and this process has been contrasted with activities carried out during a longitudinal case study.

7.2 Literature Review

7.2.1 Overview

The main areas of literature reviewed fall within an overall view of the business ecosystem which is seen as the commercialisation context. The resultant innovation ecosystem, open innovation, technology readiness levels and new product development all contribute to an understanding of the commercialisation path from research to a product. The area of new product development is seen as informed by knowledge of entrepreneurship, business models and supply chain (Fig. 7.1).

7.2.2 Commercialisation Context: The Business Ecosystem

Companies evolve rapidly with the creation of innovative new business. Therefore, they need to attract resources of all sorts, drawing capital, forming partnerships and securing suppliers and customers. The collaborative networks formed become the

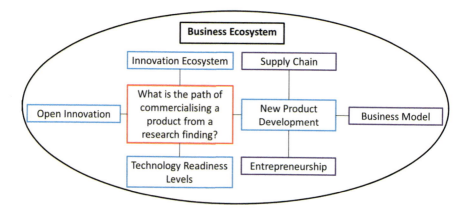

Fig. 7.1 Overview of involved literature in commercialisation process

7 Commercialisation Journey in Business Ecosystem: From Academy to Market

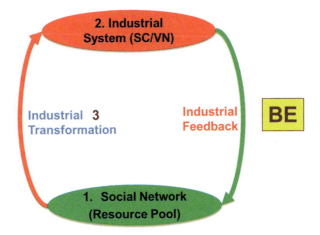

Fig. 7.2 Research focus on the commercialisation process within a business ecosystem (Adapted from Shang and Shi 2013)

business ecosystem (Moore 1993). Taking the business ecosystem concept further, Shang and Shi (2013) argued that the four key building blocks of the business ecosystem are social network (or resource pool), value network, interaction mechanisms and business context. Figure 7.2 adapts their proposed framework and proposes that one form of interactive mechanism (3) is the industrial transformation or commercialisation process between research within the social network (1) and its expression as a product in the industrial system (2, supply chain/value network).

7.2.3 Commercialisation Path: The Related Research Fields

The relevant research fields that have been identified in the literature review need to be integrated to present a larger view of the whole commercialisation path. By arranging and effectively integrating them, it also provides a chance to take a closer look on how these fields of knowledge interact and overlap with each other. Knowing these interactions can also help to enrich the existing knowledge of business ecosystem. Some of the researchers and their key research papers have been identified as their research focuses are related to the commercialisation path. Table 7.1 lists some of the papers identified in each field. It summarises the main findings of each paper and the crucial resources identified as being related to the commercialisation process.

The whole commercialisation path is a complicated and long journey. The research fields stated focus on parts of the journey, solving certain problems that might be faced in the commercialisation process.

Table 7.1 Identified relevant research papers

Field	Author and year	Comments	Resources identified
Innovation ecosystem	Adner and Kapoor (2010)	Focal firms should innovate together with complementary innovators	Industrial knowledge
			Market information
	Wang (2009)	There are interactions between different innovation ecosystems	Industrial recognition
	Adner (2012)	Make sure that the adoption chain is linked and all players along the chain are positive about the new product	Industrial standards and requirements
Open innovation	Traitler et al. (2011)	Firstly, winning respect, establishing trust, building goodwill and finally creating value	Industrial know-how
			Industrial requirement
Technology readiness level	Mankins (2009)	Test the readiness of the technology through prototyping and testing	Funding
			Academic knowledge
	Lin et al. (2007)	It is also important to understand the customer perception of usefulness alongside technology readiness	Customer perception
New product development	Cooper (2006)	5-gate new product development procedure	Academic and industrial knowledge
	Phaal et al. (2011)	It is a transformation process from science to technology to application and then to market	Academic and industrial knowledge
	Fraser et al. (2003)	Fuzzy front-end product development process	Collaboration
Supply chain	Petersen et al. (1999)	Involving suppliers/manufacturers in the new product development process	Suppliers
Business model	Chesbrough and Rosenbloom (2002)	The model requires consideration of both technical and economic domains	Academic knowledge
			Industrial knowledge
		There is a range of possible value capture strategies for resources, control and marketing implications	Market information
			Customer perception
	Morris et al. (2005)	Business model can be dissected into six components	Industrial knowledge
			Customer perception
			Market information

7.2.4 Integration of the Literature

In order to obtain a picture of the whole commercialisation path, the research fields mentioned above need to be integrated.

The research fields identified focus on four main levels, namely, strategy and business model management (strategy), resource and organisation (resource), product and service (product) and technology and science (knowledge) level. The research focusing on the strategy level tends to help companies forming plans and tactics to grow the business further. At the resource level, research focuses on obtaining external resources and allocating internal resources to fit the needs of operation. At the product level, research talks more about the process of developing a successful new product. Knowledge is also crucial in the commercialisation process. At the knowledge level, research focuses on ways to obtain scientific knowledge and convert it into a commercial product.

In the commercialisation process, there are four main stages to a typical new product development (Phaal et al. 2011). The process starts with science and gradually develops into a technology. After reaching maturity, a technology can be tested as part of an application to solve industrial problems. Finally, it can then reach the market as a mature product/service. These four stages are very typical in a research-based new product commercialisation process; therefore it is chosen to be included in the integration as the key stages.

Within these four main stages, there are several key milestones in the whole commercialisation process. The key milestones are research, scope, customisation, prototype, tests and modifications, second prototype, tests and modifications, finalised product, business model formation and launch. These key milestones are being developed from the existing new product development processes and include an element of iteration.

By plotting the individual research fields on a graph with four levels on the vertical axis and the four stages and ten key milestones on the horizontal axis, an integrated view is obtained as shown in Fig. 7.3.

The three boxes below the horizontal axis summarise the key resources identified from the research papers listed in the previous table to transfer the process to the next stage. In order to transfer from science to a technology, funding/capital is important. Academic knowledge is also crucial to further develop the promising science research. In order to move to the application stage, industrial knowledge and requirement is crucial as it tells the developer how to further develop this technology to fit industrial needs and standards. Information regarding customer perception is also vital as the developer wants to design a product that meets the requirements of customers. In order to push the process to the market stage, recognition from the industry, information about the market and suppliers are essential.

Looking at the individual research areas plotted:

Technology Readiness Level: technology readiness level covers the very beginning part of the commercialisation journey. Focusing on testing the maturity of the technology, this framework helps users at both knowledge and product level. The

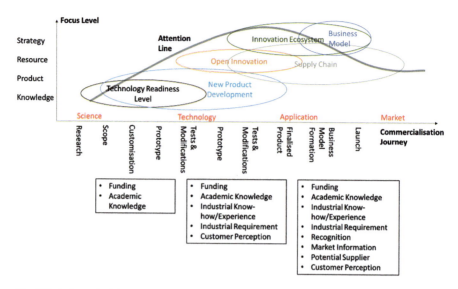

Fig. 7.3 A theoretical framework for commercialisation based on literature mapping

knowledge obtained through testing will feed back to the design with suitable modifications. At the end of the process, a mature technology should have been developed.

New Product Development: the new product development process starts slightly after the technology readiness level framework and lasts much longer. This process typically starts with scoping. The process also covers both product and knowledge level. Through prototyping, testing and modification processes, the knowledge obtained will feed back to the product design to improve the quality and performance. It can also be seen that the new product development plot has an overlapping area with technology readiness level framework plot. This is because both approaches help to test and modify the current technology/product. However, technology readiness level stops at the technology stage, while new product development continues until a product has been finalised and produced.

Open Innovation: open innovation talks about building trust and sharing resources between different players in the business ecosystem focusing on the resource level. According to the research, this process usually starts with a developed mature technology. It is a process where companies are actively looking for new technologies to develop their next-generation products. Therefore, it starts from the technology stage and ends at the application stage. There is also an overlap between new product development and open innovation. As part of the new product development process, developers are looking externally for resources which they are lacking through open innovation to complete the new product development process.

Supply Chain: there are an increasing number of research papers mentioning the importance of involving suppliers in the new product development process. When producing the prototype of the product, there is a need of involving suppliers, so that once the product is successfully launched, a supply chain can be set up very smoothly. Therefore, the involvement of supply chain should start at the prototyping of the product (typically second prototype) and continues even after the launch of the product. Supply chain overlaps with the new product development process, as it should be considered in the process. There is also an overlap between supply chain and open innovation. This is because suppliers are a resource which can be accessed through open innovation.

Innovation Ecosystem: innovation ecosystem focuses on the strategic level. The developer should co-evolve with suppliers and complementors to ensure the successful launch of the product. When the prototype of the product has been made, the developer should apply the theory of innovation ecosystem by aiming to develop alongside the different players needed to ensure a successful product launch. This theory overlaps with open innovation as it is a process of building trust and obtaining resources to collaborate with different players in the market. It also involves suppliers, as co-evolving with suppliers is an important step to ensure the success of new product development.

Business Model: the business model is the overall strategy a company should formulate to sell its product. This process usually starts after a product/service has been successfully developed. It overlaps with supply chain and innovation ecosystems as it considers and includes suppliers, collaborators and competitors.

After obtaining the relative positioning of the key areas, a thick dark line has been plotted on the graph. This is the 'attention line' which indicates the level where most attention is required at each point of time during the commercialisation. The attention focus starts from the knowledge level and moves through product and resource level to reach the strategic level. Then it falls back to the resource and product level and remains there finally.

By integrating the existing bodies of relevant knowledge, a broader view of the whole commercialisation journey has been obtained. There are several overlaps identified, and the movement of the 'attention line' for the whole process across the different levels has been highlighted. Summarising all the existing knowledge reviewed, it can be seen as a process of obtaining lacking resources from both industry and supporting organisations to complete a new product development. With the appropriate business model generated, the new product can then successfully enter the market and be applied by the customers.

7.3 Methodology

7.3.1 Overview

Based on the current literature, there are several individual research domains which collectively cover the commercialisation journey. These research fields have been identified, arranged and then integrated to provide an overall view of the theoretical commercialisation path. By means of the case study on the development of fibre optic sensor analyser in Cambridge Centre for Smart Infrastructure and Construction, the practical behaviour in research commercialisation was compared to the theoretically suggested approach. During this research, the whole commercialisation journey has been considered and framed under the business ecosystem scope.

This type of case study is being categorised as single revelatory. It is the preferred choice when an investigator has access to information not commonly accessible (Yin 2002). When building up the single revelatory case study, the common ways to obtain information are reviewing the possibility to access internal information and interview relevant people and building the case based on private information.

7.3.2 Case Study Design

A case study has been built around the development of fibre optic sensor analyser (FOSA), a technology that has been developed from the laboratory by a group of scientists. Although the commercialisation path has not been yet completed, it is now close to the final launch of the product. As the case study ran while the product was still under development, some data has been gathered through observation and participation in the process. At the same time, some data complements have been gathered through individual interviews. The access to Cambridge Centre for Smart Infrastructure and Construction (CSIC) technology development meetings, past project documentation and interviewing key stakeholders in the FOSA project allowed identification of FOSA's key development stages and CSIC's approach to expedite its product development. As part of the case study, an interview with Cambridge Enterprise was also held to confirm the accuracy and representativeness of the data collected from this case study. Cambridge Enterprise is the commercialisation arm of the University of Cambridge, formed to help students and staff commercialise their expertise and ideas.

7.3.3 Phases of the Research

The whole research has been divided into three phases:

Phase 1 focused on understanding the existing theories and background of the research area. Determining and obtaining the relevant existing academic literature was the first step. There are eight academic fields that were identified to be relevant to the whole journey from scientific research to commercialisation. The next task was to integrate the relevant academic research obtained into a theoretical framework of the commercialisation process.

Phase 2 focused on obtaining the academic and industrial data regarding the case study. The past project reports, interviews and participating in project meetings with CSIC regarding the FOSA served as important inputs to understand the case study more thoroughly. Analysing this data helps to understand the whole development process of this new product. The next task was to understand and visualise the whole development process of the FOSA project which is the case study for this work using the theoretical framework as a structure.

Phase 3 followed after the first two phases were completed, where the framework formed from integrating the existing research can then be tested and improved through comparison with the development process of FOSA in CSIC. The aim was to enrich existing academic research of the commercialisation process and enable the drawing of preliminary conclusions.

7.4 Case Study

7.4.1 Background

CSIC is a research institute based in Cambridge aiming to develop and commercialise emerging technologies which will provide radical changes in the construction and management of infrastructure, leading to considerably enhanced efficiencies, economies and adaptability. Civil engineering infrastructure is generally the most capital-intensive national investments of any country and has a long service life expectation. It is costly to maintain and difficult to replace. Therefore, routine manual visual inspection must be performed periodically to ensure the buildings are safe and there are no signs of degradation and corrosion. Fibre optic sensors have been spotted to be an ideal tool to complete the inspection tasks more effectively and accurately. By attaching the fibre to the infrastructure, scans of the whole building are possible as measurements are taken and recorded using an analyser. Although the initial tests have shown the method performs to a high level, there still exist several major disadvantages. One of them is the high expense of the equipment, and another major disadvantage is the bulky size of the equipment. These two major disadvantages are preventing this technology from being adopted in the civil industry. Therefore, CSIC decided to develop a portable, low-cost and high-performance fibre optic sensor analyser (FOSA) product to fit the needs of the civil industry.

7.4.2 Data Gathering

7.4.2.1 Reports

There were nine major construction events that have been conducted since the beginning of the FOSA development programme in 2005. This information was obtained from past industrial reports (Shi 2014) and updated during the research. These events are summarised in Table 7.2.

It can be observed that these major events happened throughout the development programme. With collaborative relationships set-up with the industrial companies, the researchers could test their technology and product in the industrial projects of the companies. The results obtained from the projects are used to modify the design further. Therefore, it can be concluded that the theory of open innovation and innovation ecosystem has been applied from the beginning of the project till today. It can be also observed that through these activities, the technology has been tested and new product has been gradually developed by applying the theory of technology readiness levels and new product development.

7.4.2.2 Interviews

Interviews were carried out with a range of partners and researchers related to the FOSA project from April 2014 to July 2015. These include two industrial partners, one academic partner and four members of CSIC.

In order to understand the whole development process, one of the interviews was an in-depth discussion with the project leader. Secondary data such as past industrial reports was collected and reviewed before and after the interview to obtain more information and data for this case study. The key finding from the interview was that the developer of this new technology/product started to establish good relationships with the industrial players at the very beginning of the development programme. Through these stable and long-term collaborative relationships with the industry, the developer was able to understand the industrial needs and requirements early on in order to put this information into the product design. It was also mentioned in the interview that with the collaborative relationships set-up, the developers could communicate with the industrial companies frequently, throughout the whole development process. This was particularly helpful, as the developers were able to update the companies with the current progress while obtaining feedback and modifying the product design accordingly. Through the communication processes, some valuable information was also obtained, for instance, industrial know-how and market information. With trust built up, the developers could test their technology and products in the construction projects of the partners. From the interview, it is also known that the whole process started with establishing good relationships with the industry and the supporting organisations while going through the process of research and technology testing. Almost at the end of the new product

7 Commercialisation Journey in Business Ecosystem: From Academy to Market

Table 7.2 List of major project events in 2005–2015

Events	Client type	Problem encountered	Date	Corresponding theory	
1	Thames link tunnel at King's Cross – deformation monitoring during proximity tunnelling	Tunnelling subcontractor	Delicate handling exposed cables prone to damage	Jan 05	Technology readiness levels
2	Singapore Circle Line – monitoring twin tunnel interaction	Asset owner	Change in tunnel elevation and surrounding soil type affects data output. Exposed cables prone to damage	Oct 06	Technology readiness levels
3	Lambeth College – pile loading and thermal response test	Asset owner	–	May 07	Technology readiness levels
4	Francis Crick Institute – preliminary load test	Piling contractor	Clamps introduce large change in strain about a localised spot	Sep 11	Technology readiness levels / New product development
5	Abbey Mills Pumping Station – shaft monitoring during excavation	Asset owner	Damage to cable during excavation	Dec 11	New product development
6	259 City Road – preliminary load test	Design subcontractor	FO cable damage – no signal from one side of pile	Jul 12	New product development
7	6 Bevis Marks – monitoring and reuse of piles	Piling subcontractor	–	Oct 12	New product development
8	Newfoundland project – test pile 2	Consultants	Clamps introduce large change in strain about a localised spot	May 14	New product development
9	Final product prototype	Product design consultant	Proceeding	June 15	New product development

development process now, the team is considering involving potential suppliers and looking for suitable business model for the newly developed product.

As part of the case study, an interview was also conducted with two technology consultants in Cambridge Enterprise who are currently collaborating with CSIC on the FOSA project to provide guidance on the commercialisation process. They have noticed through numerous commercialisation projects that they have worked on in the past years that the researchers who have good relationships with the industry were much more likely to succeed. The earlier the relationships with the industry were set up, the higher chances of success. Cases where researchers approached with excellent technology/product but limited connection with the industry have failed severely. The FOSA project is a very good representative case, where researchers started to communicate with the industry early on to build up the mutual understanding.

7.4.2.3 Participation

When the opportunity arose, theoretical approaches and management tools highlighted in the literature review were discussed with members of CSIC. For example, as the FOSA team was approaching the stage where an appropriate business model needed to be generated, the theory of business models was shared in meetings with the team as a discussion framework. The final business model generated was presented to a venture capital team to attract new investment. Although the commercialisation process of FOSA is not yet completed, some of the theories supporting the uncompleted part of the journey have been tested through such activities to verify their accuracy, and the outcome so far is favourable.

7.5 Results

7.5.1 Comparison of Areas of Literature with Practical Concerns in the Case Study

The theoretical behaviours listed on the left side of Table 7.3 are compared to the practical behaviours observed in the case study, listed on the right side of the table. Through comparison, it can be seen that the factors affecting the commercialisation stated in relevant research fields match with the practical behaviours in the industry. In practice, the researchers of FOSA have gone through the processes suggested in the relevant research fields unconsciously to secure the success of the commercialisation. Therefore, the practical behaviours of commercialisation largely match with the integrated research view as they both show the same consideration factors for successful commercialisation process.

Table 7.3 Comparison between literature and case study

Literature	FOSA case study
Innovation ecosystem	
Innovate together with complimentary innovators	Obtain recognition from the industry and work with the service companies
Adoption across the value chain	Working closely with industrial partners and building up good relationship with service companies
Interaction between innovation ecosystems	Started from oil and gas industry and the technology can be potentially applied to various industries
Open innovation	
Win respect, establish trust, build goodwill and finally create value	Long-term partnership with the industrial companies from the beginning of the project
Technology readiness level	
Test the readiness of the technology through prototyping and testing	Test the technology through partners' industrial projects
Customer perceived usefulness	Consistently discuss with the industrial partners to understand their needs and requirements of the product
New product development	
5-gate new product development procedure	Applying this procedure for developing the new product
It is a transformation process from science to technology to application and then to the market	The technology started off from a laboratory research and then developed into a technology that is aiming to be launched in the civil industry
Fuzzy front-end product development process	Collaborating with industrial companies to obtain industrial requirements of the product. Working with design consultancy to clarify doubts and identify wastes in product design
Supply chain	
Involving suppliers/manufacturers in the new product development process	Considering looking for manufacturers to participate in the product development process. However, it is unclear as the business model has not been determined at the moment

7.5.2 Comparison of the Commercialisation Timeline

Although both academic literature and the industrial case study considered the same factors within their commercialisation processes, the order of how things happened during the commercialisation journey of the case study is slightly different and can be seen clearly in the two commercialisation charts generated. The practical chart (top) is based on the case study findings, and the theoretical chart (bottom) is based on the literature. The commercialisation's 'current position' shows the progress of the FOSA development when this work was completed.

The data obtained from the case study illustrates that the collaboration with the industry started right at the beginning of the project in order to build trust and obtain resources which were lacking. Therefore, the theory of innovation ecosystem and open innovation has been applied at the beginning of the project. In addition, it can

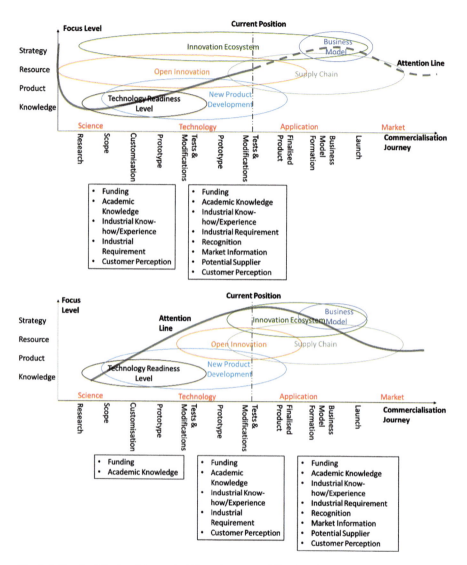

Fig. 7.4 Practical (top) and theoretical (lower) commercialisation charts

be seen from Fig. 7.4 that the thick dark line plotted which is presenting the 'attention line' moves differently. In the case study, it starts from resource and strategy level and moves down quickly to the knowledge and product level. Then it gradually shifts to the highest strategic level and eventually comes down to the resource and product level. As noticed from the interviews, a large amount of resource was required at the early stage to help the researchers to set the correct direction for their research. With larger resources and information provided at an earlier stage, the results of the research have more chance of meeting the industrial needs more

7 Commercialisation Journey in Business Ecosystem: From Academy to Market 143

quickly and with fewer and smaller modifications. The vertical dotted line represents the current stage of FOSA project. Finishing the final product prototyping, the researchers are making the final modifications before finalising the product design. This project is close to the application stage.

7.5.3 Future Projections

As the whole commercialisation process has not yet been completed, therefore the 'attention line' after the current stage is plotted in a thick dotted line. This information was obtained through interviewing the project leader of the commercialisation programme regarding their future plan. Based on the theoretical chart, the researchers should be thinking about forming a suitable business model in order to push the product to the market. Based on the interviews, this is exactly what the team is trying to work out now together with the help from Cambridge Enterprise.

7.5.4 Key Stages Observed in the Practical Commercialisation Process

The practical commercialisation chart generated showed an early start of applying the approaches stated in open innovation and innovation ecosystem research. The research focuses on the strategy and resource level of the commercialisation path. Therefore, the attention in the practical process of commercialisation starts from a high level (strategy and resource level) before it comes to a lower level (product and knowledge level). After this early stage, the behaviour observed in the practical commercialisation path becomes more similarly behaved to the theoretical commercialisation path. By paying attention to the flow of the 'attention line', a four-stage process can be observed from the chart which is presented in Fig. 7.5.

By observing the behaviour of the 'attention line', it can be seen from the figure that there are four main stages in the whole commercialisation process. With 'attention line' lying on the strategic and resource level, the first stage is relationship building, where it focuses on building good relationships with the industrial companies and supporting organisations to facilitate the development of technology and product. The second stage is technology and product development stage. Most of the resources are required at this stage, which can be seen from the two boxes in the figure. At this stage, the attention is more focused on the product and knowledge level. The next stage is business strategy formation. At this stage, with the attention on the strategic level, business model is generated in consideration of the characteristics of the product and the management model. After this stage, it enters business growth and maintenance stage where products and technologies enter the market and profit is generated. Currently, the FOSA project is at the end of the second stage

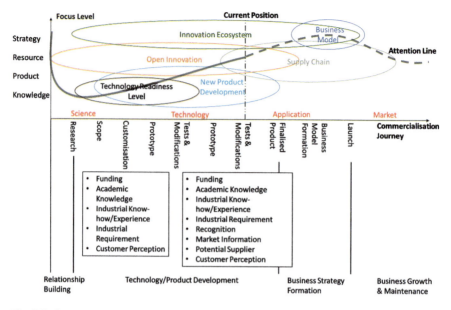

Fig. 7.5 Commercialisation process flow

(technology/product development) and the beginning of the third stage (business strategy formation). These stages help to determine the use of appropriate tools to support the commercialisation process.

7.5.5 Dissecting Commercialisation Process by Derived Four-Stage Process

With the aim of helping users to complete the commercialisation path, the whole journey is broken down into smaller tasks by applying the derived four-stage commercialisation process as shown in Table 7.4.

The table summarises the tasks at each stage of the process. In order to move on to the next stage of the process, the tasks at all attention levels in the previous stage need to be completed. When tasks in all stages are completed, commercialisation is then accomplished.

With the goal to assist users on the selection of the applicable tools to address each one of the tasks, Table 7.5 summarises the available tools in the literature to guide the users towards achieving every stage of the process.

These tools are summarised from the literature reviews and categorised using the four-stage commercialisation process derived from this work. The tools under each stage can be used to help the users accomplishing the tasks of the stage and then move on to the next stage of the four-stage process.

7 Commercialisation Journey in Business Ecosystem: From Academy to Market

Table 7.4 Tasks in commercialisation

| | Commercialisation stages | | | |
Attention level	Relationship establishment	Technology/product development	Business strategy formation	Business growth and adaptation
Strategy and business model management (strategy)	Trust formation	Forming strategic partnership with complimentors	Obtaining overall business strategy	Business model modifications
	Partnership building		Business model formation	
Resources and organisation (resource)	Knowledge sharing	External resources obtaining	Supply chain establishment	Value chain management
	Idea exchanging	Supplier selection		Industry formation
Product and services (product)	Scoping	New product development	Finalising product	Product launch
	Idea refining	Prototyping and testing		
Technology and science (knowledge)	Scientific research	Research and development	Obtaining matured technology	Further research and development
		Technology maturity testing		

Table 7.5 Tools for commercialisation

| | Commercialisation stages | | | |
Attention level	Relationship establishment	Technology/product development	Business strategy formation	Business growth and adaptation
Strategy and business model management (strategy)	Wide-lens view	Adoption chain	Six-question framework	
			Business model canvas	
Resources and organisation (resource)	Share-is-winning framework	Innovation strategy map	Supplier integration frameworks	Business ecosystem nurturing strategy
		Chess vs poker management process	New product ramp-up	
Product and services (product)		Stage-gate new product development process		
		S-T-A-M process		
Technology and science (knowledge)		Technology readiness levels		
		Technology readiness and acceptance model		

7.6 Discussion

The theoretical commercialisation path derived focuses on the view of established companies. Established companies usually hunt for new technologies that can be used in their design of the next-generation product. Through the approach stated in open innovation and innovation ecosystem, the established companies can obtain developed technologies very quickly and apply them in their new products. Therefore, from the academic point of view, the collaboration with external organisations can start slightly later, which is after the scope of the new product development has been determined.

However, the commercialisation journey of a research finding by a group of scientists is different. Coming from an academic background, the scientists have limited knowledge about the industry and the needs of the final customers. Therefore, in order to make sure that their research can be developed into a product that is meeting the industrial requirements and the needs of the customers, the scientists and researchers need to approach industrial companies and customers to obtain the necessary information. These communications enable the industry to become better informed about the scientists' ongoing research. This mutual understanding and working relationships help the scientists in the later part of the commercialisation journey. The industrial companies understand and know the technology/product that has been made in the research institute, and they save time in the due diligence process when they are trying to decide on whether to closely collaborate or purchase these technologies or products. A newly formed relationship is less favourable, as the companies need to spend a significant amount of time understanding the technology/product that has already been developed and there is a higher chance that it will not fit the industrial needs. Therefore, in order to ensure a successful commercialisation and reduce the risk as early as possible, the scientists need to start from a high level (i.e. the strategy and resource level) when they are trying to develop a new technology/product with a view of commercialising it eventually. It is worth noting at this point the iterative and resource-dependent nature of commercialisation, especially within an academic environment. There is a difference between what could be done and what is possible to do at each point of the process, with investment (time/attention as well as capital)-related progress being achieved.

In summary, the research suggests that there is importance in a collaborative path towards commercialisation for research, drawing upon the awareness and resources of the encompassing business ecosystem. Continuous communication with the industry and supporting organisations helps the scientists and researchers to obtain the resources needed. Through the continuous interactions and communications, the product can be developed meeting all the requirements of the industrial needs and ready to be deployed into the market with a suitable business model in place (Fig. 7.6).

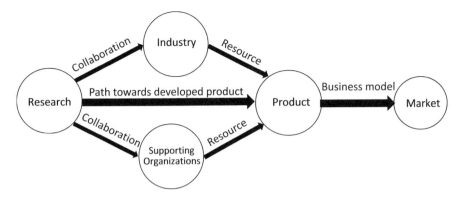

Fig. 7.6 Simplified commercialisation path highlighting collaboration

7.7 Conclusion

This work has identified and discussed the similarities and differences between theoretical and practical behaviours in the commercialisation journey. Although major similarities in behaviour have been identified, there is still a difference in the timing/order of doing things in practice compared to the perceived order derived from the literature. In practice, the scientists and researchers started with their attention on a high level where strategic alliances are formed and resources are obtained. Based on the specific case where a group of scientists and researchers are commercialising their research into a technology or product, a simplified roadmap has been developed to guide similar programmes in the future.

The key findings are as follows:

- Practical guidance on commercialisation of research is not readily accessible to entrepreneurial scientists although they welcome timely interventions from both academics and support agencies.
- The comparison between theoretical approaches to commercialisation based mainly on large companies and the practical behaviour found in one case study of commercialisation of academic research revealed differences in timing and behaviour.
- Continuous communication with industrial partners and supporting organisations from the very beginning is necessary to obtain useful information and resources to ensure the success of commercialisation.
- Awareness of the relevant business ecosystem could help to keep the commercialisation process dynamic and make available support networks more visible.

The research findings contribute to both academia and industry. For academia, this research recognised a wider commercialisation process as a relatively new body of knowledge which requires further attention. In addition, this work identified and integrated the relevant individual research fields of commercialisation process providing an overall view of commercialisation. This integration can also be used to enrich the interaction mechanism in the theory of business ecosystem. For industry, this research discusses the commercialisation process in a way that could be used as a discussion prompt to guide future commercialisation projects in research institutes and support the application of appropriate tools and techniques. Further research could include further case studies, with perhaps advanced materials, to explore the proposed commercialisation process in more depth and more focus on the role of enterprise support organisations and practical materials that they might find useful.

Acknowledgement The case study used is fibre optic sensor analyser as developed by the Cambridge Centre for Smart Infrastructure and Construction (CSIC) and pioneered by Professor Kenichi Soga and Professor Robert Mair.

References

Adner, R. (2012). *The wide lens – A new strategy for innovation*. London: Portfolio/Penguin.

Adner, R., & Kapoor, R. (2010). Value creation in innovation ecosystems: How the structure of technological interdependence affects firm performance in new technology generations. *Strategic Management Journal, 31*(3), 306–333.

Chesbrough, H., & Rosenbloom, R. S. (2002). The role of the business model in capturing value from innovation: Evidence from Xerox Corporation's technology spin-off companies. *Industrial and Corporate Change, 11*(3), 529–555.

Cooper R. (2006). Winning at new products: Pathways to profitable innovation – What are the keys to success in product innovation. Proceedings of 2006 project management, pp.1–19. And at http://www.five-is.com/wp-content/uploads/2013/12/Cooper_2005_Pathways_to_Profitable_Innovation.pdf

Fraser, P., Farrukh, C., & Gregory, M. (2003). Managing product development collaborations: A process maturity approach. *Proceedings of the Institution of Mechanical Engineers Part B: Journal of Engineering Manufacture, 217*(11), 1499–1519.

Huang, Z. (2015). Commercialisation journey in business ecosystem: From academy to market, ISMM MPhil Dissertation, University of Cambridge.

Lin, C., Shih, H., & Sher, P. J. (2007). Integrating technology readiness into technology acceptance: The TRAM model. *Psychology and Marketing, 24*(7), 641–657.

Mankins, J. C. (2009). Technology readiness assessments: A retrospective. *Acta Astronautica, 65*(9–10), 1216–1223.

Moore, J. F. (1993). Predators and prey – A new ecology of competition. *Harvard Business Review, 71.*, May–June, 75–86.

Morris, M., Schindehutte, M., & Allen, J. (2005). The entrepreneur's business model: Toward a unified perspective. *Journal of Business Research, 58*(6), 726–735.

Petersen, K. J., et al. (1999). Involving suppliers in new product development. *California Management Review, 42*(1), 59–82.

Phaal, R., et al. (2011). A framework for mapping industrial emergence. *Technological Forecasting and Social Change, 78*(2), 217–230.

Shang, T., & Shi, Y. (2013). Nurturing emerging industries through business ecosystems: The evolutionary processes and key building blocks. IfM CIM 2013 Symposium_Proceedings

Shi, B. (2014). Development of fibre optic sensor analyser in Civil and Construction Industry, ISSM MPhil Dissertation, University of Cambridge.

Traitler, H., Watzke, H. J., & Saguy, I. S. (2011). Reinventing R&D in an open innovation ecosystem. *Journal of Food Science, 76*(2), 62–68.

Wang, P. (2009). Advancing the study of innovation and globalization in organizations. Advancing the study of innovation and globalization in organizations, pp. 301–314.

Yin, R. K. (2002). *Case study research: Design and methods*. Thousand Oaks: Sage.

Part II
Benchmarking Cases

Chapter 8
Creating a Supportive Entrepreneurial Ecosystem for Street Vendors: The Case of the National Association of Street Vendors of India (NASVI)

Ranjini Swamy and Arbind Singh

Abstract Like many other emerging economies, India has made steady progress towards social and economic development since liberalization. However, poverty and inequality continue to be critical social challenges, driving the poor to seek employment in the informal sector. A significant proportion of the working age population is employed in the informal sector as street vendors or informal entrepreneurs. In the early years after liberalization, street vendors lacked legal and social status and therefore were unable to protect themselves from the harassment by authorities. They could not access critical resources like credit and training. As a result, they remained poor while the rich benefitted from the liberalized regime.

The National Association of Street Vendors of India (NASVI) emerged as a response to the street vendors' predicament. Through tireless advocacy, it helped create a better entrepreneurial ecosystem for street vendors and thereby improve their quality of life. This paper will describe what NASVI did to build an entrepreneurial ecosystem and the outcomes of its initiatives so far. It will conclude with some ideas about how the entrepreneurial ecosystem for street vendors could become sustainable.

Keywords Street vendors • NASVI • Informal entrepreneurs • Informal sector

---

The first author is grateful to Mr. Arbind Singh and Ms. Sonal Sinha of the National Association of Street Vendors of India (NASVI), New Delhi, India for their support and for sharing data for writing the case.

R. Swamy (✉)
Goa Institute of Management, Sanquelim Campus, Poriem, Goa, India
e-mail: ranjini@gim.ac.in

A. Singh
National Association of Street Vendors of India, New Delhi, India
e-mail: singharbind@hotmail.com

© Springer International Publishing AG 2018
J. Leitão et al. (eds.), *Entrepreneurial, Innovative and Sustainable Ecosystems*, Applying Quality of Life Research,
https://doi.org/10.1007/978-3-319-71014-3_8

8.1 Introduction

Like many other emerging economies, India has made steady progress towards economic and social development since liberalization. However, balancing the goals of economic growth on the one hand and full employment on the other has been challenging. Economic reforms were characterized by privatization, deregulation and the rapid substitution of labour with capital. Thus, while output (GDP growth) accelerated substantially since the 1990s, employment growth in the formal economy has been low. As a result, more than 75% of the working population in India continue to be employed in the informal economy. The trend is echoed in other developing regions like sub-Saharan Africa and other parts of Asia (Kannan and Papola 2007). However, the proportion of India's working age population employed in the informal economy is slightly higher than the proportion of the global working population working in the informal economy (Jutting and de Laiglesia 2009).

The informal economy is "…characterized by (a) ease of entry; (b) reliance on indigenous resources; (c) family ownership; (d) small scale operations; (e) labour intensive and adaptive technology; (e) skills acquired outside of the formal sector; (g) unregulated and competitive markets" (International Labour Organization 1972). In India, the informal (or *unorganized*) economy includes all unincorporated private enterprises owned by individuals or households that (a) engage in the sale and production of goods/services, (b) operate on a proprietary or partnership basis and (c) have less than ten workers.

Table 8.1 details the employment patterns in India's formal and informal economy during three periods after liberalization. Informal employment includes all employment in the informal (unorganized) economy and employment *without social protection* in the formal economy. Clearly, the informal employment as a percent of total employment has remained relatively stable across time. It continues to be significantly higher than formal employment two decades after liberalization. While employment in the formal economy has increased, the increase has largely been in informal employment (characterized by lack of job- and social- security).

Table 8.1 Formal and informal employment as percent of total employment during three time periods: 1999–2000, 2004–2005, 2011–2012

Sector of economy	1999–2000[a]	2004–2005[b]	2011–2012[b]
Formal economy			
Formal employment		6.98%	7.84%
Informal employment (no social security/job security)		6.43%	9.43%
Percent of total employment	8.8%	13.41%	17.27%
Informal economy			
Percent of total employment	91.17%	86.59%	82.72%

[a]Source: National Commission for Enterprises in the Unorganised Sector (NCEUS) (2008)
[b]Source: Srija and Shirke (2014) An analysis of the informal labour market in India. http://www.ies.gov.in/pdfs/CII%20EM-october-2014.pdf.

8 Creating a Supportive Entrepreneurial Ecosystem for Street Vendors: The Case... 153

Table 8.2 Informal employment in the non-agricultural sector across two periods: 2004–2005 and 2011–2012

Non-agricultural sectors	Employment millions (2004–2005)	% informal employment in the sector (2004–2005)	Employment millions (2011–2012)	% informal employment in the sector (2011–2012)
Manufacturing	47.92 mill	79.8%	52.49 mill	74%
Trade, hotels, restaurants	46.02 mill	96%	50.17 mill	94.8%
Construction	24.9 mill	77.5%	48.92 mill	67%
Transport/storage	14.66 mill	90.1%	18.02 mill	87%
Total working population in non-agriculture sector	160.83 million		204.03 million	

Source: Adapted from Srija and Shirke (2014). An analysis of the informal labour market in India. http://www.ies.gov.in/pdfs/CII%20EM-october-2014.pdf.

In India, informal employment appears to be more prevalent in agriculture (99% informal employment), manufacturing, trade, construction, and transport/storage. Together these sectors of the economy employ about 83% of the working age population. Table 8.2 details the percent of formal and informal employment in non-agricultural sectors of the economy across two periods. Trade, hotels and restaurants and transport/storage appear to have higher informal employment than manufacturing and construction.

Employment in India's informal economy is risky and non-remunerative for the poor. At least two sets of factors contribute to this situation: (a) at the enterprise level, the lack of legal recognition for informal enterprises and the restricted access to operating permits, credit, training and spaces to transact business; (b) at the worker level, the lack of social protection mechanisms and secure employment relationships. The first set of factors deters entrepreneurial activity among the poor in the informal sector. The second set of factors deters productive employment among the poor in the informal sector. Together, they conspire to keep down the livelihoods of informal workers.

As a result, inequality and poverty continued to be social challenges despite rapid economic growth. The National Sample Survey data for the period 1993–1994 and 1999–2000 suggest that following liberalization, inequality increased both in rural and urban India. Income disparities between the rural and urban sectors increased during this period (Pal and Ghosh 2007). In 2007, about three-quarters of the Indian population lived with a per capita expenditure of less than US$2 per day (in terms of purchasing power parity). *Seventy-nine percent of informal workers were among those living on less than US $2 per day* (NCEUS 2007).

Economic development that promotes the rights of a few people at the cost of the rights of the majority is not sustainable. Ideally, all citizens must have access to a progressively better quality of life. Given the proportion employed in the informal economy, this is more likely when economic development is accompanied by entrepreneurship[1] and better working conditions in the informal economy. According to the literature on "entrepreneurial ecosystems", entrepreneurship takes place in a social context comprising interdependent actors. This context could facilitate or impede entrepreneurship (Stam 2015). Policy makers can facilitate informal entrepreneurship by formulating and implementing supportive policies (Kannan and Papola 2007).

This paper will describe the role played by National Association of Street Vendors in India (NASVI) in developing a supportive entrepreneurial ecosystem for street vendors or informal entrepreneurs. The first section details the profile of street vendors, what they do and the challenges they face. The second section presents the formation of NASVI to address their challenges. The third section details the steps NASVI took to build a supportive ecosystem for street vendors and some of the critical challenges it faced. The fourth section explores some of the outcomes of NASVI's interventions for improving the ecosystem of street vendors. The last section reviews NASVI's initiatives and suggests some steps that NASVI could take to sustain a supportive entrepreneurial ecosystem for street vendors.

8.2 The Profile of Street Vendors

Street vendors are *self-employed workers or informal entrepreneurs*[2] who produce/sell perishable and non-perishable products from a temporary static structure or a mobile stall (Government of India 2004). They constitute about 45% of the informal workers in India. In the years before liberalization and shortly thereafter, poor people were driven by poverty and the lack of education/skills to become street vendors. The low entry barriers – for instance, modest financial and skill requirements- made street vending an attractive occupational choice for them (Bhatt 2006). Most street vendors in India tended to be males with low literacy who belonged to scheduled castes, scheduled tribes or other backward classes. Often the whole family was engaged in street vending. For instance, in case of production of perishable products like snacks, the wife prepared the snacks, the husband looked after the customers and the children washed the utensils. The street vendors walked 10–12 km every day to practise their trade. They worked between 10 and 12 h per day, with little or no access to institutional credit, crèches or toilets. Daily earnings for male street vendors ranged between Rs 50 and 100 (Bhowmik 2001).

---

[1] Entrepreneurship is a process in which opportunities for creating new goods and services are explored, evaluated and exploited. Source: Shane, S and Venkataraman, S (2000). 'The promise of entrepreneurship as a field of research'. *Academy of Management Review*, volume 25, issue 1, pp. 217–226. doi:https://doi.org/10.5465/AMR.2000.2791611

[2] Informal entrepreneurs are people who are actively involved in starting a business or who are owners/managers of a business and engage in monetary transactions that are legal but not declared to the state for tax and/or benefit purposes. They could be mobile or operate from a specific location.

8 Creating a Supportive Entrepreneurial Ecosystem for Street Vendors: The Case... 155

Street vendors needed a supportive entrepreneurial ecosystem to operate commercially. They needed supportive relationships with stakeholders to obtain the following critical resources: (a) legal status, acknowledging their right to trade; (b) a license from the relevant authorities permitting them to trade at a natural market; (c) working capital for investing in consumables (including raw materials/finished goods or services); (d) specific vending zones with access to water, electricity and other facilities in areas where they traded; (e) markets; (f) knowledge of regulations such as food safety standards or waste management policies; (g) skills to improve efficiencies, access markets and enhance earnings and (h) social legitimacy.

However, a supportive entrepreneurial ecosystem did not exist. No national law or policy gave street vendors legal status. Lacking legitimacy, they were often seen as "outsiders," "illegal operators," and "encroachers" both by the public as well as the authorities. In some states, the laws treated street vending as a public nuisance, much like the slaughtering of animals. Police officers could arrest the street vendors without a warrant and fine them (Sundaram 2008). Given the general hostility towards street vendors, many urban bodies did not develop specific vending zones for them. Some urban bodies even stopped issuing vending licenses to them. (The Mumbai municipality for instance had stopped issuing vending licenses since 1978). As a result, vendors experiencing harassment by local authorities could neither protest nor request for better facilities (Bhatt 2006). They had to bribe implementing authorities to continue their trade. Street vendors in Delhi alone annually paid Rs 600 crores[3] as bribes to the authorities (Economic and Political Weekly Editorial 2007). Despite this, they were subject to surprise demolition drives that created much uncertainty, stress and loss of income (Anjaria 2006).

Access to critical resources like credit and knowledge/skills remained a challenge. Street vendors largely obtained credit at very high (up to 110%), non-standard interest rates from moneylenders (Bhowmik 2001). This pushed them further into debt, significantly limited their growth and increased their vulnerability (Anjaria 2006). Illiteracy and lack of organization prevented access to knowledge and skills required to practise their trade. Women entrepreneurs additionally faced dangerous working conditions and gendered violence which compromised their safety and health. They were confined to traditional roles such as selling flowers at the temple or selling fruits. They operated from places close to their homes to balance vending with taking care of their children (Bhatt 2006). These constraints affected their productivity and livelihood. Women street vendors earned minimal amount despite long hours of work (Bhowmik 2001). The lack of alternate employment was a significant concern to all street vendors. They wanted formal training and support to improve their work prospects.

Worker-led Trade Unions in India did not pay much attention to informal workers or entrepreneurs (Venkata Ratnam 1999). This could be because these unions were preoccupied with the demands of workers in the formal economy or because informal workers/entrepreneurs were too poor to invest resources for unionization (Bonner and Spooner 2011). However, some NGO-led unions -such as the *Shetkari*

---

[3]A US $= Rs 64.31 as of June 05, 2017.

Mazdoor Sanghatan for farmers, and *Self-Employed Women's Association (SEWA)* for women craft workers – emerged to fill the gap (Kapoor 2007). These unions addressed the rights of informal workers (in specific occupations) to social security and to "decent work". There was no such national organization for street vendors, partly because they were very dispersed and disparate. In some cities, street vendors therefore organized themselves into small, local associations to protect their interests and collectively address common challenges. However, their small numbers, lack of legitimacy, poor awareness of their rights and responsibilities and low bargaining power made it difficult to obtain collective benefits. They needed an organization with a national presence to bring in a supportive entrepreneurial ecosystem.

8.3 The Formation of NASVI

The National Alliance of Street Vendors of India was born in 1998 to (a) represent the interests of street vendors to policy makers at the national level; (b) coordinate across various national and state-level agencies for a transformative change in the street vendors' ecosystem. The Alliance emerged as an independent but loose network of various informal street vendors' groups across the country. It surveyed street vendors across several cities to understand and document their challenges. The surveys highlighted some of the common challenges faced by street vendors across India such as the low legitimacy among various stakeholders (such as police, citizens' associations and judiciary), non-issuance of licenses by municipal bodies, and the presence of mafia-dominated 'tax' collection. Additionally, the implementation of the Police Act in many states led to arrests (*without a warrant*) and imposition of fines on street vendors for causing 'inconvenience' to the public.

Alliance members realized that supportive national policies and legislations required the cooperation of the Department of Urban Poverty Alleviation in the Ministry of Urban Development. Their initial interactions with the concerned Minister- often called "the bull-dozer man"- were characterized by fear and suspicion. Eventually the interactions helped promote a deeper understanding of the plight of street vendors and an appreciation of their need for government support. In 2001–2002, the Ministry of Urban Development joined hands with Self Employed Women's Association (SEWA) and the Alliance of Street Vendors to organize a national workshop on street vendors. During the workshop, the Ministry announced the setting up of a National Task Force to draft a National Policy on Street Vending (Bhowmik 2010).

As more vendors became members of the Alliance, there was need to transit from a loose network of street vendor groups to a more organized set-up. Typically, such loose networks were captured by a few promoters, lacked democratic decision-making, and allegedly had financial irregularities. In 2002, the Alliance members and its stakeholders explored the formation of a trade union for street vendors. However, this was rejected for several reasons: one, several trade unions were already part of their network and forming another could be viewed as a competition to them; two, mere protest demonstrations and court orders were not likely to provide a long term solution to the challenges faced by the street vendors (Bhowmik 2001).

They decided to form a membership-based organization called the National Association of Street Vendors of India (NASVI). NASVI was formally registered as an Association in 2003 under the Societies Registration Act, 1860. It was an advocacy-oriented organization aimed at providing a supportive entrepreneurial ecosystem for street vendors in India. It focussed on workplace, employment and livelihood issues of India's street vendors. Membership was open to professionals and to trade unions, community based organizations and NGOs that worked with street vendors. An Executive Committee -with representatives of street vendors (including women street vendors) – managed the Association. Members of the Association elected the Committee every 3 years.

Rather fittingly, the first elected President of the Association was Mr. Sodhan Singh, a street vendor who had approached the Supreme Court to declare that street vending was a fundamental right under the Constitution of India. Among NASVI's first activities was the organization of general body meetings across India, wherein members interacted with stakeholders to discuss wide-ranging issues of relevance to street vendors. As local groups of street vendors realized the potential of the NASVI, more became members of the Association and participated in developing its agenda.

In 2004, the Government of India set up the National Commission for Enterprises in the Unorganized Sector (NCEUS), to promote faster growth of and better working conditions in the informal enterprises. The NCEUS drafted a policy and a model law to protect the rights of street vendors, based on inputs from street vendors' associations, several state governments, government departments, municipal bodies, unions and academics. Based on studies of the informal economy, the NCEUS also recommended various legislative and policy interventions to improve the working conditions in informal enterprises (Kapoor 2007). However, more was needed, given the disparate types of workers and employment in the informal economy.

8.4 Building the Entrepreneurial Ecosystem for Street Vendors

The formation of NASVI gave street vendors the strength to demand legal and social status. Several of the most experienced and vocal street vendors went to Delhi and participated in an indefinite hunger strike to press for supportive legislations. Thousands of street vendors across India demonstrated their support. On several occasions, street vendors stood outside a political leader's house or outside a police station, to voice their opinions. In Mumbai, Lucknow and other cities, they waged a battle against the harassment by the municipal and police authorities. NGOS like Nidan -an NGO that worked with self-help groups in Bihar state-worked behind the scenes to feed information to NASVI, draw media attention to protests and incidents, and arrange strategic meetings with political leaders on the street vendors' agenda.

In response, the national government created some support systems for the street vendors through the Micro, Small and Medium Enterprises Development Act, 2006. The Act provided informal enterprises with opportunities for skill- and technology-upgradation, marketing assistance, infrastructure facilities, and stronger backward and forward linkages. It also provided for the timely and smooth flow of credit, thus enhancing competitiveness of the informal enterprises. However, subsequent surveys suggested that the potential benefits had not reached the street vendors.

In 2009, the NCEUS proposed a separate national policy and legislation to govern street vendors. By 2014, the Parliament of India i.e., the Lok Sabha and Rajya Sabha,[4] adopted the National Policy for Urban Street Vendors and passed The Street Vendors (Protection of Livelihood and Regulation of Street Vending) Act. Broadly, the policy and the Act acknowledged the right of street vendors to equal protection before the law and to practice their trade in a responsible manner. The objective of the National Policy was to provide street vendors with a supportive environment for earning livelihoods while ensuring the absence of congestion and maintenance of hygiene in public spaces and streets. See Annexure 1 for details of the main features of the Policy. The Act recognized and protected the right of street vendors to practice their trade, regulated their behavior and provided a uniform legal framework for street vendors across the country (Mathur 2014). The main provisions of the Act are detailed in Annexure 2.

The new policies and legislations held the states responsible for formulation of supportive state legislations and for implementation of the Act. State policies and legislations also needed to give street vendors legal status and protect their right to trade on street pavements, public places and lands belonging to the government. They needed to provide street vendors with access to services like credit, housing, social security and capacity building so that income inequalities could be reduced and all citizens had the right to adequate means of livelihood. In addition, all city municipal corporations within the state had to create City/town master plans that identified vending zones and provided for new street vending markets. They had to constitute Town Vending Committees (TVCs) –comprising the municipal commissioner and representatives of local planning authorities, residents' associations and street vendors[5]- to help plan, organize and regulate street vending activities. The Committees would specify the number of vendors in each zone, issue vending certificates[6] and identity cards to vendors, maintain updated records of registered street vendors, survey the street vendors once in 5 years and regulate their activities. They

---

[4] Members of Lok Sabha are directly elected by the eligible voters. Members of Rajya Sabha are elected by the elected members of State Legislative Assemblies in accordance with the system of proportional representation by means of single transferable vote.

[5] Street vendors were to constitute about 40% of the members. They would be elected among themselves. Other members of the committee would be government nominees.

[6] The certificate would specify the category of vending, the vending zone, when the vendor can practise his trade.

would give preference to vendors who were from the vulnerable sections[7] of society (Mathur 2014). Decisions taken in the Committee had to be participatory and involve the stakeholders in decisions. Some states such as Orissa, adopted policies and legislations supportive of street vendors.

Instituting such supportive policies and legislations was an important first step. Implementing these legislations across states required the support of local implementing authorities such as municipal bodies, local politicians and bureaucrats, police personnel and the judiciary. NASVI organized several meetings with political and social leaders to create awareness about the plight of street vendors and the need to apply the new policies and legislation. However, implementation continued to be a problem due to the following reasons:

First, there were differences in the provisions of the national and state laws with respect to street vendors. While the national Act overrode the state and municipal laws on Street Vending, the differences were bound to create confusion among the implementing agencies (Economic and Political Weekly Editorial 2014). This could potentially increase the harassment of street vendors.

Second, there were discrepancies between the National Policy and the Act. For instance, the National policy provided for registering existing street vendors *before registering new vendors* in a vending zone while the Act did not reinforce this provision. The National policy suggested that eviction of vendors should be the last resort and those evicted should be provided with alternate vending sites, while the Act did not mention this (Bhowmik 2010). Such discrepancies could again cause confusion among the implementing authorities and increase the harassment of street vendors.

Third, in many states, local stakeholders were yet to accommodate the concerns of street vendors. Street vendors were either not included in the Town Vending Committees (TVCs) or were not consulted as members. Contracts for utilization of public spaces and infrastructure did not take cognizance of street vendors' interests. There was a significant chance that powerful interests in the TVCs could capture and influence decisions on whom to certify as a street vendor and on what vending zone to allot. These powerful people could seek a 'rent' from vendors wanting a certificate or allotment to a vending zone. Paying off such 'rents' could potentially reduce the net earnings of the street vendors.

NASVI took up these issues with the national and state governments. At the national level, NASVI worked with the Attorney General of India and the Ministry of Housing & Urban Poverty Alleviation to help implement the law across the country and thereby ensure legal status to the vendors. It offered members legal aid to address problems of police harassment, eviction and the non-issuance of identity cards.

NASVI worked with the state governments to set up Town Vending Committees, ensure representation of street vendors in these committees and address operational

---

[7] Vulnerable sections include Scheduled Castes and Tribes, women, people with disabilities and minorities.

challenges. In some states, very few of the stipulated Town Vending Committees were set up. In others, the TVCs did not have the mandated proportion of street vendors in the Committees. In yet others, some listed members were fake. NASVI ensured that street vendors were represented in many Town Vending Committees (TVCs).

Within the TVCs, street vendors had to navigate strong opposition from and biases among other stakeholders. Street vendors were believed to be a nuisance to society (Anjaria 2006). Therefore, representatives of residents' associations and business associations opposed the creation of vending zones in towns. NASVI helped street vendors navigate such opposition. It assisted some TVCs in fee collection from street vendors and ensured that street vendors minimized inconveniences to the public.

When councillors in some TVCs attempted to provide street vending licenses to their relatives or friends and not to other strong contenders, NASVI ensured that these decisions were made in public meetings. Each vendor was identified and his credentials verified through collective consensus.

Once vending zones were identified and licenses awarded appropriate infrastructure such as toilets and kiosks had to be planned at these zones. NASVI worked with business enterprises in some states such as Orissa, to create the necessary infrastructure at street vending zones. Many local businesses funded the infrastructure development. Some vendors tried to secure additional kiosks for their non-eligible kith and kin. NASVI announced a "no-tolerance" policy towards such actions and adopted a democratic and transparent decision-making process for allotment of kiosks.

To improve street vendors' access to credit at more reasonable interest rates, NASVI sought the support of several public and private financial institutions. The financial institutions recommended that street vendors opened bank accounts for the purpose. They insisted that street vendors provided identity proof, permanent address proof and a guarantor's consent to open the bank accounts. Migrant street vendors often did not have such supporting documents and therefore found it difficult to open accounts. Even those who opened accounts found it difficult to access credit because the financial institutions believed that street vendors would not repay the loans. NASVI organized several workshops to promote a better understanding between representatives of financial institutions and street vendors. However, it became clear that public and private financial institutions were unable or unwilling to address the concerns of street vendors.

NASVI decided to offer street vendors membership in the Sanchay Thrift and Credit Cooperative Society. This was a member-owned cooperative started by NASVI and Nidan in 2001 to meet the financial requirements of informal workers (Registrar of Cooperative Societies 2014).

The Cooperative aimed to improve the social and economic well-being of its members through provision of social security, financial assistance and education. Members could save, deposit money and take loans to meet working capital or family needs. Field agents of the Cooperative visited the members daily, collected money for depositing and issued a receipt for the amount taken. Members earned 4% interest on their deposits and could avail loans between Rs 5000 and Rs 75,000 at 18% rate of interest.

8   Creating a Supportive Entrepreneurial Ecosystem for Street Vendors: The Case...

Accessing appropriate markets was also a challenge for street vendors, given their lack of knowledge and limited means. They adopted an impulsive, unplanned approach to accessing markets – for example, preferring markets that were closer to their homes. NASVI formed local market-committees comprising street vendors, to identify and address market and other local challenges. The market committees met once a month to discuss problems and find solutions. Representatives of the market committees were elected to form a Town Level Federation to share experiences and explore how to improve livelihoods. Some members from the Town Level Federations were elected to form a State Level Federation of Street Vendors. As of 2016, the state level federations of street vendors were formed in 42 of the 3600 urban level bodies in India (Chaubey 2003). The State Level Federations represented the interests of the street vendors to state authorities. NASVI helped formally register the Federations with the state's Cooperative Department, to help establish their legitimacy for negotiating with the state governments.

Following public concerns about hygiene, NASVI provided street vendors with training in areas related to street vending. NASVI partnered with Institutes of Hotel Management to help street vendors adopt safe and hygienic practices in compliance with the laws. It worked with the National Urban Livelihoods Mission (NULM)[8] to provide street vendors and their families with opportunities to learn various occupations such as beautician, drivers and computer operation.

In the course of interacting with various stakeholders, NASVI observed that many policy makers and representatives of civil society still saw street vendors as a problem rather than as vital service providers. The lack of social legitimacy was adversely affecting the demand for their services. In 2010, the organization initiated a "Street Food Festival" at Delhi, offering an opportunity for all residents to enjoy safe street foods, and understand the vendors' legitimate contributions to the city's fabric. More than 50,000 people attended the 3-day event. Customers paid an entry fee of Rs. 60[9] and a premium for the street food they ate at the Festival. The vendors earned more in the Street Food Festival than they did in months. These street festivals became an important cultural event of Delhi. The local government and business supported these events.

In 2013, the Association started a new company called NASVI Street Food Private Ltd. to enlarge street food business across India. Street food vendors became shareholders of the company. The company planned to expand Street Food Festival to other states/cities of India (i.e., Srinagar, Jaipur and Bangalore and Mumbai). It is exploring the possibility of hiring spaces in Malls and setting up food joints and food streets. NASVI members planned to participate in the International Food Festivals at Islamabad and Manila in 2017. It was expected that many street vendors in urban India would benefit from the more formal business models being created. In this way, the Association has helped and continues to help build a supportive entrepreneurial ecosystem for street vendors across India.

---

[8] The NULM is a Government of India initiative set up to (among other things) facilitate street vendors' access to suitable vending spaces, institutional credit, social security and skills.

[9] One dollar= INR 64.44.

8.5 Outcomes

NASVI aimed to provide urban street vendors with a supportive entrepreneurial eco-system and thereby improve their quality of life.[10] Research on Quality of Life suggests that it has two components: (a) the subjective experience of satisfaction on the work, family, community and personal fronts (b) the objective experience of accessing external objects/resources valuable to an individual and measurable by 'others' (Paraskevi 2013). There has been no national survey of street vendors in India to study their perception of the quality of their life. A recent survey of street vendors in Bhubaneswar, Orissa, (Kumar 2012) found that street vendors reported less harassment, greater legitimacy and a more conducive environment for practising their trade in vending zones. There is need for more systematic studies across the country on street vendors' perceptions of the quality of their lives. However, several objective indicators suggest that street vendors have more access to critical resources, especially in states with progressive laws for street vendors. These could be indicative of improved quality of life. Some of these objective indicators are described below:

However, despite these apparent improvements, challenges remain. Street vendors who have not been accommodated in vending zones in the more vendor-friendly states and those operating in less vendor-friendly states continue to face harassment, poor working conditions and demands for bribe. Relationships with local implementing authorities, residents' associations and business associations continue to be challenging in several parts of the country. The lack of vending sites in the proposed Smart Cities has also increased the uncertainty for street vendors about their future. Some are acquiring skills for other occupations (e.g., beautician) to transit to the formal sector. Whatever the choice, the struggle to participate in the economy with dignity continues.

8.5.1 Greater Legitimacy Established

NASVI's sustained advocacy has provided street vendors with the much needed legal status. The new policies and legislations recognize street vending as a legitimate activity and acknowledge the right of street vendors to practice their trade responsibly. They mandate the setting up of Town Vending Committees across States and the inclusion of street vendors in these Committees. Street vendors thus have an opportunity to participate in the Committees and influence town planning, especially the creation of vending zones.

By 2016, the Town Vending Committees in 42 (out of about 3600) urban level bodies became operational. More than a hundred women street vendors became members of these Committees. About 300 vending zones were proposed by these Committees and 40 of them were approved by the urban level bodies.

---

[10] Data for this section was supplied largely by NASVI office bearers.

8 Creating a Supportive Entrepreneurial Ecosystem for Street Vendors: The Case... 163

In Bhubaneswar, Orissa, these developments have allowed street vendors to operate from a fixed place in the city's vending zones. As a result, the public's trust in street vendors improved. NASVI was able to collect an annual fee from the street vendors on behalf of the municipality and ensure that street vendors met their commitments to various stakeholders. The municipal bodies therefore became more trustful of the vendors. The success of the Bhubaneswar model has evoked curiosity among municipalities of other states like Andhra Pradesh, Maharashtra, Bihar and West Bengal. Many of their office bearers have visited Bhubaneswar to understand the model (Kumar 2012).

With NASVI's legal advice and guidance, street vendors are now asserting their rights. They are approaching the courts for relief from eviction orders by local authorities. Many have stopped paying an illegal tax to local contractors and thereby improved their daily net earnings.

8.5.2   Enhanced Access to Credit

Following the formation of the Sanchay Thrift and Credit Cooperative Society, Street vendors in some states can deposit savings and access credit at more reasonable interest rates through membership in the Sanchay Thrift and Credit Cooperative Society. The cooperative is presently operational in three districts of Bihar state – Patna (the capital), Vaishali and Muzaffarpur only. Annexure 3 give details of the membership growth, deposits and loan amount availed since the inception of the Cooperative Society. The Annexure indicates that the membership of individuals (including street vendors) in the Cooperative has increased across years. However, the rate of membership growth has decreased in the period 2010–2016. While the total deposits received by the Cooperative have been growing unevenly across time, the amount deposited in the period 2010–2016 has grown annually by about 53% on average. Similarly, while the total loan amount disbursed to members has grown unevenly across time, the amount disbursed annually during the period 2010–2016 has grown by about 29% on average. Though the exact figures are not available, at least some part of the aggregate growth in deposits and loans could be attributed to the savings and investments made by street vendors. The data suggests that the Cooperative could be meeting a felt need of the street vendors. As of 2016, NASVI helped about 38,500 vendors access banking services, government insurance- and pension-schemes through the Cooperative.

8.5.3   Enhanced Access to Training

The Cooperative has helped train street vendors in food safety regulations, to ensure hygiene and safety of their offerings. It also helped street vendors learn new occupations. Between 2011 and 2016, about 8875 street vendors and their family members received skills training. About 940 street vendors from different urban bodies were trained to be computer operators, drivers, beauticians and so on. About 288 street vendors received training in food safety at the Institutes of Hotel Management (Sonal Sinha 2017, pers. comm.). It is however, not clear whether and how such training has improved the livelihood and effectiveness/innovativeness of street vendors.

8.5.4 Better Knowledge of and Access to Markets

Street vendors learnt about customer expectations through their experiences at the street food festivals. They saw that the public was willing to pay well for safe and good quality food. They were motivated to acquire knowledge and information about the street vending business, customer expectations, food safety standards and the regulatory context. NASVI's move to create a separate company to promote street food offers street vendors opportunities to widen their markets. Participation in street food festivals has apparently resulted in more earnings. The movement into the formal sector - through malls and other formal retail or entertainment spaces- also offers an opportunity to improve their livelihoods.

Street vendors in many states have greater opportunities to improve their earnings. They have begun to use their strength in numbers to protect and promote their interests. In Bihar for instance, over 100,000 street vendors and their family members offered to vote enbloc for an aspiring mainstream political party provided the party fielded a candidate who had fought tirelessly for their cause (Dey 2014).

8.6 Discussion and Review

NASVI has succeeded in providing street vendors with a more supportive entrepreneurial ecosystem by first mobilizing street vendors across India under a common umbrella organization, understanding their concerns and articulating these to policy makers. Its tireless advocacy with political parties, judiciary and other government functionaries helped in the formulation and improved implementation of national and state-level regulatory framework for street vendors. Partnerships with other non-government organizations like Nidan, and with various government agencies helped street vendors access financial products/services and markets. Their partnership with academic institutes such as Institutes of Hotel Management helped street vendors access the knowledge and skills required to practice responsible vending. Continuous interaction and trust-building activities with municipal authorities and residents' welfare associations helped establish a more cooperative environment and greater social legitimacy.

NASVI faced many challenges in persuading the government and financial institutions to support street vendors. Many government functionaries were not aware of the predicament of street vendors. Others in the TVCs saw street vendors as "nuisances" or "outsiders" and treated them accordingly. They often favored the interests of "insiders" like relatives over "outsiders" like migrant/minority street vendors even though the latter were more qualified. Changing the perceptions and norms of the various stakeholders required much time and effort. This could explain why only 13 of the 29 states established supportive legislation and only 42 of the over 3600 urban level bodies implemented Town Vending Committees.

Sustaining the entrepreneurial ecosystem for street vendors requires building two independent but related subsystems: (a) the research economy, whose purpose is to produce new knowledge; (b) the commercial economy whose purpose is to transform knowledge into commercially viable products, processes and management practices.

NASVI has concentrated more on building the commercial economy, so that street vendors could improve their income and quality of life as soon as possible. It has developed strong partnerships with some NGOs, the national government and the governments of some states to ensure legitimacy and access to valued resources. However, NASVI needs to scale up its efforts to improve the ecosystem of street vendors across all states. This may require expansion and/or working through partnerships, besides access to more resources. Large business enterprises could potentially support this effort through their Corporate Social Responsibility (CSR) departments or Foundations. First, large businesses could provide street vendors with training in entrepreneurship and subsequently mentor them, to enhance the chances of their success. In some cases, these trained entrepreneurs could be absorbed into the distribution networks of businesses, to enhance the reach of business into new market segments and simultaneously improve the livelihood of street vendors. Second, large businesses could enable the development of supportive infrastructure –such as dustbins, kiosks and toilets- across the country so that street vendors can improve the quality and hygiene of street-food.

NASVI has built knowledge about its stakeholders that was useful in the formulation of supportive policies and legislations. However, there is need for new knowledge to scale up the efforts and to help street vendors transit into new markets. NASVI has to establish stronger partnerships with financial institutions and academic institutions to build the research economy. Some of the potential areas of collaboration are as follows:

Partnerships with financial institutions. NASVI has helped about 38,500 of the ten million street vendors in India access banking and insurance services. Clearly, there are immense opportunities for financial institutions to address the credit and insurance requirements of street vendors. They could collaborate with NASVI to develop a greater variety of customized financial products and services –such as health insurance, microfinance- for street vendors. They could develop innovative business models that (a) permit street vendors easy access to these financial products/services and (b) assure financial institutions of reasonable profits. They could organize programs to (a) inform street vendors about the banks' products and services and about how to access them, (b) instill credit discipline and where possible (c) help them switch to cashless transactions for greater flexibility.

Partnerships with educational institutions. Educational institutions can develop and disseminate knowledge/skills that could be useful for street vendors to maintain or expand their business. For instance, colleges (in partnership with civil society) can improve the street vendors' proficiency in English and in the use of mobile technology. The Institute of Hotel Management (IHM) could generate and disseminate knowledge about (a) the nutritive value of street foods, (b) safe food handling, preparation and storage practices, (c) display/presentation of street foods and (d) responsible waste disposal. They could also help street vendors develop and share new recipes to cater to the changing tastes. Business schools could generate and disseminate knowledge about how street vendors could improve their operational efficiencies and retain customers even as they expanded their business. They could also help NASVI to rapidly scale up their efforts and reach out to many more street vendors across India. Lastly, research institutions could generate and disseminate knowledge on the nutritive value and cultural significance of many street foods. They could help street vendors find simple, cost-effective ways of minimizing adverse impacts of street foods on people and the environment.

Clearly, there are several opportunities for creating a sustainable entrepreneurial ecosystem for street vendors in India. For NASVI, the challenge will be scaling up while remaining strongly committed to improving the quality of life of street vendors.

8.7 Summary and Conclusion

India has been one of the faster growing economies of the world. While unemployment rates are low, a significant proportion of people are employed in the informal economy. Street vending is an important occupation in the informal economy. Many poor people become street vendors out of necessity and because it has low entry barriers. However, earning a decent livelihood from the street vending business is difficult, in the absence of a supportive ecosystem. NASVI helped create a more supportive entrepreneurial ecosystem for street vendors in India.

This chapter described NASVI's experience of creating a supportive entrepreneurial ecosystem for street vendors in India and the outcomes thereof. There is no systematic survey of street vendors' perception of the quality of their life following NASVI's interventions. A recent survey of street vendors in Bhubaneswar, Orissa, found that street vendors reported less harassment, greater legitimacy and a more conducive environment for practising their trade in vending zones. This is a likely outcome in states with more progressive and supportive legislations for street vendors. More objective indicators suggest that street vendors have better access to critical resources.

NASVI's progress has been heartening. However, sustaining the entrepreneurial ecosystem requires NASVI to build the commercial economy and the research economy of the ecosystem. To improve the commercial economy, NASVI needs collaborate with business and business schools to scale up its efforts across states. To improve the research economy, NASVI needs to collaborate with educational and financial institutions to generate and disseminate new and relevant knowledge. The challenge for NASVI is to manage growth while remaining committed to the welfare of street vendors.

Annexure 1

Elements of National Policy for Urban Street Vendors

- Reflect the spirit of the Constitution of India on the right of citizens to equal protection before the law as well as right to practice any profession, trade, business or occupation.[11]
- The duty of the State is to strive to minimize the inequalities in income and to adopt policies aimed at securing that the citizens have the right to adequate means of livelihood as enshrined in article 38(2), 39 (a) and 41 of the Constitution. Procedure to regulate such right of street vending when reasonable restriction is warranted in public interest.
- States must organize Town Vending Committees (TVC), adopt a participatory approach and supervise the entire process of planning, organization and regulation of street vending activities. They must facilitate the implementation of socioeconomic policies for the street vendors. They must delegate authority to local municipal bodies to frame necessary rules for identification of street vendors/vending zones and for implementation of policy. All matters related to street vendors like, i-card, vending zones, eviction, survey, should be decided by TVC only.
- The TVC should make a committee [Headed by a woman official] to take into account the Domestic Violence Act, 2005 and also a committee to be formed under Vishakha Guidelines against Sexual Harassment at workplace (Prevention, Prohibition, Redressal) Act 2013 – it will lead to a new mechanism of protecting women from sexual harassment for informal sector. Grievance Redressal Forum should be developed to help the dissatisfied in a meaningful way.
- City/town master plans need to recognize the need for developing vendor market/outlets and weekend markets and make provisions for creating new vending markets. They must provide street vendors with civic facilities for appropriate use of identified places for vending markets.
- Street vendors must be given a legal status by formulating an appropriate law and thereby providing for legitimate vending/hawking zones in the city/town master plans. Ensure that the laws are enforced. Recognize the fundamental right of street vendors to carry on trade and business mentioned in Article 19 (1)g on street pavements, public places and land belonging to state and union governments.

---

[11] Source: Sonal Sinha, NASVI, pers. comm. 2016.

- Promote access of street vendors to such services as credit, skill development, housing, social security and capacity building.
- Promote organizations of street vendors to facilitate their collective empowerment.

Annexure 2

Elements of the Street Vendors (Protection of Livelihood and Regulation of Street Vending) Act

The Act aims at creating a conducive atmosphere where street vendors, are able to carry out their business in a fair and transparent manner, without the fear of harassment and eviction.[12]

(i) The Act provides for constitution of a Town Vending Authority in each Local Authority, which is the fulcrum of the Act, for implementing the provisions of the Act.

(ii) In order to ensure participatory decision making for aspects relating to street vending activities like determination of natural market, identification of vending zones, preparation of street vending plan, survey of street vendors etc. the TVC is required to have representation of officials and non-officials and street vendors, including women vendors with due representation from SC, ST, OBC, Minorities and persons with disabilities. It has been provided that 40% members of the TVC will be from amongst street vendors to be selected through election, of which one-third shall be women.

(iii) To avoid arbitrariness of authorities, the Act provides for a survey of all existing street vendors, and subsequent survey at-least once in every 5 years, and issue of certificate of vending to all the street vendors identified in the survey, with preference to SC, ST, OBC, women, persons with disabilities, minorities etc.

(iv) All existing street vendors, identified in the survey, will be accommodated in the vending zones subject to a norm conforming to 2.5% of the population of the ward or zone or town or city.

(v) Where the number of street vendors identified are more than the holding capacity of the vending zone, the Town Vending Committee (TVC) is required to carry out a draw of lots for issuing the certificate of vending for that vending zone and the remaining persons will be accommodated in any adjoining vending zone to avoid relocation.

(vi) Those street vendors who have been issued a certificate of vending/license etc. before the commencement of this Act, they will be deemed to be a street vendor for that category and for the period for which he/she has been issued such certificate of vending/license.

---

[12] Source: Sonal Sinha, NASVI, pers. comm. 2016.

8 Creating a Supportive Entrepreneurial Ecosystem for Street Vendors: The Case… 169

(vii) It has been provided that no street vendor will be evicted until the survey has been completed and certificate of vending issued to the street vendors.

(viii) It has also been provided that in case a street vendor, to whom a certificate of vending is issued, dies or suffers from any permanent disability or is ill, one of his family member i.e. spouse or dependent child can vend in his place, till the validity of the certificate of vending.

(ix) Thus the mechanism is to provide universal coverage, by protecting the street vendors from harassment and promoting their livelihoods.

(x) Procedure for relocation, eviction and confiscation of goods has been specified and made street vendor friendly. It is proposed to provide for recommendation of the TVC, as a necessary condition for relocation being carried out by the local authority.

(xi) Relocation of street vendors should be exercised as a last resort. Accordingly, a set of principles to be followed for 'relocation' is proposed to be provided for in the Act, which states that (i) relocation should be avoided as far as possible, unless there is clear and urgent need for the land in question; (ii) affected vendors or their representatives shall be involved in planning and implementation of the rehabilitation project; (iii) affected vendors shall be relocated so as to improve their livelihoods and standards of living or at least to restore them, in real terms to pre-evicted levels (iv) natural markets where street vendors have conducted business for over 50 years shall be declared as heritage markets, and the street vendors in such markets shall not be relocated.

(xii) The Local authority is required to make out a plan once in every 5 years, on the recommendation of TVC, to promote a supportive environment and adequate space for urban street vendors to carry out their vocation. It specifically provides that declaration of no-vending zone shall be carried subject to the specified principles namely; any existing natural market, or an existing market as identified under the survey shall not be declared as a no-vending zone; declaration of no-vending zone shall be done in a manner which displaces the minimum percentage of street vendors; no zone will be declared as a no-vending zone till such time as the survey has not been carried out and the plan for street vending has not been formulated. Thus the Bill provides for enough safeguards to protect street vendors interests.

(xiii) The thrust of the Act is on "natural market", which has been defined under the Act. The entire planning exercise has to ensure that the provision of space or area for street vending is reasonable and consistent with existing natural markets. Thus, natural locations where there is a constant congregation of buyers and sellers will be protected under the Act.

(xiv) There is a provision for establishment of an independent dispute redressal mechanism under the chairmanship of retired judicial officers to maintain impartiality towards grievance redressal of street vendors.

(xv) The Act provides for time period for release of seized goods, for both perishable and non-perishable goods. In case of non-perishable goods, the local authority is required to release the goods within two working days and incase of perishable goods, the goods shall be released the same day, of the claim being made.

(xvi) The Act also provides for promotional measures to be undertaken by the Government, towards availability of credit, insurance and other welfare schemes of social security, capacity building programs, research, education and training program etc. for street vendors.

(xvii) The Act provides for protection of street vendors from harassment by police and other authorities and provides for an overriding clause to ensure they carry on their business without the fear of harassment by the authorities under any other law.

(xviii) The Act specifically provides that the Rules under the Act have to be notified within 1 year of its commencement, and Scheme has to be notified within 6 months of its commencement to prevent delay in implementation.

Annexure 3

Membership, savings deposited and loans availed by members of the Sanchay Thrift and Credit Cooperative Society across three districts of Bihar where the Cooperative is presently operational: 2001–2016.[13]

Year	Individual members (excluding self-help groups)[a]	Savings (rupees) deposited by individuals and self-help groups (percent growth over preceding year)	Savings (in US $)[b] deposited by individuals and self-help groups	Loans (rupees) availed by individuals and self- help groups (percent growth over preceding year)	Loan (in US $) availed by individuals and self-help groups from cooperative
2001–2002	886	Rupees 02,63,880	US $ 3951.54	Rupees 01,64,020	US $ 2456.16
2002–2003	1372 (35%)	06,97,696 (165%)	10,447.83	07,32,817 (346%)	10,973.76
2004–2005	2340 (70%)	19,88,182 (65%)	29,772.56	20,72,551 (182%)	31,035.97
2005–2006	2115 (−9.5%)	27,80,131 (40%)	41,631.81	32,53,757 (57%)	48,724.25
2006–2007[c]	3141 (48%)	41,91,824 (50%)	62,771.59	49,55,834 (52%)	74,212.46
2007–2008	4170 (33%)	47,11,416 (12%)	70,552.36	62,80,551 (27%)	94,049.79
2008–2009	5017 (20%)	47,66,467 (01%)	71,376.73	65,65,130 (4%)	98,311.29
2010–2011	7090 (41%)	73,15,867 (53%)	109,553.41	84,23,308 (28%)	126,137.08

(continued)

---

[13] Dollar-rupee conversion: $1 = Rs 66.779, as of 12 September, 2016.

Year	Individual members (excluding self-help groups)[a]	Savings (rupees) deposited by individuals and self-help groups (percent growth over preceding year)	Savings (in US $)[b] deposited by individuals and self-help groups	Loans (rupees) availed by individuals and self-help groups (percent growth over preceding year)	Loan (in US $) availed by individuals and self-help groups from cooperative
2011–2012	9769 (38%)	116,02,516 (59%)	173,744.98	126,19,096 (50%)	188,968.03
2012–2013	11,817 (20%)	187,36,763 (61%)	280,578.67	159,01,181 (26%)	238,116.49
2016 Sep	14,037 (19%)	265,60, 856 (41%)	397,742.64	140,00,000 (13.5%)	209,646.74

[a]Source: Sonal Sinha, NASVI, pers. comm. 2017
[b]Individual members are largely street vendors and their family members. Self-help groups have about 15–20 members each. There were 792 self-help groups across the three districts of Bihar by end 2016
[c]Until this year, expansion was largely confined to Patna district. After this year the Cooperative expanded to another two districts of Bihar

References

Anjaria, J. S. (2006). Street hawkers and the public space in Mumbai. *Economic and Political Weekly, 41*(21), 2140–2146. http://www.epw.in/journal/2006/21/review-labour-review-issues-specials/street-hawkers-and-public-space-mumbai.html. Accessed 17 Jan 2017.

Bhatt, E. (2006). *We are poor but so many: The story of self employed women in India.* Oxford: Oxford University Press.

Bhowmik, S. K. (2001). Hawkers and the urban informal sector. A study of street vending in seven cities. http://wiego.org/sites/wiego.org/files/publications/files/Bhowmik-Hawkers-URBAN-INFORMAL-SECTOR.pdf. Accessed 17 Jan 2017.

Bhowmik, S. K. (2010). Legal protection for street vendors. *Economic and Political Weekly, 45*(51), 12–15. http://www.epw.in/search/site/legal%20protection%20for%20street%20vendors. Accessed 17 Jan 2017.

Bonner, C., & Spooner, D. (2011). Organizing in the informal economy: A challenge for Trade Unions. http://library.fes.de/pdf-files/ipg/2011–2/08_a_bonner.pdf. Accessed 16 Jan 2017.

Chaubey, P. K. (2003) Urban local bodies in India: Quest for making them self-reliant. Paper presented at the National Seminar on Municipal Finances at the Indian Institute of Public Administration, New Delhi under the auspices of the Twelfth Finance Commission. http://fincomindia.nic.in/writereaddata/html_en_files/oldcommission_html/predocs/speech/chaubey_ulb.pdf. Accessed 16 Jan 2017.

Dey, S. (2014). Over a lakh hawkers to support Cong if Sahai gets Ranchi ticket. *Hindustan Times.* March 12. http://www.hindustantimes.com/ranchi/over-a-lakh-hawkers-to-support-cong-if-sahai-gets-ranchi-ticket/story-47fDsbx7wRx4DZP100TnnI.ht. Accessed 17 Jan 2017.

Economic and Political Weekly Editorial. (2007). Street vendors: Denied credit. *Economic and Political Weekly.* http://epw.in/journal/2007/29/editorials/street-vendors-denied-credit.html#sthash.pMdbE9Vj.dpuf. Accessed 17 Jan 2017.

Economic and Political Weekly Editorial. (2014). A law for street vendors. *Economic and Political Weekly, 49*(10), 08. http://www.epw.in/journal/2014/10/editorials/law-street-vendors.html. Accessed 17 Jan 2017.

Government of India. (2004). *National policy on urban street vendors of India.* New Delhi: Ministry of Urban Employment and Poverty Alleviation. http://www.prsindia.org/uploads/media/1167478283/bill82_2006123082_National_Policy_for_Urban_Street_Vendors.pdf. Accessed 17 Jan 2017.

International Labour Organization. (1972). *Employment, incomes and equality: A strategy for increasing productive employment in Kenya.* 72B09_608_engl. Geneva: ILO.

Jutting, J. P., & de Laiglesia, J. R. (Eds.) (2009). *Is informal normal? Towards more and better jobs in developing countries.* Development Centre of the OECD. http://www.oecd.org/dev/inclusivesocietiesanddevelopment/isinformalnormalmessagesfiguresanddata.htm. Accessed 18 Jan 2017.

Kannan, K. P., & Papola, T. S. (2007). Workers in the informal sector: Initiatives by India's National Commission for Enterprises in the Unorganized Sector (NCEUS). *International Labour Review, 146*(3/4), 321–329.

Kapoor, A. (2007). The SEWA way: Shaping another future for informal labour. *Futures, 39,* 554–568.

Kumar, R. (2012). The regularization of street vending in Bhubaneswar, India: A policy model. WEIGO Policy Brief No. 7. http://wiego.org/sites/wiego.org/files/publications/files/Kumar_WIEGO_PB7.pdf. Accessed 17 Jan 2017.

Mathur, N. (2014). The street vendors bill: Opportunities and challenges. *Economic and Political Weekly, 49*(10), 22–25. http://www.epw.in/journal/2014/10/commentary/street-vendors-bill.html. Accessed 17 Jan 2017.

National Commission for Enterprises in the Unorganised Sector (NCEUS). (2008). Contribution of the unorganized sector to the GDP: Report of the sub-committee of a NCEUS task force. Working Paper 2. http://nceuis.nic.in/Final_Booklet_Working_Paper_2.pdf. Accessed 17 Jan 2017.

National Commission for Enterprises in the Unorganized Sector (NCEUS). (2007). Report on the condition of work and promotion of livelihoods in the unorganized sector. http://dcmsme.gov.in/Condition_of_workers_sep_2007.pdf. Accessed 9 Jan 2017.

Pal, P., & Ghosh, J. (2007). Inequality in India: A survey of recent trends. DESA Working Paper No. 45, United Nations Department of Economic and Social Affairs.

Paraskevi, T. (2013). Quality of life: Definition and measurement. *Europe's Journal of Psychology, 9*(1), 150–162.

Registrar of Cooperative Societies. (2014). Status of registration application. http://delhi.gov.in/wps/wcm/connect/doit_rcs/RCS/Home/General+Information/Status+of+Registration+Application. Accessed 17 Jan 2017.

Shane, S., & Venkataraman, S. (2000). The promise of entrepreneurship as a field of research. *Academy of Management Review, 25*(1), 217–226. https://doi.org/10.5465/AMR.2000.2791611.

Sinha. S. (2017). NASVI. Personal Communication.

Srija, A., & Shirke, S. V. (2014). An analysis of the informal labour market in India. http://www.ies.gov.in/pdfs/CII%20EM-october-2014.pdf. Accessed on 9 Jan 2017.

Stam, E. (2015). Entrepreneurial ecosystems and regional policy: A sympathetic critique. *European Plannign Studies, 23*(9), 1759–1769.

Sundaram, S. S. (2008). National policy for urban street vendors and its impact. *Economic and Political Weekly, 43*(43), 22–25. http://www.epw.in/journal/2008/43/commentary/national-policy-urban-street-vendors-and-its-impact.html#sthash.W3AG8Sxd.dpuf.Accessed 17 Jan 2017.

Venkata Ratnam, C. S. (1999). India. In *International labour organization: Trade unions in the informal sector: Finding their bearings. Nine country papers.* Labour Education 1999/3 No.116. ILO.

Williams, C. C. (2014). *Informal sector entrepreneurship.* OECD Centre for Entrepreneurship, SMEs and Local Development. https://www.oecd.org/employment/leed/Background-Paper-PB-Informal-Entrepreneurship-final.pdf. Accessed 18 Jan 2017.

Chapter 9
Sustainable Ecosystems Through Indigenous Social Enterprises

Mario Vázquez-Maguirre

Abstract The aim of this chapter is to explore the mechanisms by which an indigenous social enterprise in southern Mexico is building a sustainable ecosystem that improves the quality of life of the community. The research suggests that indigenous social enterprises have developed novel mechanisms based on its culture and cosmovision, which ultimately generate an ecosystem that promotes community welfare. These mechanisms are accountability and transparency, legitimacy, equality policies, a participatory organizational structure, social innovation, and entrepreneurial orientation. This case shows how the communitarian perspective of the entity increases the quality of life of employees and their households, fosters the local economy, and consolidates an ecosystem that promotes development in the community. From a public policy perspective, the case also suggests actions that might promote the generation of business models that integrate vulnerable communities to the global economy from a sustainable, collaborative perspective.

Keywords Social enterprises • Sustainable development • Indigenous communities • Sustainable ecosystem • Quality of life • Social innovation

9.1 Introduction

The planet is in a dangerous period for the survival of ecosystems as we know them. Climate change presents new challenges: the extinction of species at accelerated rates, food shortages, and stronger meteorological phenomena, all of which can have catastrophic consequences to humankind. One of the responses to this phenomenon has been the search for more sustainable living methods. In this scenario, consumers, shareholders, civil organizations, and other stakeholders have demanded

M. Vázquez-Maguirre (✉)
Universidad de Monterrey, Avenida Ignacio Morones Prieto 4500 Pte., 66238, San Pedro Garza García, N.L., Mexico
e-mail: mario.vazquez@udem.edu

© Springer International Publishing AG 2018
J. Leitão et al. (eds.), *Entrepreneurial, Innovative and Sustainable Ecosystems*, Applying Quality of Life Research,
https://doi.org/10.1007/978-3-319-71014-3_9

that corporations adopt more environmentally friendly operations, while creating more value to society. Relatively new terms have been introduced in the corporate world such as sustainability, corporate social responsibility, social enterprises, green companies, corporate citizen, etc.

Within this trend, companies have promoted that their supply chain also adopts sustainable practices, accountability, and an ethical behavior. In this context, this chapter presents the case of Ixtlán Group, a social enterprise located in southern Mexico that has built an ecosystem that seeks sustainable operations, while generating welfare in the region. The following section defines social entrepreneurship, social enterprises, and their main attributes. Next, the methodology that allowed documenting this case is described. The main results are presented in Section 9.4, where mechanisms and policies that generated this ecosystem are examined; traditionally one of the most marginal regions of southern Mexico, Ixtlán, is now a pole of development and a national example of sustainable development. At the end of the chapter, the main conclusions are presented, as well as a summary of the elements that shape Ixtlán's ecosystem.

9.2 Social Entrepreneurship and Social Enterprises

Profit maximization is not individuals' only motivation; people are multidimensional actors who may derive utility from improving the welfare of other members of society (Yunus 2010). With this idea, some people start ventures to address social or environmental issues in a sustainable way; this individuals are known as social entrepreneurs. The concept of social entrepreneurship has been poorly defined, and its boundaries with other fields of study remain fuzzy (Mair and Martí 2006). In a broad sense, a social entrepreneur is someone who organizes or operates a venture or corporation which features social goals (Peredo and McLean 2006). Bornstein and Davis (2010) are more specific and characterize it as a process by which citizens build or transform institutions to advance solutions to social problems, such as poverty, illness, illiteracy, or environmental destruction, in order to make life better for many. Similarly, Peredo and Chrisman (2006) define social entrepreneurship as an individual or group of people seeking the creation of social value by seizing opportunities, taking risks, and making innovative use of their resources. Martin and Osberg (2007) add that these enterprises should be scalable to create new balances and ensure a permanent benefit. Ashoka (2015) defines it as an individual which unceasingly conceives and pursues a new idea to solve social problems at a great scale, generating impact and permanently changing the systems that originate the problem. What distinguishes social entrepreneurship is a predominant focus on value creation as opposed to commercial entrepreneurship, which has a predominant focus on value appropriation (Santos 2012).

A characteristic of social entrepreneurship, which differentiates it from commercial entrepreneurship, is the need to adopt a logic of empowerment, which is somehow opposite to the search for control. Self-interest actors, such as corporations and commercial entrepreneurs, usually follow a logic of control in order to appropriate a substantial part of the value they create (Santos 2012). Empowerment is defined by the World Bank (2011) as the process of increasing the capacity of individuals or groups to make choices and to transform those choices into desired actions and outcomes. The empowerment of actors outside and inside the organizational boundaries seems to be one of the main characteristics of social entrepreneurship, which differentiates it from other fields. This implies that social entrepreneurs usually create mechanisms and tools that both reduce stakeholders' dependencies on the organization and increase stakeholders' ability to contribute to the solution and to their own welfare. For this purpose, they often establish partnerships with some stakeholders (Santos and Eisenhardt 2006).

The traditional vehicle that social entrepreneurs form to achieve their goal is through social enterprises. These entities seek sustainable solutions and approaches that systematically address a problem, maybe through the development of a new market mechanism or through alliances with other actors such as the government, nonprofit organizations, or corporations (Santos 2012). Nonprofit organizations also address social and environmental problems, redistributing resources from more affluent to less wealthy members of society, but they usually do not seek to develop and validate sustainable solutions. Yunus (2010) believes that relying on charitable donations is not sustainable. It forces nonprofit organizations to spend important resources on fundraising. In contrast, social enterprises are designed to be sustainable, purpose oriented, and scalable and to create value while empowering its stakeholders and seek permanent solutions through social innovation (Vázquez and Portales 2014).

9.3 Methodology

The work follows a qualitative methodology and uses case study as a research technique. The case of Ixtlán Group is analyzed, an indigenous social enterprise in southern Mexico. This case, purposefully selected, represents the most successful example of a sustainable business model that generates well-being in the region. Data collection instruments included 70 semi-structured interviews collected between September 2011 and July 2012. Most of the interviewees were employees, former employees, and people from the community. Other stakeholders interviewed in a smaller number were people from financial entities, local universities, Forest Stewardship Council (FSC), clients, government, suppliers, and people from neighboring communities. The transcripts account for more than 500 pages; the interviews range from half an hour to 2.5 h. The average interview is 50 min long. Interviews include questions divided into social, economic, and environmental aspects of the particular individual, the social enterprise, and the community. The interviews are complemented with more than 120 h of observation in the organization facilities and the community.

Also, secondary data analysis includes around 1000 pages of internal documents that help data triangulation. Data analysis follows the process of categorization, abstraction, comparison, dimensionalization, integration, iteration, and refutation described by Spiggle (1994). In order to verify the inferences made from the collected data, three informants were consulted: two former employees (one of them

176 M. Vázquez-Maguirre

still serves in the organization as an external advisor) and an expert in community-based enterprises that works for a nonprofit organization.

9.4 Results

Forest-related activities are currently the main source of income in Ixtlán, but these are relatively new activities as inhabitants used to live under a subsistence economy system primarily based on agriculture and cattle. Timber exploitation in Ixtlán started in the 1940s when a concession was granted to a foreign firm. The only benefit that the community obtained from this concession was the creation of employment under poor conditions, but no other payment was given to the community for the exploitation of its natural resources (Rainforest Alliance 2001).

In 1968, 14 communities created an organization to increase the employee's bargain power against the foreign corporation, also boycotting its operations and with the ultimate goal of regaining control of their natural resources. In 1974, the government finally yielded and created a new local organization to exploit the forest. Four neighboring communities formed this new entity: Ixtlán, Capulálpam, La Trinidad, and Santiago Xiacuí. The new enterprise was called Ixcasit and had around 60 workers. These four communities began to learn about sustainability and conservation strategies, as well as how to manage their forests and logging operations. Internal problems among the four communities increased and they split in 1988; thus, the Unidad Comunal Forestal Agropecuaria y de Servicios (UCFAS) was established in 1988 (Ixtlán Group's first enterprise) with the goal of providing quality jobs for the community and stopping the emigration to northern parts of Mexico and the USA. UCFAS remained the sole entity in charge of an increasing variety of industries and business opportunities that the organization exploited until 2007, when the *comuneros* (first dwellers that still keep land rights in the community, nowadays around 300 people) decided to split the enterprise into eight entities (see Table 9.1). In 2012, the organization had over 200 employees.

Table 9.1 Enterprises of Ixtlán Group and number of workers in 2012

Enterprise	Main activity	Total
UCFAS	Sawmill and furniture factory	116
UNFOSTI	Timber exploitation	50
Servicios Técnicos Forestales (STF)	Forest sustainable management	20
Tienda Comunitaria Ixtleca	Building materials and hardware store	9
Gasolinera Comunidad Agraria	Gas station	9
Ecoturixtlán SPR de RI	Ecotourism park	10
Fideicomiso de Ixtlán (SOFOM)	Productive microlending	3
TIP Muebles	Furniture retail stores	10
Total		227

Source: Elaborated by author

9 Sustainable Ecosystems Through Indigenous Social Enterprises

Ixtlán Group has built an ecosystem around these eight entities that is based on creating sustainable value to its main stakeholders: employees and the local community. To this end, the organization has also created mechanisms to address other stakeholder's needs: accountability and transparency, legitimacy, equality policies, a participatory organizational structure, social innovation, and entrepreneurial orientation. These mechanisms are examined in the next paragraphs.

9.4.1 Accountability and Transparency

The state of Oaxaca has more municipalities than any other state in Mexico, among which about three-quarters are governed under a traditional electoral system known as *usos y costumbres* (uses and traditions). *Usos y costumbres* is rooted in an indigenous system of community service that attaches particular importance to elders, open assemblies, and consensus (Gu and Subramanian 2012; p. 38). The community of Ixtlán is also governed under this system, which means that government authorities are democratically elected every 3 years in an open general assembly under a one-person one-vote approach. Ixtlán Group maintained the democratic system when electing the principal authorities of the companies. The Commissariat of Common Goods (CCG) is the entity that controls the eight companies of Ixtlán Group. The CCG is also the highest authority regarding land issues and primary resources in the community. This organization is democratically elected in a general assembly where every *comunero* has a vote. Reelection is not allowed, so every elected authority should serve a 3-year period and then go back to his previous activities. The CCG has a Surveillance Committee (SV) that guards the actions of general managers within the group. Every company has also an Advisory Board (AB) that also supervises the manager's activities.

Transparency and accountability are strictly promoted at this level. The general manager of Tienda Comunitaria explains how the financial information needs to pass through different filters before it can be presented to the general assembly for final approval: "First, the information is analyzed by the board, we verify with them any irregularity… then the second filter is the AB, which also checks the information; their members make observations so that, when we present the information to the general assembly, everything goes well." Every enterprise follows the same process; all the information must be available to any committee that wants to check anything in particular, that is, the implicit policy. Transparency is also encouraged at lower levels. Every company holds periodical assemblies where managers explain their actions and results to workers; there is also an open-door policy where the community can witness the enterprises' actions and procedures.

Transparency and accountability come at a cost. The manager of the human resources department at UCFAS admits that surveillance procedures can be extremely bureaucratic. He adds: "there is an emphasis on accountability, but most of the issues could be solved within the enterprises… it is quite bureaucratic and a waste of time." Pedro Torres, CBC's president at the time, acknowledges that reaching a general agreement in the general assembly of *comuneros* is messy and time-consuming, which is why the advisory committee was created. This group analyzes the problem and finds alternatives before approaching the general assembly. This mechanism has proven to be more effective.

Accountability is also encouraged with external stakeholders. These actions are described next, as their main objective is to gain legitimacy to operate in the community.

9.4.2 Legitimacy

Ixtlán Group maintains a high degree of legitimacy within the community and the region due to its stakeholder approach and the synergies reached with every actor. For example, every company has a strict policy to buy its supplies from local businesses, even though some managers argue that it is often more expensive. However, they also acknowledge that if the money remains in the community, it creates more wealth than if expended in transnational retail stores. This policy also fosters employment in the community. One of the managers explains it: "We think that supporting local ventures is better; we do not want to be employees of these big retail stores, we want to support local people so that they can establish their own enterprises… why lose money? Those retail stores are going to take their profits somewhere else. The more money that circulates in the community the better, and we also do not want to lose our identity." Ixtlán is now the main trade center of the region. UCFAS' general manager believes that Ixtlán Group has generated a stronger economy: "you may have seen when you walk in the main blocks of the community that there are a lot of micro businesses, a drugstore, 20 taxis; you see trucks that come and go… there is a lot of employment here."

Ixtlán Group also works closely with universities and high schools. The organization gives students the opportunity to do paid internships and mandatory social work; some of these students have ended up working there. The worker that manages the tours at Ecoturixtlán learned his job while doing his social work. When he graduated from high school, he started working at Ecoturixtlán and was later promoted to that job. UCFAS also has established a summer program where students can work for 2 months and earn some money to cover their personal expenses. A human resources assistant explains that Ixtlán Group tries to help the students financially, mainly in summer when classes are over; they are usually placed in low-risk areas, and they are assigned a lower amount of work than full-time workers. The local university also partners with Ixtlán Group to do research about forest management and alternative productive projects. The academic programs are also based in some of Ixtlán's main activities, since the organization is the largest employer in the region.

The objective of the organization is to create jobs in the community; this stakeholder is the most important for the group. The former president of the CCG, UNFOSTI's general manager, argues that they want the wood to have as much value added as possible: "that is why we have created other enterprises along the supply chain, so that there can be more employment in the community, by creating more enterprises." Ixtlán Group has also invested in social projects to improve public facilities. A fraction of their annual profits is destined every year to community projects. They have financed roads, the central plaza, the main government building, and also public schools. During the general assemblies, people from the community can suggest new projects that could improve public spaces. Also, the machinery some companies of the group own is lent to local people. Tractors and backhoes are employed by the community to undertake productive ventures such as building rooms for rent or planting corn, beans, and vegetables. The CCG charges a rent for the equipment, but it is cheaper than the market price. One of the beneficiaries notes: "I pay a daily rent of 200 pesos [USD 15] for the tractor, the market price is around 270 pesos [USD 20] an hour."

The president of the CCG admits that a minority of local people are against forest exploitation for productive ends, which is why the CCG has taken some actions to legitimize this activity. The CCG organizes *tequios* (unpaid community work) where families get to see how the different enterprises take care of the environment, the reforested areas, the greenhouse, and the methods used to preserve the fauna, forests, and rivers. Through these events, families can see tangible results of how the existence of the enterprises benefits the environment. He adds that, during these *tequios*, a special emphasis is placed on explaining the forest management program to the children, as they are going to be the main beneficiaries of these actions. A pine tree that is planted today will be ready for exploitation in 40 years. Ixtlán Group is currently reforesting almost 100% of the exploited areas and has obtained the Forest Stewardship Council certification for sustainable forest management.

Workers are also a relevant stakeholder. Every employee has all legal benefits provided by law (social security, housing, paid vacations, profit sharing, retirement pension, paid overtime, and a 48 h a week schedule). Only 58.2% of the Mexican workers have such benefits, given the high rates of informality in the country (Dinero en Imagen 2016). The administrative assistant at the CCG recalls that when she worked in the local government as an assistant to the municipal authority, she did not get any benefits, just the salary and the Christmas bonus; she adds: "I worked for three years there and I did not have any vacations."

The plant manager at UCFAS admits that the employees are what differentiate this enterprise from others. He believes the most valuable asset is people's commitment, passion, and availability. He adds: "there is an implicit, stronger commitment to the enterprise; that may be consequence of the situation we live in, the sense of community, the needs they face." Employees are also encouraged to learn different jobs, so they can be promoted more easily; they are advised to speak up when something is wrong or needs to be addressed differently and to participate in the organization's decision-making.

Also, most workers that were interviewed believe their work is not as stressful as it could be in other enterprises. A STF worker that used to work in Mexico City recalls how he was treated: "They only wanted production, they brought industrial physiologists so we gave everything we had, to kill ourselves at work in order to get the productivity and punctuality bonuses... it was very hard, they exploited the worker to the maximum, but here managers are more conscious... they are more tolerant."

As a result, most employees at Ixtlán Group are solidary with the organization, a cultural value that seems to be deeply rooted in Ixtlán. A UCFAS worker expresses proudly that when she notices that there is a lot of work in the factory, she prefers to postpone her holidays until a more convenient time for the enterprise: "I like very much helping... I like my job, I have vacations schedule in March but I will not take them because we have work to do." In this sense, working at Ixtlán Group is also a form of contributing to the community, a way of building a stronger society. The director of the legal department at UCFAS remembers that his parents taught him values that made him want to contribute to the community; that is why he decided to come back to Ixtlán after college.

Ixtlán Group is the entity that generates more employment in the community; however, one-third of these jobs are taken by people from other communities. They have found better job conditions at Ixtlán, and they are willing to travel every day from neighboring communities to work. Ixtlán Group has a transportation service that facilitates the journey. A 40-year-old employee from Capulálpam explains why she prefers to work at Ixtlán Group instead of the local sawmill: "Here at UCFAS I have job stability. At Capulálpam, employees suddenly stop working [factory shuts down seasonally], and they do not have benefits like here. Even more, it is difficult to find a job, I am an old person, and it is not the same than before." A UCFAS worker from Ixtlán adds: "I think they get a better payment here, they told me that they make less money in other communities, and they do not even have benefits. Here, we also have emergency, no-interest loans [for up to USD 750]."

Some managers believe this phenomenon has contributed to having better relations with neighboring communities. In fact, Ixtlán Group made a joint venture with other two furniture factories located in communities nearby in order to open furniture retail stores in the state capital. Under the commercial name of TIP Muebles, this joint venture has now four stores and plans to open more in nearby states.

9.4.3 Equality

A successful ecosystem that promotes well-being would not be possible if equality was not strongly enforced. Mexico, and this region in particular, is a male-dominated society where "*machismo*" culture has deterred women from taking proactive measures to increase their well-being. Since the formation of Ixtlán Group in 1988, women have slowly gained jobs that were usually exclusive for men. Most interviewees agree that nowadays women have a more participatory role in both the organization and the community. A 68-year-old former UCFAS worker remembers that in the 1940s and 1950s, women were relegated, but now he notices a change: women participation in political and managerial positions has increased. He is glad that things are changing because "women are smarter than men in many situations," he believes. Most of the employees in the factory are women; the production manager believes they have proven to be very committed to their work. Salaries are determined by position, not gender. One of the former workers, now retiree, remembers that when a gender equality salary policy was introduced (in the 1990s), some men protested; however, after witnessing that women were as or even more productive than men, they ran out of arguments to keep fighting the new policy.

Equality has also permeated the community. The receptionist of Ecoturixtlán, who once lived in the Mixes region, explained the differences between both places: "Over there [Mixes region], people tell female children to quit school, to learn how to cook, stuff like that... but here [Ixtlán] there is not *machismo* culture, maybe a little bit... maybe that is because some people practice different religions or just the local culture."

Ixtlán's citizens also perceive gender equality both in the community and the organization. The president of the committee of San Pedro neighborhood points out that, in other communities, women are not allowed to participate in the general assemblies and they cannot work at the local enterprises, but at Ixtlán they can. Women actively participate in productive activities. Even more, he thinks women have better skills to do jobs such as furniture manufacturing. In this sense, women are the main economic provider in 211 of the 675 households that Ixtlán had in 2012. Approximately one-third of the employees are women.

Ixtlán Group is also well-known for providing job opportunities to young people. Four out of eight enterprises of the group are managed by people under 40 years old, three of them women. Guillermo, Ecoturixtlán's former manager, who is in his early 30s, describes that, when people from other communities visit Ixtlán, they ask why there are so many young people in managerial positions; he answers: "they are people from the community, how are they supposed to gain experience if we [Ixtlán Group] do not give them the opportunity to work."

Opportunities for self-growth are another important distinction of Ixtlán Group. There are countless stories about employees who have been promoted due to their effort and ability to learn. The gas station's general manager explains that she began working there 7 years ago as an accountant assistant. She remembers that many men employees opposed when she was offered a higher position because she had only finished high school, but the president of the CCG gave her the opportunity anyway. She now has 2 years as head of the gas station, and she has turned it into one of the most profitable entities. She also believes that if Ixtlán Group had not existed, she probably would have migrated to New Jersey, USA, where her sisters work as housekeepers.

9.4.4 Participatory Organizational Structure

The structure of Ixtlán Group is similar to the one Bray et al. (2006) found in their study of 42 communities in the state of Oaxaca. The authors concluded that massive agrarian reforms reflected in the agrarian law limited and overlaid other indigenous forms of governance. This may be the reason why there is a common organizational structure for communal forestry enterprises, although there are differences directly related with the level of integration of the community enterprises (Bray 1991). Ixtlán Group's level of integration makes it an example to community-based enterprises around Mexico and Latin America. Although the agrarian law establishes the general governance structure for communities, the main differences between Ixtlán Group and similar entities are the respect and discipline that most of the citizens and *comuneros* of Ixtlán have for the organizational structure and participatory mechanisms in place. The assemblies, boards, and committees usually follow an agenda, and members stick to it strictly, both in time and themes. They also respect everybody's opinion and let everyone express their point of view, and once an agreement is achieved democratically, everyone acts accordingly. "Even if someone thinks it is unfair, it does not matter, the assembly or committee made a resolution and that is the law," recalls a worker; that is how the community and the enterprises keep governability. When people from other communities are told of this fact, they usually admit that it is admirable how so many people can maintain order during assemblies. One member of another community describes that, during assemblies in his community, people usually end up fighting, they do not stick to the time allotted to each issue, and they tend to jump from issue to issue. So, naturally, they never reach an agreement, assemblies are endless, they distrust their fellow partners, and as soon as the local enterprise makes some money, they want to cash out. Discipline, respect for institutions, and a deep sense of community work seem to be an important characteristic that may have facilitated the growth of these enterprises and the sustainable ecosystem around them.

Besides formal participatory structures such as general assemblies and committees, Ixtlán Group has a horizontal structure that seems to favor employee empowerment through a closer relationship between operative workers and managers. Every worker has the opportunity to approach a manager directly and make complaints or recommendations. Although Ixtlán Group has 227 employees, middle positions are not frequent among managers and operative workers. The factory manager assistant argues that managers invite employees to provide feedback: "we are open to any comments; the area supervisor is the first instance to make any suggestion. If he or she does nothing, the office is always open; they can come up and tell us." A former UCFAS' accountant remembers that she always asked employees about the best way to solve a problem: "workers have a lot of knowledge, I used to go and ask them how they would solve this or that, and many times it worked. I talked to them and then I made my own conclusions." The horizontal structure facilitates interaction among employees since hierarchical distance between first-line employees and managers is almost nonexistent.

The organizational structure is constantly changing to find more efficient forms of governance while maintaining a high degree of accountability. In the past, the organization tried different corporate structures in order to coordinate various activities such as microloans, forest management, agriculture, ecotourism, furniture manufacturing, etc. Nowadays, the size of Ixtlán Group has forced the creation of new bodies such as boards in every enterprise and an advisory committee in order

9 Sustainable Ecosystems Through Indigenous Social Enterprises

to improve the quality and speed of decision-making. The advisory committee, the CCG, and the managers of each entity are currently planning to change the organizational structure once again to create a corporate model. Flexibility has been essential to success. Former workers and current managers agree that one of the keys that favored Ixtlán Group's growth was the ability to form a horizontal and flexible structure that combines managerial jobs with democratically elected positions.

9.4.5 Sustainable Social Innovation

Ixtlán Group has built an innovative social business model that creates social, environmental, and economic benefits to every stakeholder. The way the organization addresses the needs of its stakeholders has contributed to its legitimacy and sustainable growth.

Ixtlán Group's business model is explained to other entities in "community to community seminars," which are sponsored by the government agencies. The objective of the seminars is to share the experience of Ixtlán Group and how it dealt with issues regarding financing, growth, structure, strategy, empowerment mechanisms, governance, stakeholder management, etc. The seminars are usually held at Ecoturixtlán's convention center and generally last a week; they are led by the general managers and members of the CCG. One of the key workshops is about sustainable forest exploitation.

Sustainable social innovation can better be appreciated in the way the organization takes care of the environment and multiply resources for future generations. STF has developed an experimentation camp where the entity monitors seed and soil quality. Pest fighting squads are also responsible for collecting seeds from the best pines of the forest. Then, engineers examine if the characteristics of those trees are determined by field conditions (soil, water, altitude) or genetic predisposition. The objective is to reduce the life cycle of the forest and to obtain pine trees that are taller, stronger, and more resistant to pests, in a natural and sustainable way. Pest fighting squads are also highly renowned for the innovative ways to fight pests and fires and combat illegal logging and hunting.

The best seeds are then taken to the greenhouse. The greenhouse is a government facility built in 2008 but currently managed by the community. The greenhouse can produce half a million trees. One part of the facility is operated by STF as part of an agreement with the government. STF can plant up to 100,000 pine trees each year, which allows the organization to reforest 91 ha at a rate of 1100 trees per hectare. This number is similar to the annual exploitation surface. The system of programmed prunings and pest control has decreased the life cycle of the pine trees from 65 years to 40. The organization does not use pesticides or other chemicals because they believe they can pollute the soil and nearby rivers.

Ixtlán Group recently obtained the Forest Stewardship Council certification for sustainable forest management. This certification also includes social aspects, such as social impact assessment, security equipment for employees, salary structure, and periodic trainings about safety and productivity. UCFAS' assistant manager, who also writes the reports needed to obtain this certification, mentions that the social parameters were covered long before the certification asked for their implementation.

9.4.6 Entrepreneurial Orientation

The mission of Ixtlán Group is to provide quality job in order to generate better living standards in the community. To achieve this, the organization has also designed mechanisms that promote the creation of new ventures that can help to achieve this mission.

Ixtlán Group provides emergency loan to its employees for up to USD 750. The objective is twofold: to provide insurance in case of a medical emergency, celebration, or unexpected expenditure and to finance new ventures. These no-interest loans are an empowering tool as employees can finance productive projects to complement their income. They also provide a source of economic relief in case of emergencies or when celebrating a festivity, like a wedding or baptism. For example, a worker at Ecoturixtlán has a laundry store that he operates after work. Other employees rent rooms for students, sell groceries, or have small restaurants. A STF worker is planning to ask for a loan to raise deer. He wants to build a ranch close to the ecotourism facilities so that tourists who visit Ecoturixtlán can also pay to watch these animals. UCFAS' general manager admits that many local people have asked for loans and they have started new ventures; that is one of the reasons why they are not filling new vacancies and the organization has to recruit workers in neighboring communities.

Local citizens also prefer to focus on self-employment by starting businesses because they can easily ask for a loan. Ixtlán Group's microlending institution promotes ethical banking, that is, it charges an interest loan enough to cover its expenses and make a small profit. Financial institutions in Mexico that focus in micro-credits charge on average an annual interest rate of 63%, one of the highest in Latin America, where the figure is around 28% (Alfaro 2014). The microlending institution of Ixtlán Group charges on average 20% annually. The general manager of this institution (a woman under 40 years old) explains that she could charge a higher interest rate, but the idea is to promote entrepreneurship in the community, not to maximize profits. Some workers have taken both an emergency loan and a micro-credit, started a business, and later on they have left the organization to focus entirely on their ventures. This was the case of Enriqueta, who left UCFAS in 2008 to manage a video club, grocery store, and small hotel she built with two loans. Similarly, the person in charge of the greenhouse mentions that, as more people come to Ixtlán to work or study, local people have established new ventures: taxis, trucks, moto-taxis, bakeries, grocery stores, trout farms, and restaurants. Upcoming projects include industrialization of tree bark, hardware stores, and trading of stone materials.

9.5 Discussion

9.5.1 Building a Sustainable Ecosystem

Ixtlán Group has developed novel mechanisms based on the prevailing indigenous culture and cosmovision, which generated an ecosystem that promotes community well-being. The mechanisms described in the previous paragraphs (accountability and transparency, legitimacy, equality policies, a participatory organizational structure, social innovation, and entrepreneurial orientation) contribute to empower every stakeholder. Ixtlán Group also has developed relationships with different organizations in order to obtain resources and gain legitimacy. Figure 9.1 shows an analysis of the type of linkage that Ixtlán Group maintains with the most important stakeholders.

Ixtlán Group has developed strong linkages with four stakeholders that are deeply intertwined: *comuneros*, employees, municipal authority, and the local community. As the mission of the organization is to create quality jobs, these four actors have collaborated closely with Ixtlán Group as direct beneficiaries of its mission. *Comuneros* have managed and led the development of the organization; they concentrate decision-making and get a small dividend annually. Employees have all the legal benefits plus some other incentive such as emergency loans, bonuses, and

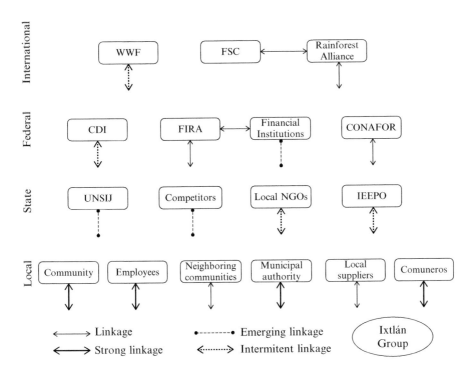

Fig. 9.1 Type of linkage (Source: Self-elaboration with primary data)

uniforms. Most of them have assumed a commitment with the organization that ultimately has contributed to its success. Similarly, the community is the main beneficiary of this social enterprise; around one-third of the profits are designated for social projects in the community. Even more, the members of the community have a formal source of employment. Lastly, the local government collaborates with Ixtlán Group to improve the inhabitant's quality of life through infrastructure projects and the funding of celebrations and fairs. Collaboration has been constant, strong, and close as both entities' mission is similar, and *comuneros* hold most of the key positions in both the local government and Ixtlán Group.

The organization has also developed other linkages that, while not as strong, promote continued collaboration. Rainforest Alliance is a nonprofit organization that is constantly supervising Ixtlán Group in order to evaluate FSC's requirements. The relationship has been constant but distant, as both parties have met, on average, once a year since 2001. FIRA (financial institution specialized in primary activities) has been a closer partner than Rainforest Alliance. It meets more often with Ixtlán Group in order to design training courses about forest management and finding convenient funding mechanisms. The relationship with FIRA is becoming stronger every day as more enterprises from the group need access to financial resources and expertise.

Meanwhile, Ixtlán Group's relationship with its neighboring communities has been respectful but distant. Conflict among neighboring communities is frequent in this region, but that has not been the case of Ixtlán. The enterprises need workers from these communities because they can no longer be found in Ixtlán, and these communities need formal employment for their inhabitants. The first attempt to a closer collaboration is a joint venture between Textitlán, Ixtlán, and Pueblos Mancomunados (two of its main competitors in the region) that seeks to share risks by creating a stronger agent in the furniture retail industry. These three entities also decided to build a furniture design center near the city of Oaxaca. The objective is to add more value to every piece of furniture they produce and identify trends and consumer's needs more promptly. Other stakeholders that share this kind of linkage are local suppliers. In general, they have preference over foreign suppliers, but the relationship with them is strictly commercial. Ixtlán Group is aware that buying supplies locally strengthens the economy, but the group has not involved local suppliers more deeply in its supply chain yet. Finally, CONAFOR (National Forest Commission) is another entity that collaborates with Ixtlán Group, mainly with STF and UNFOSTI. The relationship has been constant since its creation, and it is primarily focused on project funding and the meeting of legal requirements regarding sustainable forest management.

The organization has also developed intermittent linkages with a variety of entities that have been fundamental to the execution of specific projects. After these projects have been completed, the collaboration has stopped. However, in some cases, it has been restored after a while. The WWF (World Wildlife Fund) was an important partner when the ecotourist park was created, as it provided training and expertise. Nonetheless, this nonprofit organization has not developed any other projects with Ixtlán Group. Nowadays, IEEPO (State Institute for Public Education) is one of the largest clients of UCFAS, but due to the constant problems within IEEPO's union, this institution has not been able to develop a closer relationship with any supplier. Local nonprofit organizations such as Estudios Rurales y Asesoría (ERA) and Servicios Comunitarios (SERCO) provided training for the creation of sawmills in the region, including UCFAS, but then the relationship with Ixtlán Group ended.

Finally, there are emergent linkages that the organization is currently developing with the local university (UNSIJ), financial institutions, and some competitors. The UNSIJ is a recently created university with four forestry-related academic programs that generates research and human capital in the region. Ixtlán Group is starting to benefit from it, currently employing two of its first graduates. Additionally, the organization is also collaborating with the university through research projects that explore new productive businesses such as a CO_2 absorption project. Financial institutions are also beginning to partner with Ixtlán Group in order to fund projects. As the enterprises grow, they are becoming attractive for private banks, some of which have already offered preapproved credit lines to the organization.

The Institute of Advanced Studies of the United Nations University reached similar results (to the ones described in this chapter) in a study of the environmental impacts of Ixtlán's forest management program: Although the organization manages the forest with autonomy, Ixtlán Group has maintained a good relationship with regulatory and supportive agencies, the community, and nonprofit organizations. The case of Ixtlán highlights the importance of community ownership and governance in promoting better livelihoods and environmental stewardship (Gu and Subramanian 2012; p. 38).

The sustainable ecosystem promoted by Ixtlán Group has boosted prosperity in the community. The new services available in Ixtlán are evidence of better living standards. A retired worker explains that the pension he receives is not enough to pay for the services he has now: "today I have to pay the phone, electricity, gas, and I do not receive enough money… my wife now uses gas for cooking, has a washing machine and a television to watch soap operas." The last census indicates that 93% of the households have a television, 33% have a computer, 18% have internet, and 99% have electricity, access to water, and drainage. Also, 74% of the inhabitants have social security, and 96% of the children between 6 and 14 years old go to school (INEGI 2010). These numbers are superior to those of any surrounding community.

Although the ecosystem seems to be generating the intended results, there are undesired consequences that the participants need to address. As prosperity has increased in Ixtlán, crime rates have also started to go up. Bars have also opened in the community, raising concerns among community leaders. Regarding Ixtlán Group, some accountability mechanisms slow down decision-making, and as the organization grows, efficiency has been affected by increasing some transaction costs. Also, consumers in the furniture market seem to be price sensitive; most of them are not willing to pay extra money to support a social enterprise or a sustainable use of resources. One future strategy to mend this situation is trying to expand to new markets, maybe internationally, where the consumer is willing to pay for these attributes. Finally, as CCG authorities are democratically elected, some managers believe that the CCG expertise is lost every 3 years and the new elected authorities usually do not have the knowledge to manage the organization. Maybe a new corporate structure may allow authorities to remain linked to the organization after their term.

Ixtlán Group represents a case of how a social enterprise in a subsistence economy context can build a sustainable ecosystem that promotes well-being and prosperity. The six mechanisms designed to build a functioning organization while addressing the stakeholders' needs are the result of local values, indigenous governance systems, Mexican agrarian law, and traditional managerial practices. Although this case is deeply embedded in a particular context, the mechanisms described in this chapter can be further explored to examine their contribution to the creation of sustainable ecosystems in other regions.

References

Alfaro, O. (2014). Microcréditos mexicanos, los más caros de Latam. El Financiero. http://www. elfinanciero.com.mx/economia/mexico-con-los-microcreditos-mas-caros-de-america-latina. html. Accessed 20 Jan 2017.

Ashoka. (2015). *Emprendimiento social en México y Centro América*. Ashoka.

Bornstein, D., & Davis, S. (2010). *Social entrepreneurship: What everyone needs to know*. New York: Oxford University Press.

Bray, D. B. (1991). The struggle for the forest: Conservation and development in the Sierra Juarez. *Grassroots Development, 15*(3), 14–25.

Bray, D., Antinori, C., & Torres-Rojo, J. M. (2006). The Mexican model of community forest management. *Forest Policy and Economics, 8*, 470–484.

Dinero en imagen. (2016). ¿Cómo se define a los informales y cuántos hay en México? http://www.dineroenimagen.com/2016-02-17/68875. Accessed 10 Jan 2017.

Gu, H., & Subramanian, S.M. (2012). *Socio-ecological production landscapes: Relevance to the green economy agenda*. United Nations University Institute of Advanced Studies. http://collections.unu.edu/eserv/UNU:5509/Socioecological_production_landscapes.pdf

INEGI. (2010). *Compendio de información estadística y geográfica municipal*. México: INEGI.

Mair, J., & Martí, I. (2006). Social entrepreneurship research: A source of explanation, prediction, and delight. *Journal of World Business, 41*, 37–44.

Martin. L. & Osberg, S. (2007). Social entrepreneurship: The case for definition. *Stanford Social Innovation Review* 30–39.

Peredo, A. M., & Chrisman, J. J. (2006). Toward a theory of community-based enterprise. *Academy of Management Review, 31*(2), 309–328.

Peredo, A. M., & McLean, M. (2006). Social entrepreneurship: A critical review of the concept. *Journal of World Business, 41*, 56–65.

Rainforest Alliance. (2001). Resumen público de certificación de comunidad Ixtlán de Juárez. SmartWood Program. http://www.rainforest-alliance.org/business/forestry/documents/comunidad-ixtlan.pdf. Accessed 10 Jan 2017.

Santos, F. M. (2012). A positive theory of social entrepreneurship. *Journal of Business Ethics, 111*(3), 335–351.

Santos, F. M., & Eisenhardt K. M. (2006). *Constructing markets and organizing boundaries: Entrepreneurial action in nascent fields*. INSEAD. http://www.insead.edu/facultyresearch/research/doc.cfm?did=1837. Accessed 10 Jan 2017.

Spiggle, S. (1994). Analysis and interpretation of qualitative data in consumer research. *Journal of Consumer Research, 21*(3), 491–503.

The World Bank. (2011). *Empowerment*. The World Bank. http://siteresources.worldbank.org/INTEMPOWERMENT/Resources/486312-1095094954594/draft2.pdf. Accessed 14 Sept 2016.

Vázquez-Maguirre, M., & Portales, L. (2014). La empresa social como generadora de calidad de vida y desarrollo sustentable en comunidades rurales. *Pensamiento y Gestión, 37*, 255–284.

Yunus, M. (2010). *Building social business: The new kind of capitalism that serves humanity's most pressing needs*. New York: Public Affairs.

Chapter 10
Re-imagining the Forest: Entrepreneurial Ecosystem Development for Finnish Cellulosic Materials

Ainomaija Haarla, Henri Hakala, and Greg O'Shea

Abstract This case narrates the story of the creation of a Finnish Cellulose Entrepreneurial Ecosystem and its emergence through a series of community-based phase transitions during the years 2013–2017.

The case is explained by participants in the process who conducted and took part in a combination of more than 100 interviews and meetings. In the case, we explain the transition through phases of community: from a community of dreams through a community of inquiry towards a community of commerce, as the ecosystem emerges. The phases and transitions are characterised and driven by actors playing critical roles. These roles are identified in the phases along with the key processes that the actors lead and participate in.

The implications of the case are that entrepreneurial ecosystems can be created and driven through a bottom-up, community-based approach, driven by forms of public finance, as opposed to the creation of a hub-centred, more top-down model of development, and further that an understanding of roles and microprocesses can contribute to the building, organising and coordinating of ecosystem development.

Keywords Entrepreneurial ecosystem • Communities • Actor roles • Phase transitions

A. Haarla
Aalto University School of Chemical Engineering, Espoo, Finland

H. Hakala
School of Business and Management, Lappeenranta University of Technology, Lappeenranta, Finland

G. O'Shea (✉)
Aalto University School of Business, Helsinki, Finland
e-mail: gregory.oshea@aalto.fi

© Springer International Publishing AG 2018
J. Leitão et al. (eds.), *Entrepreneurial, Innovative and Sustainable Ecosystems*, Applying Quality of Life Research,
https://doi.org/10.1007/978-3-319-71014-3_10

10.1 Introduction

Entrepreneurial ecosystems are formed by a diverse set of interdependent actors and are characterised by 'high rates of entrepreneurship in a local region' (Spigel 2015) and 'rapid job creation, GDP growth, and long-term productivity' (Isenberg 2010). But how might such an ecosystem be planned or designed by policymakers or other national or local authorities? It is clearly a major challenge requiring a conducive culture, enabling policies and leadership, availability of appropriate finance, quality human capital, venture-friendly markets for products and a range of institutional support (Isenberg 2010). The context is also important, as each ecosystem emerges under a unique set of conditions and circumstances.

The setting or geographical region needs to have a certain set of resources to facilitate entrepreneurial success (Zacharakis et al. 2003), and it is 'the interaction between them which determines the success of the ecosystem' (Stam 2015, p.9), and that interaction builds 'one holistic system which turbocharges venture creation and growth' (Isenberg 2010, p. 43). Such holistic interaction activities develop networks, align priorities, build network capabilities (Vesalainen and Hakala 2014) and foster synergies between different stakeholders (Rodríguez-Pose 2013).

An ecosystem is marked by a mutual dependence between actors (den Hartigh and van Asseldonk 2004) and the co-evolution between, or shared fate of, organisations (Iansiti and Levien 2004). In the entrepreneurship literature, most studies adopt the perspective that opportunities are either discovered or created by an innovative individual, a process often described as a *eureka* (Gaglio and Taub 1992) or a *light bulb* (Fletcher 2006) moment. Shepherd (2015) suggests that more social perspectives, such as looking at ecosystem interactions, could advance our understanding of the formation of new opportunities. Such an approach would consider potential opportunities in terms of a process of social interaction (between a community and the entrepreneur) and therefore as a social construction, rather than solely as an outcome of thinking (in the mind of the entrepreneur) (Shepherd 2015). Furthermore, Autio and Thomas (2014) have called for research on the creation process of an ecosystem. The process of working inside the community is critical to the overall emergence of the ecosystem and to negotiating the development phase transitions. The ecosystem emerges through co-creative, microprocesses of interaction, through critical learning and reflection events, and is orchestrated by key actors as key role players. This kind of interaction perspective focuses on the process of activities and events involved in the emergence of a new opportunity within a community (Delmar and Shane 2004), which metamorphoses into an ecosystem.

To further the understanding of ecosystem development, this study elaborates the development phases and identifies the key actor roles of a Finnish project for creating a cellulose entrepreneurship ecosystem (CEE). Finland has a long tradition in highly sustainable forest resource management, and the forest-based industry has a major impact on Finnish society as a whole. The industry is, however, facing threats arising from global competition and other trends such as a reduction in the global demand for paper.

10 Re-imagining the Forest: Entrepreneurial Ecosystem Development for Finnish... 193

Novel methods of using cellulose have become an active research topic due to its abundance in nature, biodegradability and chemical formability and tunability. The development of high-value adding and sustainable entrepreneurial ecosystems using cellulose as their raw material therefore appears to offer an interesting opportunity for a country like Finland that derives much of its welfare from forests. This study is based on longitudinal research in which the authors have followed the development of this Finnish CEE through archival records, active participation in the project and over 100 research meetings and interviews. In Finland, 86% of the land is covered by forests, and the goal of the CEE is to accelerate the transformation of the current large-scale Finnish forest industry into a dynamic ecosystem for the bio-economy, containing both large- and small-scale businesses, producing more products with added value.

We outline how the CEE has undergone several phases of development. The ecosystem transitions from a community of dreams (Koenig 2012) to a scientific research-focused community of inquiry (Shepherd 2015) and finally to a go-to-market-focused community of commerce. This emergence process could also be perceived as a form of self-organisation. During the phase transitions, the community has stakeholders that provide feedback on the feasibility of the potential opportunity (Autio et al. 2013), and within the community, potential opportunities are suggested by individuals (Swedberg 2009) who can test that opportunity with other people and organisations with the expertise and experience to revise and improve their ideas (Pardales and Girod 2006). Another missing dimension in existing research into ecosystems and community as a form of ecosystem is micro-social interactions. The focus on geographical variables within the well-known Isenberg (2010) framework, while important, needs to be informed by an understanding of these concrete interactions between actors, the roles they play, and what they do together (Heikkinen et al. 2007; Gemünden et al. 2007). Hence, our study also contributes by identifying different actors and their roles in an emerging cellulose ecosystem. Finally, we provide a working model of a multidisciplinary approach to the emergence of a bio-economy-based entrepreneurial ecosystem and an analytical framework for understanding the context and the process of this emergence through actors and ecosystem phases.

10.2 Literature

The concept of ecosystems in the business literature describes cross-industrial interactions between companies with certain characteristics. It refers to a network of companies that evolve together both co-operatively and competitively, around a core innovation, to fulfil their goals (Moore 1993). Iansiti and Levien (2004) recognised that ecosystems could include sub-contractors, outsourcing partners, financiers, technology providers, and even customers and – to a lesser extent – regulatory agencies and media. Peltoniemi and Vuori (2004) defined a business ecosystem as a dynamic structure composed of interconnected populations of different types of organisations, including corporations, universities, research centres, public sector organisations, and other actors influencing the system.

The ecosystem analogy allows the study of the interconnectedness of organisations, the resulting dynamics, and possible explanations for the phenomena (Anggraeni et al. 2007). A closely related concept is an innovation ecosystem, which shares similar characteristics to the business ecosystem, and the two terms are often used interchangeably. Adner (2006) explains innovation ecosystems as collaborative arrangements firms use to combine their offerings into a mutual, customer-based solution.

Moore (1993, 2006) claimed that business ecosystems have the following economic model at their core: core capabilities become the basis for providing value to end customers that generate sales volumes, which in turn enable economies of scale and the total experience, which comprises both the core product or service and the complementary offering, and are then delivered to the end customers. Nambisan and Baron (2013) refer to this kind of structure as a hub-based innovation ecosystem. The central company holding the ecosystem leadership – which can also be called the keystone or hub company – usually has need of niche expertise, which causes new, smaller companies to spawn, ultimately leading to more entrepreneurial activity (Iansiti and Levien 2004; Nambisan and Baron 2013).

Entrepreneurship or entrepreneurial ecosystems were highlighted by Valdez (1988), who recognised certain dynamic elements in the formation of new businesses: the entrepreneur and the entrepreneurial environment. Entrepreneurship is said to be a process by which opportunities to create novel goods and services are discovered, evaluated, and exploited (Shane and Venkataraman 2000). More broadly defined, it is the process by which individuals pursue opportunities for innovation. Innovation involves creating new value in society. This innovation can be oriented towards exploration (i.e. pursuing opportunities that are radically new) or towards exploitation, in that the orientation focuses on refining existing opportunities (Lester and Piore 2004).

Cohen (2006, p.2) defined an entrepreneurial ecosystem as 'a diverse set of interdependent actors within a geographic region that influence the formation and eventual trajectory of the entire group of actors and potentially the economy as a whole'. The entrepreneurial ecosystem is also then seen as a local, geographical construct (Spigel 2015). The entrepreneurial ecosystem may be geographically bounded but not confined to a specific geographical scale (e.g. campus area, city, or a region) and could be seen as a specialised type of organisational-industrial cluster, which develops over time within a specific geographical region and is replenished or expanded by new ventures (Cohen 2006). This form of cluster embodies the co-evolution of firms around particular innovations, technologies, or markets. The ecosystem generates incentives for entrepreneurial activity, linking potentially surplus resources to extant ecosystem participants and other opportunity-oriented individuals outside of the system (Spilling 1996). Storper and Venables (2004) and Bathelt et al. (2004) have emphasised the importance of locality and what the latter research terms '*local buzz* – an information and communication ecology created by face-to-face contacts, co-presence and co-location of people and firms within the same place or region' (Bathelt et al. 2004,p.9).

The entrepreneurial ecosystem concept stresses how entrepreneurship is enabled by a comprehensive set of resources and actors that play an important role in enabling entrepreneurial action. Most of these are present locally, often requiring face-to-face contact or local mobility. The entrepreneurial ecosystem literature particularly focuses on the role of the (social) context in enabling or constraining entrepreneurship, the interdependencies between actors within the system, or a community of interdependent actors.

A community or a type of business ecosystem only emerges and holds together if its members are in agreement about the development of a common project. Our study focuses on the process of activities and events involved in the emergence of a new opportunity within a local, Finnish ecosystem which begins and emerges as a form of community (Delmar and Shane 2004). Koenig (2012) proposed a typology based on the type of reciprocity and control of key resources. The model includes four types of business ecosystems: supply systems; platforms; critically for our case, communities of destiny; and expanding communities. Both supply and platform systems feature centralised control or resources. Supply systems (similar to the model presented by Iansiti and Levien (2004)) are a centralised network in which a hub company controls key resources and surrounding companies take the role of a sub-contractor. Platform ecosystems are also centralised, but in contrast to supply systems, the hub company does not define the actions of smaller contributors but essentially provides the rules for the platform that other contributors must follow. In these centralised networks, the strategic centre gathers a small number of important partners together to engage in mobilising, designing, and controlling, to make a competitive offer to its customers.

The third and fourth types of design have non-centralised forms of control. For example, communities of destiny are organised around an existential solidarity which unites a heterogeneous group of actors. The system is not centralised, even if certain actors contribute more than others to its leadership. The final type of design groups a large number of members around an essential resource perceived to be a common good. This is an *expanding community*, and its design differs from that of the platform design in its non-proprietary character regarding the key resource, while it comes closer to the platform design in its member interdependence, while the contribution of each is distinct and isolable. The type of development for this design is expansion, which distinguishes it from a community of destiny. In such expanding communities, stakeholders cooperate without locking themselves into rigid contracts. Value creation is the product of a joint effort in a context of open participation. A number of empirical studies offer significant results on the importance of these ecosystems to fostering the dynamics of innovation (Adner 2006; Gawer and Cusumano 2014; Iansiti and Levien 2004; Maniak et al. 2014). These contributions demonstrate that the more interactions between stakeholders are open but organised within given platforms, the more likely their contributions are to be a source of value for the largest possible number.

In recent years, there has been a growing momentum behind the process view (Steyaert 2007; Van de Ven and Engleman 2004). The process literature is rich in explanations of non-linear pathways of emergence (Lichtenstein and Plowman 2009) as well as conceptualisations of the entrepreneurial journey as an emergent process in which abstract ideas are converted into tangible ventures (Dimov 2007; Lichtenstein and Kurjanowicz 2010; Venkataraman et al. 2012). As Shepherd (2015) suggests, this kind of more social perspective could advance our understanding of the formation of opportunities. The process explanation is usually developed by first eliciting sequences of events from narrative accounts (Van de Ven and Engleman 2004) and then operationalising explanatory mechanisms to explain the contingent pathway of an entrepreneurial journey (Lichtenstein et al. 2006).

A critical role in the functioning of entrepreneurial ecosystems appears to be fulfilled by forms of governance that combine sufficient structure and stability in their connections to enable investment but are also flexible enough to permit recombination and innovation. The form of governance and the process of deciding and agreeing, according to Moore, are important, and therefore an understanding of the processes being used is important. Moore himself saw a place for the use of the theory of complex adaptive systems (2006), while Peltoniemi (2006) saw a business ecosystem as fundamentally an evolving and developing structure. Business ecosystem discourse can be seen as part of larger complex systems research in social sciences which looks at complex adaptive systems characterised by distributed control, emergence, and self-organisation (Peltoniemi and Vuori 2004). Emergence here means that properties, qualities, patterns, and structures of a system rise out of interactions between actors (Peltoniemi and Vuori 2004). In the case of an entrepreneurial ecosystem, these actors are individuals, and emergence is a bottom-up process, starting from local micro-level interactions, which take place over time between interconnected actors.

The entrepreneurial creation process has constituent activities, processes, conditions and roles and can also be seen as one of the generating and refining potential opportunities through constituent activities, processes, conditions and roles. Despite the proposition that business ecosystems emerge from local interactions and negotiations between organisations (Peltoniemi and Vuori 2004), there has been no analysis of the tools and the processes that cause such ecosystems to emerge that would enable researchers to truly benefit from the ecosystem analogy (Adomavicius et al. 2006). A framework that establishes the elements and boundaries of the journey within a community has not yet been developed by process theorists (McMullen and Dimov 2013). Peltoniemi (2006) distinguishes a mutualistic form of business ecosystem, in which organisations cooperate and develop complementary capabilities in order to tackle a common enemy. In our case, mutual collaboration and agent level interactions, involving co-creation and sense-making actions taken by key actors playing key roles, lead to the emergence of, first, a community based on a compelling vision or dream (similar to Koenig's (2012) destiny) and then a community based on a need for enquiry (Shepherd 2015) and then to a community of commerce.

It is this series of microprocesses and actor roles that we seek to understand. Accordingly, we will borrow concepts taken from actor roles in innovation projects (Gemünden 2007), actor roles in innovation networks (Heikkinen et al. 2007), the facilitating of innovation networks (Kristiansen 2014) and the processes proposed in collective forms of sense-making (Nahi and Halme 2015).

10.3 Research Methodology

Our research involved a multistage and longitudinal study that spanned several Finnish organisations and a broad range of individual experiences in a project seeking to create a new entrepreneurial ecosystem. The research was conducted in several steps: preliminary investigation, in-depth interviews and data gathering, coding and analysis and finally validation.

First, exploratory interviews were conducted with five key participants within the project to understand the nature of their ecosystem development efforts and to map the community in which they work. Second, we conducted 44 semi-structured interviews with 20 members of the project working in the science and design fields, covering different locations, job roles and units. These interviews were conducted between December 2015 and May 2017.

We interviewed five people several times to gather additional evidence and discuss our interpretation of the information gained from previous interviews. Our interviews focused on individuals' direct experience with the processes in the project. We asked interviewees to describe how the community worked; what kept it together, to outline its success factors; and how entrepreneurial ideas and opportunities were developed. We also asked the interviewees to reflect on which aspects they saw as key to effective community-style ecosystem development. The interviews lasted between 45 and 60 min and were recorded and transcribed.

These preliminary and second round interviews were part of an in-depth case study of the ecosystem creation project of which the authors are part. Our role as business specialists in the project was to develop the conditions for a fully-fledged ecosystem around the new cellulosic materials. We were therefore present at all project meetings and seminars, internal and external, and helped to suggest what technologies might become commercial propositions and how new venture ideas could become opportunities. To this end we have attended more than 50 internal meetings.

The transcripts and notes comprise almost 200 pages of data. In the first-order analysis, we made little attempt to distil categories, so the number of categories was large. Fundamentally, we were looking for all forms of enablers that advanced the development of the ecosystem. As the research progressed, we started to see similarities and differences among the many categories and were able to group categories into labels or phrasal descriptors. By the time of the third-order analysis, we were asking whether the emerging themes suggested concepts that might help us describe and explain the phenomena we were observing. Once we had these third-order themes, we could then configure our data into a visual aid, which also provided a graphic representation of how we progressed from raw data to terms and themes in conducting the analyses, a key component of demonstrating rigour in qualitative research (Pratt 2009; Tracy 2010). The fourth stage of the study involved discussing our findings with a range of stakeholders in the project to validate our thinking. A steering group of the project's most accomplished technologists provided detailed feedback in meetings. We then participated in informal meetings with other senior technologists from the project, where we presented our findings, and engaged in discussions to test the generalisability of the challenges identified and the feasibility of the solutions documented in this chapter.

10.4 The Finnish Cellulose Entrepreneurship Ecosystem

10.4.1 Context of the CEE

The central goal for the CEE project is to actively and consciously combine new wood-based technology, materials design and new business creation using state innovation funding as an initial resource to kick-start the emergence of a new entrepreneurial ecosystem. The project officially began in the spring of 2013 and will run until spring 2018. The project brings together businesses and researchers from different fields including engineering, chemistry, materials science, design and business studies. The project has already developed a number of promising technologies (see Table 10.1) that may catalyse or form a backbone for a new sustainable and innovative ecosystem around cellulosic products.

Finland has a long tradition in sustainable forest resource management, and also in the design and research of forest-based products, and well-developed supply networks for handling wood materials. The chemical treatment of cellulose, called pulping, was invented in the nineteenth century. Traditionally, pulp and all products made from it – mainly paper and board – have been major exports from Finland, and the forest-based industry has had a major impact on Finnish society as a whole. The long history of the wood-based economy has left Finland with high-technology plants and an extensive knowledge of wood processing, which have in turn contributed to a willingness to utilise wood resources in a sustainable manner. The Finnish forest industry can be characterised as a mature industry, in which innovation has not previously been seen as a high priority (Peltoniemi 2013) and where the focus has been on efficient and effective systems for harvesting the wood from the forests, transporting it to cellulose mills and turning the wood into pulp suitable for producing paper, cardboard and other products. Demand for the most important products, paper and board, has been relatively stable, and the products themselves are bulk, low-value and offer limited opportunity for innovation (Järvinen and Linnakangas

10 Re-imagining the Forest: Entrepreneurial Ecosystem Development for Finnish...

Table 10.1 New technologies and materials in focus in the CEE

Ioncell-F is a process for producing man-made cellulosic fibres. These are synthetic polymers made from natural resources. Yarns produced by dissolving birch and eucalyptus pulp have been used to create pieces of clothing for demonstration purposes.
Foam forming is an enabling technology that can be applied in several application fields for example: specialty papers, filter materials, and technical textiles.
Swelling fibre yarn is a cellulose filament preparation process using fibrous cellulose I particles (i.e. pulp fibres and potentially other cellulosic materials such as (nano-fibrillated cellulose).
Nano-cellulose is cellulose that has been hydrolysed to form very small fragments. Nano-cellulose exhibits many unusual physical and chemical properties in terms of stiffness and ability to bind water, in addition to being biocompatible and biodegradable (Lin and Dufresne 2014).

2012). The need for these traditional wood and paper products is not going to disappear any day soon, but the emergence of an electronic media has reduced the global demand for printing paper. The historical capabilities developed in the forestry industry are no longer sufficient to guarantee a competitive advantage, which leaves the Finnish forestry sector with two choices: to capitalise on the existing capabilities in new ways and to develop totally new ones (Järvinen and Linnakangas 2012), and an awareness of the need for strategic change and the exploration of additional sustainable ways to derive wealth from the forests has begun.

In the largest Finnish forest corporations there is growing interest in the high-technology, high-value use of nano-cellulose in biomedical applications (e.g. using a cell culture matrix made from nano-cellulose for growing tissue from stem cells), but in terms of revenue, this kind of business is still in its infancy. However, firms are currently investing in new production capacity that could be flexibly used to produce new cellulose applications, an example being the construction of the new bio product factory in Äänekoski, Central Finland, which is the biggest ever single investment in the industry (von Weymarn 2015).

Such large-scale projects also present opportunities for small companies with novel business models built around cellulose, and there are start-up companies developing products based on unconventional uses of cellulose. At the political level, the current Finnish government is also emphasising the role of the bio-economy and clean solutions in building the future competitiveness of the nation (Anon, Finnish Prime Minister's Office 2015). The future-oriented Finnish Innovation Fund, Sitra, published a vision of a distributed bio-based economy in 2011, and the National Bio-economy Strategy was launched in May 2014 as an initiative by the Ministry of Employment. Hence, there appears to be strong political support for developing new cellulose-based businesses.

The foremost new cellulose-based materials and technologies are described in Table 10.1.

10.4.2 Emergence of the CEE: Phases of Community, Transitions, Roles and Processes

10.4.2.1 Phases of Community

The German sociologist Tönnies highlighted the distinction between *Gemeinschaft* and *Gesellschaft* communities (Community and Society) as early as 1887 (Waters 2016). In a *Gemeinschaft*, relationships emerge out of social interactions of a personal nature, and personal emotional attachments are maintained through private sentiment and loyalty, rather than through a connection involving concepts of productivity or the marketplace. In contrast, in *Gesellschaft* societies, interactions are more rational and reflect impersonal relationships, explained through the medium of money. Tönnies saw *Gemeinschaft* relations as being absorbed into a more modern rational *Gesellschaft* society.

More recently, Shepherd, in the context of entrepreneurship research (2015), has called for investigations into communities capable of developing entrepreneurial opportunities (entrepreneurial communities) and has also suggested that communities may morph in different directions. Essentially, this type of strategic learning, leading to a transition of the community, is not a straightforward process (Sirén et al. 2017), and hence our study of the CEE aligns with these ideas and proposes that there is not one form of community that emerges (as a specific type of ecosystem), but a series of emergent forms or phases of a community that transition and eventually become the entrepreneurial ecosystem. Our observations suggest that the CEE transitions from a *community of dreams* to a *community of inquiry* and finally to a *community of commerce*.

This emergence process that we see as transitioning or morphing within the entrepreneurial ecosystem is a form of self-organisation or a spontaneous coming together of a group for a purpose. A helpful precondition for self-organisation would be a symbiotic relationship between the participants such that they each provide a particular input that makes up the system, and that are complementary, and can co-evolve sympathetically (Thomas and Autio 2012) through generating and sharing new knowledge. This systemic learning process is based on the interaction of individuals creating new patterns of thought at the macro and micro levels. Mitleton-Kelly (2003) suggests that this generation and sharing of knowledge must be facilitated by providing the appropriate sociocultural and technical conditions to support connectivity and interdependence and to catalyse self-organisation (and emergence).

One such condition that we see clearly in the CEE is governance based on a horizontal as opposed to a hierarchical structure, which facilitates the phase transitions by fostering multiple local and cross collaborations between actors belonging to partner organisations (Donada and Attias 2015).

Other previous research also identifies a number of roles that are crucial for innovation, for example, gatekeepers (Allen 1970) and champions (Markham and Griffin 1998). By *roles* we mean behaviours displayed and actions taken by actors in particular positions and in particular contexts and in particular on the critical roles in the ecosystem development.

Such types of actor roles have been widely discussed in the social sciences for several decades, with a particular emphasis on role theory, which traditionally places individuals as the primary unit of analysis. In the case of the CEE, we also include dyads (two persons acting together) and triads (three persons acting together) alongside organisations as key actors performing in the ecosystem. The roles played in the case are only occasionally determined by actors' formal positions; in other words, the actor is adopting an expected and established position and then behaves accordingly. In this case, the majority of roles are not consequences of a formal position in a social structure, but must be claimed. Consequently, certain individuals change roles and might even play multiple roles. The roles are therefore a situation-specific construct and are dynamic and processual, describing what actors are doing within the overall process of the emergence of the ecosystem via phase transitions of community.

Research with partners in the CEE has shown that individuals pushing the emergence of the ecosystem recognise certain key promoter-style roles (Hauschildt and Schewe 2000) and, further, that different forms of key promoter-style roles are required for phase transitions to occur from the initial *dream* of an entrepreneurial ecosystem through the more detailed investigation of such possible opportunities in an *inquiry-focused* community through to the rational economic focus of the community of commerce. Each phase has certain characteristics in terms of these key roles, key actions and key processes.

10.4.2.2 Dream Phase

In the *dream phase*, a *Gemeinschaft*-type community of small collectives containing just a few people that know each other well (Waters 2016) shares a common understanding of what needs to be done. As in Koenig's community examples (2012), this community of dreams is a decentralised, heterogeneous group of actors bound together by a desire or a dream, an emotional and compelling common purpose. This phase has some similarities with forms of social movement, in that it is a collective process that looks to remedy perceived social and ecological problems by mobilising networks of individuals, groups and organisations bound by a shared collective identity (Hargrave and Van de Ven 2006). The dream phase in the case of the CEE began during a university summer project where technology students, art students and staff from Aalto University in Helsinki created concepts they called *World of Cellulose* and *Luxurious Cellulose Finland*. The teams were exploring a dream within the field of cellulosic materials, that a real paradigm change could occur in cellulose-based product portfolios by combining the fresh approach of art and design students with experts in advanced and non-conventional technological approaches and concepts, which were not being used by the Finnish forest industry at that time. The dream community was therefore based on an engaging and compelling vision to transform the current large-scale forest bio-economy into a vibrant ecosystem that would make Finland a source of novel and sustainable value-added cellulosic products.

The first and perhaps most important of the key roles in this phase is that of the **visionary,** played by the original senior research scientists. At this point the few individuals in the community envision the need for some form of large-scale institutional change to address future opportunities that will arise as part of their vision being enacted. Without such a driving and future-oriented role, new entrepreneurial opportunities would not have been imagined and funding would not have been acquired to push the phase transition towards the community of inquiry manifestation. A fundamental challenge at this stage is that these individuals do not have the resources, power or legitimacy to introduce such change by themselves. They therefore investigate what resources and networks are available and start to organise coalitions and to ally themselves with complementary interests and resources.

As a result, more diverse actors became engaged and embedded in the process where they can contribute to the larger dream by recombining existing practices, technologies and institutions. This collection and organisation of existing resources is done by a **resource explorer** who organises the exchange of information, seeking appropriate actors to come together, and looks for external sources of funding to transition towards and through the community of inquiry phase.

The **diplomat** is required in this phase to show political awareness in understanding the interests of the other actors in the expanding community, as well as the ability to frame the dream agenda in ways that appeal to the interests and identities of those other actors, and, critically, of the funding body or bodies that will allow the following inquiry phase to take place. The diplomat and the resource explorer together encourage the mutual understanding of new knowledge and technologies and continually contribute to the diffusion of information.

For the community to generate even greater commitment and a *local buzz* requires the creation of meaningful stories on the importance of the vision and the need to make institutional changes and actions that interested parties and actors can take to help promote such a change. **Missionaries** then act to tell these stories. Missionaries believe that the committed community can be a powerful agent of change in society and engage in trying to create a base from which they can pursue the community vision and advance the cause.

For this dream phase to succeed and transition to a more formal inquiry phase required key structures to be available for the (small) network of actors to mobilise and together engage in a form of collective action. The critical opportunity structure turned out to be the state innovation fund (the Finnish Funding Agency for Innovation or TEKES) which provided resources to take the dream forward based on a persuasive framing process delivered by the community and an altruistic form of leadership, acting without reward, in the belief that their dream of an ecosystem could be publicly promoted without major involvement from large companies or entrepreneurs at this point.

10.4.2.3 Transition from Dream to Inquiry Phase

The community of inquiry is fundamentally a place of learning, sharing and motivation. In this phase, the community focuses on more resource gathering and initial materials technology and conceptualising (product/service) development. Achieving the vision and developing the potential opportunities within a fully functioning entrepreneurial ecosystem require an extended number of community members to group around the essential forestry and technology resources in a process of social interaction and as a community to investigate the viability of the potential opportunity (Autio et al. 2013). Consistent with this interactive view of opportunity identification and refinement, the notion of potential opportunity is not in the mind of an individual, the initial creator, but is grounded in the community and in the way that actors act together to co-create and explore that opportunity.

Also in this phase, the ecosystem participants cooperate to define a collective purpose (a collective purpose being less clear for community ecosystems in which collaboration problems are more likely to arise), a refined collective identity to encompass the added members and then to co-opt key customers and partners to define value logics. Actors interact dynamically with each other to realise the purpose of the collective (i.e. the dream to be fulfilled) and to help individuals identify mutual opportunity ideas, by enabling a similar interpretation of data and employing similar vocabulary to express their emerging understanding.

At the beginning of the phase of inquiry a fundamental challenge is to bridge the various languages and thought processes that exist within the community, between designers, scientists, engineers, funders and business actors. A main aim is to enhance the networking and collaboration of the community, so that actors from different fields understand each other's roles and ways of working. Such work starts and continues at key events with networking and meetings to develop collaborative processes and functions. The leadership has a central role during the inquiry phase involving nurturing membership by building on everyday conversations and agreeing how to ensure transparent decision-making processes (Kristiansen 2014).

As the community becomes more formalised, a **conductor** becomes very important, as that person nurtures membership and helps the structuring necessary for effective self-organizing. An element critical to the productive coordination of interactions is the underlying structure of processes that connect all the participants together. One such collaborative process is the choice of governance mechanism to foster the adherence of actors to the community and to coordinate and control the actions of stakeholders. An example would be the introduction of procedures for regular monthly meetings to support networking and the building of trust. In these monthly meetings, all members or actor representatives should be present to discuss their part of the project in a language that is accessible to the all other attendees.

Once inhibitors are removed and enablers put in place, new behaviours and ways of working emerge, which enable a form of agent interaction that is not centrally or hierarchically controlled. The various actor stakeholders involved in the project begin to identify cross-dependencies in the community relationships, which lead to new ideas for opportunity development and for ways of working. Individuals self-organise to decide upon and take appropriate actions to take opportunities forward.

This mutuality and self-organising is a form of collective sense-making. Sense-making refers to a process whereby people attempt to make sense of unfamiliar contexts and unexpected events (Weick 1995). Individuals construct common mental frameworks that offer explanations for an event (Nahi and Halme 2015), turning emerging understandings into words (Weick et al. 2005). In order to do this successfully, certain ground rules or norms must be adhered to. Beinhocker (2007) formulates a list of norms that offer a specification of the internal culture elements that are required (for collective sense-making), and these include a desire for continuous and improving excellence as well as a commitment to honesty and a meritocracy. Several community actors mention the fundamental role of openness in the cross-disciplinary relationships and also of a feeling of trust and equality that encourages all participants to speak freely.

In order to keep the diverse and cross-disciplined group together, certain other actors work as **interpreters**. The interpreter role mediates the dialogue between the domains of expertise represented at the meetings, workshops and during conversations. The interpreter facilitates the communication process by helping diverse actors to understand each other by applying a knowledge of different sets of cultural norms and values. Interpreters can therefore be described as bilingual in the field of knowledge areas and institutional practices and routines. This enables them to act as negotiators if there are conflicting value systems, by providing explanations and synthesising conversations to help parties arrive at a meaningful set of shared understandings and actions.

One of the challenges in collective sense-making is the perceived fuzziness of work and interaction at the individual actor level. This inquiry phase of the community's development is characterised by fuzzy goals and relatively few signposts. Actors can often envision a future state but have great difficulty in portraying how to get there (Nahi and Halme 2015). Therefore, road mapping work to predict and enact the future is a significant part of the phase and helps with the general, collective and prospective sense-making process. The **sense helper** is an actor who creates and presents frameworks and roadmaps to help with the mutual and individual sense-making processes that are necessary to give individuals within the community some clarity of direction in the medium to longer term. These roadmaps help to conceptualise what Kristiansen (2014) calls *the problem space* and to visually summarise the work of the community and its progress. This is particularly important, as in this phase the community has evolved into a multidisciplinary, multi-actor network and this collective sense-making helps to identify the correlations and interactions between actors, factors and events, thus supporting the implementation of the roadmap.

Towards the end of this inquiry phase, the community starts another phase transition towards becoming a community of commerce, which involves a stronger focus on opportunities created. Technology readiness assessments are conducted in order to integrate various streams of technology and materials development and to prepare to converge on specific opportunities identified within the technologies and materials. Internal and external co-creation workshops are used to ideate and develop new concept opportunities, often using fortunate accident scenarios, where certain individuals take something considered mundane in one discipline across a boundary into their own discipline, where a different value proposition then becomes apparent.

Such **boundary crossers** recognise, gather, interpret and disseminate nonredundant information across boundaries (Allen 1977; Tushman 1977) by entering into unfamiliar territory and negotiating and combining ingredients from different contexts to achieve hybrid solutions (Engeström et al. 1995). A compatible role which operates at a more macro-level to drive the transition from the community of inquiry to one of commerce is that of the **helicopter pilot**. This is someone who stands apart from the local actor interactions and is aware of the greater strategic and national-regional possibilities and of the opportunities that the community is producing that have the potential to become concrete business opportunities that might trigger the creation of new companies. The helicopter pilot looks across formal organisational and technology boundaries to reduce barriers to the flow of information between other like-minded communities and networks that are also looking to transform the greater bio-economy and promote higher-level opportunity identification at the level of a technology paradigm.

10.4.2.4 Transition from Inquiry to Commerce Phase

In the dream phase, there are a small number of active participants. There is now a need in this later phase for richer interactions with more market-based external actors to co-create functionalities of services and product, and to further define the logics that drive the co-creation of value. This series of interactions now helps the community to produce and then sustain a more entrepreneurial culture.

The absorption of new knowledge and new ideologies from these external actors is the process through which community members eventually find the motivation to act entrepreneurially (Marti et al. 2013), to become 'entrepreneurised'. This process, which is here described as 'entrepreneurisation', helps actors within the community to develop a collective entrepreneurial culture, being progressively equipped with ideas and values coming originally from inside and latterly from outside of their community. There is now the combination of *Gemeinschaft* and *Gesellschaft* elements of an entrepreneurial culture and at the same time communitarian ties of mutuality.

The community has now transitioned beyond multidisciplinary co-creation into multi-organisational and multidisciplinary co-creation, creating a highly experimental and fuzzy environment, which is demanding for all actors involved. Organic structures have been found to be more favourable to the success and emergence of entrepreneurial initiatives (Hakala et al. 2016), but this fuzziness again requires a common language, a curious and respectful attitude towards different disciplines and an understanding of diverse working methods. The co-creation process requires articulation of emerging understandings by each of the actors and group level elaboration that can yield new and congruent understandings as a basis for joint action. This requires a specialist **co-creator** to facilitate an open and equal innovation approach, where internal actors and more recent external newcomers can interact to make key decisions together (Lee et al. 2012).

In this phase of the CEE, co-creation is used to develop and commercialise technological innovations through collectively constructing an industrial infrastructure. The collective constructions must then be implemented through negotiation and persuasion, and this requires an **architect** role. A more proprietary and business focus requires more understanding and action to construct critical institutional arrangements such as clarity on property rights, materials standards and certification, supply chain flows and future financing arrangements.

Joint venture and partnering expertise are also required to lead collaboration with larger partners, SMEs or possible in-house start-ups or spin-offs that would evolve from technology pilots. Former entrepreneurs within the community who have previously built successful companies and intrapreneurs with previous corporate entrepreneurship expertise who reinvest their experience in the community during this phase in order to build a bridge between community intrapreneurs and possible funders or consortium actors can be described as adopting a **bridger** role. The role also involves creating and supporting activities that enhance the entrepreneurial environment, for example, by lobbying government and establishing new organisations that support entrepreneurial activity. Similarly, a **mentor** contributes directorial experience acquired through positions on start-up or spin-off boards of directors and in the CEE also engages in teaching entrepreneurship, acting as a mentor in student start-up competitions connected to future commercial development of the cellulosic materials opportunities.

The involvement of a critical mass of experienced entrepreneurs who have contributed time, energy and wisdom to support the ecosystem is particularly helpful to **intrapreneurs**. Intrapreneurship within the CEE describes entrepreneurial behaviours within an existing organisation in terms of the creation of new ventures. They develop business models built on market knowledge of consumption patterns, pricing, market structure and supply chain structure.

The key roles and phase transitions are summarised in Table 10.2.

A visual representation of the community transitions and the emergence of the ecosystem through the community phase transitions can be seen in Fig. 10.1.

10 Re-imagining the Forest: Entrepreneurial Ecosystem Development for Finnish...   207

Table 10.2 Key roles and role descriptions in the phase transitions

Phase	Key roles	Description
Dream	Visionary	A driving and future-oriented role, imagines and clarifies new entrepreneurial opportunities and large-scale institutional change to address future opportunities
Dream	Resource explorer	Collects and organises existing resources and networks, influences external actors and helps in the process of recombining existing practices, technologies and institutions as a resource
Dream	Diplomat	Shows political awareness in understanding the interests of the other actors in the expanding community, helps frame the dream agenda to appeal to the interests and identities of actors outside of the initial community and liaises closely with the funding body and local and national government
Dream	Missionary	Helps create and then convey meaning and meaningful stories on the importance of the entrepreneurial ecosystem vision, on the need to make institutional changes and actions that actors and others can take to help promote such a change
Inquiry	Conductor	Nurtures membership by building on everyday conversations, creates agreement on how to ensure transparency in decision-making processes, helps the structuring needed for effective self-organising
Inquiry	Interpreter	Keeps the diverse and multidisciplined group together, mediates the dialogue between the domains of expertise, facilitates the open communication process
Inquiry	Sense helper	Creates and presents frameworks to help with the mutual and individual sense-making processes that are needed to give individuals within the community some clarity of direction in the medium to longer term
Inquiry	Boundary crosser	Takes the mundane from one discipline across a boundary into their own discipline, recognises, gathers, interprets and disseminates relevant information across boundaries to create new opportunity ideas
Inquiry	Helicopter pilot	Operates at a macro-level to drive the transition from the community of inquiry to commerce, stands apart from the local actor interactions and is aware of the greater strategic and national-regional possibilities and opportunities that the community is producing
Commerce	Co-creator	Facilitates, helps articulate and support emerging understandings and opportunity ideas of the partners and of the group level collaboration needed as a basis for joint action, facilitates an open and equal innovation approach
Commerce	Architect	Leads the construction process of an industrial infrastructure for commercialisation, implements through negotiation and persuasion and helps design critical institutional arrangements such as clarity on property rights, materials standards and certification, supply chain construction and future financing arrangements
Commerce	Bridger	Has joint venture and partnering expertise to lead collaboration with larger partners, SMEs or possible in-house start-ups or spin-offs that evolve from pilots; creates and supports activities that enhance the entrepreneurial environment, for example, lobbying government and establishing organisations that support entrepreneurial activity

(continued)

Table 10.2 (continued)

Phase	Key roles	Description
Commerce	Mentor	Contributes director-level experience through positions on start-up or spin-off boards of directors. Acts as a teacher and judge for new student start-up competitions
Commerce	Intrapreneur	Exhibits entrepreneurial behaviours within an existing organisation and within the community, in terms of the creation of new ventures; develops business models built on acquired market knowledge of consumption patterns, pricing, market structure and supply chain structure

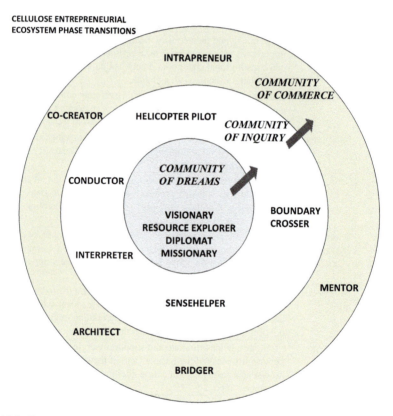

Fig. 10.1 Phase transitions

10.5 Conclusions and Implications

The *Finnish Road Map to a Circular Economy* published in 2016 (Sitra 2016) highlights the determination of the Finnish state to work with key public, private and third-sector organisations to pioneer a circular economy aiming to decouple economic development from environmental degradation. The road map sets Finland a target to be a global leader in the circular economy by 2025. This vision of Finland succeeding as a pioneer in sustainable wellbeing sees cellulose-based bio-materials as playing a significant role in the future of the planet. Fossil oil-based materials such as plastics and resource-intensive materials such as cotton or aluminium can be increasingly replaced by cellulose-based materials as technologies develop and markets become more favourable.

The forest element of the road map aims to promote economic growth and create new jobs in Finland by supporting the development of new products and services derived from the country's forests that can add high levels of value (Sitra 2016). New forest-based entrepreneurial ecosystems can have a great impact on the creation of a future Finnish economy. In the case of cellulose, the opportunity can be seen alongside the development of the circular economy. Nano-cellulose, fibres from lignin and biochemicals from hemicelluloses have a multitude of future applications ranging from bionics materials to superconductors to growth substrates for synthetic biology. These future applications and specialised high-value products will add value to cellulose and the current value chains.

A dynamic model of entrepreneurial ecosystem development represents an important step forward in our understanding of ecosystems that emerge based on technology transfer (Autio et al. 2014; Autio and Thomas 2014). This dynamic model includes an enabling environment or context in which actors play key roles using critical processes that cause phase transitions and the emergence of the Finnish cellulose entrepreneurial ecosystem (the CEE). The systemic conditions are the foundation for the ecosystem: networks of large and small companies, community leadership, sources of finance, local talent, knowledge and sophisticated support services. The presence of these elements and the interaction between them help to ground the success of the ecosystem. Leadership, through its actions in the community phases, provides direction and role models for the entrepreneurial ecosystem. This leadership is critical in building and maintaining the ecosystem. This involves a set of visible visionary leaders who are committed to the creation of the Finnish CEE. Access to financing, preferably provided by actors with knowledge of entrepreneurship, is crucial for investments in such technology-driven entrepreneurial projects with a longer-term horizon where market returns may be quite distant (Kerr and Nanda 2009).

An important source of opportunities for entrepreneurship can be found in knowledge from both public and private organisations (Audretsch et al. 2005), and perhaps the most important element of the CEE is the presence of a diverse and highly skilled group of committed actors. These actors have different goals, expectations and attitudes, and many authors have called for more research on this topic in entrepreneurial ecosystems. In this case we highlight 14 roles that actors adopt and show how the roles work during phase transitions and the emergence of the ecosystem. These roles help understand how ecosystems characterised by openness and the coexistence of mutually shared and diverse individual motives can be built.

From a practitioner perspective, the study contributes to managerial knowledge by providing a framework tool to identify the prerequisites for open and bottom-up ecosystem emergence in terms of actor roles. The CEE is fundamentally built on

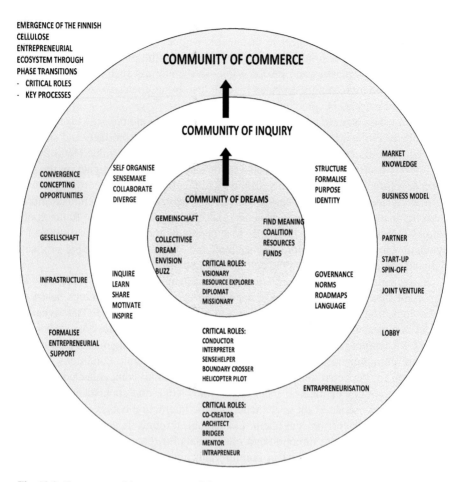

Fig. 10.2 Emergence of the entrepreneurial ecosystem

innovation discovery, but the idea of innovation should not only be applied to products; it also should be applied to ecosystem people practices (Birkinshaw et al. 2008), ecosystem structures and governance models. In this context, the key success factors are those that relate to the ability to mutually orchestrate, conduct and structure the creation of innovations within an open-innovation style system designed to foster collaboration between actors who may not typically have communicated openly with one another, for example, in a centralised ecosystem controlled by a hub-type organisation (Chesbrough et al. 2006; Damanpour and Aravind 2012).

A visual representation of the roles, processes and transitions is shown in Fig. 10.2.

There is a need for a detailed understanding of the processes by which ecosystems are created. In our case, new knowledge on cellulosic materials should be shared to generate further new learning and opportunities, and the process is about understanding connectivity, interdependence, emergence and self-organisation. We extend research linking collective sense-making to ecosystem development, and, specifically, our findings help identify the specific mechanisms that drive sense-making, including the conditions that facilitate learning and the generation and sharing of knowledge.

This case offers further reflection on the governance model, which is suitable for community-based ecosystems, based on decentralised control. To successfully develop community-based ecosystems, leaders will need to manage new operating models and learn new ways of collaborating and of creating and capturing value and a process for co-creation encompassing various actors. That last process will also have to allow for the chance emergence of breakthrough ideas in the areas of products, services and business models. Policymakers have primarily supported the creation of knowledge ecosystems assuming that these ecosystems will automatically trigger the development of business ecosystems. However, the value creation processes in the bottom-up, emergent, knowledge-driven ecosystem and those in the traditional hub-based business ecosystem are fundamentally different, and policies to support each type will have to be designed accordingly.

New cellulose-based products will provide Finland with a significant competitive advantage arising from the country's sustainable source of the biomass and the infrastructure to export products around the world. The renewability, climate friendliness and biodegradability of cellulose-based biomaterials allow for a more positive vision of the future.

References

Adner, R. (2006). Match your innovation strategy to your innovation ecosystem. *Harvard Business Review, 84*(4), 98.

Adomavicius, G., Bockstedt, J., Gupta, A., & Kauffman, R. J. (2006). Understanding patterns of technology evolution: An ecosystem perspective. In *System Sciences, 2006. HICSS'06. Proceedings of the 39th Annual Hawaii International Conference on* (Vol. 8, pp. 189a–189a). IEEE.

Allen, T. J. (1970). Communication networks in R & D laboratories. *R&D Management, 1*(1), 14–21.

Allen, T. J. (1977). *Managing the flow of technology: Technology transfer and the dissemination of technological information within the R and D organization*. Cambridge: MIT Press.

Anggraeni, E., Den Hartigh, E., & Zegveld, M. (2007, October). Business ecosystem as a perspective for studying the relations between firms and their business networks. In *ECCON 2007 Annual meeting*.

Anon. (2015). *Finland, a land of solutions. Strategic Programme of Prime Minister Juha Sipilä's Government*. [Pdf] Prime Minister's Office. Available at: http://valtioneuvosto.fi/documents/10184/1427398/Ratkaisujen+Suomi_EN_YHDISTETTY_netti.pdf/8d2e1a66-e24a-4073-8303-ee3127fbfcac. Accessed 10 Apr 2016.

Audretsch, D. B., Lehmann, E. E., & Warning, S. (2005). University spillovers and new firm location. *Research Policy, 34*(7), 1113–1122.

Autio, E., & Thomas, L. (2014). Innovation ecosystems. *The Oxford handbook of innovation management*, 204–288.

Autio, E., Dahlander, L., & Frederiksen, L. (2013). Information exposure, opportunity evaluation, and entrepreneurial action: An investigation of an online user community. *Academy of Management Journal, 56*(5), 1348–1371.

Autio, E., Kenney, M., Mustar, P., Siegel, D., & Wright, M. (2014). Entrepreneurial innovation: The importance of context. *Research Policy, 43*(7), 1097–1108.

Bathelt, H., Malmberg, A., & Maskell, P. (2004). Clusters and knowledge: Local buzz, global pipelines and the process of knowledge creation. *Progress in Human Geography, 28*(1), 31–56.

Beinhocker, E. D. (2007). *The origin of wealth: The radical remaking of economics and what it means for business and society.* Cambridge: Harvard business school Press.

Birkinshaw, J., Hamel, G., & Mol, M. J. (2008). Management innovation. *Academy of Management Review, 33*(4), 825–845.

Chesbrough, H., Vanhaverbeke, W., & West, J. (2006). *Open innovation: Researching a new paradigm.* New York: Oxford University Press on Demand.

Cohen, B. (2006). Sustainable valley entrepreneurial ecosystems. *Business Strategy and the Environment, 15*(1), 1–14.

Damanpour, F., & Aravind, D. (2012). Managerial innovation: Conceptions, processes, and antecedents. *Management and Organization Review, 8*(2), 423–454.

Delmar, F., & Shane, S. (2004). Legitimating first: Organizing activities and the survival of new ventures. *Journal of Business Venturing, 19*(3), 385–410.

Den Hartigh, E., & van Asseldonk, T. (2004). Business ecosystems: A research framework for investigating the relation between network structure, firm strategy, and the pattern of innovation diffusion. In *ECCON 2004 Annual Meeting: Co-Jumping on a Trampoline,* The Netherlands.

Dimov, D. (2007). Beyond the single-person, single-insight attribution in understanding entrepreneurial opportunities. *Entrepreneurship Theory and Practice, 31*(5), 713–731.

Donada, C., & Attias, D. (2015). Food for thought: Which organisation and ecosystem governance to boost radical innovation in the electromobility 2.0 industry? *International Journal of Automotive Technology and Management, 15*(2), 105–125.

Engeström, Y., Engeström, R., & Kärkkäinen, M. (1995). Polycontextuality and boundary crossing in expert cognition: Learning and problem solving in complex work activities. *Learning and Instruction, 5*(4), 319–336.

Fletcher, D. E. (2006). Entrepreneurial processes and the social construction of opportunity. *Entrepreneurship and Regional Development, 18*(5), 421–440.

Gaglio, C. M., & Taub, R. P. (1992). Entrepreneurs and opportunity recognition. *Frontiers of Entrepreneurship Research, 12,* 136–147.

Gawer, A., & Cusumano, M. A. (2014). Industry platforms and ecosystem innovation. *Journal of Product Innovation Management, 31*(3), 417–433.

Gemünden, H. G., Salomo, S., & Hölzle, K. (2007). Role models for radical innovations in times of open innovation. *Creativity and Innovation Management, 16*(4), 408–421.

Hakala, H., Sirén, C., & Wincent, J. (2016). Entrepreneurial orientation and international new entry: The moderating role of autonomy and structures in subsidiaries. *Journal of Small Business Management, 54*(S1), 90–112.

Hargrave, T. J., & Van de Ven, A. H. (2006). A collective action model of institutional innovation. *Academy of Management Review, 31*(4), 864–888.

Hauschildt, J., & Schewe, G. (2000). Gatekeeper and process promotor: Key persons in agile and innovative organizations. *International Journal of Agile Management Systems, 2*(2), 96–103.

Heikkinen, M. T., Mainela, T., Still, J., & Tähtinen, J. (2007). Roles for managing in mobile service development nets. *Industrial Marketing Management, 36*(7), 909–925.

Iansiti, M., & Levien, R. (2004). Strategy as ecology. *Harvard Business Review, 82*(3), 68–81.

Isenberg, D. J. (2010). How to start an entrepreneurial revolution. *Harvard Business Review, 88*(6), 40–50.

Järvinen, J., & Linnakangas, J. (2012). Firm capabilities in the Finnish forest cluster: Comparisons based on self-organizing map. *Silva Fennica, 46*(1), 131–150.

Kerr, W. R., & Nanda, R. (2009). Democratizing entry: Banking deregulations, financing constraints, and entrepreneurship. *Journal of Financial Economics, 94*(1), 124–149.

Koenig, G. (2012). Business ecosystems revisited. *Management, 15*(2), 208–224.

Kristiansen, S. T. (2014). Facilitating innovation in networks composed of non-mandated relations. *International Journal of Action Research, 10*(1), 34–53.

Lee, S. M., Olson, D. L., & Trimi, S. (2012). Co-innovation: Convergenomics, collaboration, and co-creation for organizational values. *Management Decision, 50*(5), 817–831.

Lester, R., & Piore, M. (2004). *The missing dimension.* Cambridge: Harvard University Press.

Lichtenstein, B., & Kurjanowicz, B. (2010). Tangibility, momentum, and the emergence of The Republic of Tea. *ENTER Journal, 1*(1), 125–148.

Lichtenstein, B. B., & Plowman, D. A. (2009). The leadership of emergence: A complex systems leadership theory of emergence at successive organizational levels. *The Leadership Quarterly, 20*(4), 617–630.

Lichtenstein, B. B., Dooley, K. J., & Lumpkin, G. T. (2006). Measuring emergence in the dynamics of new venture creation. *Journal of Business Venturing, 21*(2), 153–175.

Lin, N., & Dufresne, A. (2014). Nanocellulose in biomedicine: Current status and future prospect. *European Polymer Journal, 59*, 302–325.

Maniak, R., Midler, C., Lenfle, S., & Pellec-Dairon, M. L. (2014). Value management for exploration projects. *Project Management Journal, 45*(4), 55–66.

Markham, S. K., & Griffin, A. (1998). The breakfast of champions: Associations between champions and product development environments, practices and performance. *Journal of Product Innovation Management, 15*(5), 436–454.

Marti, I., Courpasson, D., & Barbosa, S. D. (2013). "Living in the fishbowl". Generating an entrepreneurial culture in a local community in Argentina. *Journal of Business Venturing, 28*(1), 10–29.

McMullen, J. S., & Dimov, D. (2013). Time and the entrepreneurial journey: The problems and promise of studying entrepreneurship as a process. *Journal of Management Studies, 50*(8), 1481–1512.

Mitleton-Kelly, E. (2003). *Ten principles of complexity and enabling infrastructures. Complex systems and evolutionary perspectives on organisations: The application of complexity theory to organisations* (pp. 23–50). New York: Pergamon.

Moore, J. F. (1993). Predators and prey: A new ecology of competition. *Harvard Business Review, 71*(3), 75–83.

Moore, J. F. (2006). Business ecosystems and the view from the firm. *The Antitrust Bulletin, 51*(1), 31–75.

Nahi, T., & Halme, M. (2015). Co-creation as Sensemaking: Collaboration in inclusive business creation in low-income contexts. *Academy of management proceedings* (Vol. 2015, No. 1, p. 18544). New York: Academy of Management.

Nambisan, S., & Baron, R. A. (2013). Entrepreneurship in innovation ecosystems: Entrepreneurs' self-regulatory processes and their implications for new venture success. *Entrepreneurship Theory and Practice, 37*(5), 1071–1097.

Pardales, M. J., & Girod, M. (2006). Community of Inquiry: Its past and present future. *Educational Philosophy and Theory, 38*(3), 299–309.

Peltoniemi, M. (2006). Preliminary theoretical framework for the study of business ecosystems. *Emergence-Mahwah-Lawrence Erlbaum, 8*(1), 10.

Peltoniemi, M. (2013). Mechanisms of capability evolution in the Finnish forest industry cluster. *Journal of Forest Economics, 19*(2), 190–205.

Peltoniemi, M., & Vuori, E. (2004, September). Business ecosystem as the new approach to complex adaptive business environments. In *Proceedings of eBusiness research forum* (Vol. 18, pp. 267–281). https://www.researchgate.net/profile/Elisa_Vuoripublication/228985086_Business_Ecosystem_as_the_New_Approach_to_Complex_Adaptive_Business_Environments/links/09e415110ff11e4a99000000.pdf

Pratt, M. G. (2009). From the editors: For the lack of a boilerplate: Tips on writing up (and reviewing) qualitative research. *Academy of Management Journal, 52*(5), 856–862.

Rodríguez-Pose, A. (2013). Do institutions matter for regional development? *Regional Studies, 47*(7), 1034–1047.

Shane, S., & Venkataraman, S. (2000). The promise of entrepreneurship as a field of research. *Academy of Management Review, 25*(1), 217–226.

Shepherd, D. A. (2015). Party on! A call for entrepreneurship research that is more interactive, activity based, cognitively hot, compassionate, and prosocial. *Journal of Business Venturing, 30*(4), 489–507.

Sirén, C., Hakala, H., Wincent, J., & Grichnik, D. (2017). Breaking the routines: Entrepreneurial orientation, strategic learning, firm size, and age. *Long Range Planning, 50*(2), 145–167.

Sitra. (2016). Leading the cycle – Finnish road map to a circular economy 2016–2025, Sitra Studies 121, ISBN 978-951-563-978-3 (PDF) www.sitra.fi

Spigel, B. (2015). The relational organization of entrepreneurial ecosystems. *Entrepreneurship Theory and Practice, 41*, 49–72.

Spilling, O. R. (1996). Regional variation of new firm formation: The Norwegian case. *Entrepreneurship & Regional Development, 8*(3), 217–244.

Stam, E. (2015). Entrepreneurial ecosystems and regional policy: A sympathetic critique. *European Planning Studies, 23*(9), 1759–1769.

Steyaert, C. (2007). 'Entrepreneuring'as a conceptual attractor? A review of process theories in 20 years of entrepreneurship studies. *Entrepreneurship and Regional Development, 19*(6), 453–477.

Storper, M., & Venables, A. J. (2004). Buzz: Face-to-face contact and the urban economy. *Journal of Economic Geography, 4*(4), 351–370.

Swedberg, R. (2009). Schumpeter's full model of entrepreneurship. In R. Ziegler (Ed.), *An introduction to social entrepreneurship: Voices, preconditions, contexts* (pp. 77–106). Cheltenham: Edward Elgar.

Thomas, L., & Autio, E. (2012). Modeling the ecosystem: a meta-synthesis of ecosystem and related literatures. In *DRUID 2012 Conference, Copenhagen (Denmark)*.

Tracy, S. J. (2010). Qualitative quality: Eight "big-tent" criteria for excellent qualitative research. *Qualitative Inquiry, 16*(10), 837–851.

Tushman, M. L. (1977). Special boundary roles in the innovation process. *Administrative Science Quarterly*, 587–605.

Valdez, J. (1988). *The entrepreneurial ecosystem: Toward a theory of new firm formation*. Working Paper. Small Business Institute.

Van de Ven, A. H., & Engleman, R. M. (2004). Event-and outcome-driven explanations of entrepreneurship. *Journal of Business Venturing, 19*(3), 343–358.

Venkataraman, S., Sarasvathy, S. D., Dew, N., & Forster, W. R. (2012). Reflections on the 2010 AMR decade award: Whither the promise? Moving forward with entrepreneurship as a science of the artificial. *Academy of Management Review, 37*(1), 21–33.

Vesalainen, J., & Hakala, H. (2014). Strategic capability architecture: The role of network capability. *Industrial Marketing Management, 43*(6), 938–950.

von Weymarn, N. (2015). *Forest-based business ecosystems: Case Äänekoski bioproduct mill*. [Pdf] Metsä Group Oyj. Available at: http://www.metsa.fi/documents/10739/4144441/Part2_N.von Weymarn_150611+Mets%C3%A4+Fibre_Bioproduct+mill_ENG.pdf/4f8a4db3-5d45-47b0-ad78-8b5b9cce76ad. Accessed 26 Jan 2016.

Waters, T. (2016). Gemeinschaft and Gesellschaft societies. In Blackwell, G. R. (Ed.), *Blackwell encyclopedia of sociology* (2nd ed.). New York: Blackwell.

Weick, K. E. (1995). *Sensemaking in organizations* (Vol. 3). Thousand Oaks: Sage.

Weick, K. E., Sutcliffe, K. M., & Obstfeld, D. (2005). Organizing and the process of sensemaking. *Organization Science, 16*(4), 409–421.

Zacharakis, A. L., Shepherd, D. A., & Coombs, J. E. (2003). The development of venture-capital-backed internet companies: An ecosystem perspective. *Journal of Business Venturing, 18*(2), 217–231.

Chapter 11
Sustainable Environmental and Social Practices in Companies in the State of Santa Catarina, Brazil

Simone Sehnem and Hilka Pelizza Vier Machado

Abstract Current research, comprising a questionnaire answered by 50 companies, identifies the introduction and implementation of sustainable and social practices by the companies, their motives for implementing them, the difficulties they face, and the benefits they receive. Results reveal that environmental practices fully implemented by 68% of the companies comprise the monitoring of risks and opportunities for the organizations' activity due to climatic changes, 56% of the firms under analysis separate wastes, and 52% of the firms train personnel in health and safety procedures on work. Non-implemented practices include incineration (burning of mass) by 80% of the firms, hiring of indigenous and tribal workers by 68%, composting by 64%, and use of surface water in processing.

Keywords Sustainability • Sustainable practices • Environmental and social practices

11.1 Introduction

Sustainable entrepreneurship is the exploitation of opportunities that provide economic profits and enhance social or environmental improvement (Hockerts and Wüstenhagen 2010; Shepherd and Patzelt 2011). It may be implemented by eco-innovations, while entrepreneurs may be called strategic eco-innovators, strategic eco-implementing agents, passive eco-innovators, or non-eco-innovators (Kemp and Pearson 2008).

Coupled to commitment with environmental improvement, entrepreneur activity is relevant for economic and social development (Leitão and Alves 2016).

S. Sehnem (✉) • H.P.V. Machado
Doutorado em Administração. Universidade do Oeste de Santa Catarina,
Campus Chapecó, Seminário, Chapecó, Santa Catarina, Brazil
e-mail: simonesehnem_adm@yahoo.com.br; hilkavier@yahoo.com

© Springer International Publishing AG 2018
J. Leitão et al. (eds.), *Entrepreneurial, Innovative and Sustainable Ecosystems*, Applying Quality of Life Research,
https://doi.org/10.1007/978-3-319-71014-3_11

Consequently, the results of entrepreneur activity increase its relevance when social, economic, and environmental aspects are incorporated to the companies' strategies and practices.

Social and environmental practices are associated to the idea of life quality which, in itself, is a multidimensional concept which represents the individuals' material and subjective conditions of life within a specific context (Leitão and Alves 2016). According to Schlesinger et al. (2016), one dimension for assessing life quality is the perception of the environment's quality. The abovementioned authors evaluated life quality in cities from the residents' point of view.

The current chapter provides results of a research work which assessed administrators' perspective on the implementation of social and sustainable practices. Research was undertaken with 50 companies from different sectors to identify the introduction and implementation of sustainable and social practices by firms, their motivations, difficulties faced, and benefits received.

The southern Brazilian state of Santa Catarina was the context of current research. The policy of the state enhances sustainable development executed by the Office of the Environment and Sustainable Development and by a Foundation for the Environment.

11.2 Sustainable Social and Environmental Practices and Quality of Life

The integration of sustainable practices has become a common event in supply networks, underscoring decrease in energy consumption, introduction of innovatory packaging and mechanization, and development of laboratory processes, triggered by challenges in energy intake that provide insights with regard to increasing firms' commitment for sustainable practices (Glover et al. 2014).

Consequently, small and big companies vie for improvement in their use of natural resources, valorization of people, and economic returns which make viable the firms' survival. Sustainable practices are, consequently, validated within the organizational context (Suchman 1995).

According to Mathew and John (2016), technological progress and ecological awareness are daily on the rise. In fact, the twentieth century witnessed the development of a culture that gradually affected emerging nations and developing countries, with several consequences to the environment. Environmentalists' and conservationists' efforts in the twenty-first century have contributed toward society's awareness on the consequences of lack of care and bad use of natural resources which will surely reduce people's lifestyle and quality (Schlesinger et al. 2016).

The Global Reporting Initiative's guidelines (2013), edition n. 4, provide a series of procedures for sustainability reports through indexes of environmental, social, and economic performance and their impacts. The guidelines have been developed through a process that involves several stakeholders, comprising firms, workers, civil society, financial markets, auditors, and other experts in several subjects. They also involve dialogues with regulating and government agents hailing from different countries (GRI 4 2013).

OECD (2011) provides another parameter to measure people's life quality. In fact, a Life Quality Index may be established by a set of welfare and follow-up indicators. It also establishes a series of methodological and investigation projects to improve the welfare measurement base (Durand 2015). Welfare is measured by results achieved within life's material conditions which comprise earnings, richness, employment, incomes, and housing conditions. Life quality includes health, equilibrium between labor and living, schooling and skills, social connections, involvement and empowerment, environmental quality, personal safety, and satisfaction with life. Future welfare is assessed by taking into account the main resources that trigger well-being throughout time and which are influenced by current activities, such as economic, natural, human, and social capital (Durand 2015).

The above parameters evaluating the level of life quality encompass objective and subjective aspects. Durand (2015) subdivides the assessment of material and life quality conditions into 11 dimensions: income and richness, employment and salaries, housing, health, equilibrium between labor and life, social connections, civil involvement, environmental conditions, personal safety, and subjective well-being. In other words, life quality is assessed by discarding a multidimensional construct and comprises economic, social, psychological (Leitão and Alves 2016), and environmental aspects (Schlesinger et al. 2016).

Environmental assessment in current research has been undertaken through environmental practices suggested by Goulet (2002), Elkington (2001), GRI 4 (2013), and Dias (2014) and includes reverse logistics, cleaner production, separation of wastes, 5Rs (Reduce, Recycle, Reuse, Recover, and Reintegrate), treatment of industrial effluents, water recycling, water reuse, pollution control, eco-efficiency, eco-innovation, biotechnology, a system of environmental management, clean energies, eco-design, composting, incineration, sustainable consumption, zero wastes, integrated prevention and control of pollution, green chemistry, use of ecological packaging, auditing of suppliers, environmental auditing in production processes and in the referencing of effluents and wastes, use of surface water in industrial processes, use of underground water in industrial processes, healthy environmental management of dangerous wastes, technologies in energy reduction and consumption processes, water reduction and consumption technologies, waste reduction technologies, mitigation of environmental impacts produced, use of fuel from renewable sources, gas emission reduction technologies, evaluation of products' life span, and voluntary environmental treaties.

Several dimensions were suggested by other authors, such as Goulet (2002), Elkington (2001), GRI 4 (2013), and Dias (2014), and added to social practices. They involve social responsibility; labor practices based on internationally acknowledged norms; quota-based hiring of employees; regular provision of benefits to employees; monitoring and reporting of lesions, labor-caused diseases, absenteeism, training on matters of health, and safety on work; training on handling dangerous wastes; training in ergonomics on work; training on the prevention of accidents on work; training on human rights relevant to the organization's activities; report of formal processes and complaints by the local community; report on corruption risks identified by risk assessments; information of anticorruption policies and procedures adopted by the organization; monitoring of clients' and suppliers' complaints; observation of ergonomic aspects in the labor process (GRI, n. 4 2013); communication of sustainable performance by specific reports; green marketing; and information of the firm's ethic principles and values (GRI, n. 4 2013; Dias 2014).

Data were collected by a questionnaire with eight sections:

(a) The company's features, activity, number of employees, town or city, and implemented guidelines
(b) Profile of the questionnaire respondent, occupation, and time period at the company
(c) Environmental practices within the production process
(d) Social practices implemented by the firm
(e) Implemented economic practices
(f) Difficulties for the establishment of sustainable practices
(g) Motives for the establishment of sustainable practices
(h) Benefits from sustainable practices

Likert-type scales, between 1 and 5 (1=low; 5=high), were employed so that environmental practices established within the production process and social practices established by the firms could be identified. Data were tabulated, and a descriptive analysis was provided to pinpoint sustainable and social practices established by firms in the state of Santa Catarina, Brazil.

11.3 Sustainable Social and Environmental Practices Established by Firms in the State of Santa Catarina, Brazil

The participating firms' profiles are provided by data in Tables 11.1, 11.2, 11.3, 11.4, 11.5, 11.6, 11.7, and 11.8. Tables 11.1 and 11.2 give the activities of the *firms* under analysis.

Current research mapped firms from different industrial sectors, underscoring food products, civil construction, and metallurgy. Table 11.2 lists the firms under the heading "Other types of activity."

Table 11.3 shows companies' size, with number of employees.

Firms with up to 50 employees are predominant among the companies analyzed (36%), followed by firms with over 500 employees (30%). Table 11.4 provides the time period of the employees in the firms under analysis.

Note that 64% of participants have worked in the firm for 10 years and 22% have worked between 10.1 and 20 years. Only two participants have worked for more than 40 years.

11 Sustainable Environmental and Social Practices in Companies in the State of Santa... 219

Table 11.1 Activity

Activity	Abs. Freq.
Food products	13
Civil engineering	4
Metallurgy	4
Textile industry	3
Printing presses	2
Furniture-making	2
Paper and cardboard	2
Plastic products	2
Clothes, footwear, and cloths	2
Soft-drink industry	1
Rubberware	1
Mechanics	1
Other types of activity	13
Total	50

Source: Data collected from research

Table 11.2 Other types of activity

Activity	Abs. Freq.
Frame-making	1
Agricultural and livestock (animal rations)	1
Car industry	1
Aluminum gutters and conduits	1
Equipment for aviculture, swine culture, and livestock	1
Equipment for abattoirs	1
Sports industry	1
Manufacture and assembly of prefabricated concrete structures	1
Financial	1
Technical advice in civil engineering, agronomy, and social and environmental marketing	1
Services	1
Public works	1
Supermarkets	1
Total	13

Source: Data collected from research

Data in Table 11.5 demonstrate the variety of careers of the participants, most of whom are owners and managers. Note the number of managers, supervisors, and analysts, respectively, with relative frequency 18%, 10%, and 8%. Table 11.6 shows the geographic dispersion of the research participants.

Table 11.3 Number of employees

Number of employees	Freq. Abs.	Rel. Freq.
Up to 50	18	36%
Over 501	15	30%
Between 51 and 100	7	14%
Between 101 and 150	3	6%
Between 151 and 200	2	4%
Between 251 and 300	2	4%
Between 201 and 250	1	2%
Between 351 and 400	1	2%
Between 451 and 500	1	2%
Total	50	100%

Source: Data collected from research

Table 11.4 Time period of employees in the company

Time period of employees	Abs. Freq.
Up to 10 years	32
Between 10.1 and 20 years	11
Between 20.1 and 30 years	4
Between 30.1 and 40 years	0
Between 40.1 and 50 years	2
No reply	1
Total	50

Source: Data collected from research

Table 11.6 shows that the companies analyzed lie in 27 different municipalities, of which one is nationwide. Chapecó, São Miguel do Oeste, and Blumenau are conspicuous for having seven, four, and four firms under analysis, respectively, per municipality.

Tables 11.7 and 11.8 exhibit Certification Programs and Quality Improvement to which the companies are committed.

Table 11.7 demonstrates that 5S and Certificate ISO 9.001 are the most underscored guidelines. Only six companies emphasize practices associated to the environmental management system, with Certificate ISO 14.001. Two companies established minimum requirements for improvement practices in health and occupational safety management through Certificate Occupational Health and Safety Assessment Series (OHSAS 18.001). Table 11.8 reveals other guidelines with norms and specific tools for the companies' activities.

Table 11.5 Occupation of respondents of the questionnaire

Career	Freq. Abs.	Freq. Rel.
Manager	9	18%
Supervisor	5	10%
Analyst	4	8%
Administration officer	4	8%
Administration director	3	6%
Engineer	3	6%
Management partner	3	6%
Director of human resources	2	4%
Administrative officer	1	2%
Quality assistant	1	2%
Commercial officer	1	2%
Internal counselor	1	2%
Accountant	1	2%
Director of manufacture	1	2%
Production manager	1	2%
Financial manager	1	2%
Environmental quality manager	1	2%
President	1	2%
Owner	1	2%
Receptionist/telephone operator	1	2%
Technician	1	2%
No reply	4	8%
Total	50	100%

Source: Data collected from research

11.3.1 Environmental Practices

Although few companies have environmental certification (ISO 14.001), all environmental practices at levels 5 and 1 were mentioned by the companies.

According to Table 11.9, 54% of researches under analysis have an advanced stage in reverse logistic practices, with only 10% failing to adopt such practice. Further, 26% lie in the initial stages for eventual use of reverse logistics (level 2). Cleaner production is fully practiced in 18% of the companies under analysis, with 24% of firms at level 4. This boils down to the fact that most companies underscore the continuous application of an integrated environmental and prevention strategy for processes, products, and services.

Standard deviation for these practices ranges between 1.58 for environmental management system and 16.81 for incineration (burning of mass). Composting is another practice with high standard deviation (12.49), followed by a standard deviation of 12

Table 11.6 Municipalities of the companies under analysis

Municipalities	Freq. Abs.	Freq. Rel.
Chapecó	7	14%
São Miguel do Oeste	4	8%
Blumenau	4	8%
Videira	3	6%
Itajaí	3	6%
Xanxerê	2	4%
Not cited	2	4%
Joinville	2	4%
Concórdia	2	4%
Brusque	2	4%
Vargem Bonita	1	2%
Brazil	1	2%
São Bento do Sul	1	2%
States RS, SC, PR, and MS	1	2%
Pinhalzinho	1	2%
Palmitos	1	2%
Maravilha	1	2%
Machadinho	1	2%
Joaçaba	1	2%
Jaraguá do Sul	1	2%
Gaurama	1	2%
Faxinal dos Guedes	1	2%
Erechim	1	2%
Cunha Porã	1	2%
Catanduvas	1	2%
Campos Novos	1	2%
Braço do Norte	1	2%
Arvoredo	1	2%
Arroio Trinta	1	2%
Total	50	100%

Source: Data collected from research

for item use of surface waters in processes, and 11.29 for item separation of wastes. Practices with the lowest standard deviation comprised clean energy (s/d = 2.35), environmentally healthy management of hazard wastes (s/d = 3.08), water consumption reduction technologies (s/d = 3.54), pollution control (3.54), and reverse logistics (3.81). Fully adopted practices by the companies under analysis, at level 5, include separation of wastes, with 56% of firms, followed by treatment of industrial effluents (38%), auditing of internal processes (34%), and reverse logistics (30%). At level 4, eco-efficiency practices have been established by 34% of companies, eco-innovation by 32%, and technologies for waste reduction by 30%.

11 Sustainable Environmental and Social Practices in Companies in the State of Santa... 223

Table 11.7 Guidelines adopted by companies

Guidelines	Abs. Freq.	Rel. Freq.
Program 5S	21	36.84%
ISO 9.001	14	24.56%
ISO 14.001	6	10.53%
OHSAS 18.001	2	3.51%
None	14	24.56%
Total	57[a]	100%

Source: Data collected from research
[a]Since each company may adhere to more than 1 guideline, the number was higher than the 50 companies analyzed

Table 11.8 Other guidelines

Guidelines	Abs. Freq.	Rel. Freq.
ABVTEX–Brazilian Association of Textile Retail	1	9.09%
BPS and APPCC[a]	1	9.09%
5S in progress	1	9.09%
Quality and prevention maintenance management	1	9.09%
GMP/HACCP[b]	1	9.09%
NBR 14789	1	9.09%
ISO in progress	1	9.09%
Kaizen	1	9.09%
Inmetro legal norms	1	9.09%
Toyota quality programs	1	9.09%
Certificate IN 04 and IN 65	1	9.09%
Total	11	100%

Source: Data collected from research
[a]Hazard analysis and critical control point
[b]Good manufacturing practice and hazard analysis and critical control points

Practices which have not been established by the companies under analysis comprise incineration (burning of mass) (80%), composting (64%), use of surface waters in processes (62%), green chemistry (54%), use of underground water in processes (54%), and environmental audits in production and management processes of effluents and wastes (54%). At level 2, zero wastes (internal recycling) did not occur in 26% of companies, sustainable consumption in 24%, clean energy in 22%, and environmental management system in 22%.

Several other companies analyzed mention other practices. Recycling of electronic apparatuses, building of supply sites for sprayers, collection of hospital residues, containers in car washes, use of energy generator, and 100% of well water used by the company should be underscored.

Table 11.9 Introduction of environmental practices

Practices	1		2		3		4		5		Standard deviation
	F.A	F.R.%	F.A.	F.R.	F.A.	F.R.	F.A.	F.R.	F.A	F.R	
Reverse logistics	5	10%	8	16%	10	20%	12	24%	15	30%	3.81
Cleaner production	5	10%	5	10%	19	38%	12	24%	9	18%	5.83
Separation of wastes	1	2%	0	0	9	18%	12	24%	28	56%	11.29
5Rs[a]	3	6%	8	16%	16	32%	11	22%	12	24%	4.85
Treatment of industrial effluents	10	20%	5	10%	4	8%	12	24%	19	38%	6.04
Water recycling	21	42%	4	8%	9	18%	8	16%	8	16%	6.44
Water reuse	20	40%	6	12%	4	4%	11	22%	9	18%	6.20
Pollution control	11	22%	4	8%	12	24%	13	26%	10	20%	3.54
Eco-efficiency	14	28%	5	10%	10	20%	17	34%	4	8%	5.61
Eco-innovation	8	16%	6	12%	16	32%	16	32%	4	8%	5.66
Biotechnology	26	52%	8	16%	8	16%	6	12%	2	4%	9.27
Environmental management system	10	20%	11	22%	12	24%	9	18%	8	16%	1.58
Clean energies	12	24%	11	22%	10	20%	6	12%	11	22%	2.35
Eco-design	16	32%	10	20%	11		10	20%	3	6%	4.64
Composting	32	64%	7	14%	5	10%	1	2%	5	10%	12.49
Incineration (burning of mass)	40	80%	3	6%	4	8%	1	2%	2	4%	16.81
Sustainable consumption	5	10%	12	24%	20	40%	10	20%	3	6%	6.67
Zero wastes (internal recycling)	11	22%	13	26%	13	26%	12	24%	1	2%	5.10
Integrated prevention and control of pollution	20	40%	5	10%	15	30%	8	16%	2	4%	7.38
Green chemistry	27	54%	6	12%	11	22%	3	6%	3	6%	10.05
Use of ecological packaging	16	32%	9	18%	10	20%	11	22%	4	8%	4.30
Auditing of suppliers	22	44%	6	12%	8	16%	4	8%	10	20%	7.07
Auditing in internal processing	13	26%	4	8%	8	16%	8	16%	17	34%	5.05
Environmental auditing in production processes and in the referencing of effluents and wastes	26	54%	0	0	11	22%	6	12%	7	14%	9.77

Sustainable practice	n	%	n	%	n	%	n	%	n	%	Value
Use of surface water in industrial processes	31	62%	3	6%	3	6%	4	8%	9	18%	12
Use of underground water in industrial processes	27	54%	5	10%	6	12%	7	14%	5	10%	9.54
Healthy environmental management of dangerous wastes	13	26%	6	12%	10	20%	13	26%	8	16%	3.08
Technologies in energy reduction and consumption processes	8	16%	8	16%	20	40%	10	20%	4	8%	6
Water reduction and consumption technologies	11	22%	8	16%	14	28%	12	24%	5	10%	3.54
Waste reduction technologies	4	8%	10	20%	12	24%	15	30%	9	18%	9.75
Mitigation of environmental impacts produced	20	40%	6	12%	9	18%	9	18%	6	12%	5.79
Use of fuel from renewable sources	23	46%	8	16%	6	12%	7	14%	6	12%	7.31
Gas emission reduction technologies	20	40%	6	12%	10	20%	7	14%	7	14%	5.79
Evaluation of products' life span	17	34%	7	14%	11	22%	11	22%	4	8%	4.90
Voluntary environmental treaties	23	46%	6	12%	12	24%	4	8%	5	10%	7.91

Source: Data collected from research

a Reduce, Recycle, Reuse, Recover and Reintegrate

Table 11.10 Establishment of environmental practices

Practices	1.00	2.00	3.00	4.00	5.00	Means
Reverse logistics	5.00	8.00	10.00	12.00	15.00	3.48
Cleaner production	5.00	5.00	19.00	12.00	9.00	3.30
Separation of wastes	1.00	0.00	9.00	12.00	28.00	4.32
5Rs	3.00	8.00	16.00	11.00	12.00	3.42
Treatment of industrial effluents	10.00	5.00	4.00	12.00	19.00	3.50
Water recycling	21.00	4.00	9.00	8.00	8.00	2.56
Water reuse	20.00	6.00	4.00	11.00	9.00	2.66
Pollution control	11.00	4.00	12.00	13.00	10.00	3.14
Eco-efficiency	14.00	5.00	10.00	17.00	4.00	2.84
Eco-innovation	8.00	6.00	16.00	16.00	4.00	3.04
Biotechnology	26.00	8.00	8.00	6.00	2.00	2.00
Environmental management system	10.00	11.00	12.00	9.00	8.00	2.88
Clean energies	12.00	11.00	10.00	6.00	11.00	2.86
Eco-design	16.00	10.00	11.00	10.00	3.00	2.48
Composting	32.00	7.00	5.00	1.00	5.00	1.80
Incineration (burning of mass)	40.00	3.00	4.00	1.00	2.00	1.44
Sustainable consumption	5.00	12.00	20.00	10.00	3.00	2.88
Zero wastes (internal recycling)	11.00	13.00	13.00	12.00	1.00	2.58
Integrated prevention and control of pollution	20.00	5.00	15.00	8.00	2.00	2.34
Green chemistry	27.00	6.00	11.00	3.00	3.00	1.98
Ecological packaging	16.00	9.00	10.00	11.00	4.00	2.56
Audits for suppliers	22.00	6.00	8.00	4.00	10.00	2.48
Audits for internal processes	13.00	4.00	8.00	8.00	17.00	3.24
Environmental audit in production and management processes of effluents and wastes	26.00	0.00	11.00	6.00	7.00	2.36
Use of surface waters in processes	31.00	3.00	3.00	4.00	9.00	2.14
Use of underground waters in processes	27.00	5.00	6.00	7.00	5.00	2.16
Environmentally healthy management of hazardous wastes	13.00	6.00	10.00	13.00	8.00	2.94
Technologies that reduce energy consumption	8.00	8.00	20.00	10.00	4.00	2.88
Technologies that reduce water consumption	11.00	8.00	14.00	12.00	5.00	2.84
Technologies that reduce waste levels	4.00	10.00	12.00	15.00	9.00	3.30
Mitigation of generated environmental impacts	20.00	6.00	9.00	9.00	6.00	2.50
Use of fuel from renewable sources	23.00	8.00	6.00	7.00	6.00	2.30
Use of technologies in the reduction of gas emissions	20.00	6.00	10.00	7.00	7.00	2.50
Assessment of products' life cycle	17.00	7.00	11.00	11.00	4.00	2.56
Voluntary environmental treaties	23.00	6.00	12.00	4.00	5.00	2.24

Table 11.10 shows that, by weighed means, waste separation was the most relevant environmental practice and green chemistry the least important. On average, effluent treatment, reverse logistics, 5Rs, and cleaner production were also relevant.

Other environmental practices comprised an apparatus for solar light and wind, the use of recycled material, environmental education program, selective collection, motivation for workers and society for forest recovery by distributing native plants, environmental education, projects for environmental preservation, protection of stream and river sources, collection of used batteries from cell phones and home appliances, collection of packages of fertilizers, selective collection of garbage, recycling, use of recycled paper and separation of garbage, water reuse, costs with waste management, rules for environmental organizations, proper consumption of water in production processes, eco-emission, environmental objectives and chronograms, set of practices for the reduction of the occurrence of dengue, priority in the separation of wastes, reprocessing, the engineering of the use of surplus in prime matter, policies of minimum wastes, education and conferences on proper consumption and disposition of wastes, use of chicken manure as fertilizer, use of firewood exclusively from renewable sources, correct disposal of materials, Six Sigma project with special emphasis on the environment (a methodology based on continuous quality improvement of the processes involved in the production of services and objects while taking into account all the important aspects of the business and aimed at excellence in competitiveness, with zero deficit), environmental education project for the local community and partnerships, monitoring of water consumption to reduce the consumption of their important resource, reuse of effluents, recycling of industrialized products, reuse of water, maintenance and improvement of the environment, treatment of the sewage system, and monitoring of consumption.

11.3.2 Social Practices

Table 11.11 shows social practices identified in the companies under analysis.

Data in Table 11.11 show that training on health and work safety lies at full level (level 5) for 52% of the companies. Monitoring and reporting of types of lesions, rate of lesions, rate of occupational diseases, loss of working days, rate of absenteeism, and number of deaths related to labor as a ratio to the totality of workers were adopted by 48% of the companies under analysis, whereas trainings on the prevention of accidents in the work milieu were reported in 46% of firms analyzed. Moreover, monitoring of the number of complaints by clients and suppliers was practiced by 44% of firms.

Level 4 comprises social responsibility (36% of the companies), compliance to the ergonomic aspects in the processes (30%), information on anticorruption policies and procedures employed by the organization (26%), and information on

Table 11.11 Introduction of social practices

Practices	1 F.A	1 F.R.	2 F.A.	2 F.R.	3 F.A.	3 F.R.	4 F.A.	4 F.R.	5 F.A	5 F.R	Standard deviation
Social responsibility	6	12%	6	12%	13	26%	18	36%	7	14%	5.34
Labor practices based on internationally acknowledged norms	14	28%	7	14%	10	20%	12	24%	7	14%	3.08
Hiring of quota-discriminated workers	19	38%	7	14%	12	24%	3	6%	9	18%	6
Regular benefits to full-time workers	3	6%	5	10%	12	24%	11	22%	19	38%	6.32
Monitoring and registration of any type of lesion, rates of lesion, rates of occupational diseases, loss of a day's work, rate of absenteeism, and number of deaths as a ratio to total number of workers	7	14%	5	10%	6	12%	8	16%	24	48%	7.91
Training on health and work safety	4	8%	4	8%	5	10%	11	22%	26	52%	9.41
Training on handling dangerous wastes	11	22%	6	12%	8	16%	10	20%	15	30%	3.39
Training in ergonomics in the work milieu	8	16%	7	14%	8	16%	9	18%	18	36%	4.53
Training on accident prevention in the work milieu	3	6%	6	12%	8	16%	10	20%	23	46%	7.71
Training on human rights relevant to the company's activities	14	28%	6	12%	12	24%	10	20%	8	16%	3.16
Hiring of tribal and indigene laborers	34	68%	5	10%	4	8%	3	6%	4	8%	13.44
Report on formal processes on complaints by local communities	17	34%	10	20%	10	20%	6	12%	7	14%	4.30
Report on significant risks related to corruption identified by risk evaluations	19	38%	9	18%	7	14%	9	18%	6	12%	5.20
Information on anticorruption policies and procedures employed by the company	17	34%	6	12%	7	14%	13	26%	7	14%	4.80
Monitoring of the number of complaints by clients and suppliers	7	14%	3	6%	9	18%	9	18%	22	44%	7.14
Observation of ergonomic aspects of the processes	10	20%	5	10%	7	14%	15	30%	13	26%	4.12
Information to people on the firm's sustainability performance by means of specific reports (report on sustainability and social balance)	22	44%	5	10%	3	6%	10	20%	10	20%	7.38
Green marketing	15	30%	11	22%	10	20%	10	20%	4	8%	3.94
Information on the company's ethical principles and values in internal processes and in negotiations with interested parties (clients, suppliers, society, and shareholders)	8	16%	6	12%	8	16%	13	26%	15	30%	3.81

Source: Data collected from research

ethical principles and values of the firm in internal processes and in negotiations with interested parties (clients, suppliers, society, and shareholders) (26%).

Non-implemented social practices include the hiring of indigene and tribal workers (68%), information to interested parties on sustainable performance through specific reports (reports on sustainability and social balance) in 44% of the companies, report on significant risks related to corruption which have been identified by risk assessments (38%), and hiring of quota-discriminated employees (38%).

Standard deviation ranged between 3.08 for work practices based on internationally acknowledged norms and 13.44 for the hiring of indigene and tribal workers. Weighted averages of social practices (Table 11.12) corroborate the above results.

There were several social practices involving workers and their family, such as, internal trainings; member meetings; prize-giving to outstanding workers; relaxing break; ludic activities outside the company's working hours; family integration; conferences on health in the workshops; labor gymnastics; admittance of families in conferences on safety, principally during the Week for the Prevention of Accidents during Work (SIPAT); prizes for full attendance; financial subsidies in schooling; visits to newly born children with guidance for the parents; program for medical assistance on the spot, featuring a gynecologist; and schooling of young people and adults in the firm. Other practices for the local community were also identified: support for the community; social investment fund; program involving voluntary personnel; visits by the community; projects in schools; junior entrepreneurships; environmental education in public schools; accountability toward the community; social organization to access public policies for housing; employing people with deficiencies; donations to the community to enhance health and safety; voluntary activities; employment of foreigners; monthly distribution of ration baskets; admittance of the general community in conferences on safety, mainly during the Week for the Prevention of Accidents on Work (SIPAT); subsidizing social work; donation of products to charities; Program Future Athlete; service to the community; investment in a foundation for minors and elderly people; and support for local health schemes and donations of products.

11.3.3 Difficulties for the Deployment of Sustainable Practices

Table 11.13 reveals that investment of capital is a major difficulty to establish sustainable practices, followed by corporative culture and measuring. Other difficulties underscored by employees comprised the firm's size, with branches nationwide, impairing new activities, legislation, lack of investments, bureaucracy of public policies, lack of knowledge and of commitment to implement sustainable actions, necessity of hiring specialized consulting team, and lack of awareness by the administration on the importance of implementing sustainable practices.

In spite of the above difficulties, participants mentioned several motivations to proceed in sustainable practices as commented below.

Table 11.12 Average of social practices

Practices	1	2	3	4	5	Means
Social responsibility	6.00	6.00	13.00	18.00	7.00	3.28
Labor practices based on internationally acknowledged norms	14.00	7.00	10.00	12.00	7.00	2.82
Hiring of quota-discriminated employees	19.00	7.00	12.00	3.00	9.00	2.52
Benefits to full-time employees	3.00	5.00	12.00	11.00	19.00	3.76
Monitoring and reporting of types of lesions, rate of lesions, rate of occupational diseases, loss of working days, rate of absenteeism and number of deaths related to labor as a ratio of totality of workers	7.00	5.00	6.00	8.00	24.00	3.74
Training on health and safety on work	4.00	4.00	5.00	11.00	26.00	4.02
Training on handling of hazardous wastes	11.00	6.00	8.00	10.00	15.00	3.24
Training in ergonomics in the work milieu	8.00	7.00	8.00	9.00	18.00	3.44
Training on the prevention of accidents on the work milieu	3.00	6.00	8.00	10.00	23.00	3.88
Training on human rights relevant for the firm's activities	14.00	6.00	12.00	10.00	8.00	2.84
Hiring of indigene and tribal employees	34.00	5.00	4.00	3.00	4.00	1.76
Report formal process on complaints by the local community	17.00	10.00	10.00	6.00	7.00	2.52
Report on significant risks related to corruption based on risk assessments	19.00	9.00	7.00	9.00	6.00	2.48
Information on anticorruption policies and procedures by the firm	17.00	6.00	7.00	13.00	7.00	2.74
Monitoring of number of complaints by clients and suppliers	7.00	3.00	9.00	9.00	22.00	3.72
Compliance to ergonomic aspects in the processes	10.00	5.00	7.00	15.00	13.00	3.32
Information to interested parties on the sustainable performance through specific reports (reports on sustainability and social balance)	22.00	5.00	3.00	10.00	10.00	2.62
Green marketing	15.00	11.00	10.00	10.00	4.00	2.54
Information on the firm's ethical principles and values in internal processes and in negotiations with interested parties (clients, suppliers, society, and shareholders)	8.00	6.00	8.00	13.00	15.00	3.42

11.3.4 Motivations and Benefits for the Implementation of Sustainable Practices

Tables 11.14 and 11.15 show results of current research with regard to motives and benefits in the implementation of sustainable practices.

The main motives for the implementation of environmental practices by companies were the awareness of managers on their necessity and importance, corporative

11 Sustainable Environmental and Social Practices in Companies in the State of Santa... 231

Table 11.13 Difficulties in the deployment of the firm's sustainable practices

Practices	F.A	F.R.
Investing in capital (new machines and equipments)	19	38%
Corporation culture	9	18%
Difficulty in measuring	7	14%
Practices are unknown	5	10%
Lack of commitment by the management to implement sustainable activities	4	8%
Monitoring by suppliers	1	2%
Others	5	10%
Total	50	100%

Source: Data collected from research
[a]More than one alternative could be marked

Table 11.14 Motives for implementing sustainable practices

Practices	F.A	F.R.
Awareness of managers with regard to need and importance	18	36%
Corporative culture	5	10%
External demands (clients, shareholders, NGOs, administration, general community)	4	8%
Costs decrease	4	8%
Impact on corporative image	4	8%
Desire to be respected by the community	3	6%
Risk administration	3	6%
Profit increase	2	4%
Increase in operational efficiency	2	4%
Concern on brand	2	4%
Internal demands (by employees)	1	2%
Concern on regulation	1	2%
Others	1	2%
Total	50	100%

Source: Data collected from research
[a]More than one alternative could be marked

culture (with only 10%), external demands (clients, shareholders, NGOs, government, and the community at large), decrease of costs, and impact on the corporative image. The firm's activities were also one of the motives underscored.

Results show that firms are mainly motivated by internal decisions (36%), and only 8% were motivated by external demands. Further, 10% of firms insisted on corporative culture that enhances the implementation of sustainable practices. The above evidences the preparation level of most companies under analysis with regard to the issue whose benefits may be seen in Table 11.15.

The two most important benefits in the implementation of environmental practices were improvement of the firm's image and product quality, followed by

Table 11.15 Benefits when sustainable practices are implemented

Practices	F.A	F.R.
A better image	14	28%
Improvement in quality	10	20%
Improvement in administration	7	14%
Higher income	7	14%
Growth	6	12%
Low costs	2	4%
Improvement in research and development	2	4%
Others	2	4%
Pioneerism	0	0
Total	50	100%

Source: Data collected from research

improvement in management, income, and growth. Other less underscored motives comprised reduction of costs and contribution for research and development. Further, improvement in the work milieu and life quality for all the people involved in the production process and awareness for the preservation of the environment were also mentioned.

11.3.5 Synthesis of Results

The companies' profile demonstrated that 64% have been established for the last 10 years, 22% between 10.1 and 20 years, and 8% up to 30 years, with only two firms on the market for more than 40 years. Further, 24.56% of the firms have Certificate ISO 9.001; 10.53% have ISO 14.001, and 3.51% have OHSAS 18001. In the case of environmental practices, results reveal that several practices have been adopted fully and are thus denominated by strategic eco-adopters (Kemp and Pearson 2008) or, rather, committed to sustainable entrepreneurship (Kuckertz and Wagner 2010). However, 38% of the companies insisted that investments are the greatest difficulty to establish sustainable practices, followed by corporative culture (18%). The main motivation was managers' awareness (36%), with profit increase mentioned by a mere 4% of respondents. Image (28%) and quality (20%) improvement were the most important benefits.

Horbach et al. (2014) agree that several environmental practices have not been adopted by firms due to incomplete information and coordination issues. Results in current research showed that practically one half of the participating firms is aware on the need to implement such practices. However, Khanna et al. (2009) underscore the relevance of managers' broader vision on environmental management systems to commit the head administration and empower workers at all levels and with all techniques, such as mapping of processes, analysis of generating causes, and environmental accounts.

In the case of social benefits, the greatest emphasis lies on health and safety activities, the prevention of accidents, and compliance to ergonomic rules. Other social activities for the external community have also been identified, such as social responsibility and community support through projects and financial aid. It should be made clear that social and environmental actions identified in current research are not the only possibilities. In fact, one may also include activities already mentioned by OECD (2011): the adoption of P+L technologies; incorporation of eco-efficiency practices; preference for purchasing green products, compliance to environmental criteria to select suppliers, adoption of water recycling and, when possible, local purchases; investment in P&D, in eco-design, in the use of ecological material, and dry productive and sustainable processes; incorporation of processes which reduce natural resources in the process; selection of clean transport; use of reused or recycled packages and containers; reuse of ecological material for primary package; adoption of recovery system of materials and recycled materials; separation, preparation, and disposal of wastes; replacement of hazardous materials and pollutants; innovation of storage practices; distribution and commercialization of products to enhance social and environmental sustainability; reduction of gas emissions, liquid effluents, and solid wastes; and reduction of water consumption and energy during production processing.

The conditions of each sector and firm should be taken into account, especially their development stage. This is due to the fact that the companies analyzed in current study hail from different sectors and places. Further, the sample comprised small, medium, and big enterprises. However, through the identification of environmental and social practices undertaken by these companies, results of current research may contribute toward the elaboration of sustainable policies and the construction of cultures in other organizations by imitating the abovementioned activities. In fact, results revealed the amplitude and multidimensional aspects of the social and environmental stances associated to life quality (Leitão and Alves 2016).

11.4 Final Considerations

Current research identified the innovation levels of sustainable and social practices implemented by companies in the state of Santa Catarina, Brazil. Results reveal that fully implemented practices in the different companies comprise separation of wastes, treatment of industrial effluents, auditing of internal processes, reverse logistics; 5Rs; clean energies; training on health and safety on work; monitoring and reporting of types of lesion, rate of lesions, rate of occupational diseases, rate of absenteeism, and mortality rate related to labor as a ratio of all workers (employees and outsourced laborers); training on the prevention of labor-related accidents; monitoring the number of complaints by clients and suppliers; concession of regular benefits to full-time employees; and compliance to ergonomics in the labor milieu.

Non-implemented or hardly implemented practices by the firms analyzed include incineration (burning of mass); composting; use of surface water in the processes;

green chemistry; use of underground water in the processes; environmental auditing in production and management processes of effluents and wastes; employment of indigene and tribal workers; report for those concerned on sustainable performance by means of specific reports (reports on sustainability and social balance); report on significant risks related to corruption identified by risk assessment; quota-discriminated employees; report on formal complaints by the local community; information on anticorruption policies and procedures by the company; monitoring of risks and opportunities for the organization's activities due to climatic changes; priority in expenses with local suppliers; monitoring re-work and re-process index; identification of the company's significant indirect economic impacts, positive or negative; monitoring loss index (in BRS) in the process; and monitoring costs per unit. Results of current research may guide entrepreneurs in other Brazilian states and may contribute toward in-depth discussions on entrepreneurs' and companies' role, through practice and strategies, with regard to the lifestyle of their stakeholders.

The inclusion of different sectors has been one of the limitations in current analysis since an inter-sectorial visualization was not possible. It may be the theme for further research works.

References

Dias, R. (2014). *Eco-inovação: caminhos para o desenvolvimento sustentável*. São Paulo: Atlas.

Durand, M. (2015). The OECD better life initiative: How's life? And the measurement of well-being. *Review of Income and Wealth*, Series 61, no 1.

Elkington, J. (2001). *Canibais com garfo e faca*. São Paulo: Makron Boos.

Glover, J. L., Champion, D., Daniels, K. J., & Dainty, A. J. D. (2014). An institutional theory perspective on sustainable practices across the dairy supply chain. *International Journal Production Economics, 152*, 102–111.

Goulet, D. (2002). Desenvolvimento autêntico: fazendo-o sustentável. In C. Cavalcanti (Ed.), *Meio ambiente, desenvolvimento sustentável e políticas públicEas* (Vol. 4). São Paulo: Cortez.

GRI 4. (2013). *Diretrizes G4 para relato de sustentabilidade: princípios para relato e conteúdos padrão*. The Netherlands: Global Reporting Initiative.

Hockerts, K., & Wüstenhagen, R. (2010). Greening Goliaths versus emerging Davids: Theorizing about the role of incumbents and new entrants in sustainable entrepreneurship. *Journal of Business Venturing, 25*, 481–492.

Horbach, J., Rammer, C., & Rennings, K. (2014). Determinantes da ecoinovação por tipo de impacto ambiental: o papel da pressão regulatória, da alavancagem tecnológica e do fator de mercado. In C. Arruda & F. Carvalho (Eds.), *Inovações ambientais: Políticas Públicas, Tecnologias e Oportunidades de Negócios*. Rio de Janeiro: Elsevier.

Kemp, R., & Pearson, P. (2008). Final report MEI project about measuring eco-innovation. UM-MERIT. Maastricht. Available at www.merit.unu.edu/MEI. Accessed Aug 2016.

Khanna, M., Deltas, G., & Harrington, D. R. (2009). Adoption of pollution prevention techniques: The role of management systems and regulatory pressures. *Environmental and Resource Economics, 44*, 85–106.

Kuckertz, A., & Wagner, M. (2010). The influence of sustainability orientation on entrepreneurial intentions: Investigating the role of business experience. *Journal of Business Venturing, 25*, 524–539.

Leitão, J., & Alves, H. (2016). *Entrepreneurial and innovative practice in public institutions – A quality of life approach*. Alemanha: Springer.

Mathew, L. R., & John, D. (2016). Frugal automation of sustainable practices in Kerala. *Procedia Technology, 24*, 1211–1218.

OECD. (2011). *How's life? Measuring well-being*. OECD Publishing.

Schlesinger, W., Taulet, A. C., Alves, H., & Burguete, J. L. V. (2016). An approach to measuring perceived quality of life in the city through a formative multidimensional perspective. In J. Leitão & H. Alves (Eds.), *Entrepreneurial and innovative practice in public institutions – A quality of life approach* (pp. 59–79). Alemanha: Springer.

Shepherd, D. A., & Patzelt, H. (2011). The new field of sustainable entrepreneurship: Studying entrepreneurial action linking "what is to be sustained" with "what is to be developed". *Entrepreneurship: Theory & Practice, 35*(1), 137–163.

Suchman, M. C. (1995). Managing legitimacy: Strategic and institutional approaches. *Academy Management Review, 20*(3), 571–610.

Chapter 12
Mapping an Entrepreneurial, Innovative and Sustainable Ecosystem Using Social Network Analysis: An Exploratory Approach of Publicly Funded Innovative Project Data

Hugo Pinto and Carla Nogueira

Abstract The innovative dynamics of a region largely depends on existing actors and their connectivity, so the resilience of a particular innovation system can be analysed through the study innovation networks. Starting from the Algarve's case study, this analysis uses methods of social network structural analysis to map actors and centralities regarding cooperation and innovation in regional development. The chapter uses data collected through web content mining, starting from the list of organizations that have benefited from public support to innovation. The mapping of the innovation network in the Algarve is compared to theoretical models of resilient networks with the statistical indicators of hierarchy and homophily. The results facilitate the identification of gatekeepers, clusters of activities and constraints and potentialities to the enhancement of the regional entrepreneurial, innovative and sustainable (EIS) ecosystem. This approach has high potential for replication in other regions. The chapter concludes with policy implications for the EIS ecosystem's resilience and dynamics.

Keywords Crisis • Innovation • Regional policy • Network • Resilience

---

H. Pinto (✉)
Centre for Social Studies, University of Coimbra, Coimbra, Portugal

Faculty of Economics, University of Algarve, Faro, Portugal

Research Centre for Spatial and Organisational Dynamics, University of Algarve,
Faro, Portugal
e-mail: hpinto@ces.uc.pt

C. Nogueira
Research Centre for Spatial and Organisational Dynamics, University of Algarve,
Faro, Portugal

© Springer International Publishing AG 2018
J. Leitão et al. (eds.), *Entrepreneurial, Innovative and Sustainable
Ecosystems*, Applying Quality of Life Research,
https://doi.org/10.1007/978-3-319-71014-3_12

12.1 Introduction

High volatility and economic turmoil; increasing technological, social and environmental risks; and the successive shocks in the socio-economic systems have grown interest in the concept of resilience in social sciences, particularly in regional studies. The most common conception of resilience refers to the ability of a given system to return to a steady state after a shock. This is an approach, which is mainly used in engineering and related to the idea of *bouncing back*. A second conception of resilience emerges from the ecological studies and focuses on how a system resists without changing its essential characteristics and without exceeding a certain existing load capacity. A third concept of resilience, which has become particularly relevant in regional studies, is concerned with the processes of selection, adaptation and generation of alternative growth trajectories in systems (the idea of *bounce forward*).

This last approach refers to an evolutionary perspective of socio-economic systems by proposing an analytical framework that internalizes change and allows not only the possibility of returning to a given equilibrium or resisting an internal shock (e.g. a structural failure) or an external shock (such as a recession in the economy) but also the opportunity of creating new paths (Boschma 2015). However, the concept of resilience remains to be clarified.

Several authors have devoted attention to the concept, by trying to delimit it and to implement it at the regional level (Christopherson et al. 2010; Davoudi et al. 2012; Dawley et al. 2010; Martin and Sunley 2014; Martin and Tyler 2015; Boschma and Pinto 2015; Simmie and Martin 2010; Simmie 2014). Attention has been given to resilience as a region's ability to adapt to shocks in production and employment (Davies 2011). Regional resilience depends on productive specialization and related variety, actors and network capacities, path dependencies and *lock-ins*, specific institutional architectures and different other factors such as social capital, systemic services or the innovation ability of a territory.

One of the limits in the implementation of the concept of resilience has been choosing an adequate level of analysis. Resilience is a phenomenon that can be studied on multiple scales, from the individual, to organizational, to aggregate levels such as a region or a country. The innovation system can be a useful scale to analyse resilience (Pinto and Pereira 2014). In the systemic perspective, the innovative dynamic largely depends on the existent actors and their connectivity, and so the resilience of a certain innovation system can be analysed through the study of innovation networks. Innovation networks regard, in their essence, to groups of relations, bonds or connections, between the nodes that represent the innovation actors that exist – people, companies, and organizations – interacting in the generation, utilization and diffusion of new knowledge and allowing the collective to learn and innovate (Pinto et al. 2015).

Among other options, it is possible to consider the regional innovation system (RIS) (Uyarra and Flanagan 2012) as a unity of analysis in the study of regional resilience. In this way the attempt is to understand the capacity of a RIS to deal with a shock and be able to maintain or improve its innovative dynamic. The benefits of this choice are relatively easy to identify. Conceptually, the components of a RIS are identified as actors and existent relationships. A RIS has a specific spatial configuration related to a certain territory but rarely runs out in the territorially bounded relations. A RIS has a clear function: promoting innovation, with a broader objective – the regional development. It is relatively accessible, in empirical terms, to identify the set of central actors in a specific RIS and start the research based in these elements. Many of the problems related to innovation activities in the region are directly related to the existence of systemic failures. The RISs are objects of public policies, and it is frequent to identify an overlap between what is the RIS and the intervention territory of regional policy for research and innovation (for a reflection on the concept of RIS cf. Pinto et al. 2012). Structural network analysis (SNA) can thus be a relevant method to study knowledge and innovation networks in the region.

SNA has become a very popular approach in social sciences in recent years. From the 1990s onwards, increasing attention was being paid to social contexts. The study of networks and their structural patterns grew at a rapid pace boosted through the use of computing means (Newman 2010). Although this increase is far from recent, in some fields such as the regional economy and economic geography (Ter Wal and Boschma 2009), these analyses have not yet been consolidated. Only in the last few years has SNA begun to be applied in the study of interaction between actors in regions in a systematic way.

The present chapter is an incursion into this theme, seeking to carry out the study of a regional innovation system through the analysis of networks to generate clues about regional resilience. This study focuses on the region of Algarve (Portugal), as a case study, to, through official information on public support for innovation and a qualitative collection following an innovative approach with web content analysis, map the innovation network. This case is particularly interesting in the Portuguese context because it presents common aspects with the national reality but in an exacerbated way. It is a region based on services of low technological intensity, particularly linked to tourism, with low critical mass and a limited range of innovation actors. In addition, it was one of the territories that most felt the impact of the crisis of 2008, with a sharp fall in regional production and an explosive growth in unemployment. On the other hand, it is a region that recovered promptly with the acceleration of the economy, especially since 2015, with the introduction of new competitive sectors anchored in scientific knowledge and more sophisticated tourist products.

The chapter is organized in four parts. Firstly, the text debates the relevance of systemic perspectives of innovation to comprehend regional resilience. We debate the entrepreneurial, innovative and sustainable (EIS) ecosystems, suggested in the current volume, and compare it with the RIS approach. We tend to agree with a practical vision that suggests that even if both approaches gave more attention to some specific aspects, they are extremely related, with many overlapping elements, and almost can be used interchangeably. Then the article argues for the relevance of applying the SNA to the study of the resilience of a particular system. Next, the methodology is explained, highlighting the data collection process and the organization for the relational matrix. The main results of the SNA are presented in Sect. 4. The text ends with a set of conclusions and some implications for regional policies in order to promote innovation.

12.2 EIS Ecosystems and Network Structure

12.2.1 Entrepreneurial, Innovative and Sustainable (EIS) Ecosystems

The increase of multilevel study regarding innovative dynamics as a path for fortifying the economic fabric, expanding productive capacity and creating employment has led to the attempt to construct methodological and conceptual frameworks to respond to this need. As a result, a number of approaches to innovation systems have emerged which, although some authors identify as overlapping, they can be complementary and contribute together to the creation of frameworks with similar heuristic values.

Priority has been given to the potential of integrated policies that aim to promote entrepreneurial activities in order to foster innovation capacity and address societal challenges (Ács et al. 2015; Foster and Shimizu 2013). One of the emerging frameworks recurrently mobilized is anchored in the concept of entrepreneurial, innovative and sustainable (EIS) ecosystems, which has been receiving increasing attention over the last years (Simatupang et al. 2015) and is the motivation of this manuscript.

There are several forms to define entrepreneurial, innovative and sustainable ecosystems, which are related to the context under analysis. The innovation ecosystem encloses two different economical fields: 'the research economy, which is driven by fundamental research, and the commercial economy, which is driven by the marketplace' (Oh et al. 2016: 2). This concept tries to complement previous approaches by filling the gap between intention and result once it focuses to portray the conditions in which the key regional agents aggregate efforts to support entrepreneurial activities engaging to generate economic and social wealth (Prahalad 2005; Cohen 2006).

The regional actors or entities involved in the collective goal of cocreating and developing technology and innovation establish complex relationships resulting in a network that promotes interactions aimed to stimulate and promote entrepreneurship, innovation and regional development driven through a sustainable path within a specific environment (Jackson 2011; Simatupang et al. 2015; Brekke 2015). This network of relations within a sector or a territory, as stated previously, has the capacity to strengthen or limit the evolution of innovative ecosystems (Hage et al. 2013) once knowledge and technology compete and co-evolve through formal and informal transfer in the sector network, based on multi-stakeholder collaboration (Simatupang et al. 2015).

Despite the stated focus on technological aspects of EIS ecosystems, there are several actors who widen the concept dimensions and analyse the importance of contextual elements, such as the strategies, cultures and organizational and institutional environment, as structural factors when building up the competency and effectiveness of EIS ecosystems (Brekke 2015; Phillips 2006; Carayannis and Campbell 2009). Thus, an efficient EIS ecosystem should rely on the integration of agents' activities at three different levels, namely, the strategic level (policy-making), the institutional level (support institutions) and the enterprise level (entrepreneurs and business entities) (Simatupang et al. 2015:391).

An EIS ecosystem is a social and economic construction that operates in several co-related and interdependent levels. This multilevel nature implies the generation of synergistic effects of the system layers along with cross-level interactions (Prahalad 2005; Spigel 2015). Methodologically it implies a highly complex multilevel construct that needs to give voice to the actors involved and their connections. The context layer implies the environmental outlines of the system, such as the cultural and organizational factors and geographical characteristics (Oh et al. 2016). At the regional level, it includes stakeholders, such as political decision makers, governance bodies, business and technological organizations, R&D agencies and the networks by which they are connected (Isenberg 2011). At the niche level, it is important to underline the group and individual actions, who are engaged in micro level activities that determine posterior outcomes (Oh et al. 2016) working as micro mechanisms from where the actions are formed and emerge. This methodological and theoretical proposal can help to understand the innovative dynamics and capacities of a specific system. However, despite that it still is a concept that, per se, is not able to explain comprehensively the innovative capacity of socio-economic systems as a structural, social and economic construction (Simatupang et al. 2015). One of the reasons most referenced in the literature is because there are different types of innovation ecosystems that arrogate different explanations and analytical frameworks (Oh et al. 2016).

The innovation ecosystems are typified according to its geographical endowment, innovation processes, trigger actors and prime focus (Oh et al. 2016). Based on these features, it is possible to identify innovation ecosystems that differ from the city-based unit to hyperlocal systems (Cohen et al. 2014); that vary according to the actors that trigger it (universities, digital sector, enterprises); the type of innovation focus – usually ecosystems are engaged with processes of open and collaborative innovation (Zhang et al. 2014); and that rely on the same theoretical basis as regional and national innovation systems (Morrison 2013).

If we compare the EIS ecosystem and RIS concepts, we find that they are very similar when analysed together, although there are some differences. Regarding limitations, both concepts present fragile theoretical frameworks and methodological options. However, a great work has been done, through these approaches, trying to comprehensively analyse the innovative dynamics, capacities and outputs of a system. The similarities mainly rely on the importance given to knowledge transfer, stakeholders' collaboration, presence of intention and the acknowledged importance of governance (Oh et al. 2016). The differentiating factors of EIS ecosystem are greater reference to the evolution of systemic connections among innovation actors, focus on open innovation, a central role of information and communication technologies along with a greater impact on the media, larger emphasis on differentiated roles (niches) occupied by organizations and industries and the importance of market forces, relative to government (Simatupang et al. 2015).

However, compared with the RIS approach, the EIS ecosystem concept is still underdeveloped as the related empirical research is still under theorized. Therefore, opportunities persist for a better integration not only with the promptly accumulating research but also with general organizational theory and research. The knowledge produced slightly explains what factors and especially interactions of factors at various levels of analysis lead to desired economic development outcomes (Simatupang et al. 2015). Thus, there are some challenges to overcome, mainly a more effective distinction from national and regional innovation systems, assessing the system performance and a clear definition of the levels at which the term is used (Oh et al. 2016). We consider that the research agenda may benefit more if EIS ecosystem literature is developed in collaborative effort with the more consolidated studies about systems of innovation.

12.2.2 Network Analysis and Typologies of Resilience in Innovation Networks

From a modelling perspective, networks are relatively simple to understand since they consist of two essential elements: nodes and links. SNA is an approach that assumes that these nodes and links reflect the implicit structures between actors and institutions in society, the existing relations and the role of these actors at the individual level in the network. It is a perspective that connects micro and macro levels of analysis, resulting in a flexible tool that can also be used to study the meso level – something that is not abundant in the social sciences. SNA transcends quantitative-qualitative dichotomies, as it relies on robust statistical analysis and, at the same time, is based on data collected on actors and institutions that, in most cases, can be observable and studied regarding qualitative information. SNA can be categorized as a situated case study with an explicit temporal and spatial reference (Breiger 2004).

Research that uses SNA tends to adopt one of two approaches: the design of an egocentric network or mapping the entire network in a given domain (Marsden 2005). In the first case, the analysis focuses on studying the set of relations with other actors and objects of a certain central actor – the ego – the starting point of research. In the second case, the aim is to map the global network, finding actors and interrelated objects considered as delimiters of a certain social group. It should be stressed that in this type of analysis, the term actor can represent an individual, company or particular collective social unit (Rivera et al. 2010).

SNA seeks to study social phenomena as groups of standardized relationships between actors. The basic structure of the network retracts the relationships and interactions, as well as affiliations between the actors and certain attributes in the network. The type of association between the actors is fundamental to the definition of research. Relationships in the context of SNA represent the set of social bonds of a certain type (e.g. 'interacts with', 'negotiates with', 'collaborates with') that binds pairs of actors. Connections in SNA are usually described using two dimensions: symmetry (refers to mutual or reciprocal relations, when a relation is established between two actors and works in both directions) and homophily (refers to relations between actors with similar characteristics). These characteristics are related to the resources of the actors (Jackson 2010). Relationships are also described by their intensity. This dimension is usually associated with the debate about weak or strong ties, as a result of Granovetter's analysis (Granovetter 1973, 1983) which concluded that strong ties are structuring of networks but weak ties are essential in the search for opportunities, by introducing novelty and innovation in the network, and to the integration of new actors in certain subgroups of the network.

When connections between two subgroups within a network are dependent on a limited number of intermediaries, a structural hole can be created, resulting in isolated groups or actors within the network if the actors connecting them are removed. These structural holes give power to those actors whose relationships eliminate holes (Burt 1995, 2000) because they represent opportunities to mediate information flows, coordinate and mobilize other actors according to their own objectives. The actors between structural holes gain centrality in intermediation allowing to reveal the hierarchical structure of the network and to identify influential nodes. It should be noted that the existence of a gap between two groups does not necessarily mean that the members of one group are not aware of the other group. It simply means that they do not engage in joint activities.

A common strategy in the study of limited scale social networks has been to identify all members and track their connections. But this is far from a simple matter. Social relationships are social constructs, based on situational definitions made by the members of the group. Data in SNA is collected normally with the use of questionnaires, especially when the actors are people. These usually inquire about the relations of the respondent with other actors. Another option is the direct observation that favours an ethnographic research approach. Interviews are also a particularly suitable option for collecting data from individuals in high positions within organizations and who tend to avoid questionnaires. Archive data and official records can also be used to obtain relational information. Any study using SNA should be cautious in defining the relationships that will be analysed and make sure that the data collection techniques are appropriate for the intended level of analysis.

Recent studies have attempted to cross SNA with regional studies. This is a field which remains unexplored (Ter Wal and Boschma 2009) since networks have been viewed as a territorial phenomenon although the localized nature of social capital has been emphasized several times (Rutten et al. 2010) and the distinction between localized networks and nonlocalized networks has already been addressed in the literature (Karlsson 2011).

Recent research has attempted to perceive the essential characteristics of a given network of regional actors to structure a 'resilient network'. One of these studies is the proposal of Crespo et al. (2013) that presents three types of network as a result of statistical indicators of homophily and hierarchy: 'random network', 'resilient network' and 'core-periphery network'. Table 12.1 summarizes the topology and the essential factors in each type of network.

The existence of networks of each of these types has important consequences for public policies. Table 12.2 summarizes some of these implications in terms of the structural change that policies must promote in order for the network to become more resilient.

Table 12.1 Resilience of different types of network

Source: Crespo et al. (2013)

Table 12.2 Implications for policies in different types of network

	Hierarchy: Δlal=0	Hierarchy: Δlal>0	Hierarchy: Δlal<0
Homophily: Δb=0	*Laissez faire*	Reinforce the up part of the hierarchy of knowledge networks	Reinforce the down part of the hierarchy of knowledge networks
Homophily: Δb<0	Promote structural heterophily and disassortativity	Reinforce the up part of the hierarchy of knowledge networks	Reinforce the down part of the hierarchy of knowledge networks
		Promote structural heterophily and disassortativity	Promote structural heterophily and disassortativity
Homophily: Δb>0	Reinforce the structural homophily and assortativity	Reinforce the up part of the hierarchy of knowledge networks	Reinforce the down part of the hierarchy of knowledge networks
		Reinforce the structural homophily and assortativity	Reinforce the structural homophily and assortativity

Source: Crespo et al. (2013)

12.3 Methodology

Based on the Algarve's case study, this research uses methods of structural analysis of social networks to map actors and centralities in cooperation and innovation in regional development. The analysis uses data collected through *web content mining* from the list of organizations benefiting from public support for innovation through the regional Operational Program (OP) 2007–2013.

The official list of support/beneficiaries of the regional OP in innovation incentive systems was obtained directly from the Algarve Regional Coordination and Development Commission (CCDR Algarve) and is currently available on its institutional website. With this collected list, the next objective was to create a relational data matrix to perform the SNA. The first group of nodes and relationships collected included organizations involved in innovation projects with funding through the OP. Based on this initial listing, the websites of all beneficiary entities were gathered. The *content mining* analysis of the websites ran from March to May 2016, looking for expressions such as 'partnership', 'network', 'project' and 'protocol' to identify a second group of nodes and relationships. These new nodes and relationships have been added to the initial listing. Then it was tried to identify the websites of the new entities, and a second round of *web content mining* was executed.

The identified actors were characterized in terms of:

- Typology - 1, company; 2, governance entity; 3, innovation intermediary (business association, technology transfer office, among others); 4, university or public entity of R&D.
- Five-digit main economic activity code.
- Location in the Algarve.

The relationships identified were characterized in terms of:

- Innovation - 1, relation explicitly related to innovative activities vs. 0, other types of collaboration.
- Depth - 1, low deep (project, activity); 2, deep (partnerships, networks, projects, protocols); 3, consolidated (if collaboration was repeated among the same entities).

Based on this information, it was possible to develop the structural network analysis. In the following section, we present the main results of this study.

12.4 Results of Structural Analysis of Social Networks

12.4.1 The Algarve Innovation Network

The SNA was carried out based on the information collected, using the software NodeXL (Smith et al. 2010) and Cytoscape (Shannon et al. 2003). The final network presents a total of 929 nodes and 726 relations, with 639 not being repeated. This result has an interesting aspect. The fact that there are more nodes than links is suggestive of a large number of innovative projects funded publicly that have a single beneficiary that does not present any online information of collaboration with other actors.

The different typologies of actors were represented with the following logic in the figures: squares represent companies (COMP), lozenges are innovation intermediaries (INT), circles are the actors of governance (GOV), and triangles are universities and other public R&D entities (UNIV). Using the Fruchterman-Reingold algorithm, Fig. 12.1 presents the global network. This image represents a sparsely populated network core, where the vast majority of actors concentrate on the periphery of the network.

An alternative representation using the Harel-Koren fast multiscale algorithm, Fig. 12.2, presents the global network but allows clarifying the subgroups in the EIS ecosystem. This image presents two crucial clusters with an important variety of actors and some peripheral communities dominated by companies. There are several subgroups linked by a very limited number of actors, which on the one hand give added power to these nodes and on the other hand they are a catalyst for the creation of structural holes if these actors disappear or for some reason begin to not perform their function properly within the network.

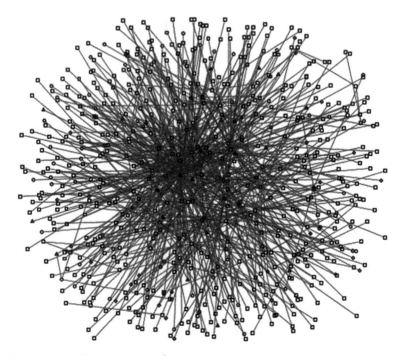

Fig. 12.1 Actors and relationships in the Algarve innovation system (Source: Own elaboration using the NodeXL, Fruchterman-Reingold algorithm)

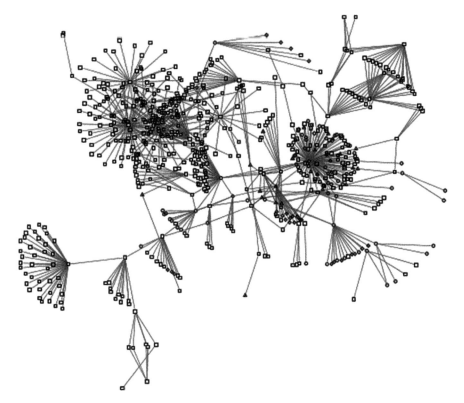

Fig. 12.2 Structural holes in the innovation system of the Algarve (Source: Own elaboration using the NodeXL, Harel-Koren Fast Multiscale algorithm)

The number of relationships is one of the main indicators of the importance of an actor in the network. An analysis of this measure, the so-called degree, the total number of connections – in and out degree – shows that the actors that concentrate the most connections are few; there are only 21 nodes with more than 10 connections (Table 12.3).

After these 21 entities, the number of relations sharply decreases. As a reference the average number of connections per actor, in this network, is 2.2. Several organizations, the CRIA – Technology Transfer and Entrepreneurship Division of the University of Algarve, CCDR Algarve, and UAlg – University of Algarve (Rectory), populate the nucleus of the network. AMAL – Intermunicipal Community of Algarve and Tourism of Portugal are also crucial entities in network connectivity.

It is worth giving some attention to the particular case of CRIA, which assumes a high relevance, with more than double the relationships identified by the second most connected actor. The creation and development of this entity has already been analysed in previous studies (namely, in Pinto and Pereira 2012). The role of this UAlg Division in the region has transcended the mere technology transfer office,

Table 12.3 Number of relationships identified of most connected entities

Actor	Degree (total number of connections)
INT1 – CRIA	119
COMP103	52
COMP60	40
GOV3 – CCDR Algarve	39
COMP187	31
COMP26	29
COMP109	25
UNIV3 – UAlg (Rectory)	25
COMP102	21
COMP248	19
COMP5	19
COMP194	18
GOV4 – AMAL	18
COMP40	17
COMP34	16
GOV2 – Institute of Tourism	15
COMP43	14
COMP9	14
COMP242	13
COMP1	12
COMP168	10

Source: Own elaboration using the NodeXL

mainly due to the lack of other intermediary actors specialized in innovation. This actor has played a catalytic role in promoting innovation in the region and has also been an instrument of regional actors, in particular the CCDR itself, when they wish to intervene in this area, with recurrent support and funding through specific projects under the regional OP.

12.4.2 Hierarchy and Homophily in the Innovation Network

The mapping of the innovation network in the Algarve can be compared with the theoretical network models previously presented through hierarchy and homophily indicators.

As stated, the hierarchy is measured by the number of relationships with other actors. In this case we use the *degree distribution* to understand if actors that have more relations are few, dominating the network, or if the relations are distributed in a balanced way by the nodes of the network. Figure 12.3 shows a scatter diagram illustrating the number of nodes with a particular degree. A very high number of nodes present a low degree, while only a very low number of nodes have a high number of relations.

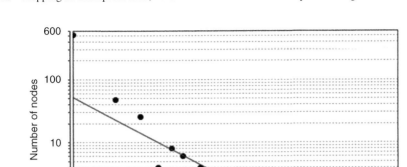

Fig. 12.3 Hierarchy in the network (Source: Own elaboration using Cytoscape)

This graphical intuition can also be confirmed, following the proposal of Crespo et al. (2013), estimating a representative function of this relation and analysing the associated coefficient (a).

$$\text{Log}(Y) = C(x)a \quad (12.1)$$

$$\text{Log}(Y) = \log(C) + a\log(x) \quad (12.2)$$

$$\text{Log}(y) = 52{,}160 - 1185x \quad (12.3)$$

In this case (cf. Eq. 12.3), the coefficient is negative, which is illustrated by the negative slope line shown in Fig. 12.3. This result translates to a high level of hierarchy, an outcome that would be expected given what was stated in Table 12.3.

The other measure of network analysis refers to homophily. It should be noted that homophily refers, as discussed above, in general terms to the fact that certain actors privilege relationships with actors that are similar to themselves. There are, of course, a number of possible perspectives on homophily (whether business entities deal more with other companies, if R&D actors relate to other R&D entities, if entities in a particular sector/economic activity relate to entities in their sector, if entities with a high number of employers and/or high business volume relate with small- and medium-sized enterprises or not). All these dimensions are possible to analyse with data collected for SNA. In our particular case, these analyses are possible to carry out. However, homophily will be studied in this article in a very particular aspect, probably the most studied by the literature: the fact that more connected entities relate to more connected entities. Homophily can thus be measured by the linear association between the number of relations of an actor and the average number of relations of its neighbours. This indicator is called *degree correlation*. Figure 12.4 shows the dispersion diagram between the number of neighbours and the average

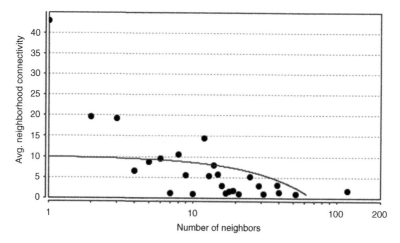

Fig. 12.4 Homophily in the network (Source: Own elaboration using Cytoscape)

number of neighbours' connections. The fact that this distribution is *flat*, having an unclear pattern, suggests that there is no obvious trend. That is, actors with a higher degree do not necessarily relate to actors with a higher degree.

This graphical intuition can be confirmed, following the proposal of Crespo et al. (2013), estimating a function of this relation and analysing the associated coefficient (b) and calculating the correlation coefficient.

$$Y = 10,049 - 0146x \qquad (12.4)$$

In this case the trend curve (cf. Eq. 12.4) is almost horizontal (practically with no defined slope pattern), and the correlation coefficient is relatively low ($c = 0.385$).

Thus, the intense negative slope of the degree distribution and the flatness of the degree correlation result in a network that characterizes the regional innovation system in the Algarve, close to the theoretical model of a 'random network'. A 'random network' is, from the structural point of view, a relatively resilient network to shocks, which dissipate by several nodes, destroying parts of the network but which tend to renew rapidly or to be replaced in their functions by other nodes. But from the point of view of effectiveness, a 'random network' has a lack of cohesion and of internal density and usually has a disconnected central structure. In order to be effective, a real social network should not over-approximate the characteristics of a 'random network', at the risk of creating rapid contagion, and transfer shock impacts through the network, from the periphery to the centre, leading to the destruction of the essential structures of the global function of the network. A innovation system should rather reveal patterns that suggest a privileged association between some of the nodes in order to structure a core of actors, varying in typology and number, densely connected to each other, approaching the theoretical model of 'resilient network'.

12.5 Conclusion

The last few years were of high economic and social turbulence. It has become fundamental for the social sciences to find concepts and methodologies capable of fostering an understanding of how socio-economic systems, at different levels, resist and recover from certain structural shocks and failures.

In this context, the concept of resilience has been used to analyse the impacts of shocks, particularly those resulting from the economic crisis. Increasingly, an evolutionary approach to resilience has been presented in regional studies, which allows not only to understand the capacity to return to certain development paths but also the capacity to construct new paths and opportunities.

In this text it is suggested that the resilience capacity of a specific territory can be analysed using the SNA. One of the limitations of the concept of resilience is the choice of the unit of analysis. Used ambiguously it can be applied from people to countries. The chapter suggested that focusing a specific system – as an EIS ecosystem or a RIS – may help to provide some precision to the comprehension of regional resilience. The exploratory study in this chapter presented a novel methodology to gather information to create a relational data matrix. This methodology consisted, in a first phase, in the creation of a list of entities and relationships in innovative projects supported by public resources and in a second phase, through web content mining, a transversal online identification of entities and collaborations for innovation in the region. Certainly, this methodological approach presents weaknesses, mainly because the information online does not necessarily reproduce the real situation of the actors but rather what they intend to make more visible. This approach of gathering relational information in two phases is useful to fill the problems of completeness that are quite common in SNA if the data is limited to use information from official public records.

The Algarve's case study pointed to an innovation system close to a 'random network', with limited internal density and excessively dependent on a very small number of intermediaries. The text suggested that the use of two indicators (degree distribution and degree correlation) provides important clues to innovation policies and the structure of EIS ecosystems. The degree distribution – which measures the hierarchy by the number of links of each actor – has impacts on the policies at the actor's individual level. In the case under study, it is necessary to connect actors with fewer connections, for example, promoting links between actors beyond market (supplier-consumer) relations or by developing collaborative activities for innovation. The degree correlation – which measures homogeneity – is a key indicator for policy design at the system's level. In this case study, the low level of connectivity between more central actors suggests the need for the promotion of more collaborative activities at the centre of the network to be accompanied by a reinforcement of the role of mediation and translation by a broader range of actors that will constitute a denser and more populated nucleus. Public policies should make efforts to stimulate cooperation for innovation by avoiding excessive weight of some actors and an exacerbated concentration of resources.

Future research using this kind of relational matrix may explore topics such as the spatial location of relations, the sectoral specialization of the actors and the related variety or specific clusters within the network.

Acknowledgements Hugo Pinto benefits from the financial support from FCT – Portuguese Science and Technology Foundation (SFRH/BPD/84038/2012). The authors are thankful to CCDR Algarve for the availability of data. They also recognize the support of Daniela Mendes, Silvia Dragomir and Jorge André Guerreiro (research internships) in the preparation of material for this study.

References

Ács, Z. J., Szerb, L., & Autio, E. (2015). *Global entrepreneurship index 2015*. Washington, DC: The Global Entrepreneurship and Development Institute.

Allan, P., & Bryant, M. (2012). Resilience as a framework for urbanism and recovery. *Journal of Landscape Architecture, 6*(2), 37–41.

Boschma, R. (2015). Towards an evolutionary perspective on regional resilience. *Regional Studies, 49*(5), 733–751. https://doi.org/10.1080/00343404.2014.959481.

Boschma, R., & Pinto, H. (2015). Resilient territories. In H. Pinto (Ed.), *Resilient territories innovation and creativity for new modes of regional development*. Newcastle upon Tyne: Cambridge SP.

Breiger, R. (2004). The analysis of social networks. In M. Hardy & A. Bryman (Eds.), *Handbook of data analysis*. India: Sage Publications.

Brekke, T. (2015). Entrepreneurship and path dependency in regional development. *Entrepreneurship & Regional Development: An International Journal, 27*(3–4), 202–218.

Burt, R. (1995). *Structural holes*. Cambridge: Harvard University Press.

Burt, R. (2000). The network structure of social capital. In B. Staw & R. Sutton (Eds.), *Research in organizational behaviour* (Vol. 22, pp. 345–423). Greenwich: JAI Press.

Carayannis, E. G., & Campbell, D. F. J. (2009). 'Mode 3' and quadruple helix: Toward a 21st-century fractal innovation ecosystem. *International Journal of Technology Management, 46*(3–4), 201–234.

Christopherson, S., Michie, J., & Tyler, P. (2010). Regional resilience: Theoretical and empirical perspectives. *Cambridge Journal of Regions Economy and Society, 3*(1), 3–10.

Cohen, B. (2006). Sustainable valley entrepreneurial ecosystems. *Business Strategy and the Environment, 15*(1), 1–14.

Cohen, B., Almirall, E., & Chesbrough, H. (2014). The city as a lab: Open innovation meets the collaborative economy. *California Management Review, 59*(1), 5–13.

Crespo, J., Suire, R., & Vicente, J. (2013). Lock-in or lock-out? How structural properties of knowledge networks affect regional resilience? *Journal of Economic Geography*. https://doi.org/10.1093/jeg/lbt006.

Davies, S. (2011). Regional resilience in the 2008-2010 downturn: Comparative evidence from European countries. *Cambridge Journal of Regions, Economy and Society, 4*(3), 369–382. https://doi.org/10.1093/cjres/rsr019.

Davoudi, S., Shaw, K., Haider, L. J., Quinlan, A. E., Peterson, G. D., Wilkinson, C., & Mcevoy, D. (2012). Resilience: A bridging concept or a dead end? "Reframing" resilience: Challenges for planning theory and practice interacting traps: Resilience assessment of a pasture management system in northern Afghanistan urban resilience: What does it mean in planning. *Planning Theory & Practice, 13*(2), 299–333.

Dawley, S., Pike, A., & Tomaney, J. (2010). *Towards the resilient region ?: Policy activism and peripheral region, SERC Discussion Papers, SERCDP0053*. London: Spatial Economics Research Centre (SERC), London School of Economics and Political Science.

Foster, G., & Shimizu, C. (2013). Entrepreneurial ecosystems around the globe and company growth dynamics, Report Summary for the Annual Meeting of the New Champions 2013, World Economic Forum.

Granovetter, M. (1973). The strength of weak ties. *The American Journal of Sociology, 78*(69), 1360–1380.

Granovetter, M. (1983). The strength of weak ties: A network theory revisited. *Sociological Theory, 1*, 201–233.

Hage, J., Mote, J. E., & Jordan, G. B. (2013). Ideas, innovations, and networks: A new policy model based on the evolution of knowledge. *Policy Sciences, 46*, 199–216.

Hamdouch, A., & Depret, M. (2012). *Mondialisation et résilience des territoires*. Québec: Presses de l'Université du Québec.

Isenberg, D. J. (2011). *"The entrepreneurship ecosystem strategy as a new paradigm for economic policy: Principles for cultivating entrepreneurship", the Babson entrepreneurship ecosystem project*. Massachusetts: Babson College.

Jackson M (2010). An overview of social networks and economic applications, Benhabib J, A Bisin and M Jackson Handbook of Social Economics, New York, Elsevier Science & Technology, 511–585.

Jackson, B. D. J. (2011). *What is an innovation ecosystem?* Washington, DC. http://erc-assoc.org/sites/default/files/topics/policy_studies/DJackson_Innovation Ecosystem_03-15-11.pdf

Karlsson, C. (2011). Clusters, networks and creativity. In D. E. Andersson, Å. E. Andersson, & C. Mellander (Eds.), *Handbook of creative cities* (pp. 85–114). Cheltenham: Edward Elgar.

Marsden, P. (2005). Recent developments in network measurement. In P. Carrington, J. Scott, & S. Wasserman (Eds.), *Models and methods in social network analysis* (pp. 8–30). Cambridge: Cambridge University Press.

Martin, R., & Sunley, P. (2014). On the notion of regional economic resilience: Conceptualization and explanation. *Journal of Economic Geography, 15*(1), 1–42. https://doi.org/10.1093/jeg/lbu015.

Martin, R., & Tyler, P. (2015). Local growth evolutions: Recession, resilience and recovery. *Cambridge Journal of Regions, Economy and Society, 8*, 141–148. https://doi.org/10.1093/cjres/rsv012.

Morrison, E. (2013). Universities as anchors for regional innovation ecosystems. http://www.edmorrison.com/universities-as-anchors-for-regionalinnovationecosystems/

Newman, M. (2010). *Networks: An introduction*. New York: Oxford University Press.

Oh, D. S., Phillips, F., Park, S., & Lee, E. (2016). Innovation ecosystems: A critical examination. Technovation, 54, 2–6. https://doi.org/10.1016/j.technovation.2016.02.004.

Phillips, F. (2006). *Social culture and high tech economic development: The technopolis columns*. London: Palgrave Macmillan.

Pinto, H., & Pereira, T. S. (2012). Institucionalização da Transferência de Conhecimento: Políticas Públicas e Formação de Actores-Rede na Universidade Portuguesa, Actas do VII Congresso da APS, http://www.aps.pt/vii_congresso/papers/finais/PAP1260_ed.pdf

Pinto, H., & Pereira, T. S. (2014). Resiliência dos sistemas de inovação face à turbulência económica, Oficinas do CES, 418. http://www.ces.uc.pt/publicacoes/oficina/ficheiros/11157_Oficina_do_CES_418.pdf

Pinto, H., Guerreiro, J., & Uyarra, E. (2012). Diversidades de Sistemas de Inovação e Implicações nas Políticas Regionais: Comparação das Regiões do Algarve e da Andaluzia. *Revista Portuguesa de Estudos Regionais 29*, 3–14. http://www.apdr.pt/siterper/numeros/RPER29/29.1.pdf

Pinto, H., Noronha, M. T., & Faustino, C. (2015). Knowledge and cooperation determinants of innovation networks. *Journal of Technology Management & Innovation, 20*(1), 83–102. https://doi.org/10.4067/S0718-27242015000100007.

Prahalad, C. K. (2005). *The fortune at the bottom of the pyramid: Eradicating poverty through profits*. Saddle River: Wharton School Publishing.

Rivera, M. T., Soderstrom, S. B., & Uzzi, B. (2010). Dynamics of dyads in social networks: Assortative, relational, and proximity mechanisms. *Annual Review of Sociology, 36*(1), 91–115. https://doi.org/10.1146/annurev.soc.34.040507.134743.

Rutten, R., Westlund, H., & Boekema, F. (2010). The spatial dimension of social capital. *European Planning Studies, 18*(6), 863–871. https://doi.org/10.1080/09654311003701381.

Scott, J. (2000). *Social network analysis: A handbook* (2nd ed.). Sage Publishers: Great Britain.

Shannon, P., Markiel, A., Ozier, O., Baliga, N. S., Wang, J. T., Ramage, D., Amin, N., Schwikowski, B., & Ideker, T. (2003). Cytoscape: A software environment for integrated models of biomolecular interaction networks. *Genome Research, 13*(11), 2498–2504.

Simatupang, T. M., Schwab, A., & Lantu, D. C. (2015). Building sustainable entrepreneurship ecosystems. *International Journal of Entrepreneurship and Small Business, 26*(4), 389–398.

Simmie, J. (2014). Regional economic resilience: A Schumpeterian perspective. *Raumforschung und Raumordnung, 72*(2), 103–116. https://doi.org/10.1007/s13147-014-0274-y.

Simmie, J., & Martin, R. L. (2010). The economic resilience of regions: Towards an evolutionary approach. *Cambridge Journal of Regions, Economy and Society, 3*, 27–43.

Smith, M., Milic-Frayling, N., Shneiderman, B., Rodrigues, E. M., Leskovec, J., & Dunne, C. (2010). (Version 1.0.1.167) [Software]. NodeXL: A free and open network overview, discovery and exploration add-in for Excel 2007/2010. Disponível em http://www.smrfoundation.org

Spigel, B. (2015). The relational organization of entrepreneurial ecosystems. *Entrepreneurship Theory and Practice, 39*(4), 1540–6520.

Ter Wal, A., & Boschma, R. (2009). Applying social network analysis in economic geography: Framing some key analytic issues. *The Annals of Regional Science, 43*(3), 739–756.

Uyarra, E., & Flanagan, K. (2012). Reframing regional innovation systems: Evolution, complexity and public policy. In P. Cooke (Ed.), *Re-framing regional development* (pp. 146–163). Cheltenham: Edward Elgar.

Wasserman, S., & Faust, K. (1994). *Social network analysis: Methods and applications.* Cambridge: Cambridge University Press.

Zhang, X., Ding, L., & Chen, X. (2014). Interaction of open innovation and business ecosystem. *International Journal Services Science Technology, 7*(1), 51–64. https://doi.org/10.14257/ijunesst.2014.7.1.05.

Chapter 13
Corporate Social Responsibility and Total Quality Management: The Stakeholders' Value Creation Debate Revisited

Luís Mendes and Dalila Dias

Abstract Since both total quality management (TQM) and corporate social responsibility (CSR) consider the interest of either internal or external stakeholders, these approaches are generally considered appropriate corporate strategies to enhance organizations' value in order to obtain sustainable competitive advantages. Through a comprehensive literature review, this chapter aims to systematize knowledge on how the implementation of strategies based on TQM and CSR principles may create stakeholders' value and generate sustainable competitive advantages. More specifically the chapter aims to examine whether there is a relationship of complementarity between both and to analyse how a strategy based on both orientations may contribute to organizations' sustainable performance while improving the quality of life. Overall the few results provide support to the idea that combined CSR-TQM approaches enable organizations to gain competitive advantages. Overall, this review highlights that when thought proactively and strategically, sustainability-based approaches combining CSR-TQM approaches are potential sources for obtaining sustainable competitive advantages and for improving quality of life of the workforce and citizens in local communities, in particular, and even of society in general.

Keywords Total quality management • Corporate social responsibility • Customer value • Sustainability • Competitive advantages • Quality of life

---

L. Mendes (✉)
Advanced Studies in Management & Economics Research Center (CEFAGE-UBI),
Department of Management and Economics, University of Beira Interior, Covilhã, Portugal
e-mail: lmendes@ubi.pt

D. Dias
University of Beira Interior, Covilhã, Portugal

© Springer International Publishing AG 2018
J. Leitão et al. (eds.), *Entrepreneurial, Innovative and Sustainable Ecosystems*, Applying Quality of Life Research,
https://doi.org/10.1007/978-3-319-71014-3_13

13.1 Introduction

Companies that embrace a high-quality, holistic approach to corporate sustainability, ensuring compliance with environmental standards and safeguard of natural resources and looking for new environmentally and socially conscious sustainability solutions that could minimize risks while delivering enhanced profitability through cost reduction, improved resource accessibility, marketing and recruiting benefits, are more likely to address short-term needs while positioning themselves for long-term success (Fust and Walker 2007).

While total quality management (TQM) has been implemented worldwide along the past three decades in several different either private or public industries (Ghobadian and Gallear 2001), corporate social responsibility (CSR) is a much more recent phenomenon.

Although several studies have shown that quality management does not always improve the sustainability of a firm, due to several factors such as lack of top management involvement (e.g. Viada-Stenger et al. 2010; Yeung et al. 2006), when responsiveness for quality is extended throughout all the levels in the organization, the success of TQM-based quality management systems is more likely to occur (Bou and Beltran 2005), and several studies have provided findings to support such positive relationship between TQM and performance (Jaca and Psomas 2015; Yeung et al. 2006; Samson and Terziovski 1999).

Considering the trade-off between CSR-based investments and profitability, regarding the relationship between CSR and organizations' performance, findings have been quite inconclusive, and although some studies have suggested negative and neutral relationships (e.g. Parast and Adams 2012; McWilliams and Siegel 2000), several studies have reported positive influences of CSR strategies in organizations' performance (Foote et al. 2010; Lu et al. 2013; Zali and Sheydayaee 2013).

The stakeholder theory suggests that, in order to create long-term value and generate sustainable wealth over time, organizations should guide decision-making, and expand the scope of their activities beyond shareholders' own interests, to several other parties with vested interests, such as customers, employees, suppliers, governmental bodies, trade associations, trade unions and the community in general, among others. Since both approaches consider the interest of either internal or external stakeholders, TQM and CSR are generally considered appropriate corporate strategies that can enhance organizations' value and potential sources in order to obtain sustainable competitive advantages (Benavides-Velasco et al. 2014).

Moreover, one of the key issues that have significantly interested scholars in the fields of TQM and CSR deals with the degree of overlap between both strategic approaches. According to McAdam and Leonard (2003), considering its greater penetration in organizations, TQM even may act as a key catalyst for developing CSR within organization.

Through a comprehensive literature review, this chapter aims to systematize knowledge on how the implementation of strategies based on TQM and CSR principles may create stakeholders' value and generate sustainable competitive advantages for organizations. More specifically, anchored in the existing literature in both fields, the chapter aims to identify similarities and differences between both strategies in order to reduce/eliminate redundancies in the use of resources, to examine whether there is a relationship of complementarity between both regarding sustainability and trust factors, to explore how TQM can act as a foundation and key catalyst for the development of CSR-based strategies and to analyse how a strategy based on both orientations may contribute to organizations' sustainable performance while improving the quality of life of the workforce and citizens in local communities, in particular, and even of society in general.

13.2 Background

While TQM has been implemented worldwide along the last decades in several different organizational contexts, CSR appears to be a much more recent phenomenon. First of all, it is important to understand what these two concepts are and how they evolved, although in the literature there is no consensus in this area.

13.2.1 Corporate Social Responsibility

Over the past decades, CSR and its effect on organizations' success has been the subject of much academic debate and criticism, with most questions focusing on whether a company that is socially responsible is more likely to be financially successful (Foote et al. 2010). Similarly, there is also a growing interest among managers in CSR's antecedents and consequences, especially for executives at multi-national and multidivisional companies (McWilliams et al. 2006).

Nevertheless, nowadays, the power of environment, citizens, potential investors, pressure groups and a wide range of other stakeholders is increasingly holding companies to account for social, environmental and economic impacts that they have on society and the natural environment, and companies, regardless of their size and target market, need to earn approval of the society to be able to remain in business (Gechevski et al. 2016).

As highlighted by Bowen et al. (2013), CSR refers to a fundamental morality regarding how a company behaves towards society, following ethical behaviour towards stakeholders and recognizing the spirit of both legal and regulatory environment. According to these authors, entrepreneurs' social responsibility refers to obligation regarding defining policies and making decisions that converge towards a strategy that converge to societies' goals and values.

As explained by Carroll and Shabana (2010), organizations' social responsibility connects economic, legal, ethical and philanthropic dimensions with the expectations society has about these organizations. Similarly, Tarí (2011) considers that social responsibility refers to the set of business practices that meet or exceed the economic, legal, ethical and philanthropic expectations of society, considering all the interested parties in this issue. Mijatovic and Stokic (2010) also emphasize organizations' ethical commitment to environmental and economic sustainability without depriving stakeholders.

The ISO 26000:2010 international standards provide guidance on how organizations should convert principles into effective actions and share best practices concerning social responsibility. As defined in these standards, CSR refers to the influences of organizations' decisions and activities (products, services and processes) on society and environment, through transparent and ethical behaviour, contributing to society's sustainable development (including its health and welfare) and taking into account stakeholders' expectations, in compliance with applicable law and international norms, integrated throughout the organization, practised in its activities within its sphere of influence, being part of the organizational culture.

Other authors have redefined the concept of organization, placing it in its socio-economic context as a living organism that is fed by society and, in return, promotes societal well-being, contrary to the reductive concept of a simple economic entity that produces goods and services (Parsa et al. 2015). From this perspective, there is a symbiotic relationship between organizations and society, a mutualist spirit that generates benefits for both parties.

13.2.2 Total Quality Management

Being for a long time framed at an operational context, quality management begins to rise interest from a strategy point of view, with a focus shift towards strategic quality management. As highlighted by Hellsten and Klefsjo (2000), the evolution of quality management reached a point where quality is considered as a key factor for competition, moving from a narrow manufacturing-based perspective to a corporate emphasis applied to all business functions and employees with broader implications for management. In this context, Garvin (1987) proposed eight critical dimensions of quality that can serve as a framework for strategic analysis: performance, features, reliability, conformance, durability, serviceability, aesthetics and perceived quality. As highlighted by the author, although the most traditional notions of conformance and reliability remain important, they are subsumed within a broader strategic framework. Considering their business strategy and their positioning, companies focus on one or more dimensions of quality; being sure with the upstream of this process, they must consider that quality is strategic and in this strategy formulation process they do not disregard the external context.

From an evolutionary perspective, quality management starts to consider organizations as a whole, originating a new approach called total quality management and focusing on both internal and external stakeholders, and is described by Miller (1996) as a continuous effort from top management to take the necessary steps to enable everyone in the organization to grasp information about quality principles to meet or exceed the expectations of internal and external customers. TQM may be conceptualized as a structured approach to refocus organizations' behaviour, planning and working practices towards an employee-driven culture, problem-solving, stakeholder oriented, values integrity and open and fear-free, in such a way that organizations' business practices are based on seeking continuous improvement, devolution of decision-making, removal of functional barriers, eradication of sources of error, teamworking, honesty and fact-based decision-making (Ghobadian and Gallear 1996).

Hansson (2003) considers TQM as an important management philosophy in the sense that it supports the organization in satisfying customers. According to Ghobadian and Gallear (1996), several values underpin the TQM concept, such as an implicit convergence of multiple interests (employees, shareholders, customers, suppliers and the wider society), an emphasis on individual/collective honesty and integrity, stakeholders' satisfaction as everyone's key priority, people as key internal success factors, management's responsibility for maintaining an environment in which employees can perform efficiently and effectively, organization viewed as a chain of interlinked processes, continuous improvement pursuing, emphasis on prevention, high interaction between parties (employees, customers, suppliers), mistakes considered as learning opportunities, employees empowerment, strategic alliances with suppliers, mutual respect concerning all relationships, decisions based on facts, functional integration and openness within and outside the organization.

Table 13.1 shows some of the main conceptualizations of TQM reported in literature.

Table 13.1 Conceptualizations of total quality management

Authors	Definition
Oakland (1989)	Approach to improve competitiveness, efficiency and flexibility throughout the organization, emphasizing values
Shiba et al. (1993)	TQM is seen as a system that brings together a set of tools and methods that aim to empower organizations in a context of rapid change
Dale (1994) and Huxtable (1995)	Important management philosophy that supports organizations regarding customer satisfaction efforts
Dahlgaard (1999)	Corporate culture oriented towards increasing customer satisfaction in a continuous process, involving all internal employees
Hellsten and Klefsjo (2000)	TQM is defined as a continuously changing management system, involving values, methodologies and tools with the aim of increasing internal and external customer satisfaction
Milosan (2014)	Organizational strategy based on performance, privileging skills, training and involvement of the whole organization in process improvement on a permanent basis
Wang et al. (2012)	TQM is a broadly recognized management philosophy that focuses on process continuous improvement within organizations, aiming at delivering superior value to customers and meeting their needs, benefiting the organization in terms of increased profitability and productivity
Gharakhani et al. (2013)	TQM is a systematic approach to improving the quality of enterprise-wide management with the purpose of improving performance in terms of quality, productivity, customer satisfaction and profitability

As can be observed from these different points of view, TQM underpins the effectiveness and efficiency in the use of resources, and, in this sense, several authors such as Isaksson (2006) or Hellsten and Klefsjo (2000) approach a TQM framework highlighting the importance of providing higher value (increasing internal and external customer satisfaction) at lower costs (resource use efficiency), which is consistent with the objectives of economic sustainability.

The efficient use of resources debate converges to the issue of sustainability, and, in this context, the evolving quality framework is upgraded and aligns with this premise, according to Al Nofal and Zairi (2002) who argue that the shift from product/service orientation to customer/market orientation shows that different focus in different time periods marks the different emphasis in TQM and sustainability.

13.3 TQM and CSR as Sustainable Competitive Advantage Sources

13.3.1 TQM and CSR Through the Lens of RBV

Authors have ground their research on different theoretical approaches to study if and how TQM-based frameworks (e.g. ISO 9001, European Excellence Model) and CSR may lead to sustainable competitive advantages, such as the resource-based view of the firm.

As proposed by several researchers, such as Barney (1991) or Peteraf (1993), sustainable competitive advantages may be defined as organizations' abilities to develop and implement a value creating strategy in such a way that current and potential competitors are unable to duplicate such strategy. Grounded in Penrose's (1959) work *The Theory of the Growth of the Firm* and later extended by other researchers (e.g. Barney 1991; Wernerfelt 1984), the resource-based view of the firm (RBV) became one of the leading and most influential theories in the management theorizing history, with a prominent role in the study of sustained competitive advantages.

A core premise of the RBV of the firm is that, rather than simply monitoring its competitive environment to identify sources of competitive advantages, organizations should look inside and compete on the basis of their own internal resources and capabilities. The supporters of this perspective argue that sustainable competitive advantages depend primarily on the application of a bundle of valuable resources (both tangible and intangible) at companies' disposal (e.g. Wernerfelt 1984). According to Galbreath's (2005) typology, (1) tangible resources would include financial and physical assets, (2) intangible resources that are assets would include intellectual property and organizational and reputational assets, and (3) intangible resources that are skills include capabilities. Resources and capabilities are the primary constants upon which an organization can establish its identity and frame its strategy, and they are the primary sources of firms' competitive advantage (sustained over time), and, thus, firms' design of strategies should exploit each one of their unique characteristics (Grant 1991).

Barney (1991), in particular, and RBV promoters in general focused on attributes that resources should possess to generate and sustain a long-term competitive advantage, arguing that resources and capabilities must be valuable, rare, imperfectly imitable and non-substitutable. According to Peteraf's (1993) model, transforming a short-term competitive advantage into a sustained competitive advantage requires four conditions that must be met: superior resources (heterogeneity within an industry), ex post limits to competition, imperfect resource mobility and ex ante limits to competition. Grant (1991) points to four characteristics of resources and capabilities which are likely to be critical determinants for firms' sustainable competitive advantage: durability, transparency, transferability and replicability.

As already shown in previous sections, TQM and CSR have manifest several concerns in this arena. Benavides-Velasco et al. (2014) consider that TQM and CSR are potential sources for obtaining sustainable competitive advantages, but this perception had an evolutionary process regarding both approaches.

As TQM concerns, its association with reaching sustainable competitive advantages dates back to the 1990s (Molina-Azorín et al. 2015). Powell (1995) argues that TQM may represent a potential source of sustainable competitiveness, opinion corroborated by Woodruff (1997) who added that relying only in innovation and product quality strategies alone does not guarantee the existence of competitive advantages. Based on the idea that organizations face growing difficulties in sustaining competitive advantages only anchored in static resources, Su et al. (2014) propose a dynamic capability-based strategy explaining how to sustain a competitive advantage in quality, arguing that meta-learning helps sustain a high level of quality performance, while sensing weak signals and resilience to quality disruptions improves the consistency of quality performance.

Based on an analysis of the seminal TQM literature, Reed et al. (2000) provide arguments showing how strategic TQM issues may generate a cost- or differentiation-based advantage; using concepts from resource-based theory, the authors show how TQM-based processes have the potential to create sustainability of advantage, highlighting that the individual components of the strategy's process embody tacitness and are a complex system, thus producing the causal ambiguity that can protect a TQM-based advantage from imitation.

Indeed, there is a large body of empirical evidences supporting a positive relationship between adopting TQM-based strategies and generating sustainable competitive advantages (e.g. Curkovic and Pagell 1999; Samson and Terziovski 1999; Hendricks and Singhal 1997; Flynn et al. 1995). For example, analysing the relationship between TQM and performance in a sample of US firms, Powell (1995) found that certain tacit, behavioural, imperfectly imitable TQM-based resources (e.g. open culture, employee empowerment and top management commitment) can drive TQM success and produce advantage, concluding that these tacit resources, and not TQM tools, allow to outperforming competitors. Escrig-Tena et al. (2001) demonstrated that the introduction of TQM can generate a wealth of distinctive competencies which partly explain how a competitive advantage can be generated or boosted.

Yunis et al. (2013) found that TQM is an important dynamic resource that competitive strategies support, allocate and enhance in order to achieve sustainable competitive advantage. Moreover, the researchers found that soft TQM elements have a higher impact on reaching operational performance and explained that these soft elements include the major forces of change, innovativeness and continuous improvement, namely, the tacit knowledge, experience and problem-solving abilities.

Although the understanding on how CSR can be aligned with corporate strategy and how firms' environmental policy can meet the needs of its key communities can be grounded on framework as the agency theory, the stakeholder theory or the institutional theory, to the extent that companies engage in CSR strategically, such behaviour can be also analysed through the lens of the resource-based view of the firm (McWilliams et al. 2006). Hart (1995), in the first theoretical paper to apply the RBV framework to CSR, highlighted that, for some organizations, environmental social responsibility may represent a resource able to lead to a sustained competitive advantage. Since then, the number of studies focused on CSR, and adopting a resource-based view (frequently combined with other theoretical approaches), has grown in recent years, beginning with a focus on environmental aspects and subsequently extending to more general issues of CSR, as, for example, corporate social disclosure (Branco and Rodrigues 2006). The RBV support of CSR, as a practice, develops from the belief that it can lead to unique characteristics that offer a competitive advantage (Foote et al. 2010).

Russo and Fouts (1997), Sharma and Vredenburg (1998) and Bansal (2005) are examples of studies approaching CSR, grounded in the resource-based view of the firm, with a high impact in literature, recording thousands of citations. For example, Russo and Fouts (1997) conclude that companies reporting higher levels of environmental performance had also higher financial performance, and McWilliams et al. (2002) stressed that, when supported by political strategies, CSR strategies may be conducted to develop sustainable competitive advantages.

Based on the initial idea that CSR has garnered much attention over the past decades, with most questions focusing on whether a company socially responsible is more likely to be financially successful, Foote et al. (2010) conclude that, although without measurable empirical evidences, there is support in literature that engaging in CSR-based approaches has a significant influence on performance. Investigating the impact of CSR activities on corporate performance, Kang and Liu (2014) argue that undertaking CSR leads to greater financial returns compared to related cost, concluding that engaging in CSR is beneficial for firms and thus worth implementing.

Drake and Rhodes (2015) consider that sustainability challenges have a relevant impact on stakeholders. Regarding CSR, these authors point out that organizations have not yet understood its true potential, because this approach is used in the perspective of cost minimization or risk prevention, while companies should go further, namely incorporating the organizational strategy and acting in the perspective of adding value to improve the competitive position. The ISO 26000:2010 international standards present this strategic framework concerning the importance of responsibility in the context of organizations' performance, namely, respecting to competitive advantages.

13.3.2 Total Quality Management and Its Impact on Stakeholders

Various studies demonstrate that TQM-based quality management systems have positive influences on several stakeholders, such as employees (Para-González et al. 2016; Dubey et al. 2015), customers (Wang et al. 2012; Tarí et al. 2010) or shareholders (Chaudary et al. 2015), among others.

Moreover, managers exhibiting a personal commitment to quality, acting as a role model and ensuring merit-based reward system have a key influence, through direct effects on several important outcomes, including employees' attitudes (Oakland 2011), increased job satisfaction and employee commitment (Clark et al. 2009). Several studies have shown that diverse HRM practices such as training, incentive systems have a positive moderating effect on the relationship between TQM-based quality management systems and customer satisfaction (e.g. Chandler and McEvoy 2000). For example, organizations engaged in TQM-based improvement programmes are more responsive to changes in internal and external customers' needs, positively influencing performance (Wang et al. 2012). TQM-based strategies and policies' effective deployment, as well as operations' systematic and continuous revision and improvement, allow firms to reach sustainable results (Oakland 2011). Organizations continuously pursuing process improvements allow mutual and long-term loyalty between organizations and their stakeholders (Oppenheim and Przasnyski 1999) and can benefit with higher operational reliability and innovation, better productivity levels and significant waste reduction (Prajogo and Sohal 2006).

Indeed, supporting quality management literature is filled with empirical evidences (surveys and case studies) on the TQM approach, as well as its influence on organizational performance. Although some studies found no evidence of a positive relation between TQM and financial performance (e.g. Kober et al. 2012), several research projects brought empirical evidences supporting a positive relationship between both variables, such as Shrivastava et al. (2006) or Rahman (2001) concerning profitability; Akgün et al. (2014) concerning ROI, gross margin and earnings; Hendricks and Singhal (2001) concerning operating income and sales; and Agus et al. (2000), concerning revenue growth, among many others.

Several studies also show empirical evidences regarding the positive influence of TQM-based quality management systems on operational performance, such as product and process innovation (Honarpour et al. 2017; Aminbeidokhti et al. 2016; Perdomo-Ortiz et al. 2009); productivity (Iyer et al. 2013); efficiency (Salhieh and Abu-Doleh 2015; Hasan and Kerr 2003); lead time (Sadikoglu and Zehir 2010; Boyer 1991); flexibility (Escrig-Tena et al. 2012); service quality (Talib et al. 2011); delivery performance (Samson and Terziovski 1999); cost-effectiveness (Modgil and Sharma 2016; Lee and Whang 2005); product quality issues, such as scrap level, rework level and waste reduction (Fuentes et al. 2006; Shrivastava et al. 2006); customer satisfaction (Fuentes et al. 2006; Hasan and Kerr 2003); market benefits (Psomas and Fotopoulos 2010); and corporate image among society (Yang 2006), among other operational benefits.

Moreover, rooted in the idea that satisfied internal customers contribute to satisfying needs and expectations of external customer, supporting quality management literature shows that, as internal customers, employees are as important as external customers (Youssef et al. 2014). As a result, TQM is frequently associated with quality of work life (QWL) issues. A QWL cultural underpinning anchors a successful TQM strategy and aims at creating a fear-free organization in which employee involvement is vigorously pursued, generating a high degree of reciprocal commitment (employee to the goals and development of the organization and the organization to the needs and development of the employee) (James 1992). Employees' identification process with the company begins with the projection of a strong clear corporate image through its outward presentation of premises and products and is fostered by the use of slogans and a clear mission statement reinforced with consistent management behaviours (Webley and Cartwright 1996).

Concerning QWL, several papers report empirical evidences regarding the positive influence of TQM-based quality management systems on many issues such as work satisfaction (Mendes 2010; Hasan and Kerr 2003; Hoonakker et al. 2000), employee morale (Sadikoglu and Zehir 2010; Samson and Terziovski 1999), job enrichment (Youssef et al. 2014), opportunity for growth and relationships with co-workers (Carayon et al. 1999), responsibility for the safety and health of employees and local community (Youssef et al. 2014; Podgórski 2000), organizational commitment (Mendes and Jesus 2017; Carlos et al. 2014; Karia and Asaari 2006; Allen and Brady 1997), organizational citizenship behaviour (Carlos et al. 2014), job involvement and career satisfaction (Karia and Asaari 2006), empowerment (Andrade et al. 2017; Sweis et al. 2013), perceived organizational support (Allen and Brady 1997), corporate image among employees (Webley and Cartwright 1996) and physical working conditions, mental state, career orientation, effect on personal life, self-respect and sense of achievement (Joseph et al. 1999), among other QWL issues.

13.3.3 Corporate Social Responsibility and Its Impact on Stakeholders

Although CSR's critics argue that CSR distracts from the fundamental economic role of businesses, which is to make money, and that CSR is nothing more than a feel-good programme, which attempts to serve as a watchdog over large and powerful corporations, proponents of CSR argue that corporations benefit in many ways by operating with a longer-term view of their organization and role in society than they do by focusing on just their own short-term profits (Foote et al. 2010).

The evolution of the CSR concept originated several categorization proposals of CSR's models based on diverse dimensions. For example, Carroll (1979) proposed the CSR pyramid, a three-dimensional social performance conceptual model including four dimensions: discretionary (e.g. philanthropic issues, community support), economic (e.g. efficiency, profitability), legal (e.g. compliance with applicable laws) and ethical responsibilities (e.g. "beyond compliance" measures).

Based on the previous works of Carroll (1991) and Swaen and Chumpitaz (2008), Palihawadana et al. (2016) found that perceived CSR is explained through four dimensions: legal, ethical, economic and philosophy responsibility. According to these authors, philosophy responsibility deals with companies' voluntarily participation in charitable projects, active sponsorship in social events, donations to charities and concerns with the enhancement of a society's quality of life.

Dahlsrud (2008) proposed a five-dimension model:

1. The environmental dimension, concerning the natural environment (e.g. cleaner environment, environment stewardship)
2. The social dimension, referring to the relationship between business and society (e.g. contributing to a better society)
3. The economic dimension, regarding socio-economic or financial aspects, including describing CSR as a business operation
4. The stakeholder dimension, involving interactions with stakeholders (e.g. employees, suppliers, customers, communities)
5. The voluntariness dimension, referring to actions not prescribed by law (based on ethical values, beyond legal obligations)

Also referred to as the three CSR's pillars (people, planet and profit), the triple bottom line (TBL) approach is certainly one of the most accepted CSR models and widely employed both in the literature and in practice known, placing emphasis on (1) responsibility for society (people), (2) responsibility for environment (planet) and (3) responsibility for financial success (profit). Coined by Elkington (1997) and characterized according to its contribution to economic prosperity, environmental quality and social capital (González-Rodríguez et al. 2015), the TBL systematic approach has become increasingly fashionable in management, consulting, investing and NGO circles over the last few years, based on the idea that firms cannot be successful in the long run if they consistently disregard the interests of key stakeholders and that the overall fulfilment of obligations to communities, employees, customers and suppliers, among other parties, should be measured, audited and reported just as the financial performance has been for more than a century (Norman and MacDonald 2004).

As stressed by Geva (2008), the concentric circle model, based on the work of the Committee for Economic Development in 1971, holds that CSR firms have direct responsibility to promote the quality of life, even at the expense of profitability; this responsibility could be extended to sustainable development, environmental health and the social determinants of health (Dimmler 2017).

In accordance with whatever the model considered, building sustainable relationships with stakeholders corresponds to a starting point for running a business ethically, paying attention to both social and ecological environment (Du et al. 2015). As highlighted by Deng et al. (2013), CSR does not involve only economic or legal responsibilities but also firms' involvement in initiatives directed at social wealth protection and thus firms' improvement in the quality of life of clients, employees and shareholders.

Indeed, there are several different reasons associated with organizations' active CSR agenda, and as highlighted by Sprinkle and Maines (2010), most of the benefits of CSR naturally mirror the reasons for engaging in CSR. As reported by several researchers, such as Lenssen et al. (2010), Graafland and Van De Ven (2006) or Solomon and Lewis (2002), several important reasons motivate companies to pursue CSR-based strategies, such as willingness to improve the organizational image or reputation of the organization, the need to comply with regulations, a way of political lobbying and pressure from clients/consumers.

According to Sprinkle and Maines (2010), there are several different reasons underlying organizations' motivations for engaging in socially responsible endeavours:

- Altruistic intentions, simply believing that their CSR efforts are part of being a good global citizen.
- A *window dressing* way to appease various stakeholder groups (e.g. nongovernmental organizations) in order to avoid negative publicity, and, in such a perspective, CSR may simply be viewed as another cost of doing business.
- Potential contracting benefits, believing that CSR helps recruit, motivate and retain employees (frequently reported as one of the most significant benefits of CSR programmes).
- Customer-related motivations, believing that CSR may entice consumers to buy companies' products/services, allowing them to reap price premiums or garner increases in market share.
- Focus on environmental concerns, leading to reductions in production costs.
- Integral part of risk management efforts, believing that CSR may be an effective lever for easing legal or regulatory constraints, regarding, for example, avoiding (or reducing) emissions' reduction and other adverse incidents and reducing the chances of lawsuits and damages to reputation.
- Supplier-related motivations.
- Believing that, just as customers may be more likely to purchase goods and services from socially responsible firms, suppliers may be keen on working with such organizations and thus allowing positive spill over effects for suppliers.
- Potential to attract capital from investors and receive better terms from creditors, believing that many individuals likely wish to align their investments with their moral aims.

Shnayder et al. (2016) systematize the several potential motivations into two main dimensions:

- Financial or profit-based (at least in part) motivations, such as competitiveness in labour market, consumer demands and safety, creating shared value, efficiency, ensuring future success, entering new markets, growth, image, increasing yield, internal assessment/self-regulation, profit, regulatory compliance, supply chain synergy and sustainability, among others
- Intrinsic or value-based motivations, such as child welfare, climate change mitigation, full landfills, human rights, improving biodiversity, improving consumer

nutrition, improving health, increasing exercise among children, influencing consumer behaviour, maintaining soil fertility, protecting environment and resources, reducing emissions, species extinction, supporting fairness/equality and supporting small-scale business

Although there are no doubts about the clear influence of CSR-based strategies on the society in general and especially in what the quality of life concerns, the relationship with organizations' performance and quality of working life is not so obvious, and many studies have been performed along the last couple of decades in order to better understand CSR's benefits for organizations.

Indeed, management and economics literature is filled with many empirical evidences (surveys and case studies) regarding the influence of CSR-based approaches on organizational performance. Although some researchers found no evidence of a positive relation between CSR and financial performance (e.g. Madorran and Garcia 2016), several studies reported empirical evidences supporting a positive relationship between CSR and several variables, such as ROA (Wei and Lin 2015), net profit margin (Kamatra and Kartikaningdyah 2015), return on invested capital and sales growth rate (Oh and Park 2015) and investor loyalty (Arikan et al. 2016), among others. As highlighted by Nollet et al. (2016), this is particularly true in the longer run.

Moreover, several empirical results also suggest a positive and significant influence of CSR-based approaches on operational performance issues such as productivity (Hasan et al. 2016; Wei and Lin 2015), customer satisfaction (Saeidi et al. 2015; Luo and Bhattacharya 2006), customer loyalty (Aramburu and Pescador 2017; Pérez and del Bosque 2015) or customer perceived value and intention to spread word of mouth (Arikan et al. 2016), among others.

Finally, as observed with TQM, CSR-based initiatives also appear to influence positively the quality of working life. Indeed, empirical evidences suggest a close relationship between CSR and organizational commitment (Asrar-ul-Haq et al. 2017; Panagopoulos et al. 2016), especially in what the affective concerns (Kim et al. 2017; Mory et al. 2016), organizational citizenship behaviour (Islam et al. 2016; Rupp et al. 2013), job satisfaction (Barakat et al. 2016; Du et al. 2015), job performance (Kim et al. 2017) and corporate image/reputation among employees (López-Fernández and Rajagopal 2016; Komodromos and Melanthiou 2014), among other issues.

13.4 Dual Strategic Approaches Based on TQM and CSR

TQM and CSR's theoretical framework shows that both approaches have been attracting the attention of several authors and suggest great similarities between them. Within this context, there is a need to understand whether these two approaches are complementary or overlapping, because both focus on internal and external stakeholders, are based on adding value to organizations and focus on efficiency and effectiveness, and their success depends strongly on their internalization in organizational culture, as explained by Benavides-Velasco et al. (2014) about CSR and Garvin (1987) about TQM.

13.4.1 Similarities Between TQM and CSR

Although organizations' image and reputation and the level of satisfaction of society regarding their actions are more related to the implementation of CSR actions (Benavides-Velasco et al. 2014), the truth is that both TQM and CSR approaches are shown in literature to have several similarities, and according to McAdam and Leonard (2003), CSR has a strong affinity with the principles of quality management.

For example, as explained by Kok et al. (2001), TQM has a foundational similarity to CSR in that it has an ethical anchor while at the same time contributing to organizational goals and measures (McAdam and Leonard 2003). TQM principles appear to be consistent with both the legitimate ethical and instrumental sides of CSR (McAdam and Leonard 2003). Vinten (1998) highlights the role that ethical considerations play in various quality award schemes, stressing that there is scant evidence in the awards that ethical issues have achieved high materiality and that organizations that constantly have a negative ethical impact may find the withdrawal of public approval and of the market for its product or services. Indeed, as highlighted by McAdam and Leonard (2003), the founders of modern quality management and business excellence (e.g. Crosby, Deming, Juran) considered ethics, principles and respect for people as key principles, such as other more recent researchers (e.g. Fisscher and Nijhof 2005; Gentili et al. 2003).

Moreover, both management approaches focus on identified needs of various stakeholders (employees, customers and society) and share common values such as proactive action, the importance of win-win relationships with partners as well as adopting an ethical perspective that exceeds the expectations of society and laws (Benavides-Velasco et al. 2014). In fact, throughout last decades, both CSR and TQM progressed towards common purposes, including ensuring customers' confidence, enhancing organizational credibility and demonstrating the focus on long-term sustainability's advantages over short-term profitability (ASQ 2009).

According to the BSR's recent report in partnership with the American Society of Quality, exploring the connection between CSR and quality and opportunities for increased collaboration, (1) both CSR and TQM are based on a set of values and beliefs, such as "do no harm", "zero waste", "make external costs visible" and "driving out fear" between management and employees, (2) both have a very strong focus on people (not just customer satisfaction but also quality of working life and employee satisfaction), and (3) both share common lines of thinking regarding several concerns, such as making hidden costs visible, corporate governance, empowerment, proactive behaviour and internal alignment (ASQ/BSR 2011).

As referred by Zink (2007), there are many similarities between TQM and CSR, and based on a stakeholder approach, corporate sustainability justifies a redefinition of TQM goals, taking into account that the (long-term) survivability of an organization is related to the survivability of society, and therefore CSR has to play a stronger role within business. Indeed, as highlighted by Zink (2005), the "implementation of a TQM system" corresponds to one of the economic and financial criteria assessed by the Sustainability Index of the SAM Sustainability Group (which is delivering data for the Dow Jones Sustainability Group Index), based on a Corporate Sustainability Questionnaire, which has a stakeholder orientation and includes specific CSR concepts.

As already seen previously, literature provides many evidences regarding the benefits provided by TQM and CSR individually, and both share common similarities. In fact, TQM and CSR are generally considered potential sources to obtain sustainable competitive advantages. The question here is whether stakeholders may benefit from a dual strategy based on both TQM and CSR approaches. The March 2008 Quality Progress Quick Poll indicated that 82.8% of respondents agreed that social responsibility and environmental sustainability should be considered a part of quality management (ASQ 2009). In TQM systems, attention is generally paid to social responsibility as far as the impact on society is recognized and implemented within the company (Fisscher and Nijhof 2005).

13.4.2 Towards a Relationship of Complementarity Between TQM and CSR

TQM and CSR practices are in many ways complementary (e.g. Benavides-Velasco et al. 2014). Several works suggest that TQM-based quality management systems can be a platform and catalyst for effectively developing CSR within organizations (e.g. Poureh 2015; Zink 2007), and, thus, CSR can be advanced more rapidly in organizations if it can be incorporated in already established TQM models, methodologies and change programmes (McAdam and Leonard 2003).

Indeed, social responsibility is somehow already reflected in the several different models of excellence such as the European Foundation for Quality Management (EFQM) Model of Excellence or the Malcolm Baldrige National Quality Award (MBNQA) Model (Nováková et al. 2014; Foote et al. 2010). As stated by Fisscher and Nijhof (2005), in general, TQM-based models (e.g. EFQM and Malcolm Baldrige National Quality Award Models), a focus on stakeholder value is embedded (customers, employees and society as a whole). Indeed, excellence models are considered valuable instruments to transfer the concept of corporate sustainability into practice (e.g. Zink 2007).

In the initial 1988 Baldrige Criteria for Performance Excellence, public responsibility was focused narrowly on mechanisms used for external communication of information concerning corporate support of quality assurance or improvement activities outside the company, but over the next years, this item was expanded to include how firms extend quality leadership to the external community and integrate responsibilities to the public for health, safety, environmental protection and ethical business practice into quality policies and activities (including how firms promote quality awareness and sharing with external groups, how firms encourage employee leadership and involvement in quality activities of external organizations, among other questions) (Foote et al. 2010).

The EFQM Excellence Model grounds on several fundamental concepts defining the underlying principles that form the foundation for achieving sustainable excellence in any organization. Two of these principles are clearly in line with the CSR approach:

- According to the *Creating a Sustainable Future* principle, "excellent organisations have a positive impact on the world around them by enhancing their performance whilst simultaneously advancing the economic, environmental and social conditions within the communities they touch" (EFQM 2012).
- According to the *Sustaining Outstanding Results* principle, "excellent organisations achieve sustained outstanding results that meet both the short and long term needs of all their stakeholders, within the context of their operating environment" (EFQM 2012).

Moreover, regarding the criteria providing the framework to help organizations to convert the fundamental concepts into practice, three of these are also clearly in line with the CSR approach:

- According to the *Leadership* criterion, "excellent organisations have leaders who shape the future and make it happen, acting as role models for its values and ethics and inspiring trust at all times" (EFQM 2012).
- According to the *People* criterion, "excellent organisations value their people and create a culture that allows the mutually beneficial achievement of organisational and personal goals. They develop the capabilities of their people and promote fairness and equality. They care for, communicate, reward and recognise, in a way that motivates people, builds commitment and enables them to use their skills and knowledge for the benefit of the organisation" (EFQM 2012).
- According to the *Society Results* criterion, "excellent organisations achieve and sustain outstanding results that meet or exceed the needs and expectations of relevant stakeholders within society" (EFQM 2012).

Similarly, some of the Baldrige Criteria for Performance Excellence are also clearly in line with the CSR approach:

- The *Leadership* criterion deals with how senior leaders' personal actions guide and sustain the organization and how the organization fulfils its legal, ethical and societal responsibilities (NIST 2015).
- The *Workforce* criterion deals with how the organization ensures workplace health, security and accessibility for the workforce, among several other issues (NIST 2015).
- The *Leadership and Governance Results* deals with several different outcomes, including results concerning meeting and surpassing regulatory and legal require-

ments, ethical behaviour, stakeholders' trust in senior leaders and governance and fulfilment of societal responsibilities and support of key communities, among others (NIST 2015).

As highlighted by Zutshi and Sohal (2005), the integration of different management approaches (e.g. quality management system, environmental system, occupational health and safety system) can result in significant tangible and intangible benefits including cost savings and more efficient use of valuable organizational resources, greater acceptance by employees and higher staff motivation, better scope for input by stakeholders and enhanced confidence of customers and positive market/community image, among others, although the authors recommend obtaining top management's full commitment, ensuring adequate resources to integrate the approaches and promoting communication and training across the organization, in order to minimize resistance for changes.

Applying quality principles, such as continuous improvement, empowerment and errors/waste reduction, contributes to the overall CSR profile of organizations that can differentiate their brands/reputation and attract top talent, when taking responsibility for protecting the future of societies and environments in which they operate (ASQ 2009).

As reported by Benavides-Velasco et al. (2014), the implementation of both TQM and CSR can *allow efficiency improvements*, a reduction of bureaucracy by eliminating duplication of policies and procedures and the alignment of goals and processes.

In fact, several CSR issues and applications can benefit from quality frameworks, including a range of tactical-level tools and approaches that can help CSR leaders to develop stronger, business-aligned cases for action and robust programmes for improvement on a variety of CSR issues: waste reduction, worker empowerment, governance, health and safety and supplier engagement, accountability and transparency. For example, waste minimization and pollution prevention, which, for CSR, address key issues regarding resource use, energy and significant environmental trends that affect a wide range of stakeholders, including consumers and communities, are at the centre of TQM-based quality improvement programmes through efficient manufacturing layouts and inventory controls aiming at reducing waste from overproduction, waiting time, transportation, inventory, overprocessing, reduced factory footprints, excessive motion, defects and raw materials (ASQ/BSR 2011).

13.4.3 Empirical Research on Strategic Approaches Based on Both TQM and CSR

As already observed in previous sections, a significant body of literature has been focusing on both TQM and CSR phenomena individually, either theoretically or empirically. However, as a combined strategy, the truth is that these issues are barely explored.

But, although only few empirical studies have been conducted around the world, approaching potential benefits gained through combined CSR-TQM approaches, grounded in both services (e.g. hospitality, finance) and manufacturing contexts (e.g. IT, energy, automotive), findings seem to support the idea discussed in several theoretical papers according to which organizations could benefit from such strategy. Findings highlight a growing awareness and commitment from organizations worldwide regarding both CSR and quality improvement issues, leading progressively to the development of systems based on the integration of CSR and TQM principles.

Overall the few results provide support to the idea that combined CSR-TQM approaches enable organizations to gain competitive advantages. As observed on the summary provided in Table 13.2, CSR appears as a valuable resource leading to sustainable competitive advantage by promoting and supporting the development of TQM, even if CSR could have a direct effect on improving internal quality results (operational) but an indirect effect on external quality results. Moreover, TQM could mediate the relationship between CSR and performance.

Table 13.2 Empirical studies focused on both TQM and CSR approaches

Study	Data collect	Context	Country	Data anal	Contributions
Benavides-Velasco et al. (2014)	a	Hotel	Spain	c	A dual strategy benefits stakeholders, with a positive effect on performance:
					TQM has a positive influence on employees and customers
					CSR benefit results concerning employees, customers and society
McAdam and Leonard (2003)	b	Energy	United Kingdom	d, e	Combined CSR-TQM approaches enable organizations to avoid applying successive unrelated change initiatives, demonstrating progress on the "quality journey"
Chiarini (2016)	b	Industry	Worldwide	d, e	Full suitability of Hoshin Kanri as an alternative system to balanced scorecard (BSC) for deploying CSR
Poureh (2015)	b	Industry	Worldwide	e	Most companies try to be certified by ISO-based quality systems and realize that CSR aspects of their business performance are key issues

(continued)

Table 13.2 (continued)

Study	Data collect	Context	Country	Data anal	Contributions
Mehralian et al. (2016)	a	Pharmacy	Iran	c	CSR as a valuable resource leading to sustainable competitive advantage by promoting and supporting TQM
					CSR promotes firms' image and reputation, which will attract more qualified and loyal stakeholders
					TQM mediates the relationship between CSR and performance
Parast and Adams (2012)	a	Energy	Worldwide	c	Top management support for quality is the main driver of CSR practices
					CSR has a direct effect on improving internal quality results (operational) but an indirect effect on external quality results
Kok et al. (2001)	b	Energy	Netherland	d, e	Excellence models do not give much direction for developing a more structured policy on social responsibility
Álvarez García et al. (2014)	a	Tourism	Spain	c	Data show the importance of top management leadership in achieving social impact results
					Process management is directly influenced by employee management, quality planning and learning and acts directly on social impact results
Tarí Guilló and García Fernández (2011)	b	Services	Spain	d, e	Greater awareness and commitment regarding CSR's dimensions in companies with higher level of quality management

Data collection: (a) survey by questionnaire; (b) case study
Data analysis: (c) structural equation modelling; (d) document review; (e) interviews

13.5 Concluding Remarks

Organizations are increasingly concerned about how their actions affect the environment and social welfare, and employees, consumers, investors, lenders, governmental agencies and other stakeholder groups are demanding that firms operate in a socially responsible manner.

Through a comprehensive literature review, this chapter systematizes knowledge on how the implementation of strategies based on TQM and CSR principles may create stakeholders' value and contribute to organizations' sustainable performance, while improving the quality of life of the workforce and citizens in local communities, in particular, and even of society in general.

Overall, this literature review shows that there are many evidences in the academic literature that sustainability-based approaches should be thought proactively and strategically. Several authors have been advocating the idea of complementarity between TQM and CSR approaches, especially regarding issues concerning sustainability and trust. Briefly, our literature review allows us to highlight several fields where similarities between both approaches seem evident: (1) process orientation, (2) stakeholder focus, (3) commitment, (4) efficacy of resources management, (5) contribution to competitiveness, (6) organizational reputation, (7) long-term planning and (8) continuous improvement assessment culture.

Although a significant body of literature has been focusing on both TQM and CSR phenomena individually, as a combined strategy, this review highlights that these issues are barely explored. Even without enough direct and measurable empirical evidences, literature supports the idea that engaging in a joint strategy combining TQM and CSR principles may increase stakeholders' value and lead to a significant influence on performance; the few empirical findings available seem to support the idea that combined CSR-TQM approaches are potential sources for obtaining sustainable competitive advantage, suggesting a growing awareness and commitment from organizations worldwide regarding both CSR and quality improvement issues, leading progressively to the development of systems based on the integration of CSR and TQM principles.

While the volume of research has increased significantly over the last decades and approached most of the issues in business theory, currently, as academic fields, TQM and CSR remain wide-ranging, and multi-faceted research fields and the nature of the relationships between TQM, CSR and advantages remain quite unexplored. For example, at the stakeholder level, many studies analysed the direct influence of each approach, but literature suggests that together TQM and CSR can have different effects on each stakeholder. Moreover, there is a need for broader and deeper studies to see if organizations can manage a balanced approach in relation to other contexts, such as adverse markets, and less developed TQM systems. These are issues that certainly deserve further empirical research, approaching several different organizational, environmental and competitive contexts and pondering the use of alternative research methods, especially in what longitudinal approaches concerns.

Moreover, there are no consistent findings concerning the contribution of adopting TQM or CSR principles to EIS (entrepreneurship, innovation and sustainability) ecosystems. Indeed, if as already observed, both TQM and CSR are generally associated to organizations' sustainability, concerning innovation and entrepreneurial orientation; the potential relation has not reached a similar academic consensus. In fact, while sustainability is a core issue in both TQM and CSR approaches, the nature of the relationship between TQM/CSR and innovation remains quite inconclusive. While some evidences point to the inexistence of relationship, some studies conclude that TQM and CSR based working environments sustain innovation, and according to other researchers, innovation can inclusive be prevented. Similarly, regarding the relationship between TQM or CSR and entrepreneurial orientation, some previous studies were found to be inconclusive, and in general they did not show agreement concerning findings. Indeed, some studies highlight a lack of relationship between variables, whereas others conclude that TQM- and CSR-based working environments promote entrepreneurial orientation, either directly or as a mediation effect.

As a result, although literature on TQM and CSR points to several long-term benefits, additional research is clearly needed to expand the influence spectrum of TQM and CSR over EIS ecosystems, in particular. For example, further research may focus on explaining how TQM and CSR can act as a supportive contextual value which interacts with other organizational phenomena (e.g. organizational ambidexterity) in promoting innovation and entrepreneurial orientation and thus contributing to effective EIS ecosystems. Because each EIS ecosystem is unique, comparisons between different EIS ecosystems exposed to different levels of TQM and CSR principles' dissemination would certainly contribute to shed light on such issue. Moreover, most of the few studies available are cross-sectional in nature. Considering that organizational behaviour is dynamic by nature, literature fails clearly in explaining the dynamic effect of TQM and CSR principles' dissemination on EIS ecosystem; longitudinal research studies would contribute with further explanations concerning long-term effects.

Acknowledgement The authors are pleased to acknowledge financial support from Fundação para a Ciência e a Tecnologia (grant UID/ECO/04007/2013) and FEDER/COMPETE (POCI-01-0145-FEDER-007659).

References

Agus, A., Krishnan, S. K., & Kadir, S. L. S. A. (2000). The structural impact of total quality management on financial performance relative to competitors through customer satisfaction: A study of Malaysian manufacturing companies. *Total Quality Management, 11*(4–6), S808–S819.

Akgün, A. E., Ince, H., Imamoglu, S. Z., Keskin, H., & Kocoglu, I. (2014). The mediator role of learning capability and business innovativeness between total quality management and financial performance. *International Journal of Production Research, 52*(3), 888–901.

Al Nofal, A., & Zairi, M. (2002). Best practices and sustainable TQM implementation. In *Proceedings of the 7th World Congress for Total Quality Management* (Business Excellence, Make it happen!), Verona, Italy, 25–27 June 2002.

Allen, M. W., & Brady, R. M. (1997). Total quality management, organizational commitment, perceived organizational support, and intraorganizational communication. *Management Communication Quarterly, 10*(3), 316–341.

Álvarez García, J., Del Río Rama, M. C., Vila Alonso, M., & Fraiz Brea, J. A. (2014). Dependence relationship between the critical quality factors and social impact. *RAE-Revista de Administração de Empresas, 54*(6), 692–705.

Aminbeidokhti, A., Jamshidi, L., & Mohammadi Hoseini, A. (2016). The effect of the total quality management on organizational innovation in higher education mediated by organizational learning. *Studies in Higher Education, 41*(7), 1153–1166.

Andrade, J., Mendes, L., & Lourenço, L. (2017). Perceived psychological empowerment and TQM-based quality management systems: An exploratory research. *Total Quality Management and Business Excellence, 28*(1–2), 76–87.

Aramburu, I.A., & Pescador, I.G. (2017). The effects of corporate social responsibility on customer loyalty: The mediating effect of reputation in cooperative banks versus commercial banks in the Basque country. *Journal of Business Ethics*. In press. Available online 17 Jan 2017.

Arikan, E., Kantur, D., Maden, C., & Telci, E. E. (2016). Investigating the mediating role of corporate reputation on the relationship between corporate social responsibility and multiple stakeholder outcomes. *Quality and Quantity, 50*(1), 129–149.

ASQ. (2009). Seeking sustainable success: ASQ integrates quality and social responsibility. Available via ASQ. http://asq.org/2009/05/iso-26000/seeking-sustainable-success-asq-integrates-quality-and-social-responsibility.pdf. Accessed 4 Jan 2017.

ASQ/BSR. (2011). *CSR and quality: A powerful and untapped connection*. White paper available via https://www.bsr.org/reports/BSR_ASQ_CSR_and_Quality.final.pdf. Accessed 21 Jan 2017.

Asrar-ul-Haq, M., Kuchinke, K. P., & Iqbal, A. (2017). The relationship between corporate social responsibility, job satisfaction, and organizational commitment: Case of Pakistani higher education. *Journal of Cleaner Production, 142*(4), 2352–2363.

Bansal, P. (2005). Evolving sustainably: A longitudinal study of corporate sustainable development. *Strategic Management Journal, 26*(3), 197–218.

Barakat, S. R., Isabella, G., Boaventura, J. M. G., & Mazzon, J. A. (2016). The influence of corporate social responsibility on employee satisfaction. *Management Decision, 54*(9), 2325–2339.

Barney, J. (1991). Firm resources and sustained competitive advantage. *Journal of Management, 17*(1), 99–120.

Benavides-Velasco, C. A., Quintana-García, C., & Marchante-Lara, M. (2014). Total quality management, corporate social responsibility and performance in the hotel industry. *International Journal of Hospitality Management, 41*, 77–87.

Bou, J. C., & Beltran, I. (2005). Total quality management, high-commitment human resource strategy and firm performance: An empirical study. *Total Quality Management and Business Excellence, 16*(1), 71–86.

Bowen, H. R., Gond, J., & Bowen, P. G. (2013). *Social responsibilities of the businessman*. Iowa City: University of Iowa Press.

Boyer, S. M. (1991). Total quality management and new product development. *Total Quality Management, 2*(3), 283–290.

Branco, M., & Rodrigues, L. (2006). Corporate social responsibility and resource-based perspectives. *Journal of Business Ethics, 69*(2), 111–132.

Carayon, P., Sainfort, F., & Smith, M. J. (1999). Macroergonomics and total quality management: How to improve quality of working life? *International Journal of Occupational Safety and Ergonomics, 5*(2), 303–334.

Carlos, V., Mendes, L., & Lourenço, L. (2014). The influence of TQM on organizational commitment, organizational citizenship behaviours, and individual performance. *Transylvanian Review of Administrative Sciences*, Special Issue, 111–130.

Carroll, A. B. (1979). A three-dimensional conceptual model of corporate performance. *Academy of Management Review, 4*(4), 497–505.

Carroll, A. B. (1991). The pyramid of corporate social responsibility: Toward the moral management of organizational stakeholders. *Business Horizons, 34*(4), 39–48.

Carroll, A. B., & Shabana, K. M. (2010). The business case for corporate social responsibility: A review of concepts, research and practice. *International Journal of Management Reviews, 12*(1), 85–105.

Chandler, G. N., & McEvoy, G. M. (2000). Human resource management, TQM, and firm performance in small and medium-size enterprises. *Entrepreneurship: Theory and Practice, 25*(1), 43–57.

Chaudary, S., Zafar, S., & Salman, M. (2015). Does total quality management still shine? Re-examining the total quality management effect on financial performance. *Total Quality Management and Business Excellence, 26*(7–8), 811–824.

Chiarini, A. (2016). Corporate social responsibility strategies using the TQM: Hoshin kanri as an alternative system to the balanced scorecard. *TQM Journal, 28*(3), 360–376.

Clark, R. A., Hartline, M. D., & Jones, K. C. (2009). The effects of leadership style on hotel employees' commitment to service quality. *Cornell Hospitality Quarterly, 50*(2), 209–231.

Curkovic, S., & Pagell, M. (1999). A critical evaluation of the ability of ISO 9000 to lead to a competitive advantage. *Journal of Quality Management, 4*, 51–67.

Dahlgaard, S. M. P. (1999). The evolution patterns of quality management: Some reflections on the quality movement. *Total Quality Management, 10*(4–5), S473–S480.

Dahlsrud, A. (2008). How corporate social responsibility is defined: An analysis of 37 definitions. *Corporate Social Responsibility and Environmental Management, 15*(1), 1–13.

Dale, B. G. (1994). *Managing quality*. London: Prentice Hall.

Deng, X., Kang, J., & Low, B. S. (2013). Corporate social responsibility and stakeholder value maximization: Evidence from mergers. *Journal of Financial Economics, 110*, 87–109.

Dimmler, L. (2017). Linking social determinants of health to corporate social responsibility: Extant criteria for the mining industry. *The Extractive Industries and Society, 4*, 216. In press, Available online 19 Jan 2017.

Drake, M., & Rhodes, D. (2015). Socially responsible supply chain management for a competitive advantage. In L. O'Riordan, P. Zmuda, & S. Heinemann (Eds.), *New perspectives on corporate social responsibility – locating the missing link* (pp. 321–340). Essen: FOM-Edition.

Du, S., Bhattacharya, C. B., & Sen, S. (2015). Corporate social responsibility, multi-faceted job-products, and employee outcomes. *Journal of Business Ethics, 131*(2), 319–335.

Dubey, R., Singh, T., & Ali, S. S. (2015). The mediating effect of human resource on successful total quality management implementation: An empirical study on SMEs in manufacturing sectors. *Benchmarking, 22*(7), 1463–1480.

EFQM. (2012). *An overview of the EFQM excellence model*. Brussels: European Foundation for Quality Management.

Elkington, J. (1997). *Cannibals with forks: The triple bottom line of 21st century business*. Oxford: Capstone Publishing Ltd..

Escrig-Tena, A. B., Bou-Llusar, J. C., & Roca-Puig, V. (2001). Measuring the relationship between total quality management and sustainable competitive advantage: A resource-based view. *Total Quality Management, 12*(7–8), 932–938.

Escrig-Tena, A. B., Bou-llusar, J. C., Roca-Puig, V., & Beltran-Martin, I. (2012). Does quality management drive labor flexibility. *Total Quality Management and Business Excellence, 23*(2), 159–176.

Fisscher, O., & Nijhof, A. (2005). Implications of business ethics for quality management. *The TQM Magazine, 17*, 150–160.

Flynn, B. B., Schroeder, R. G., & Sakakibara, S. (1995). The impact of quality management practices on performance and competitive advantage. *Decision Sciences, 26*, 659–691.

Foote, J., Gaffney, N., & Evans, J. R. (2010). Corporate social responsibility: Implications for performance excellence. *Total Quality Management and Business Excellence, 21*(8), 799–812.

Fuentes, M. M. F., Montes, F. J. L., & Fernández, L. M. (2006). Total quality management, strategic orientation and organizational performance: The case of Spanish companies. *Total Quality Management and Business Excellence, 17*(3), 303–323.

Fust, S.F., & Walker, L.L. (2007). *Corporate sustainability initiatives: The next tqm? – understanding emerging corporate sustainability practices through the lens of total quality management*. White paper available via Korn/Ferry International. http://www.kornferry.com/institute/download/download/id/16762/aid/207. Accessed 20 Jan 2017.

Galbreath, J. (2005). Which resources matter the most to firm success? An exploratory study of resource based theory. *Technovation, 25*, 919–981.

Garvin, D. (1987). Competing on the eight dimensions of quality. *Harvard Business Review, 65*(6), 101–109.

Gechevski, D., Mitrevska, M., & Chaloska, J. (2016). Corporate social responsibility based on EFQM framework. *Annals of Faculty Engineering Hunedoara – International Journal of Engineering, 14*(1), 115–120.

Gentili, E., Stainer, L., & Stainer, A. (2003). Ethical dimensions of total quality management. *International Journal of Business Performance Management, 5*(2–3), 237–244.

Geva, A. (2008). Three models of corporate social responsibility: Interrelationships between theory, research, and practice. *Business and Society Review, 113*(1), 1–41.

Gharakhani, D., Rahmati, H., Farrokhi, M., & Farahmandian, A. (2013). Total quality management and organizational performance. *American Journal of Industrial Engineering, 1*(3), 46–50.

Ghobadian, A., & Gallear, D. (1996). Total quality management in SMEs. *OMEGA: International Journal of Management Science, 24*(1), 83–106.

Ghobadian, A., & Gallear, D. (2001). TQM implementation: An empirical examination and proposed generic model. *Omega, 29*(4), 343–359.

González-Rodríguez, M. R., Díaz-Fernández, M. C., & Simonetti, B. (2015). The social, economic and environmental dimensions of corporate social responsibility: The role played by consumers and potential entrepreneurs. *International Business Review, 24*(5), 836–848.

Graafland, J., & Van De Ven, B. (2006). Strategic and moral motivation for corporate social responsibility. *Journal of Corporate Citizenship, 22*, 111–123.

Grant, R. M. (1991). The resource-based theory of competitive advantage: Implications for strategy formulation. *California Management Review, 33*(3), 114–135.

Hansson, J. (2003). *Total quality management – Aspects of implementation and performance: Investigations with a focus on small organisations*. Doctoral Thesis no. 6, Lulea University of Technology, Department of Business administration and Social Science, Division of Quality & Environmental Management.

Hart, S. (1995). A natural-resource-based view of the firm. *Academy of Management Review, 20*(4), 986–1014.

Hasan, M., & Kerr, R. M. (2003). The relationship between total quality management practices and organisational performance in service organisations. *The TQM Magazine, 15*(4), 286–291.

Hasan, I., Kobeissi, N., Liu, L., & Wang, H. (2016). Corporate social responsibility and firm financial performance: The mediating role of productivity. *Journal of Business Ethics*, In press. Available online 9 Feb 2016.

Hellsten, U., & Klefsjo, B. (2000). TQM as a management system consisting of values, techniques and tools. *The TQM Magazine, 12*(4), 238–244.

Hendricks, K. B., & Singhal, V. R. (1997). The long-term stock price performance of quality award winners. In D. B. Fedor & S. Ghosh (Eds.), *Advances in the management of organizational quality* (pp. 1–37). Greenwich: JAI Press.

Hendricks, K. B., & Singhal, V. R. (2001). Firm characteristics, total quality management, and financial performance. *Journal of Operations Management, 19*(3), 269–285.

Honarpour, A., Jusoh, A., & Md Nor, K. (2017). Total quality management, knowledge management, and innovation: An empirical study in R&D units. *Total Quality Management and Business Excellence*, In press. Available online 12 Jan 2017.

Hoonakker, P., McEniry, M., Carayon, P., Korunka, C., & Sainfort, F. (2000). Total quality management and teamwork in the public sector: The Wisconsin department of revenue study. In Proceedings of the XIVth Triennial Congress of the International Ergonomics Association and 44th Annual Meeting of the Human Factors and Ergonomics Association, 'Ergonomics for the New Millennium', Human Factors and Ergonomics Society, San Diego, California, USA, 30 Jul–4 Aug 2000, pp. 257–260.

Huxtable, N. (1995). *Small business total quality*. London: Chapman & Hall.

Isaksson, R. (2006). Total quality management for sustainable development: Process based system models. *Business Process Management Journal, 12*(5), 632–645.

Islam, T., Ahmed, I., Ali, G., & Sadiq, T. (2016). Behavioral and psychological consequences of corporate social responsibility: Need of the time. *Social Responsibility Journal, 12*(2), 307–320.

Iyer, A., Saranga, H., & Seshadri, S. (2013). Effect of quality management systems and total quality management on productivity before and after: Empirical evidence from the Indian auto component industry. *Production and Operations Management, 22*(2), 283–301.

Jaca, C., & Psomas, E. (2015). Total quality management practices and performance outcomes in Spanish service companies. *Total Quality Management and Business Excellence, 26*(9–10), 958–970.

James, G. (1992). Quality of working life and total quality management. *International Journal of Manpower, 13*(1), 41–58.

Joseph, I. N., Rajendran, C., Kamalanabhan, T. J., & Anantharaman, R. N. (1999). Organizational factors and total quality management – An empirical study. *International Journal of Production Research, 37*(6), 1337–1352.

Kamatra, N., & Kartikaningdyah, E. (2015). Effect corporate social responsibility on financial performance. *International Journal of Economics and Financial Issues, 5*, 157–164.

Kang, H., & Liu, S. (2014). Corporate social responsibility and corporate performance: A quantile regression approach. *Quality and Quantity, 48*(6), 3311–3325.

Karia, N., & Asaari, M. H. A. H. (2006). The effects of total quality management practices on employees' work-related attitudes. *The TQM Magazine, 18*(1), 30–43.

Kim, H. L., Rhou, Y., Uysal, M., & Kwon, N. (2017). An examination of the links between corporate social responsibility (CSR) and its internal consequences. *International Journal of Hospitality Management, 61*, 26–34.

Kober, R., Subraamanniam, T., & Watson, J. (2012). The impact of total quality management adoption on small and medium enterprises' financial performance. *Accounting and Finance, 52*(2), 421–438.

Kok, P., Van Der Wiele, T., McKenna, R., & Brown, A. (2001). A corporate social responsibility audit within a quality management framework. *Journal of Business Ethics, 31*(4), 285–297.

Komodromos, M., & Melanthiou, Y. (2014). Corporate reputation through strategic corporate social responsibility: Insights from service industry companies. *Journal of Promotion Management, 20*(4), 470–480.

Lee, H. L., & Whang, S. (2005). Higher supply chain security with lower cost: Lessons from total quality management. *International Journal of Production Economics, 96*(3), 289–300.

Lenssen, G., Bevan, D., Fontrodona, J., Minoja, M., Zollo, M., & Coda, V. (2010). Stakeholder cohesion, innovation, and competitive advantage. *Corporate Governance: The International Journal of Business in Society, 10*(4), 395–405.

López-Fernández, A. M., & Rajagopal, R. (2016). Analysis of stakeholder value derivation through corporate social responsibility for business growth and society's collateral benefits. *International Journal of Business Performance Management, 17*(4), 413–427.

Lu, W. M., Wang, W. K., & Lee, H. L. (2013). The relationship between corporate social responsibility and corporate performance: Evidence from the US semiconductor industry. *International Journal of Production Research, 51*(19), 5683–5695.

Luo, X., & Bhattacharya, C. B. (2006). Corporate social responsibility, customer satisfaction, and market value. *Journal of Marketing, 70*(4), 1–18.

Madorran, C., & Garcia, T. (2016). Corporate social responsibility and financial performance: The Spanish case. *RAE Revista de Administracao de Empresas, 56*(1), 20–28.

McAdam, R., & Leonard, D. (2003). Corporate social responsibility in a total quality management context: Opportunities for sustainable growth. *Corporate Governance: The International Journal of Business in Society, 3*(4), 36–45.

McWilliams, A., & Siegel, D. (2000). Corporate social responsibility and financial performance: Correlation or misspecification? *Strategic Management Journal, 21*(5), 603–609.

McWilliams, A., Van Fleet, D. D., & Cory, K. (2002). Raising rivals' costs through political strategy: An extension of the resource-based theory. *Journal of Management Studies, 39,* 707–723.

McWilliams, A., Siegel, D., & Wright, P. M. (2006). Corporate social responsibility: Strategic implications. *Journal of Management Studies, 43*(1), 1–18.

Mehralian, G., Nazari, J. A., Zarei, L., & Rasekh, H. R. (2016). The effects of corporate social responsibility on organizational performance in the Iranian pharmaceutical industry: The mediating role of TQM. *Journal of Cleaner Production, 135,* 689–698.

Mendes, L. (2010). Motivations behind ISO 9000, early implementation problems and perceived benefits in manufacturing SME: A Portuguese case study. *Actual Problems of Economics, 4*(106), 262–283.

Mendes, L., & Jesus, J. (2017). Influence of total quality-based human issues on organisational commitment. *Total Quality Management and Business Excellence,* In press. Available online 9 May 2016.

Mijatovic, I., & Stokic, D. (2010). The influence of internal and external codes on CSR practice: The case of companies operating in Serbia. *Journal of Business Ethics, 94*(4), 533–552.

Miller, W. J. (1996). A working definition for Total Quality Management (TQM) researchers. *Journal of Quality Management, 1*(2), 149–159.

Milosan, I. (2014). Studies about the total quality management concept. *Acta Technica Corvininesis – Bulletin of Engineering, 7*(3), 453–445.

Modgil, S., & Sharma, S. (2016). Total productive maintenance, total quality management and operational performance an empirical study of Indian pharmaceutical industry. *Journal of Quality in Maintenance Engineering, 22*(4), 353–377.

Molina-Azorín, J. F., Tarí, J. J., Pereira-Moliner, J., López-Gamero, M. D., & Pertusa-Ortega, E. M. (2015). The effects of quality and environmental management on competitive advantage: A mixed methods study in the hotel industry. *Tourism Management, 50,* 41–54.

Mory, L., Wirtz, B. W., & Göttel, V. (2016). Factors of internal corporate social responsibility and the effect on organizational commitment. *International Journal of Human Resource Management, 27*(13), 1393–1425.

NIST. (2015). *Malcolm excellence framework.* Gaithersburg: United States Department of Commerce.

Nollet, J., Filis, G., & Mitrokostas, E. (2016). Corporate social responsibility and financial performance: A non-linear and disaggregated approach. *Economic Modelling, 52,* 400–407.

Norman, W., & MacDonald, C. (2004). Getting to the bottom of triple bottom line. *Business Ethics Quarterly, 14*(2), 243–262.

Nováková, R., Ďurková, K., Ovsenák, V. (2014). Indicators of social responsibility in the wood processing industry in terms of quality management. In: Proceedings of the 7th International Scientific Conference on Position and Role of the Forest Based Sector in the Green Economy, Zvolen (SLOVAKIA), 21–23 May 2014.

Oakland, J. S. (1989). *Total quality management.* Oxford: Butterworth-Heinemann.

Oakland, J. (2011). Leadership and policy deployment: The backbone of TQM. *Total Quality Management and Business Excellence, 22*(5), 517–534.

Oh, W., & Park, S. (2015). The relationship between corporate social responsibility and corporate financial performance in Korea. *Emerging Markets Finance and Trade, 51,* S85–S94.

Oppenheim, B. W., & Przasnyski, Z. H. (1999). Total quality requires serious training. *Quality Progress, 32*(10), 63–73.

Palihawadana, D., Oghazi, P., & Liu, Y. (2016). Effects of ethical ideologies and perceptions of CSR on consumer behaviour. *Journal of Business Research, 69,* 4964–4969.

Panagopoulos, N. G., Rapp, A. A., & Vlachos, P. A. (2016). I think they think we are good citizens: Meta-perceptions as antecedents of employees' reactions to corporate social responsibility. *Journal of Business Research, 69*(8), 2781–2790.

Para-González, L., Jiménez-Jiménez, D., & Martínez-Lorente, Á. R. (2016). Do total quality management and the European Foundation for Quality Management model encourage a quality-oriented human resource management system? *International Journal of Productivity and Quality Management, 17*(3), 308–327.

Parast, M. M., & Adams, S. G. (2012). Corporate social responsibility, benchmarking, and organizational performance in the petroleum industry: A quality management perspective. *International Journal of Production Economics, 139*(2), 447–458.

Parsa, H. G., Lord, K. R., Putrevu, S., & Kreeger, J. (2015). Corporate social and environmental responsibility in services: Will consumers pay for it? *Journal of Retailing and Consumer Services, 22*(1), 250–260.

Penrose, E. T. (1959). *The theory of the growth of the firm*. New York: Oxford University Press.

Perdomo-Ortiz, J., González-Benito, J., & Galende, J. (2009). An analysis of the relationship between total quality management-based human resource management practices and innovation. *International Journal of Human Resource Management, 20*(5), 1191–1218.

Pérez, A., & del Bosque, I. R. (2015). Corporate social responsibility and customer loyalty: Exploring the role of identification, satisfaction and type of company. *Journal of Services Marketing, 29*(1), 15–24.

Peteraf, M. (1993). The cornerstones of competitive advantage: A resource-based view. *Strategic Management Journal, 14*(3), 179–191.

Podgórski, D. (2000). Occupational health and safety management in polish enterprises implementing total quality management systems. *International Journal of Occupational Safety and Ergonomics, 6*, 85–101.

Poureh, S.A. (2015). *A corporate social responsibility review within a total quality management framework*. Bachelor of Science Thesis in Industrial Engineering and Management, University of Gävle, Faculty of engineering and sustainable development, Department of Industrial Development, IT and Land Management (Sweeden).

Powell, T. C. (1995). Total quality management as competitive advantage: A review and empirical study. *Strategic Management Journal, 16*, 15–37.

Prajogo, D. I., & Sohal, A. S. (2006). The relationship between organization strategy, total quality management (TQM), and organization performance: The mediating role of TQM. *European Journal of Operational Research, 168*(1), 35–50.

Psomas, E. L., & Fotopoulos, C. V. (2010). Total quality management practices and results in food companies. *International Journal of Productivity and Performance Management, 59*(7), 668–687.

Rahman, S. (2001). Total quality management practices and business outcome: Evidence from small and medium enterprises in western Australia. *Total Quality Management, 12*(2), 201–210.

Reed, R., Lemak, D. J., & Mero, N. P. (2000). Total quality management and sustainable competitive advantage. *Journal of Quality Management, 5*, 5–26.

Rupp, D. E., Shao, R., Thornton, M. A., & Skarlicki, D. P. (2013). Applicants' and employees' reactions to corporate social responsibility: The moderating effects of first-party justice perceptions and moral identity. *Personnel Psychology, 66*(4), 895–933.

Russo, M. V., & Fouts, P. A. (1997). A resource-based perspective on corporate environmental performance and profitability. *Academy of Management Journal, 40*(3), 534–559.

Sadikoglu, E., & Zehir, C. (2010). Investigating the effects of innovation and employee performance on the relationship between total quality management practices and firm performance: An empirical study of Turkish firms. *International Journal of Production Economics, 127*(1), 13–26.

Saeidi, S. P., Sofian, S., Saeidi, P., Saeidi, S. P., & Saaeidi, S. A. (2015). How does corporate social responsibility contribute to firm financial performance? The mediating role of competitive advantage, reputation, and customer satisfaction. *Journal of Business Research, 68*(2), 341–350.

Salhieh, L., & Abu-Doleh, J. (2015). The relationship between total quality management practices and their effects on bank's technical efficiency. *International Journal of Commerce and Management, 25*(2), 173–182.

Samson, D., & Terziovski, M. (1999). Relationship between total quality management practices and operational performance. *Journal of Operations Management, 17*(4), 393–409.

Sharma, S., & Vredenburg, H. (1998). Proactive corporate environmental strategy and the development of competitively valuable organizational capabilities. *Strategic Management Journal, 19*(8), 729–753.

Shiba, S., Graham, A., & Walden, D. (1993). *A new American TQM. Four practical revolutions in management.* Portland: Productivity Press, Centre for Quality Management.

Shnayder, L., van Rijnsoever, F. J., & Hekkert, M. P. (2016). Motivations for corporate social responsibility in the packaged food industry: An institutional and stakeholder management perspective. *Journal of Cleaner Production, 122*, 212–227.

Shrivastava, R. L., Mohanty, R. P., & Lakhe, R. R. (2006). Linkages between total quality management and organisational performance: An empirical study for Indian industry. *Production Planning and Control, 17*(1), 13–30.

Solomon, A., & Lewis, L. (2002). Incentives and disincentives for corporate environmental reporting. *Business Strategy and the Environment, 11*(3), 154–169.

Sprinkle, G. B., & Maines, L. A. (2010). The benefits and costs of corporate social responsibility. *Business Horizons, 53*(5), 445–453.

Su, H. C., Linderman, K., Schroeder, R. G., & Van De Ven, A. H. (2014). A comparative case study of sustaining quality as a competitive advantage. *Journal of Operations Management, 32*(7–8), 429–445.

Swaen, V., & Chumpitaz, R. (2008). Impact of corporate social responsibility on consumer trust. *Recherche et Applications en Marketing, 23*(4), 7–33.

Sweis, R. J., Al-Mansour, A., Tarawneh, M., & Al-Dweik, G. (2013). The impact of total quality management practices on employee empowerment in the healthcare sector in Saudi Arabia: A study of king Khalid hospital. *International Journal of Productivity and Quality Management, 12*(3), 271–286.

Talib, F., Rahman, Z., Qureshi, M. N., & Siddiqui, J. (2011). Total quality management and service quality: An exploratory study of quality management practices and barriers in service industry. *International Journal of Services and Operations Management, 10*(1), 94–118.

Tarí, J. J. (2011). Research into quality management and social responsibility. *Journal of Business Ethics, 102*(4), 623–638.

Tarí Guilló, J. J., & García Fernández, M. (2011). La gestión de la calidad y la responsabilidad social en empresas de servicios. *Revista de Dirección y Administración de Empresas, 18*, 77–93.

Tarí, J. J., Claver-Cortés, E., Pereira-Moliner, J., & Molina-Azorín, J. F. (2010). Levels of quality and environmental management in the hotel industry: Their joint influence on firm performance. *International Journal of Hospitality Management, 29*(3), 500–510.

Viada-Stenger, M. C., Balbastre-Benavent, F., & Redondo-Cano, A. M. (2010). The implementation of a quality management system based on the Q tourist quality standard. The case of hotel sector. *Service Business, 4*(3), 177–196.

Vinten, G. (1998). Putting ethics into quality. *The TQM Magazine, 10*(2), 89–94.

Wang, C.-H., Chen, K.-Y., & Chen, S. C. (2012). Total quality management, market orientation and hotel performance: The moderating effects of external environmental factors. *International Journal of Hospitality Management, 31*(1), 119–129.

Webley, P., & Cartwright, J. (1996). The implicit psychology of total quality management. *Total Quality Management, 7*(5), 483–492.

Wei, Y.-C., & Lin, C. Y.-Y. (2015). How can corporate social responsibility lead to firm performance? A longitudinal study in Taiwan. *Corporate Reputation Review, 18*(2), 111–127.

Wernerfelt, B. (1984). The resource-based view of the firm. *Strategic Management Journal, 5*(2), 171–180.

Woodruff, R. E. (1997). Customer value: The next source for competitive advantage. *Academy of Marketing Science Journal, 25*(2), 139–153.

Yang, C.-C. (2006). The impact of human resource management practices on the implementation of total quality management. *International Journal of Quality and Reliability Management, 18*(2), 162–173.

Yeung, A. C. L., Cheng, T. C. E., & Lai, K.-H. (2006). An operational and institutional perspective on total quality management. *Production and Operations Management, 15*(1), 156–170.

Youssef, E. M., Youssef, M. A., & Ahmed, A. M. M. B. (2014). Total quality management intensity and its impact on HRM practices in manufacturing firms. *International Journal of Productivity and Quality Management, 13*(4), 495–512.

Yunis, M., Jung, J., & Chen, S. (2013). TQM, strategy, and performance: A firm-level analysis. *International Journal of Quality & Reliability Management, 30*(6), 690–714.

Zali, R., & Sheydayaee, J. (2013). Determinants of corporate social responsibility, dynamic capability and financial performance (Cases study: Accepted firms in Tehran stock exchange market). *International Journal of Financial Management, 3*(2), 29–37.

Zink, K. J. (2005). Stakeholder orientation and corporate social responsibility as a precondition for sustainability. *Total Quality Management and Business Excellence, 16*(8–9), 1041–1052.

Zink, K. J. (2007). From total quality management to corporate sustainability based on a stakeholder management. *Journal of Management History, 13*(4), 394–401.

Zutshi, A., & Sohal, A. (2005). Integrated management system: The experiences of three Australian organisations. *Journal of Manufacturing Technology Management, 16*(2), 211–232.

Chapter 14
From Broker to Platform Business Models: A Case Study of Best Practices for Business Model Innovation in Hybrid Interorganizational Partnerships

Paula Ungureanu and Diego Maria Macri

Abstract This study is concerned with how hybrid partnerships – i.e., multiparty cross-sector partnerships dealing with broad problems that go beyond the scope and scale of single partners – set up, implement, and then innovate business models. In particular, we draw on a hybrid partnership for open innovation where six public and private organizations came together with the intention to set up and implement joint innovation projects with large-scale impact at the regional level. Two business models of hybrid partnerships are discussed in this chapter, the brokering model and the platform model, as well as the mechanisms of transition from the first to the latter. Our findings suggest that while the platform model seems more appropriate for complex projects in which a wide number of heterogeneous interests coexist, both models present advantages and disadvantages. We suggest that advantages and disadvantages of hybrid partnership business models should be considered in a relational manner, by focusing on how the business model innovation will impact on each parameter of the current model and, at the same time, on how manageable the parameters of the new model are in terms of partnership strategy, structure, and mobilizable resources.

Keywords Hybrid partnerships • Cross-sector • Broker • Business model innovation • Open innovation

---

P. Ungureanu (✉) • D.M. Macri
Department of Sciences and Methods for Engineering (DISMI), University of Modena and Reggio Emilia, Reggio Emilia, Italy
e-mail: paula.ungureanu@unimore.it; dmacri@unimore.it

© Springer International Publishing AG 2018
J. Leitão et al. (eds.), *Entrepreneurial, Innovative and Sustainable Ecosystems*, Applying Quality of Life Research,
https://doi.org/10.1007/978-3-319-71014-3_14

14.1 Introduction

This chapter is concerned with business model innovation in cross-sector collaborations for complex innovation projects. Most research in business model innovation has focused on organizations' ability to create innovation and improvement processes in order to build new value propositions or enter new markets and industries (Massa and Tucci 2013), but less is known about what happens when business models need to be set up, assessed, and revisited in a collaboration ecosystem with multiple private and public organizations, each mobilizing distinct interests, goals, and objectives. We draw on a longitudinal case study of a hybrid partnership in the north of Italy that brought together multiple private and public actors such as the local government, a Chamber of Commerce, several industrial and trade associations, a Public Utility Company, and a Regional European Development Office, with the goal to support open innovation projects at the regional level. The case study is particularly relevant for the entrepreneurial, innovative, and sustainable (EIS) ecosystem approach. In particular, it describes the birth and evolution of a local ecosystem focused on innovation, knowledge transfer, and sustainability, in which heterogeneous organizations constantly stepped in and out of the boundaries of the project, according to their own interests while struggling to create an adequate business model for the ecosystem, which would have also reflected their own interests at hand. The case follows the evolution of a new organization called RIO that partners created in support of the partnership and to which they delegated the management of the partnership ecosystem. By following the evolution of RIO, we were able to trace the evolution of the ecosystem itself, identifying collaboration stages, critical turning points, and best practices for managing the critical points of the partnership. In particular, we discuss three stages in the ecosystem: a brokering model stage, a transition stage, and a platform model stage and show how multiple adjustments were made from one stage to the next in order to suit more closely the nature and dynamics of the ecosystem. Unpacking the assumptions of each model, their critical points, the consequences, and the coping mechanisms that they triggered, allowed us to adopt a practice-based perspective on business model innovation in hybrid partnerships. We propose a discussion on ecosystems organized according to brokering versus platform models. We suggest that a careful analysis of the characteristics of the ecosystem can favor the identification of best practices for its organization.

The chapter is organized as follows. We first discuss the importance of hybrid partnerships for open innovation. We then streamline what is known about business model innovation at the interorganizational setting and highlight a set of critical points that still need to be investigated to understand the challenges that setting up and modifying a business model at the interorganizational level entail with respect to the organizational level. We then describe the context of the case study and give an account of the main findings which are organized around three stages: the broker model stage, the transition stage, and the platform model stage. In the discussion section, we summarize a series of advantages and disadvantages of the two models and comment on how they inform best practices about business model innovation in the case of hybrid partnerships.

14.2 Toward an Understanding of Business Model Innovation in Hybrid Partnerships

14.2.1 Hybrid Partnerships as Tools for Open Innovation

Interorganizational collaborative activities have become more prominent and extensive not just in the private sector but in the public sector as well, with hybrid forms of collaborative engagement between business, government, and civil society being stipulated every day (Bryson et al. 2006; Hartley et al. 2013; Kivleniece and Quelin 2012; Selsky and Parker 2005). Many of these cross-sector collaborations are constituted to address *metaproblems* – broadly defined overarching frames entailing interests that have to do with the public good and go beyond the jurisdiction and competencies of single organizations. Examples of metaproblems addressed through public-private collaborations are fostering industrial competitiveness, managing urban development, improving social welfare and fostering social innovation, or programming the sustainable development of a given region (Le Ber and Branzei, 2010a; Linder and Rosenau 2000; Selsky and Parker 2005).

A case that entails significant challenges is that of cross-sector partnerships for collaborative (i.e., open) innovation where public and private organizations get together with the intention to set up and implement joint innovation projects with large-scale impact. As far as the public sector is concerned, there has been growing attention to intrapreneurial and entrepreneurial processes (Damanpour and Schneider 2009; Leitao and Alves 2016; Morris and Jones 1999). For instance, trends in public entrepreneurship are increasingly pushing public actors toward innovation ecosystems that encompass crosscutting organizations, groups, teams, and communities (Bernier and Hafsi 2007; Hjorth 2013). Accordingly, not only governments become interested in promoting and supporting the innovation of private organizations but they also turn into active project stakeholders. Motivations include expanding jurisdiction to new sectors by retrieving skills and competencies that are not available internally, achieving legitimation in new markets and fields, or simply adjusting to the institutional logics of the new public management (Bryson et al. 2006; Skelcher 2005). Similarly, private organizations that try to enter fields and markets where private initiative is viewed with suspicion are increasingly considering long-term partnerships with public organizations, governmental institutions, or NGOs (Googins and Rochlin 2000; Rondinelli and London 2003). By lowering costs, reaching new groups of customers, and more broadly filling institutional voids through new product or service offerings, open innovation is considered a tool to create bundles of social and economic value (Koschmann et al. 2012; Le Ber and Branzei 2010a; Selsky and Parker 2005). As a consequence, it becomes important to understand how organizations engaged in long-term cross-sector multiparty partnerships manage to collaborate inside complex innovation projects and, in particular, how they set up, negotiate, implement, and revisit the business model of the partnership throughout its life cycle.

It has been argued that ecosystems that entail heterogeneous partners present multiple challenges for those who enact them. For instance, there is evidence that although collaboration between cross-sector organizations mobilizes broadly defined objectives as to allow partners' divergent interests to coexist, collaborations are often permeated by tensions between self versus common interest, especially as the number of partners increases (Turcotte and Pasquero 2001; Waddell and Brown 1997). It is thus important to understand the main advantages and challenges faced by public and private organizations that decide to collaborate in complex innovation projects. More importantly, it is important to keep track of how the partnership evolves through time. The creation of a common ground for collaboration has been said to play a fundamental part in partnerships' ability to adjust through time (Majchrzak et al. 2015). Koschmann and colleagues (2012) have argued, for instance, that the overall value of cross-sector partnerships is not merely in connecting interested parties but, rather, in their ability to substantially influence the people and issues within the domains of the interested parties. This ability, they argue, comes from the constitution of organizational forms that are distinct from their members and that display collective agency – the capacity to influence a host of relevant outcomes beyond what individual organizations could do on their own. New structures such as functional roles, organizational teams, common projects, and common goal structures have been found useful for negotiating tensions and fueling partnership interaction because they can act as scaffolds for the creation of a common ground (Doz and Baburoglu 2000; Le Ber and Branzei 2010b). On the one hand, attempts to create a common strategy allows actors to draft premises and rules of the game, but on the other, given the different interests and logics at stake, it paves the way for additional conflicts and misunderstandings that organizations might not be prepared for upfront (Selsky and Parker 2005; Turcotte and Pasquero 2001). We thus argue that business models and partners' ability to set up, negotiate, and revise business models (i.e., business model innovation) may play a fundamental role in understanding, diagnosing, and establishing best practices for the evolution of hybrid partnerships through time.

14.2.2 Business Model Innovation in Hybrid Interorganizational Partnerships

Although no generally accepted definition of the term "business model" has yet been reached – for instance, terms such as "business model," "business strategy," or even "economic model" are often used interchangeably (Morris et al. 2005) – business models reflect "management's hypothesis about what customers want, how they want it and what they will pay, and how an enterprise can organize to best meet customer needs, and get paid well for doing so" (Teece 2010, p. 20). In other words, business models offer a holistic approach explaining how firms "do business" encompassing basic insights of innovation, business processes, and routines (Casadesus-Masanell and Ricart 2010; Cavalcante et al. 2011; Zott et al. 2011). A good business model is a relatively comprehensive description of the organization's situation, structures and capabilities, the partners, the target market, the value proposition, who is creating and capturing value, the value chain, as well as which activities will be conducted by the focal firm, by partners, or through arm's length transactions, as well as revenue and cost structures. It is important to note that a business model will include not just a description of the organization but also, critically, a description of its environment, including the broader (economic, social, and political) institutional context, competitors, customers, consumers, suppliers, and – especially relevant for our discussion – partners (Dahan et al. 2010).

According to extant research, both the design of business models and the ability to constantly introduce innovations to the business model are key issues for any organization looking for better performance and higher value capture. In literature, this has been discussed under the name of business model innovation (BMI) (Amit and Zott 2012; Chesbrough 2010; Mitchell and Coles 2003). Accordingly, BMI is associated to the ability to create innovation and improvement processes at the firm level that can be used to build new value propositions or enter new markets and industries. Adding new firm activities, linking existing activities in new ways, and changing their distribution inside the firm have been all discussed as relevant BMI processes (Massa and Tucci 2013).

While most research has been concerned with business model innovation at the firm level, there is still little understanding of the challenges of first setting up and further on innovating the business models of hybrid interorganizational partnerships (Chesbrough and Schwartz 2007; Dahan et al. 2010). Studies suggest that a main factor to shape the developmental path of an alliance is partners' ability to first assess and then react to discrepancies between initial and emergent conditions (Arino and de la Torre 1998; Eden and Huxham 2001; Le Ber and Branzei 2010b; Majchrzak et al. 2015). It is interesting to point out that in many of the cases in which cross-sector partnerships are set up, there is no preestablished business model, such that in some cases partners use a business model of one of the partnering firms that they gradually modify and adjust to reflect the logics and functioning of the entire partnership or, most commonly, they build a business model from scratch (Dahan et al. 2010). From such standpoint, creating a business model for a cross-sector partnership is a step-by-step, trial and error project which might have important consequences for the trajectory of the partnership and the dynamics between partners. From such standpoint, it is thus important to define a list of does and don'ts for those who are considering engaging in such projects and outline critical points in the adoption and use of partnership business models (Bryson et al. 2015).

14.3 Context Description

In this chapter, we draw on a multiple-year case study of a hybrid collaboration in Italy between one municipality, one public university, three trade and industrial associations, one Chamber of Commerce, a Public Utility Company, and a Regional European Development Office that came together with the broad goal of supporting innovation and knowledge exchange at the regional level. The EU Cohesion Policy has been supporting for many years cross-sector collaborations between government, universities, and the private sector to deliver innovation in EU regions (CEC 2014), and Italian regions have been no exception to this trend. For instance, not only is strengthening research, technological development, and innovation singled out in the EU Cohesion Policy for 2014–2020 as a leading way to generate "smart specialization" across European regions but also highly prioritized by the long-term strategies of Italian local governments (Romano et al. 2014; Zerbinati and Souitaris 2005).

In line with the institutional context in which it was inserted, the partnership that we studied was founded in 2009 in support of open projects for local innovation. To this purpose, stakeholders signed an Innovation Agreement in which they committed to "join resources to obtain mutual benefits related to innovation and knowledge transfer" by putting together "an innovative local government," "highly competitive industrial region," and "distinctive research competencies of the local University" (cfr.). Following the Agreement, a new organization was created – the Regional Innovation Office (RIO) which had the purpose to implement the partnership agenda. This implied identifying concrete market opportunities for shareholders' innovation projects, managing innovation projects on behalf of the shareholders, and negotiating, throughout the process, their heterogeneous goals and interests.

By studying the evolution of RIO from its foundation to the present date, we trace the evolution pattern of the partnership and identify a series of critical points which have determined partners to reconsider the initial business model of the partnership as to move toward more customized and at the same time enabling business models.

14.4 Main Findings

The case study describes three stages in the evolution of RIO: *the broker stage*, *the transition stage*, and the *platform stage*, emphasizing how the shortcomings of the first business model and the subsequent threat of partnership failure in the transition stage have led to the setup of the second model. The setup of the platform model will be here proposed as best practice for collaborations between (multiparty, cross-sector) private institutions with highly diversified and heterogeneous interests and a set of trade-offs with respect to the broker model will also be identified.

14.4.1 The Broker Model Stage

14.4.1.1 Assumptions

In the first phase of the collaboration (2009–2014), RIO was designed as broker –as a boundary organization that was expected to collect, assemble, and enact the multiple interests of its shareholders. Since partners had collaborated only occasionally and predominantly in dyads but never around long-term projects and never together in formalized partnerships, they had little knowledge of each other's goals and interests, and even less understanding about how to interconnect them. As a consequence, all participating institutions expressed the intention to create a broker that would mediate interorganizational differences and contribute to the creation of a dense network of interorganizational actors, resources, and projects. Besides, since partners felt the pressure to act as a whole, they expected RIO to scout, manage, and carry out projects on their behalf. At the end of this timespan, RIO traversed financial and legitimacy crises, mostly due to partners' reluctance to make further investments. As time passed, RIO started being perceived as a third party, a boundary organization that no longer represented their interests. In particular, partners' intention to delegate to RIO all aspects of managing the partnership, on the one hand, and their unwillingness to give up control, on the other hand, generated an environment full of contradictions, ambiguities, malfunctions, and unexpected events. Figure 14.1 represents graphically the assumptions of the brokering model.

14.4.1.2 Shortcomings

Several factors concurred to the fact that, as time passed, RIO started to be perceived as a third party, a boundary agent that did not represent shareholders' interests:

1. *Overflowing goals:* Partners were animated by different goals that proliferated in uncontrollable ways.[1] Since these goals were manifold and highly specific, partners continued to pursue them individually or in dyads despite the partnership frame. As a consequence, RIO's assignment remained excessively broad and generic.
2. *Split hierarchy:* RIO was assigned the responsibility to coordinate common projects but not also the authority to do it. Each organization continued to run decision-making processes internally.

---

[1] To give an example, the municipality was concerned with urban development, social welfare, and cultural initiatives and the university with obtaining new research funding, the Chamber of Commerce was interested in legitimating its choices for allocation of public funds, the Public Utility Company was concerned with a specific urban regeneration project, the European Office aimed at implementing a network of science parks across the region, and the trade and industrial associations were animated by the need to defend the interests of the firms they represented and their own interests as well (e.g., competition and collaboration with other industrial associations).

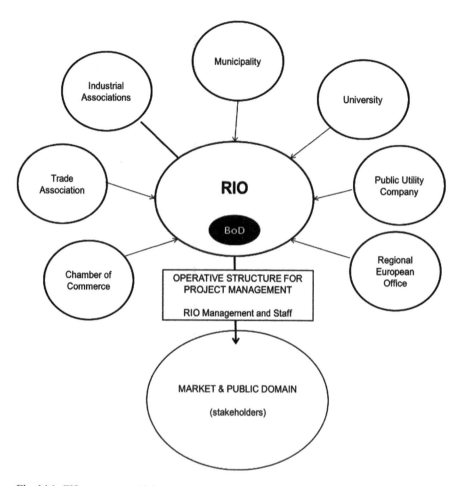

Fig. 14.1 EIS ecosystem with brokering model

3. *Double unaccountability:* RIO was evaluated each year based on a generic mission of "innovation and technological transfer," rather than on specific projects or on well-defined goals assigned to each project. This was motivated by partners' will to ensure that RIO had enough autonomy and flexibility on the market, on the one hand, but also by their intention to avoid direct responsibility for joint projects. The double unaccountability loop had led, on the one hand, to partners' perception that RIO was not generating value for their organizations and for the public domain in general, and, on the other hand, enhanced RIO's belief in founders' lack of interest and responsibility.
4. *Opportunistic behavior:* Actors either did not delegate their projects to RIO or decided to opportunistically delegate those projects with scarce resources or with limited internal support.

5. *Marginal assignments:* Most of the projects that the partner organizations delegated to RIO were not concerned with their core activities but with marginal activities. These were either activities that partners felt comfortable sharing with outsiders because they were not strategic for their organizations, activities that did not count significantly toward the organizational performances, or activities for which they did not have internal funding or support.
6. *Limited entrepreneurial initiative:* RIO only rarely manifested initiatives such as proposing new projects or creating new opportunities for its stakeholders. RIO attributed the limited entrepreneurial initiative to the scarce resources and the limited institutional legitimation that partners invested them with.
7. *Decreasing investments:* Shareholder's financial investment in RIO was limited and diminished each year. This was also reinforced by the perception that RIO was not generating value.
8. *Information gaps:* RIO and its stakeholders had limited information about each other's projects, initiatives, goals, and activities. The communication system was deemed insufficient by all parties. It mostly ran through RIO's informal relations and largely depended on RIO's ability to use informal relations with each of the partnering organizations. However, the flow of projects, plans, objectives, and expectations that each partner brought to the partnership was much more than RIO's organizational structure could process.

14.4.2 The Transition Stage

The 2014–2015 timespan marked a critical stage of transition. In particular, after the implementation of the brokering model and the first dissatisfactions with the model, RIO traversed a period of financial and legitimacy crisis. The municipality, the university, and the Chamber of Commerce saw their institutional roles altered by national legislation changes. The difficulties faced by these organizations in committing to the collaboration project on the long term, together with the perception of RIO's inability to generate value for each single partner, determined partners to inquire about whether maintaining or terminating the partnership. This caused a period of paralysis as far as decision-making about existing projects and launch of new projects is concerned. After a long and hurdled period of transition, partners decided to keep the partnership alive and to restructure RIO according to a new model that would reflect more closely their specific needs and interests. We identified several reasons that contributed to this decision:

1. *Pressures to avoid partnership failure:* Manifold institutional pressures for legitimation and accountability prevented partners from declaring the failure of the partnership. Since stakeholders were inserted in a natural ecosystem in which they coexisted (i.e., the region), the failure of the partnership was perceived as a potential threat for the public domain – a "point of no return" in the evolution of

the local community. As a consequence, partners were motivated to avoid break-points at all costs.

2. *Persistence of collaboration goals:* Just as in 2009 when they had decided to found RIO, partners still had the pressing need to engage in innovative collaborations with other institutions as to generate more value for themselves and for the local community. Accordingly, during the transition phase, the leaders of the partnering organizations had come to believe that the complex activities of the partnership could have been only dealt with by persevering in the project of collaboration.

3. *Compulsion to complete the collaboration infrastructure.* Despite rising conflicts, tensions, and mistrust, partners evaluated that they were halfway in the realization of a common structure to enable open innovation. As such, delegating the management of the partnership to a boundary organization such as RIO was still considered the best, if not the only possible solution. However, there was considerable confusion about how the project could have been restructured as to avoid the traps experienced in the first phase and to overcome the paralysis that characterized the second phase.

14.4.3 The Platform Model Stage

14.4.3.1 Assumptions

All the organizations that had initially founded RIO decided to preserve the partnership and to restructure RIO according to a new model that would have reflected more closely their specific needs and interests. Starting with the second half of 2015, partners engaged in a 1-year consultation process aimed at reorganizing the business model of RIO. This process reconsidered the relational and instrumental structure of the partnership, from goal setting and authority settlements to resource allocation and levels of commitment. The platform was designed and prototyped and is currently being experimented, as follows:

1. *Loosely coupling heterogeneous interests within a multilayered platform*: RIO was transformed from a boundary organization that operated on the market with the mandate of its shareholders to a boundary-less organization that coopted projects from a large number of local stakeholders. To this purpose, RIO encourages not only its shareholders but also other local shareholders interested in open innovation, to launch projects of interest and to lobby those projects to other organizations, in the attempt to obtain necessary resources to take the project further.

2. *Concentrating governance and widening participation*: Partners decided to reduce the shareholders base in order to concentrate authority, responsibility, and decision-making inside a circumscribed perimeter. Moreover, they redesigned the Board of Directors to give voice to the top management of the partnering

organizations (Mayor, University Dean, Presidents of Industrial Associations, President of Public Utility Company, President of European Regional Agency and President of RIO). This also contributed to the creation of an informal circle of decision-makers in the ecosystem.

Whereas the shareholders' base, the stakeholders base was widened in order to attract as many resources as possible, to encourage diffusion of the partnerships' initiatives, and to gain legitimacy in the local community.

3. *Disintermediating*: Rather than delegating projects to RIO, the stakeholders are encouraged to launch the projects themselves. A project must be launched by a triggering organization/institution that manifests a strong interest in a project which requires collaboration with other organizations and/or institutions (e.g., setting up a regional science park, creating a joint industry-academia PhD, designing a national database on technology transfer projects). With the help of RIO, the triggering actor identifies and mobilizes relevant partners.

4. *Abolishing generic missions*: RIO's old mission regarding generic activities of innovation and knowledge transfer was abolished. Instead, its action became the direct expression of stakeholders' interests.

5. *Creating project units*: Each project constitutes a separate organizational structure which is designed, managed, and evaluated only by those organizations that manifest a direct interest in its realization. These structures received the name of "innovation units." Innovation units are characterized by juridical and financial autonomy – i.e., they constitute as separate organizational units inside RIO or even as separate firms within the firm. Their responsibilities include defining the purpose of the project, clarifying goals and subgoals, budgeting the project activities, and composing project management teams.

6. *Managing a multilayered platform*: In the platform model, the main mission of RIO is the coordination of the platform. First, RIO is responsible for providing a set of basic services to the innovation units (physical space, administrative staff, communication, etc.). Second, RIO develops a service catalogue from which each innovation unit can choose the services of interest (e.g., project management, legal support, public relations, funding proposal drafting, etc.). This allows to create a personalized offer according to the contextualized needs of each unit. While for the basic services a fixed cost is imputed to RIO's shareholders on an annual basis, for catalogue services costs are assigned to each innovation unit (thus to stakeholders) by perceiving a service fee with variable percentages to be defined at the moment of creation of the innovation unit. Such services are delivered by RIO in collaboration with a pool of external collaborators – consulting firms, professionals and freelancers, etc. Services that are not contemplated in the catalogue might also be offered to innovation units provided the renegotiation of the annual fee.

7. *Mobilizing network externalities*: In addition to managing the ecosystem of innovation units, RIO has the mission of creating synergies between innovation units, scouting for new resources, encouraging new entrances and anticipating exits, managing the overall portfolio of innovation units, and planning its short and long-term evolution.

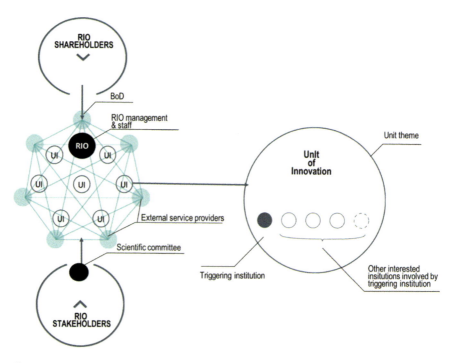

Fig. 14.2 EIS ecosystem with platform model

8. *Building communication and reporting infrastructures*: RIO also plays an active role in facilitating information flows inside, across, and outside the innovation units. Each innovation unit communicates the evolution of the project to RIO management. In turn the latter documents the composition and evolution of the platform's projects portfolio, reporting results to the BoD and to the platform's scientific committee. The latter is composed of scientists, influent managers, and technology gurus that are responsible for identifying general technological innovation trends in the market and studying their compatibility with the platform's features and requirements.

Figure 14.2 represents graphically the assumptions of the platform model, as described in the eight points above.

14.5 Discussion and Implications for Practice

Although it has become almost commonplace to think about public and private organizations in open innovation systems, it has been less straightforward to think that such initiatives can assume various forms – especially when they imply collaboration with other organizations. It is also important to consider that such forms

Table 14.1 Characteristics of the EIS ecosystem and consequences for the adoption of brokering and platform models

Characteristics of EIS ecosystem	Brokering model	Platform model
1. Heterogeneous goals	Overflowing goals	Loosely coupling heterogeneous interests within a platform
2. Multiple individual governance systems and common governance systems run in parallel (e.g., RIO BoD)	Split hierarchy	Concentrating governance and widening participation
3. Responsibilities are dispersed in the network	Double unaccountability	Disintermediating
4. Collaboration goals and subgoals are broadly defined and highly inclusive	Opportunistic behavior related to generic missions	Abolishing generic missions
5. Priorities are assigned differently by network organizations according to internal systems of relevance and modify over time	Marginal assignments	Defining project units
6. Initiatives are born spontaneously and go extinct spontaneously, as actors interact in the ecosystem	Limited entrepreneurial initiative	Managing the multilayered platform
7. The growth of the ecosystem depends on the extent to which actors allocate and mobilize resources across boundaries	Decreasing investments	Mobilizing network externalities
8. Information flows fast, asymmetrically, and unpredictably	Lack of shared information	Creating communication and reporting infrastructures

are highly dependent on the characteristics of the environments in which they develop and that different partnership business models can lead to different partnership configurations and different partnership outcomes (see also Vurro et al. 2010).

A paradox of cross-sector partnerships is that by which partnering organizations might designate brokers to accomplish innovation activities on their behalf rather than act as innovators themselves. Table 14.1 summarizes the characteristics of the EIS ecosystem and shows their consequences when a broker model or a platform model are adopted. By comparing the brokering model with the platform model, it becomes visible that the latter was established to answer shortcomings experienced with the first. Specifically, setting up brokerage units to which organizations broadly delegate the responsibility of managing complex interorganizational projects has become a common practice. The complexity of the partnership objectives, the uncertainty of its long-term outcomes, and the difficulty of negotiating heterogeneous interests, among others, are some of the reasons why partnerships might opt for a brokering model (Ungureanu et al. 2016).

As summarized in Table 14.1 and described throughout the case study, the adoption of a brokering business model can generate a sort of ambidexterity in the partnership such that the partnering organizations (i.e., the partnership shareholders) remain focused on their core missions and, at the same time, create boundary organizations that operate on their behalf in new fields of interests. We have exemplified some of the reasons why the brokering model has high likelihood of failure in cross-sector partnerships. This does not mean that the brokering model is destined to fail in any situation but that in the environmental conditions here described (see Table 14.1), only difficultly could have partners' goodwill and best practices avoided the failure of the model. We do not imply that there are no examples of boundary organizations that use the brokering model successfully to deal with complex innovation projects. Instead, we suggest that although brokering organizations operate with success in different sectors of the private and public economy, the likelihood that these units reach the goals for which they were created decreases as the number and the heterogeneity of the goals assigned to them increase (see Bryson et al. 2006; Lunnan and Haugland 2008). Furthermore, the circumscribed nature of brokering models renders them less subject to exponential growth than platform models: While in the brokering model partners assigned to RIO, a general mission of innovation and technological transfer which in turn RIO had to first articulate and then implement according to its own understanding and competencies, in the platform model, a higher number of actors played a more active role.

What is interesting to notice is that even if both the platform model and brokering model were designed to meet their interests, partnering organizations were more willing to mobilize resources within innovation units than they were willing to assign them to RIO during the brokering years. This is also connected to the risk that partners may reach a certain point in which they perceive the broker as a third party that is not the expression of their strategic vision, either as single organizations or as partnership. If allocating resources to RIO is perceived in the first case as a contribution to a higher (and more generic) goal, in the latter it is seen as an investment in a strategic project for one's organization. To give an example, in Italy, the brokering model is mostly used by single organizations or by bipartite partnerships to set up complex projects with external stakeholders (e.g., universities that set up independent organizations to deal with industry relations, municipalities that create independent organizations to deal with local fundraising for public innovation, private firms that create a task force for social innovation projects, etc.). These projects still represent a very small fraction of the total expenditure in research and development of Italian public and private organizations, but they are on the rise, just as the hybrid multi-stakeholder project that we have presented in this study (see Muscio 2010). Our findings suggest that while brokering organizations with few shareholders can thrive by hyper-specializing in a set of goals that their shareholders have in common, this is not applicable to brokering organizations that are accountable for broad and potentially divergent goals pertaining to a high number of shareholders from different sectors. The risks that we emphasized in this case study are distributed across a continuum that goes from difficulties to negotiate heterogeneous goals, on the one hand, to the tendency to establish overarching goals that are broad enough to encompass shareholders' divergent interests, on the one hand, but also ambiguous enough to be misrecognized by them, on the other hand (see overflowing goals).

Another important risk is the difficulty that brokering organizations encounter in maintaining both authority and responsibility on the goals assigned to them by shareholders (see split hierarchy and unaccountability), as well as maintaining shareholders' commitment to financing their activities (see opportunistic behavior, marginal assignments, and decreasing investments). In particular, we have shown that the difficulty to capture investments might determine brokering organizations to spend more time looking for shareholders' financial support than reaching the objectives assigned to them. This, in turn, impacts negatively on their image and on the perception that they can generate value for the shareholders and for the community of stakeholders at large.

The platform model overcomes such problems because it gives space to public institutions, businesses, and other social institutions to come together directly, without intermediation. The units of innovation (UI) here described represent self-determined groups that, by making use of the supportive functions of the platform, collaborate to carry forward projects of direct concern for shareholders. When a cross-sector partnership becomes organized like an open platform, the boundaries between shareholders and stakeholders (interested individuals, organizations, or communities that are situated outside the partnership) become blurred. The UI can be thus seen as small businesses that plan, finance, implement, promote, and monitor projects of direct concern but which have the particularity that their members represent both the innovation unit and the partnering organizations. Then what matters is that the parties that create an innovation unit maintain full control on goal setting, resource allocation, and project implementation, regardless of their more or less stable affiliation with the partnership. Since the destiny of the UI depends directly on their efforts, they must act as entrepreneurs, actively looking for support for the innovation unit, rather than delegating to the broker. In other words, the previously mentioned paradox is resolved such that organizations no longer delegate broad objectives but work with other interested parties to select and make them come to life. Needless to say, this can also trigger some negative consequences, such as the increasing complexity that involved parties confront with inside and outside the partnership, scarcity of competent resources, or tendency to stabilize some coalitions in order to lower the complexity of managing a highly diverse portfolio of innovation units. Another particularity of the platform business model is that by emphasizing the active roles of the partnering organization, the role of the brokering organization becomes one of technical support. While this may appear like a downgrade, it actually deals more realistically with what a small organization can do for a high number of partners which manifest little willingness to make large investments in joint projects of uncertain outcomes. As we have seen, precisely because of the uncertain outcomes that a collaboration with diverse stakeholders will bring for each of the involved parties, actors may feel entitled to push their own goals in the partnership agenda and show reluctance in delegating the control over partnership decisions (see also Austin and Seitanidi 2012).

It is important to notice that in addition to the abolishment of the generic mission and to disintermediation, another fundamental advantage provided by the platform model has to do with the capacity to mobilize network externalities. While in the broker model, the brokering organization is responsible for finding resources and assembling them around specific shareholder interests; in the platform model, the boundary organization has a mere support role, identifying synergies between projects and suggesting more efficient recombination across innovation units. Yet, as stressed earlier, it is the innovation unit that maintains at all times full responsibility for making the project grow – i.e., creating connections with other potential interested parties and promoting projects to the community at large. The brokering organization can offer a broad range of services in support of these activities but only if the members of the innovation unit have clearly indicated the nature and direction of their needs. From this standpoint, the boundary organization acts as a warranty for the rationalization of the activities hosted on the platform, creating communication and reporting infrastructures inside and across units of innovation. Most importantly, the brokering organization in the platform model identifies synergies and establishes a strategic direction to ensure the growth of the platform over time, on the one hand, and the reinforcement of its identity, on the other.

We would like to point out that the platform model is not without flaws and risks. First, the flow on the platform depends heavily on the strength of the entrepreneurial interests of the partnering organizations. Second, it depends on their ability to attract the interests of other actors inside and outside the partnership as to create functioning and autonomous innovation units. In the absence of these conditions, the network becomes less dense, and the ability to mobilize network externalities also becomes more modest. The network effect in the platform model is highly important because the main advantages of participating to an innovation platform derive not so much from the services provided by the boundary organization but from the opportunities arising from complex networks of social and economic interests (see Koschmann et al. 2012). Most importantly, innovation units are also difficult to manage because they entail actors with different backgrounds and partially divergent objectives. The management of such units can provide significant challenges for partners and for members of the brokering organizations who are called to act as facilitators. Although this last aspect has received less attention both in research and in practice, it is particularly important to set up appropriate infrastructures in support of the professionalization of boundary brokers, such as training offers, policy guidelines, or access to existing best practices (Hundal 2014; Jupp 2000; Warner 2003).

Another key aspect for understanding business model innovation in cross-sector partnerships is the transition between business models. As the literature on business model innovation suggests, questioning the current business model, and going through trial and error processes to modify it, constitutes without doubt a trigger for change, on the one hand, but it also brings along potential negative consequences, such as higher levels of uncertainty, rising complexity, and spirals of conflicts and mistrust (Massa and Tucci 2013). If this is true for organizations, it can be even more so for cross-sector interorganizational partnerships that entail high levels of uncertainty, complexity, and conflictuality per se. Our case study testifies the thin line between questioning the actual business model, innovating it, and declaring the failure of the partnership. For instance, we have shown that in the transition stage, partners' problems with the business model led them to experience a generalize state of paralysis in decision-making and project management, which almost caused the dissolvement of the partnership. It was only thanks to the presence of some catalyzing factors – i.e., pressures to avoid failure, persisting need to accomplish the goals that brought them in the partnership in the first place, and compulsion to complete the initiated collaboration – that partners decided to keep looking for alternative solutions. However, in cases in which these catalyzing factors are missing or are less impactful, partners might decide to throw in the towel rather than sustain the efforts and uncertainties entailed by a new business model. The question that rises spontaneous is: Given the fragility of hybrid partnerships, especially in the beginning phases (Doz and Boburoglu 2000; Austin and Seitanidi 2012), is it worthy to try a business model innovation if there are signs that the model in place is not performing well, or is it more convenient to try to ensure partnership stability and wait for the consolidation of the current model? Evidence from the literature suggests that the ability to continuously adjust plays a very important aspect in the evolution of a partnership (Eden and Huxham 2001; Majchrzak et al. 2015). Future research might investigate when and whether small steps of business innovation can allow for swifter and less destabilizing translations (see also Sosna et al. 2010).

All in all, ecosystems that encompass the public and the private domain develop around fuzzy sets of relations between multiple organizations with heterogeneous goals and interests (Hartley et al. 2013; Selsky and Parker 2005; Waddell and Brown 1997). Although interest in the nature, evolution, and conceptualization of hybrid partnerships has been remarkable, literature has shared a tendency to portray these forms of collaboration as win-win situations of which all stakeholders benefit (Austin and Seitanidi 2012; Linder and Rosenau 2000). Yet little is known about business model adopting in such settings, and the logics and mechanisms that allow actors to innovate their business models (Vurro et. 2010; Dahan et al. 2010). Two business models of hybrid partnerships have been discussed in this chapter, the brokering model and the platform model. While the platform model seems more appropriate for complex projects in which heterogeneous cross-sector interests coexist, both models present advantages and disadvantages. We have suggested that attention should be given to identifying, signaling, and managing both advantages and disadvantages in a relational manner, by focusing on how the business model innovation will impact on each parameter of the current model and, at the same time, on how manageable the parameters of the new model are in terms of partnership strategy, structure, and mobilizable resources.

References

Amit, R., & Zott, C. (2012). Creating value through business model innovation. *MIT Sloan Management Review, 53*(3), 41.

Arino, A., & De La Torre, J. (1998). Learning from failure: Towards an evolutionary model of collaborative ventures. *Organization Science, 9*(3), 306–325.

Austin, J. E., & Seitanidi, M. M. (2012). Collaborative value creation: A review of partnering between nonprofits and businesses. Part 2: Partnership processes and outcomes. *Nonprofit and Voluntary Sector Quarterly.*, 0899764012454685, *41*, 929–968.

Bernier, L., & Hafsi, T. (2007). The changing nature of public entrepreneurship. *Public Administration Review, 67*(3), 488–503.

Bryson, J. M., Crosby, B. C., & Stone, M. M. (2006). The design and implementation of cross-sector collaborations: Propositions from the literature. *Public Administration Review, 66*, 44–55.

Bryson, J. M., Crosby, B. C., & Stone, M. M. (2015). Designing and implementing cross-sector collaborations: Needed and challenging. *Public Administration Review, 75*(5), 647–663.

Casadesus-Masanell, R., & Ricart, J. E. (2010). From strategy to business models and onto tactics. *Long Range Planning, 43*(2), 195–215.

Cavalcante, S., Kesting, P., & Ulhøi, J. (2011). Business model dynamics and innovation: (Re) establishing the missing linkages. *Management Decision, 49*(8), 1327–1342.

Chesbrough, H. (2010). Business model innovation: Opportunities and barriers. *Long Range Planning, 43*(2), 354–363.

Chesbrough, H., & Schwartz, K. (2007). Innovating business models with co-development partnerships. *Research-Technology Management, 50*(1), 55–59.

Commission of the European Communities. (2014). *An introduction to EU cohesion policy 2014–2020*. http://ec.europa.eu/regional_policy/sources/docgener/informat/basic/basic_2014_en.pdf

Corbett, A., & Katz, J. A. (2012). Introduction: The action of entrepreneurs. In A. C. Corbett & J. A. Katz (Eds.), *Entrepreneurial action* (Advances in entrepreneurship, firm emergence and growth, volume 14). Emerald Group Publishing Limited.

Dahan, N. M., Doh, J. P., Oetzel, J., & Yaziji, M. (2010). Corporate-NGO collaboration: Co-creating new business models for developing markets. *Long Range Planning, 43*(2), 326–342.

Damanpour, F., & Schneider, M. (2009). Characteristics of innovation and innovation adoption in public organizations: Assessing the role of managers. *Journal of Public Administration Research and Theory, 19*(3), 495–522.

Doz, Y., & Baburoglu, O. (2000). From competition to collaboration: The emergence and evolution of R&D cooperatives. In *Cooperative strategy: Economics, business and organisational issues* (pp. 173–192).

Eden, C., & Huxham, C. (2001). The negotiation of purpose in multi-organizational collaborative groups. *Journal of Management Studies, 38*(3), 373–391.

Googins, B. K., & Rochlin, S. A. (2000). Creating the partnership society: Understanding the rhetoric and reality of cross-sectoral partnerships. *Business and Society Review, 105*(1), 127–144.

Hartley, J., Sørensen, E., & Torfing, J. (2013). Collaborative innovation: A viable alternative to market competition and organizational entrepreneurship. *Public Administration Review, 73*(6), 821–830.

Hjorth, D. (2013). Public entrepreneurship: Desiring social change, creating sociality. *Entrepreneurship and Regional Development, 25*(1–2), 34–51.

Hundal, S. (2014). The role partnership brokers play in creating effective social partnerships. In *Social partnerships and responsible business: A research handbook* (p. 420).

Jupp, B. (2000). *Working together: Creating a better environment for cross-sector partnerships* (Vol. 23). London: Demos.

Kivleniece, I., & Quelin, B. V. (2012). Creating and capturing value in public-private ties: A private actor's perspective. *Academy of Management Review, 37*(2), 272–299.

Koschmann, M. A., Kuhn, T. R., & Pfarrer, M. D. (2012). A communicative framework of value in cross-sector partnerships. *Academy of Management Review, 37*(3), 332–354.

Le Ber, M. J., & Branzei, O. (2010a). (Re)forming strategic cross-sector partnerships relational processes of social innovation. *Business & Society, 49*(1), 140–172.

Le Ber, M. J., & Branzei, O. (2010b). Value frame fusion in cross sector interactions. *Journal of Business Ethics, 94*, 163-195.

Leitão, J. & Alves, H. (2016). *Entrepreneurial and innovative practices in public institutions: A quality of life approach, applying quality of life research: best practices*. Cham: Springer.

Linder, S. H., & Rosenau, P. V. (2000). *Mapping the terrain of public-private policy partnership: Public-private policy partnerships*. Cambridge, MA: MIT Press.

Lunnan, R., & Haugland, S. A. (2008). Predicting and measuring alliance performance: A multidimensional analysis. *Strategic Management Journal, 29*(5), 545–556.

Majchrzak, A., Jarvenpaa, S. L., & Bagherzadeh, M. (2015). A review of interorganizational collaboration dynamics. *Journal of Management, 41*(5), 1338–1360.

Massa, L., & Tucci, C. L. (2013). Business model innovation. In *The Oxford handbook of innovation management* (pp. 420–441). Oxford: Oxford University Press.

Mitchell, D., & Coles, C. (2003). The ultimate competitive advantage of continuing business model innovation. *Journal of Business Strategy, 24*(5), 15–21.

Morris, M. H., & Jones, F. F. (1999). Entrepreneurship in established organizations: The case of the public sector. *Entrepreneurship: Theory and Practice, 24*(1), 71–71.

Morris, M., Schindehutte, M., & Allen, J. (2005). The entrepreneur's business model: Toward a unified perspective. *Journal of Business Research, 58*(6), 726–735.

Muscio, A. (2010). What drives the university use of technology transfer offices? Evidence from Italy. *The Journal of Technology Transfer, 35*(2), 181–202.

Romano, A., Passiante, G., Del Vecchio, P., & Secundo, G. (2014). The innovation ecosystem as booster for the innovative entrepreneurship in the smart specialisation strategy. *International Journal of Knowledge-Based Development, 5*(3), 271–288.

Rondinelli, D. A., & London, T. (2003). How corporations and environmental groups cooperate: Assessing cross-sector alliances and collaborations. *The Academy of Management Executive, 17*(1), 61–76.

Selsky, J. W., & Parker, B. (2005). Cross-sector partnerships to address social issues: Challenges to theory and practice. *Journal of Management, 31*(6), 849–873.

Skelcher, C. (2005). Public-private partnerships and hybridity. In *The Oxford handbook of public management* (pp. 347–370). Oxford: Oxford University Press.

Sosna, M., Trevinyo-Rodríguez, R. N., & Velamuri, S. R. (2010). Business model innovation through trial-and-error learning: The Naturhouse case. *Long Range Planning, 43*(2), 383–407.

Teece, D. J. (2010). Business models, business strategy and innovation. *Long Range Planning, 43*(2), 172–194.

Turcotte, M.-F., & Pasquero, J. (2001). The paradox of multistakeholder collaborative roundtables. *The Journal of Applied Behavioral Science, 37*(4), 447–464.

Ungureanu, P., Bellesia, F., Bertolotti, F., & Mattarelli, E. (2016, January). Institutional Frames and Collaboration Expectations in Hybrid Interorganizational Partnerships. *In Academy of Management Proceedings, 2016*(1), 15769. Academy of Management.

Vurro, C., Dacin, M. T., & Perrini, F. (2010). Institutional antecedents of partnering for social change: How institutional logics shape cross-sector social partnerships. *Journal of Business Ethics, 94*, 39–53.

Waddell, S., & Brown, L. D. (1997). *Fostering intersectoral partnering: A guide to promoting cooperation among government, business, and civil society actors* (Vol. 13). Boston: Institute for Development Research (IDR).

Warner, M. (2003). *Partnerships for sustainable development: Do we need partnership brokers*. London: ODI.

Zerbinati, S., & Souitaris, V. (2005). Entrepreneurship in the public sector: A framework of analysis in European local governments. *Entrepreneurship and Regional Development, 17*(1), 43–64.

Zott, C., Amit, R., & Massa, L. (2011). The business model: Recent developments and future research. *Journal of Management, 37*(4), 1019–1042.

Chapter 15
Development of an Innovation Ecosystem in a Fast-Paced Economic Environment: The Case of the Vodafone Open Innovation Program

Alexander Kerl

Abstract Many companies experience a blurring of traditional industry boundaries. This challenge forces companies from various industries to look for alternative ways toward being innovative. One approach is to start initiatives for multi-cross-industry innovations. These cross-industry activities may lead to the development of new innovation ecosystems. In this context, I pose the central research question: By what kind of organizational framework are initiatives for multi-cross-industry innovation supported, and how can companies utilize this approach for the generation of new innovation ecosystems?

Following this research question, I conduct an in-depth case study of the Vodafone Open Innovation Program which can be characterized as a multi-cross-industry innovation network of the Vodafone GmbH. I present the organizational model of the Vodafone Open Innovation Program and show key characteristics of the case, before I establish that multi-cross-industry activities may lead to the generation of new innovation ecosystems. In this context, the structured approach of the entire program and the staged intellectual property rights mechanism will especially be highlighted as key characteristics.

Keywords Innovation ecosystem • Multi-cross-industry innovation • Organizational structure • Converging industries • Case study • IP management

---

A. Kerl (✉)
Institute of Project Management and Innovation, University of Bremen, Bremen, Germany
e-mail: Alexander.Kerl@innovation.uni-bremen.de

© Springer International Publishing AG 2018   305
J. Leitão et al. (eds.), *Entrepreneurial, Innovative and Sustainable*
Ecosystems, Applying Quality of Life Research,
https://doi.org/10.1007/978-3-319-71014-3_15

15.1 Introduction: The Need for Innovation Across Industry Boundaries

The open innovation paradigm elaborated by Chesbrough (2003) states a shift from a "closed to an open innovation paradigm" (Chesbrough 2003). At first, companies opened their innovation departments to their respective industries (Gillier et al. 2010), as the integration of interorganizational knowledge results in innovative products (Rosell and Lakemond 2012). Initially, this did lead to more innovative products and also to a decrease in efficiency in the long term, as developed solutions started showing fewer variations (Emden et al. 2006; Datta and Jessup 2013). In order to obtain more distant knowledge, companies took to cooperating with enterprises beyond the boundaries of their industries (Heil 2015). Obvious examples of products or services that originated from cross-industry development activities are Smart TVs or Smart Homes.

The development process of such products involves a variety of companies from different industries. Companies that aim at developing innovative products contribute to increasing industry convergence. The latter phenomenon is intensively discussed in scientific literature and describes a continuous blurring of traditional industry boundaries (e.g. Curran et al. 2010; Jaspers et al. 2012; Dowling et al. 1998; Gambardella and Torrisi 1998, 2009; Kim et al. 2015). Hacklin et al. (2009) describe this phenomenon as a sequential process. They identified four stages of convergence in the information and communication technology (ICT) industries, namely, (1) knowledge convergence, (2) technological convergence, (3) applicational convergence, and (4) industry convergence.

According to Jaspers et al. (2012), the industry convergence spawns new segments which are located in between formerly distant industrial branches. Innovations originating from segments like these are called multi-cross-industry innovations, according to Khan et al. (2013). This concept leads to new challenges regarding established innovation management literature, as elaborated by Hauschildt and Salomo (2011), Ahmed and Shepherd (2010) and Goffin et al. (2009), which deals with the innovation management of individual companies rather than with the management of more than two companies from different industries.

While we know a lot about the reasons why companies cooperate with one another (e.g. cost and risk sharing, reducing time to market, development of skills and competences, etc. (Gillier et al. 2010; Hagedoorn and Duysters 2002)), we still know fairly little about how companies can foster their engagement in such initiatives (e.g. Khan et al. 2013; Kerl and Moehrle 2015; Gillier et al. 2010). Especially the organizational framework of these partnerships and the key characteristics of such collaborative initiatives may be assumed to differ from what existing innovation management literature describes (van Lente et al. 2003). Furthermore, I think that the engagement in cross-industry collaborations may be a starting point for the development of a new innovation ecosystem, as this concept is typically defined as "collaborative arrangements through which firms combine their individual offerings into a coherent, customer-facing solution" (Adner 2006). Hence, an innovation ecosystem may comprise different companies from various industries that collaborate with one another toward a common goal (West and Wood 2013).

Consequently, the following research question is posed: By what kind of organizational framework are initiatives for multi-cross-industry innovation supported, and how can companies utilize this approach for the generation of new innovation ecosystems? In order to investigate this research question, an in-depth case study of the Vodafone Open Innovation Program, which can be characterized as a German multi-cross-industry innovation network of one of the largest telecommunication companies worldwide, is conducted.

15.2 Multi-Cross-Industry Innovation Initiatives and Innovation Ecosystems: Conceptual Aspects

Multi-cross-industry innovation as a specific type of cross-industry innovation derives from scientific literature of the 1980s. According to Jaffe (1986), a technical spillover across industries has a positive influence on a company's R&D productivity. Kotabe and Scott Swan (1995) state that cross-industry alliances tend to be indicative of more innovative products than the cooperation of companies with partners from their own key business industries. Today, the phenomenon of cross-industry cooperation is intensively discussed in the scientific literature (e.g. Alves et al. 2007; Brockhoff et al. 1991; Couchman and Beckett 2006; Enkel and Gassmann 2010; Enkel and Heil 2014; Fischer and Varga 2002; Fukugawa 2006; Gassmann et al. 2010; Levén et al. 2014; Lew and Sinkovics 2013; Murphy et al. 2012; Sammarra and Biggiero 2008). It is based on two strategic management approaches: the knowledge-based view (Grant 1996; Grant and Baden-Fuller 2004; Kogut and Zander 1992) and the open innovation theory, as elaborated by Chesbrough (2003). Khan and Möhrle (2012) first introduced the concept of multi-cross-industry innovation as a specific form of cross-industry innovation. They describe multi-cross-industry innovation as the process of creating new products, services, or combinations thereof by combining core knowledge elements from at least three different industries in a significantly new way in order to successfully develop and implement new businesses (Khan and Möhrle 2012).

The differentiation between cross-industry innovation and the concept of multi-cross-industry innovation chiefly pertains to the number of actors involved in the cooperation process. Multi-cross-industry innovation activities are characterized by cooperation activities of at least three organizations from different industries. However, an increasing number of actors involved in the development process seem to enhance the network complexity and lead to new challenges in terms of innovation management literature (Khan and Möhrle 2012). The key challenges regarding multi-cross-industry innovation concern overcoming the cognitive distance between representatives of different industries, developing an environment characterized by trust and personal relationships, and transferring knowledge from one industry partner to another (Cohen and Levinthal 1990; Enkel and Gassmann 2010; Gassmann et al. 2010; Lichtenthaler and Lichtenthaler 2010).

As initiatives for multi-cross-industry innovation typically take place in externally managed innovation networks, these networks may be seen as starting points for the emergence of new innovation ecosystems. The concept of innovation ecosystems is based on an analogy between biological ecosystems and business ecosystems proposed by Moore (1993), who suggests that "a company be viewed not as a member of a single industry but as part of a business ecosystem that crosses a variety of industries" (Moore 1993) and defines a business ecosystem as an environment in which "companies coevolve capabilities around a new innovation: they work co-operatively and competitively to support new products, satisfy customer needs, and eventually incorporate the next round of innovations" (Moore 1993). According to this definition and to other influential researchers in the field of innovation ecosystems, like Iansiti and Levien (2004) and Adner (2006), companies "should increasingly move away from industry-focused strategic planning towards strategizing within and around ecosystems" (Autio and Thomas 2014). Therefore, the concept of innovation ecosystems seems to be a promising opportunity for companies to engage in open innovation activities like multi-cross-industry innovations within an ecosystem environment. Especially companies faced with challenges resulting from converging industries may benefit from cross-industry collaborations within an innovation ecosystem, because the ecosystem as a whole gives its members access to a highly diverse knowledge base.

In the following chapters, I use the term innovation ecosystem instead of business ecosystem in order to place an emphasis on the innovation activities within such ecosystems. The term innovation ecosystem is also used in other scientific literature (e.g. Adner 2006; Adner and Kapoor 2010; Mercan and Goktas 2011; Dedehayir and Seppänen 2015).

15.3 Selection of the Case Example and Research Setting

For the exploration of the phenomenon of multi-cross-industry innovation in an ecosystem environment, I choose an exploratory approach in accordance with Yin (2014) and Eisenhardt (1989), as the identification of comparable cases and the analysis of cases are of a complex nature. There are many networks which are recognizable as innovation networks, but there are few innovation networks which meet the requirements of a multi-cross-industry innovation network as described above. In addition, to sharpen the selection, I specify the following three criteria:

- The multi-cross-industry innovation network should be managed by an own and specific management entity in order to distinguish between characteristics of a leading organization and the innovation ecosystem.
- Since I regard innovation as a continuous activity of an organization, the multi-cross-industry innovation network should aim for a long-term focus.

- Furthermore, the multi-cross-industry innovation network should be active in a fast paced economic environment, as the challenges of innovation management are particularly high in this kind of environment.

Consequently, the form of the study is contemporary, and the identification of suitable research objects is an ongoing task for researchers and companies alike.

The exploratory approach is realized in form of an in-depth case study. A case study analysis allows the deduction of new concepts, hypotheses, and theories and is the preferred method "in situations when (1) the main research questions are 'how' or 'why' questions; (2) a researcher has little or no control over behavioral events; and (3) the focus of study is a contemporary (as opposed to entirely historical) phenomenon" (Yin 2014).

I select the case example of the Vodafone Open Innovation Program due to the program's general organizational structure and aim. Compared to other German multi-cross-industry innovation networks, the Vodafone Open Innovation Program is embedded in the Vodafone Innovation Park and primarily aims at the development of innovative business models. The Vodafone Open Innovation Program deals with multi-cross-industry innovations and consequently heads for cross-industry collaborations with companies, start-ups, research institutions, and universities. Alongside with existing bi- and multilateral development partnerships, the program periodically allows the initiation of new multi-cross-industry initiatives. In contrast to other German multi-cross-industry innovation networks, the Vodafone Open Innovation Program can be categorized as a commercial network to which every organization effectively has access as long as it is willing to pay the required participation fee.

In 2015, the network activities of the Vodafone Open Innovation Program are concerned with the focal points of digital economy and smart living. In one section of digital economy, the participating members deal with topics like customer experience, e-commerce, and machine-to-machine communication. The focal point of smart living combines the ongoing digitalization of home appliances, wearable technologies in the field of mobile health, general mobility (like autonomous driving), sustainability, and sharing. In summary, the program is aimed at facing the challenges that companies have to deal with in times of progressing digitalization and the dissolution of established industry boundaries. All these points make the Vodafone Open Innovation Program a highly suitable research object.

Case study relevant primary data was generated through semi-structured in-depth interviews with four representatives of the Vodafone Open Innovation Program and by 2 days of participation in the Vodafone Open Innovation Program in April and again in June 2015. All interviews are conducted on different organizational levels, speaking with the managing director, the head of department, a senior consultant, and a consultant from the Vodafone Innovation Park. All in all, six interviews with the four representatives mentioned above were conducted. The first round of interviews was conducted in 2013, and the second round in 2015 and 2016. Each round comprised three interviews of differing duration. The length ranged from 26 to 107 min, with an average of 62 min. Five of these six interviews were conducted in personal meetings, and one was conducted by telephone. I chose to conduct the interviews in two rounds with nearly the same interview partners (two of all four representatives were identical in both interview rounds) in order to gain a better understanding of the implementation process of the Vodafone Open Innovation Program and the decisions made during the interval between both rounds.

The questions for the interviews were developed before the empirical process started. A general interview guide was developed which was then modified according to the respective interview partner's position in the Vodafone Company. All in all, the interview guide was divided into four sections: Sect. 1 involved questions about the interview partner's position, Sect. 2 was concerned with the company and the network, Sect. 3 with the specific organizational structure of the network, and Sect. 4 consisted of questions regarding key characteristics based on previous literature.

To avoid a possible bias, all data was triangulated with secondary data. The secondary data consists of presentations, brochures, publications, business reports, and materials collected during participation in the program. For analysis purposes, the data was coded in accordance with Miles et al. (2014) and Silverman (2010). Coding was performed in two successive steps: first, all interview data was coded with concepts used by the participants, also referred to as in vivo coding (Corbin and Strauss 2015), and second, the initial coding was enhanced by means of analysis characteristics based on the work of Kerl and Moehrle (2015), Khan et al. (2013), and Pittaway et al. (2004). In cases of ambiguous information, follow-up talks were conducted.

15.4   Observations in the Case of the Vodafone Open Innovation Program

Due to its aforementioned characteristics, the Vodafone Open Innovation Program proves to be a suitable research object for investigating the organizational structure and specific key characteristics of a multi-cross-industry innovation network in a fast-paced economic environment. Furthermore, it allows investigating the question whether multi-cross-industry innovation activities are a suitable instrument for the development of an innovation ecosystem.

In the following section, the organizational model and specific network characteristics of the Vodafone Open Innovation Program are described. Furthermore, I present the results of the case analysis, based on previously identified key elements of success.

15.4.1 The Organizational Model of the Vodafone Open Innovation Program

The following description of the organizational model of the Vodafone Open Innovation Program focuses on its basic organization, network type, and network composition.

Basic organization: Being part of the Vodafone Innovation Park, the Vodafone Open Innovation Program is organized as a spin-off organization. According to the head of the Vodafone Innovation Park, a spin-off organization ensures the flexibility and responsiveness required by a multi-cross-industry network acting in the field of digital communication. Moreover, a spin-off organization is able to commercialize research and development results, align the innovation system with the open innovation approach, and facilitate networking on the company level (EIRMA 2003; Parhankangas 2001; Rohrbeck et al. 2009). A lack of know-how and methodical competence regarding the management of a cross-industry network initiative like the Vodafone Open Innovation Program led to the appointment of an external open innovation company which took over the general management of the Vodafone Open Innovation Program in 2015.

The basic structure of the program is illustrated in Fig. 15.1 and follows a standard stage-gate approach. The program is divided into four key elements: before potential participants attend the first workshop, they are informed about the basic concept, idea, and structure of the Vodafone Open Innovation Program by means of so-called preliminary information talks. After these preliminary information talks, companies are given the option to pay a participation fee that allows them to take part in either the first workshop, respectively, think tank or in the entire process depicted in Fig. 15.1.

During the semi-structured think tank, the participating companies are asked to develop new innovative ideas for business models either in the field of digital economy or smart living, depending on the program's focus. For the idea-generating process, all members are asked to think up to five ideas in 5 min time in tandem teams. After the first 5 min, each team member elaborates the ideas generated by his/her tandem partner for another 5 min. This process can be categorized as a standard brainwriting method, which is not specially designed for the generation of innovative business models like the integrated approach by Halecker and Hartmann (2013), who posited a systems thinking approach for the generation of business

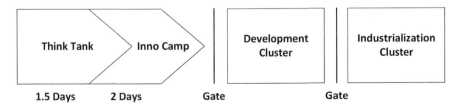

Fig. 15.1 Structure of the Vodafone Open Innovation Program (Source: Author)

model innovations. Subsequently, all generated ideas are discussed by the tandem teams, and three have to be selected for specification. The specification process follows a light version of the Business Model Canvas approach developed by Osterwalder and Pigneur (2010) and seems to be helpful to the participants in terms of structuring and specifying their business models. After working on three ideas for innovative business models, the whole group is asked to rate all ideas by means of points. Each participant is allowed to give up to six points to each individual idea. On the basis of this analysis, new working groups are assigned. The size of these groups is not standardized but based upon the previous voting process. At the close of the workshop, all specified ideas for business models are presented, discussed, and documented in order to enable a further discussion and development of ideas in an online workspace accessible to registered participants only.

Comparable to the think tank workshops, the inno camp workshops are also semi-structured and aimed at the ongoing development and specification of ideas generated in the preceding think tank. There is a mix of structured phases with moderated discussions and the application of creativity techniques, and there are unstructured phases in which the participants are asked to refine their business models in heterogeneous working groups. In 2013 the results of the inno camp workshop were documented by the participants themselves. They did not have the advantage of any tool or method like the Business Model Canvas. Considering the newly assigned network management, it is probable that the upcoming inno camp workshops will see the application of specific methods or tools such as the Business Model Canvas and the like.

After being processed in the think tank and inno camp workshops, the generated ideas have to pass a decision gate. Interested members have to find cooperation partners with whom they sign a development agreement. This agreement is highly customized and deals with intellectual property rights and resource allocation issues. The aim of the third stage, the so-called development cluster, is to realize first prototypes and refine the business models. This stage is marked by profoundly individual cooperation activities. So far, one development cluster could be reached by one initiative in 2013.

After its successful development in the development cluster, an initiative has to pass another gate where all participating companies decide whether the business model is economic and whether further investments should be made. The operational aim of the industrialization cluster is to finalize the business model and to achieve market maturity.

Network type: The Vodafone Open Innovation Program can be characterized as a hybrid network type. On the one hand, the Vodafone Open Innovation Program shows characteristics of an informal network as described by Fischer and Varga (2002) — especially in the first stages of the organizational structure. Although there is a defined structure in place, the initiating company Vodafone does not stipulate many regulations. On the other hand, the more the process reaches a matured stage in the organizational structure, the more regulations have to be met. On the whole, the program seems to involve more standardized processes than "network relations of a mainly informal nature" (Fischer and Varga 2002).

Network composition: The Vodafone Open Innovation Program aims at a high degree of heterogeneity. There are basically no limitations that concern the application for participation, except for the requirement that potential companies are asked to depute representatives from their innovation departments or at least representatives who are deeply involved in the company specific innovation process and except for the fact that all participants, i.e. companies, have to pay a participation fee to an amount depending on the number of workshops they wish to attend. According to Nooteboom et al. (2007), the effect of cognitive distance related to the overall innovation performance is U-shaped. In consequence, there is an optimal cognitive distance respectively heterogeneity of the participating members in relation to the innovation performance. However, the aim should not be a preferably high degree of cognitive distance but rather "to find partners at sufficient cognitive distance to tell something new, but not so distant as to preclude mutual understanding" (Nooteboom et al. 2007). Melander and Lopez-Vega (2013) suggest that in development projects, which can be characterized by a high degree of technological uncertainty, a detailed selection of cooperation partners is of pivotal importance. Even though their research deals especially with supplier cooperation, their findings can be applied to multi-cross-industry cooperation activities, too. Moreover, Bergendahl and Magnusson (2015) state that the intended type of innovation has an impact on the concept of cognitive distance as well as the supporting knowledge creation processes. Thus, the concept of cognitive distance requires a multidimensional measure which does not only take into account "geographical and organizational distance, but also [...] other dimensions such as technology" (Bergendahl and Magnusson 2015; Konsti-Laakso et al. 2012).

Established initiatives: So far, the Vodafone Open Innovation Program has led to one digital prototype of an innovative business model. Due to nondisclosure agreements between the participating companies and the Vodafone GmbH, I am not permitted to refer to this finalized multi-cross-industry innovation in detail before market launch. As regards perceived successes, the organizational model of the Vodafone Open Innovation Program seems to be partially suitable for the program's strategic aim of initiating multi-cross-industry innovations in a fast-paced economic environment and establishing new cooperation links with interindustry as well as cross-industry companies and research institutes in the form of an innovation ecosystem. Participation in the Vodafone Open Innovation Program allows companies to gain insight into foreign industries, to find potential cooperation peers regarding innovative ideas for business models, to develop ideas in the course of network activities, and, as mentioned before, to establish or tighten new or already existing links with other companies and research institutions.

15.4.2 Key Characteristics of the Organizational Model Derived from Case Analysis

The interviews indicate that the Vodafone Open Innovation Program is aimed at facing specific challenges of a fast-paced environment such as the telecommunication industry, which is Vodafone's core business (Hilmola 2012). In order to be able to develop innovative business models in an industry that is characterized by relatively short product life cycles, a more structured and formalized approach seems to be beneficial. Furthermore, the interviews suggest that a high level of absorptive and desorptive capacity and support from the top management seem to have a positive effect on the output performance. On the other hand, an insufficient ability to develop a high level of trust and personal relationships caused by the unstable composition of the network and the absence of multi-cross-industry innovation architects seem to impair development processes at more advanced stages of the program's structure.

Structured approach: In comparison with other German innovation networks that aim to develop an innovation ecosystem, the approach of the Vodafone Open Innovation Program is more structured and formalized. As pointed out above, participants are stimulated by the application of creativity techniques such as the group structured brainwriting technique during workshops. According to Thompson (2003) and Heslin (2009), "Brainwriting groups consistently generate more and better ideas than groups who follow their natural instincts" (Thompson 2003). Hence, the concept of brainwriting may enable the generation of innovative ideas at an early stage of the innovation process. Moreover, a combination of structured and coordinated individual and group working phases seems to have a particularly positive influence on the idea generation process.

Staged intellectual property rights mechanism: As mentioned before, the participating companies are not required to sign any protective contract or agreement dealing with intellectual property rights or nondisclosure in the first two stages of the Vodafone Open Innovation Program structure. After passing the first gate, only those companies which decide to refine the innovative business model or product have to sign a nondisclosure agreement and, if necessary, further contracts dealing with intellectual property rights and resource allocation. Buss and Peukert (2015) state "that there is a link between research and development (R&D) outsourcing and intellectual property (IP) infringement" (Buss and Peukert 2015). Furthermore, they point out that this link is of a positive nature. Hence, development activities occurring in cross-industry networks or R&D cooperations in general increase the infringement risk, depending on the degree of interaction. Jiang et al. (2013) identify two dominant governance mechanisms — trust and formal contracts — which may both influence the degree of knowledge leakage and the occurrence of intellectual property infringements in consequence of this. As mentioned before, the Vodafone Open Innovation Program represents a case in which trust cannot easily develop over a period of several years due to the volatile network composition. Consequently, a staged intellectual property rights mechanism seems to be beneficial in terms of a high degree of interpersonal trust on the one hand and a relatively low risk of intellectual property infringement on the other. Nevertheless, formal contracts may diminish the risk of knowledge leakage at an early stage of a cooperative innovation process. Although Jiang et al. (2013) state that trust (especially competence trust) is a more effective safeguard compared to formal contracts, the latter still allow companies to minimize the risk of knowledge leakage and consequential intellectual property infringements at an early stage of a cooperation.

Absorptive and desorptive capacity: According to Lichtenthaler and Lichtenthaler (2010) as well as Müller-Seitz (2012), a high absorptive and desorptive capacity may lead to a better network innovation performance. Furthermore, Khan et al. (2013) state that "for a profitable co-operation in the multi-cross-industry innovation context, the transfer and implementation of knowledge from as well as to the knowledge base of an enterprise are essential" (Khan et al. 2013). Three characteristics which seem to have a positive influence on the absorptive and desorptive capacity, on either the network or the company level, have been identified in the case of the Vodafone Open Innovation Program. First, the avoidance of restrictions at the early stage of an idea generation process seems to create a common interest in potential multi-cross-industry innovation initiatives by bringing together different knowledge bases. Second, the heterogeneity of the network composition seems to increase the absorptive and desorptive capacity by bringing together different knowledge bases from different industries. Third, all network members can be characterized by their industry-specific knowledge which enables them to actively enhance network knowledge by participating in network activities. Thus, the network as an entity is able to absorb knowledge on the network level, processes knowledge in the course of network activities, and desorbs knowledge on the company level into the respective innovation departments. The ongoing acquisition of new potential network participants also seems to increase the absorptive and desorptive capacity.

Volatile network composition: Due to the fact that the Vodafone Open Innovation Program aims to develop innovative business models in a fast paced-environment like the telecommunication industry, the program has to deal with the corresponding challenges as mentioned before. Therefore, the network structure is not geared to a long-term existence, evolving over several years, but to intensive short-term workshops. Potential members have the option to participate in the entire program or only in its first stage, depending on the purchased workshop package. The consequence is an unstable composition of the network, which may, on the one hand, lead to a high absorptive and desorptive capacity but on the other hand seems to impair a long-term network cooperation. According to findings by Kerl and Moehrle (2015), trust may be a key success factor for a long-term oriented network.

Multi-cross-industry innovation architect: In order to be successful in a network environment with an initial idea, different companies have to cooperate intensively over a specific time frame. Khan et al. (2013) identified the role of the multi-cross-industry innovation architect, hereinafter referred to as architect, in a different German multi-cross-industry innovation network. The architect takes over two key roles within the development process. One is that he "provides the first problem or need from which the subject is derived and additionally acts as a booster by being more active and committing more resources" (Khan et al. 2013). Other case studies show that the role of the architect is of pivotal importance for the overall network innovation performance (Khan et al. 2013; Kerl and Moehrle 2015). The interviews I conducted and the information gathered by attending the Vodafone Open Innovation think tank and inno camp workshops suggest that the involvement of at least one architect is also of pivotal importance in the Vodafone Open Innovation Program. The architect's role resembles that of a promoter according to Hauschildt and Salomo (2011) as well as that of a product champion according to Markham and Aiman-Smith (2001). The "promoter theory focuses on several specialists to overcome different barriers to innovation, while champion theory concentrates on generalists playing multiple roles" (Rese et al. 2013). Furthermore, the architect has a stronger need to solve a specific problem or develop a specific business model or product. Hence, the architect is willing to invest more resources and convince other representatives to participate in a specific initiative. In the case of the Vodafone Open Innovation Program, this role is partly taken on by the network itself. Nevertheless a study by Rese et al. (2013) shows that successful interorganizational innovation projects are characterized by the existence of role players who bear characteristics of champions. So the incidental lack of at least one architect seems to be one reason for the low-output rate of the first Open Innovation Program in 2013.

15.4.3 Development of an Innovation Ecosystem

The case of the Vodafone Open Innovation Program is an example of a single company aiming at the establishment of (multi-)cross-industry innovation activities by engaging several organizations from different industries in organized multiday workshops. As shown above, the Vodafone Open Innovation Program bears characteristics of a multi-cross-industry innovation network. In order to answer the research question as to how multi-cross-industry activities lead to the development of new innovation ecosystems, we have to investigate the starting point of an innovation ecosystem. The theoretical definitions of innovation networks and innovation ecosystems are not clear-cut. Several definitions of both concepts exist simultaneously, which is why I define activities that take place during the organized program as network activities. In the case of the Vodafone Open Innovation Program, some initiatives for collaborations are carried out outside the program, including new collaboration partners who are not part of the Vodafone Open Innovation Program yet.

Although it is hard to define where network activities end and where innovation ecosystem activities start, I regard the long-term involvement of new collaboration partners from outside the program's organizational setting as a starting point for the emergence of a new innovation ecosystem. From this point on, all involved parties collaborate with one another outside the program's structure, acquiring or simply involving new partners from various industries.

Figure 15.2 visualizes three different types of innovation ecosystems aimed at by the management of the Vodafone Open Innovation Program. The first ecosystem, as

15 Development of an Innovation Ecosystem in a Fast-Paced Economic Environment...   317

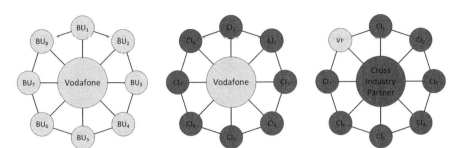

Fig. 15.2 Different types of innovation ecosystems aimed for by the Vodafone Open Innovation Program (Source: Author)

depicted in Fig. 15.2, shows an internal innovation ecosystem of the Vodafone GmbH, in which the company acts as a central member of the ecosystem, collaborating with several internal business units (BU_x) of the same company. The idea of this approach is to create links between different business units of a multinational company like the Vodafone GmbH in order to achieve cross-industry innovation results without having to go beyond the company boundaries. The second and third ecosystems, as depicted in Fig. 15.2, visualize two types of the cross-industry innovation ecosystem. Both comprise the Vodafone GmbH in collaboration with cross-industry partners (CI_x). In the second one, the Vodafone GmbH acts as a leading/centric member of the ecosystem, whereas in the third, it acts like a regular member of an innovation ecosystem, which is mainly steered and influenced by a different organization.

Ultimately, both the interview data and the self-assessment of the management of the Vodafone Open Innovation Program indicate that multi-cross-industry innovation activities are generators of new innovation ecosystems.

15.5 Conclusions

The explorative in-depth case study deals with the questions of what kind of organizational framework serves to support initiatives for multi-cross-industry innovation and how companies can utilize this approach for the generation of new innovation ecosystems. In order to answer these questions, I analyzed a German multi-cross-industry innovation network known as the Vodafone Open Innovation Program, which is part of the Vodafone Open Innovation Park. This multi-cross-industry innovation network can be characterized by its strategic aim to develop innovative business models, setting it apart from other German multi-cross-industry innovation networks which mainly aim at developing innovative products or solutions. Moreover, the Vodafone Open Innovation Program has a management unit of its own, it is focused on long-term innovations, and it is active in the fast-paced economic environment of the telecommunication industry. The study reveals two new key characteristics of a multi-cross-industry innovation network: the use of a staged intellectual property rights mechanism and a formally structured organizational model. Furthermore, I suggest that the Vodafone Open Innovation Program may be seen as a generator of new innovation ecosystems.

From a theoretical perspective, the in-depth case study contributes to multi-cross-industry innovation as well as innovation ecosystem literature, especially in terms of the organizational framework that is required to achieve a high innovation performance and key characteristics that depend on the environment in which the innovation ecosystem is active. Furthermore, the case leads to new questions concerning the concept of multi-cross-industry innovation. One key question is: What organizational model is needed to meet the industry specific challenges, and what characteristics serve to support the organizational model in regard to a high innovation performance? Another question is: How do the different key characteristics affect each other? To answer questions like these, further research in the field of multi-cross-industry innovation and, respectively, innovation ecosystems has to be undertaken.

From a managerial perspective, the study offers a 'good practice' example of how to develop an innovation ecosystem in order to achieve open innovation cross-industry results. Managers may take up this example and transfer it to their institution, taking into account the contingencies of environments. As we have isolated different mechanisms (such as the staged intellectual property rights mechanism) and roles (such as the multi-cross-industry innovation architect), managers may also use these in different settings — for instance, while improving a "closed" innovation process within a company.

One major shortcoming of this study is the fact that I merely analyzed one German multi-cross-industry innovation network that aims at developing innovative business models. Although all case study relevant data has been triangulated, the development of the organizational model of the Vodafone Open Innovation Program has to be further observed to ensure the consistency of the findings. Additionally, further research has to be done in more diverse environments to answer the above-mentioned research questions.

References

Adner, R. (2006). Match your innovation strategy to your innovation ecosystem. *Harvard Business Review, 84*(4), 98.

Adner, R., & Kapoor, R. (2010). Value creation in innovation ecosystems: How the structure of technological interdependence affects firm performance in new technology generations. *Strategic Management Journal, 31*(3), 306–333.

Ahmed, P. K., & Shepherd, C. (2010). *Innovation management: Context, strategies, systems and processes*. Pearson Harlow.

Alves, J., Marques, M. J., Saur, I., & Marques, P. (2007). Creativity and innovation through multidisciplinary and multisectoral cooperation. *Creativity and Innovation Management, 16*(1), 27–34.

15 Development of an Innovation Ecosystem in a Fast-Paced Economic Environment... 319

Autio, E., & Thomas, L. (2014). Innovation ecosystems. *The Oxford Handbook of Innovation Management*, 204–288.

Bergendahl, M., & Magnusson, M. (2015). Creating ideas for innovation: Effects of organizational distance on knowledge creation processes. *Creativity and Innovation Management, 24*(1), 87–101.

Brockhoff, K., Gupta, A. K., & Rotering, C. (1991). Inter-firm R&D co-operations in Germany. *Technovation, 11*(4), 219–229.

Buss, P., & Peukert, C. (2015). R&D outsourcing and intellectual property infringement. *Research Policy, 44*(4), 977–989.

Chesbrough, H. W. (2003). *Open innovation: The new imperative for creating and profiting from technology*. Harvard Business Press.

Cohen, W. M., & Levinthal, D. A. (1990). Absorptive capacity: A new perspective on learning and innovation. *Administrative Science Quarterly*, 128–152.

Corbin, J. M., & Strauss, A. L. (2015). *Basics of qualitative research: Techniques and procedures for developing grounded theory* (4th ed.). Thousand Oaks: SAGE Publications.

Couchman, P. K., & Beckett, R. (2006). Achieving effective cross-sector R&D collaboration: A proposed management framework. *Prometheus, 24*(2), 151–168.

Curran, C.-S., Bröring, S., & Leker, J. (2010). Anticipating converging industries using publicly available data. *Technological Forecasting and Social Change, 77*(3), 385–395.

Datta, A., & Jessup, L. M. (2013). Looking beyond the focal industry and existing technologies for radical innovations. *Technovation, 33*(10), 355–367.

Dedehayir, O., & Seppänen, M. (2015). Birth and expansion of innovation ecosystems: A case study of copper production. *Journal of Technology Management & Innovation, 10*(2), 145–154.

Dowling, M., Lechner, C., & Thielmann, B. (1998). Convergence–Innovation and change of market structures between television and online services. *Electronic Markets, 8*(4), 31–35.

EIRMA. (2003). Innovation through spinning in and out. *Research-Technology Management, 46*, 63–64.

Eisenhardt, K. M. (1989). Building theories from case study research. *Academy of Management Review, 14*(4), 532–550.

Emden, Z., Calantone, R. J., & Droge, C. (2006). Collaborating for new product development: Selecting the partner with maximum potential to create value. *Journal of Product Innovation Management, 23*(4), 330–341.

Enkel, E., & Gassmann, O. (2010). Creative imitation: Exploring the case of cross-industry innovation. *R&D Management, 40*(3), 256–270.

Enkel, E., & Heil, S. (2014). Preparing for distant collaboration: Antecedents to potential absorptive capacity in cross-industry innovation. *Technovation, 34*(4), 242–260.

Fischer, M. M., & Varga, A. (2002). Technological innovation and interfirm cooperation: An exploratory analysis using survey data from manufacturing firms in the metropolitan region of Vienna. *International Journal of Technology Management, 24*(7), 724–742.

Fukugawa, N. (2006). Determining factors in innovation of small firm networks: A case of cross industry groups in Japan. *Small Business Economics, 27*(2–3), 181–193.

Gambardella, A., & Torrisi, S. (1998). Does technological convergence imply convergence in markets? Evidence from the electronics industry. *Research Policy, 27*(5), 445–463.

Gassmann, O., Zeschky, M., Wolff, T., & Stahl, M. (2010). Crossing the industry-line: Breakthrough innovation through cross-industry alliances with 'non-suppliers. *Long Range Planning, 43*(5), 639–654.

Gillier, T., Piat, G., Roussel, B., & Truchot, P. (2010). Managing innovation fields in a cross-industry exploratory partnership with C–K design theory. *Journal of Product Innovation Management, 27*(6), 883–896.

Goffin, K., Herstatt, C., & Mitchell, R. (2009). *Strategien und effektive Umsetzung von Innovationsprozessen mit dem Pentathlon-Prinzip*. München: FinanzBuch.

Grant, R. M. (1996). Toward a knowledge-based theory of the firm. *Strategic Management Journal, 17*(S2), 109–122.

Grant, R. M., & Baden-Fuller, C. (2004). A knowledge accessing theory of strategic alliances. *Journal of Management Studies, 41*(1), 61–84.

Hacklin, F., Marxt, C., & Fahrni, F. (2009). Coevolutionary cycles of convergence: An extrapolation from the ICT industry. *Technological Forecasting and Social Change, 76*(6), 723–736.

Hagedoorn, J., & Duysters, G. (2002). Learning in dynamic inter-firm networks: The efficacy of multiple contacts. *Organization Studies, 23*(4), 525–548.

Halecker, B., & Hartmann, M. (2013). Contribution of systems thinking to business model research and business model innovation. *International Journal of Technology Intelligence and Planning, 9*(4), 251–270.

Hauschildt, J., & Salomo, S. (2011). Innovationsmanagement. Vahlen.

Heil, S. (2015). *Cross-industry innovation – A theoretical and empirical foundation on the concept of absorptive capacity.* Dissertation, Zeppelin University.

Heslin, P. A. (2009). Better than brainstorming? Potential contextual boundary conditions to brainwriting for idea generation in organizations. *Journal of Occupational and Organizational Psychology, 82*(1), 129–145.

Hilmola, O. (2012). Technological change and performance deterioration of mobile phone suppliers. *International Journal of Technology Intelligence and Planning, 8*(4), 374–388.

Iansiti, M., & Levien, R. (2004). *The keystone advantage: What the new dynamics of business ecosystems mean for strategy, innovation, and sustainability.* Harvard Business Press.

Jaffe, A. B. (1986). Technological opportunity and spillovers of R&D: Evidence from firms' patents, profits and market value. *The American Economic Review, no., 5*, 984–1001.

Jaspers, F., Prencipe, A., & Ende, J. (2012). Organizing interindustry architectural innovations: Evidence from mobile communication applications. *Journal of Product Innovation Management, 29*(3), 419–431.

Jiang, X., Li, M., Gao, S., Bao, Y., & Jiang, F. (2013). Managing knowledge leakage in strategic alliances: The effects of trust and formal contracts. *Industrial Marketing Management, 42*(6), 983–991.

Kerl, A., & Moehrle, M. G. (2015). *Initiatives for multi cross industry innovation: The case of universal home.* Technology Management in the ITDriven Services (PICMET), Proceedings of PICMET'15 (pp. 2223–2229).

Khan, A., & Möhrle, M. G. (2012). Multi cross industry innovation: Eine Herausforderung an das Innovationsmanagement. *Innovative Produktionswirtschaft: Jubiläumsschrift zu 20 Jahren produktionswirtschaftlicher Forschung an der BTU Cottbus, 20*, 45–58.

Khan, A., Möhrle, M. G., & Böttcher, F. (2013) Initiatives for multi cross industry innovation: The case of future_bizz. In: *Technology Management in the IT-Driven Services (PICMET), 2013 Proceedings of PICMET'13.* IEEE, pp. 616–622.

Kim, N., Lee, H., Kim, W., Lee, H., & Suh, J. H. (2015). *Dynamic patterns of industry convergence: Evidence from a large amount of unstructured data.* Research Policy.

Kogut, B., & Zander, U. (1992). Knowledge of the firm, combinative capabilities, and the replication of technology. *Organization Science, 3*(3), 383–397.

Konsti-Laakso, S., Pihkala, T., & Kraus, S. (2012). Facilitating SME innovation capability through business networking. *Creativity and Innovation Management, 21*(1), 93–105.

Kotabe, M., & Scott Swan, K. (1995). The role of strategic alliances in high-technology new product development. *Strategic Management Journal, 16*(8), 621–636.

Levén, P., Holmström, J., & Mathiassen, L. (2014). Managing research and innovation networks: Evidence from a government sponsored cross-industry program. *Research Policy, 43*(1), 156–168.

Lew, Y. K., & Sinkovics, R. R. (2013). Crossing borders and industry sectors: Behavioral governance in strategic alliances and product innovation for competitive advantage. *Long Range Planning, 46*(1), 13–38.

Lichtenthaler, U., & Lichtenthaler, E. (2010). Technology transfer across organizational boundaries: Absorptive capacity and desorptive capacity. *California Management Review, 53*(1), 154–170.

Markham, S. K., & Aiman-Smith, L. (2001). Product champions: Truths, myths and management. *Research-Technology Management, 44*(3), 44–50.

Melander, L., & Lopez–Vega, H. (2013). Impact of technological uncertainty in supplier selection for NPD collaborations: Literature review and a case study. *International Journal of Technology Intelligence and Planning, 9*(4), 323–339.

Mercan, B., & Goktas, D. (2011). Components of innovation ecosystems: A cross-country study. *International Research Journal of Finance and Economics, 76*, 102–112.

Miles, M. B., Huberman, A. M., & Saldaña, J. (2014) *Qualitative data analysis: A methods sourcebook* (3rd ed.).

Moore, J. F. (1993). Predators and prey: A new ecology of competition. *Harvard Business Review, 71*(3), 75–83.

Müller-Seitz, G. (2012). Absorptive and desorptive capacity-related practices at the network level–the case of SEMATECH. *R&D Management, 42*(1), 90–99.

Murphy, M., Perrot, F., & Rivera-Santos, M. (2012). New perspectives on learning and innovation in cross-sector collaborations. *Journal of Business Research, 65*(12), 1700–1709.

Nooteboom, B., van Haverbeke, W., Duysters, G., Gilsing, V., & Van den Oord, A. (2007). Optimal cognitive distance and absorptive capacity. *Research Policy, 36*(7), 1016–1034.

Osterwalder, A., & Pigneur, Y. (2010). *Business model generation: A handbook for visionaries, game changers, and challengers*. Hoboken: Wiley.

Parhankangas, A. (2001). *From a corporate venture to an independent company: A base for a typology for corporate spin-off firms*. IEEE.

Pittaway, L., Robertson, M., Munir, K., Denyer, D., & Neely, A. (2004). Networking and innovation: A systematic review of the evidence. *International Journal of Management Reviews, 5*(3–4), 137–168.

Rese, A., Gemünden, H., & Baier, D. (2013). "Too many cooks spoil the broth": Key persons and their roles in inter-organizational innovations. *Creativity and Innovation Management, 22*(4), 390–407.

Rohrbeck, R., Döhler, M., & Arnold, H. (2009). Creating growth with externalization of R&D results—the spin-along approach. *Global Business and Organizational Excellence, 28*(4), 44–51.

Rosell, D. T., & Lakemond, N. (2012). Collaborative innovation with suppliers – A conceptual model for characterizing supplier contributions to NPD. *8*(2), 197–214.

Sammarra, A., & Biggiero, L. (2008). Heterogeneity and specificity of inter-firm knowledge flows in innovation networks. *Journal of Management Studies, 45*(4), 800–829.

Silverman, D. (2010). *Qualitative research*. London: Sage Publications.

Thompson, L. (2003). Improving the creativity of organizational work groups. *The Academy of Management Executive, 17*(1), 96–109.

van Lente, H., Hekkert, M., Smits, R., & van Waveren, B. (2003). Roles of systemic intermediaries in transition processes. *International Journal of Innovation Management, 7*(03), 247–279.

West, J., & Wood, D. (2013). Creating and evolving an open innovation ecosystem: Lessons from Symbian ltd. In R. Adner, J. E. Oxley, & B. S. Silverman (Eds.), *Collaboration and competition in business ecosystems* (1st ed., pp. 27–67). Bingley: Emerald.

Yin, R. K. (2014). *Case study research: Design and methods*. London: Sage Publications.